BURNING
AT
THE
GRASSROOTS

Inside the Dean Machine

BURNING
AT
THE
GRASSROOTS

Inside the Dean Machine

Dana Dunnan

BURNING AT THE GRASS ROOTS: INSIDE THE DEAN MACHINE

Copyright © 2004 by Dana Dunnan

A list of significant changes and updates to this document, and the dates on which they occur, will be found on this page, as well as the website
http://www.burningatthegrassroots. com

Updated July 22, 2004	Iraq Fatalities
Updated August 16, 2004	Iraq Fatalities
Updated	Howard Dean portrait added
Updated	Barack Obama picture added

ISBN 1-58961-261-2

PageFree Publishing, Inc.
109 South Farmer Street, Otsego, MI 49078
www.pagefreepublishing.com
Second Printing August 2004

DEDICATION

Larry Nunes

This book came about as a result of a conversation with Larry and Mary Nunes in late October of 2003. Ironically, it occurred in Middletown, Rhode Island, where Howard Dean went to St. George's Preparatory School.

After describing to them my exhaustive efforts on behalf of the Dean campaign, I was stunned to have Larry say that I should write everything down. I felt as if he was indicating that I could work harder, or smarter, which I didn't feel was possible. Three months later that suggestion, which had initially planted a seed for the idea of a magazine article, began to sprout.

That is but one reason for dedicating this book to Larry Nunes. His unflagging commitment to our political system, his unfailing courage through the hardest moments in his life, his unsurpassed devotion to Mary - all of these things have long inspired me. His humility would have served Howard Dean well.

I hold little hope that this book will sway him. The tenacity that has kept him going through his eighty-two years has also kept him an unbending Republican.

Judy and I will, nonetheless, continue to pray for him.

Dana Dunnan
April 18, 2004

The Grassroots Team- We really *do* have the power

Shannon McCarty
Adam Drapcho
Judy Dunnan
Dana Dunnan
Rob Lyons

The Grassroots Team wishes to thank: Supportive friends and family, PageFree Publishing, Inc. of Otsego, Michigan, Printed Matter of Newfields, New Hampshire, the Weeks Public Library of Greenland, New Hampshire, Ozzie's Market of Greenland, New Hampshire, the National Press Club of Washington, DC, Sugar Mill Farm of Barton, Vermont, Water Street Bookstore of Exeter, New Hampshire, Sue, Maggie and Cindy of the Greenland Post Office and the Crown Plaza Hotel of Washington, DC.

TABLE OF CONTENTS

Lincoln must come again.

When Lincoln comes this time, our eyes must be open to the fact that he will not look the way we remember him. He will probably be a woman, a minority, or someone who is physically challenged. Most of all, he must come from within the hearts of all Americans.

MOVING FORWARD

Why does this magnificent applied science, which saves work and makes life easier, bring us so little happiness? The simple answer runs: Because we have not yet learned to make sensible use of it.
ALBERT EINSTEIN, in an address at Cal Tech, 1931

I have observed the New Hampshire (NH) primary as a voter since first casting a ballot for George McGovern. My home now is in Greenland, but for 25 years I lived in Exeter, where I taught journalism at Phillips Exeter Academy. I could watch candidates speak at the town bandstand 50 yards from my front door. I did learn from the Secret Service, however, that we would not be allowed to peer out of our own windows, since our viewing the candidate in such a manner might be viewed as intent to do harm.

My involvement in the Dean campaign in the 2004 Democratic primary season gave me a look into the window of politics. My commitment sprang from a deeply felt revulsion at the direction in which America was headed, both domestically, and abroad.

Furthermore, for the first time, I found a candidate with whom I felt a personal connection, one whose growth had traversed paths similar to my own, and whose values largely seemed to mirror my own.

The commitment I would make to that campaign would take an enormous toll. I would suffer from exhaustion, exhilaration, depletion of financial resources, and the emotional trauma of a roller coaster ride unparalleled in the annals of American politics.

At the end of that ride, I would find myself with more questions than answers.

Where did my money go? Who had decided how to spend it? Why didn't America see the same person I saw in Howard Dean? Who is Howard Dean, really?

So my campaign journey had not ended - but rather, just begun. The reflection on an experience that transpired at cyber speed would also mandate asking the right questions, of the right people.

Many of them, nationally recognized experts, were asking the same questions. All of them wanted the answers, and virtually all of them told me that they hoped I would share my conclusions with them, as soon as I got them.

You hold those conclusions in your hand.

Presidential campaigns have long featured insurgent candidacies. Most recently, Ralph Nader elected George W. Bush, with Supreme help. As Bush faces a titanic political struggle against his re-election, the interest of great numbers of Americans will focus on politics.

In researching this book, I interviewed the Reverend Jesse Jackson, whose presidential campaign gave him the mantle of change agent that Howard Dean assumed two decades later. An insurgent, who opened Democratic Party doors to other minority candidates, Jackson said to this author in February 2003,

"This will be a campaign of great historical proportions. Howard Dean made a contribution that will be as big as (the selection of) the nominee. In the last two months, the other eight bludgeoned him into submission. He set the pace, and sometimes the pace-setter doesn't win. The change that we see (in the electoral process) never comes from the top down, from the candidate, but bottom up."

Jackson provided a list that might point to the failings of the Dean campaign:

"Before you run, you need a message, money, a sound infrastructure and an army of volunteers."

Again, in February 2003, BBC producer Gordon Corera noted the international interest the Dean campaign generated:

"Dean registered here because of the war issue. He got more coverage here. We see everything here through the lens of (American) foreign policy. Dean was the only one on the radar. Everyone in Britain was genuinely interested in the Dean movement, as well as the man. When the history books are written, he'll get as much space as the winner."

The arc of the Dean candidacy is unparalleled. A key to the upward trajectory of the Dean campaign was the Internet. The Internet is not a Mobius strip; it is constantly expanding. The story of the Dean movement is constantly evolving. In my best of all possible worlds, this book will be its Genesis, a book about the first great American political phenomena of the 21st Century.

Walter Shapiro of USA Today captured the Dean drama:

"If we're going to understand how we pick presidents, or the nominating process, or the compacted primary season, we will need to understand the Dean campaign. This story will impact the next forty years of American politics. Never has an insurgent candidate risen so far before the primaries, nor has a purported front runner fallen so fast without a sex scandal. It is one of the great Icarus moments in American political history."

This book didn't start as an exercise in participatory journalism. When my wife and I began working as volunteers in the Dean campaign last September, we joined because Howard Dean was a man we had met, whose career we followed, and whose causes were in alignment with ours. Instead of waiting to be contacted by the campaign and drawn in, as I was, I might have contacted the campaign earlier, had I believed he had a chance to win. By September, he was acknowledged to have created a full-blown phenomenon.

Pulitzer Prize winner David Halberstam said to me that, "Where wise men fear to tread, fools rush in, in batalllion strength." There were very few fools involved in my experience in the Dean campaign. However, the campaign soared in the face of George Santayana's oft-quoted wisdom, "Those who do not remember the past are condemned to relive it."[1] Malcolm X put it another way: "Of all of our studies, history is best qualified to reward our research."

All too often, the past is prologue to the future.

Dean's campaign failed to utilize the lessons of past insurgent campaigns, and, sometimes, even of traditional politics. USA Today reporter Walter Shapiro summed it up: "They got caught up in their own hubris."

When the idea that you have become a part of a new and different campaign is repeated so often that you internalize it as a mantra, you can accept directions from people who are supposedly experts in politics, even if they fly in the face of your own common sense.

When our direction, as volunteers, came from a 23 year-old, the fact that he had been in politics for 17 years (distributing political leaflets at the age of 6), made him an expert to us. When directions came from persons unknown, or voices unseen, in the state party headquarters, one assumed they were experts.

The people who worked in the office with me were far from fools. I've spent time as a student at Stanford and Berkeley, as adjunct faculty at Harvard, and a visiting scholar at MIT and have worked as a Teamster. Yet I found the people I had around me on the Dean campaign were the best cadre I've ever joined. They, too, trusted the direction they were given, and were equally prepared to attack the most tedious or onerous task with a zeal that they may have never felt before in their lives.

The siren song was Dean's often repeated "You have the power." By empowering us, he encouraged a level of participation that few of us had ever had in our lives. Being onstage with the candidate, having him look you in the eye, shake your hand, and actually listen to what you said to him, entranced his supporters. The visceral reinforcement of empowerment, however, would be jarred by the campaign's surreal rise and fall.

While the feeling that maybe something wasn't being done right had been with me from the beginning, it wasn't until December that I began to think that the campaign's misjudgments would be its undoing. I'd had some interesting and amusing experiences on the campaign trail.

Every writer probably evaluates life experiences through the lens of having something they might write about, but I didn't have such a conscious thought until December, when I started saving e-mails and clipping newspaper articles.

My vision began as writing a clever little tale of the campaign trail, one that would resonate with tens of thousands of Dean supporters. However, as the sense of foreboding increased, I began to think that understanding the errors of the campaign was more important than my little story.

Once I began to commit myself to the idea of writing about the campaign, I began to see the wheels coming off the bus. The phenomena that had been so elevated was now marked by its meteoric fall. Whatever part of me that is intellectual began analyzing that decline. Similar analysis was beginning to occur throughout the media. Howard Dean was being described as *the* presidential candidate of 2003, which, unfortunately, was a year too soon.

MIT sociologist and ethnologist Susan Silbey provided an academic perspective on the role of the media in the demise of the Dean campaign, in clear accessible language:

"Life is controlled by complex, abstract systems, like banking and finance. Citizens place a trust in these systems without understanding them. Even experts in one system don't understand the working of other systems. All of this goes on behind the backs of ordinary citizens…There is a contradiction here - people don't trust the media, but don't have other sources. The way the media generates its audience (is) by salacious emotional appeal and also by appearing, by creating an illusion of being objective. (This is done by) criticizing itself and by offering opposing but flat and un-nuanced cartoon-like views, suggesting that those are the extremes. In the process, (the media) eliminates other points of view."

The same week Silbey said this, *Time* magazine referred to Dean as a "choleric cartoon."

As I began contacting "experts" in political analysis in February, it became clear that politics was also somewhat of the expert system that Silbey had described. It wasn't rocket science, but something closer to an art.

An artist's eccentricities are generally accepted as part of the package. James Carville is widely seen as rather strange, (not merely for his eerie similarity to the Gollum in "Lord of the Rings") but he is an artist.

Joe Trippi, the man seen as the "mad genius" behind the Dean campaign, was the artist, and Dean was both benefactor and beneficiary. Unfortunately, both may have believed that the self-proclaimed "campaign unlike any before it" was not required to know the lessons of past insurgent's successes and failures.

MIT political science professor, Stephen Ansolabehere comments that *"The ads weren't any worse, or better, than anyone else's. The ads should have captured what was at the core of him, being a doctor."*

Trippi's firm produced the ads, and his financial windfall would look like conflict of interest. Still worse, the campaign dabbled in the black art of negative advertising.

Referring to negative ads in Iowa, Ansolabehere notes that, *"Dean and Gephardt was a little like the tar baby. Gephardt was the wrong campaign to tangle with, because he wasn't going anywhere.*" The Gephardt campaign would describe the effect as a murder-suicide. Was it also, perhaps, a physician-assisted suicide?

Dean was a physician, and a governor in "a small New England state." The personal politics of such a small state wouldn't be possible on a national scale. But as his campaign sailed on, Dean kept his faith in Trippi, until foundering on the shoals of New Hampshire.

Then Trippi was gone.

Stephen Ansolabehere reflects on this event: "*Reorganizing in the middle of a campaign is a nightmare. He should have kept Trippi on. It's nearly impossible to change horses in midstream.*"

By that time, the media had seemed to turn on Dean, poll numbers had plummeted, and the cosmology of expansion of the core of the truly committed had become negligible.

Along with the party machinery, led by Terry McAuliffe, the media performed an autopsy on Dean. The label of "unelectable" given him in the media, and by the multi-headed monster of opponents he had faced, created a self-fulfilling prophecy. And so my work, writing a living history and analysis of his campaign's historic arc, began.

BEGINNINGS

Is it a fact, or have I dreamt it — that, by means of electricity, the world of matter has become a great nerve, vibrating thousands of miles in a breathless point of time?
NATHANIEL HAWTHORNE, The House of the Seven Gables

"Howard Dean is really the only candidate who has been able to inspire, at the grassroots level, all over this country, the kind of passion and enthusiasm for democracy and change and transformation of America that we need in this country."

By the time Al Gore endorsed Dean with these words, Gore and his wife had received more than 2,500 letters supporting Dean, in early October 2003 alone. The letters were generated by a new political tool, the Meetup.

Gore continued to say that Dean's "…supporters are breathing fresh air into the lungs of our democracy. In a world in which politics is a spectator sport, and for many people, campaigns mean sitting at home passively being manipulated by attack ads and half-truths, the Dean candidacy engages active participation, not from those who want special favors later, but from those who dream of building a better world now. And that's why the Dean campaign is one of the best things that's (sic)happened to American democracy in decades."

When former New Jersey Senator Bill Bradley endorsed Dean on January 6, 2004, he had received more than a thousand letters from Meetup participants. Following on the endorsement of Dean by Al Gore, his opponent in the 2000 primaries, Bradley's endorsement made it look as if the Democratic establishment was unifying behind this former Vermont governor, who had been a nonentity in the nation's mind just a year earlier.

The day after the Bradley endorsement in New Hampshire, Dean was riding high. In a campaign press release, Dean wrote that his "campaign has built the greatest grassroots campaign presidential politics has ever seen."

Dean's campaign manager Joe Trippi enthused in the same press release that "...this type of campaign is how our founders envisioned politics happening - neighbor to neighbor, friend to friend, co-worker to co-worker. They never meant for it to be a battle of sound bytes on TV - and neither do we."

But one month later, the post-mortems were pouring in.

David Paul Kuhn wrote on CBSNews.com: "A fast month, and a political light year, after Howard Dean stood poised to win the Iowa caucuses, the former Vermont governor took the stage at a rally Wednesday and ended the campaign that once seemed unstoppable. How did the mighty fall? The answer is complicated, and the rise and fall of Howard Dean will keep political coroners busy for years."[2]

The now-departed campaign manager Joe Trippi was among the forensics specialists:

"I mean, there is no one that can change the fact that by using the Internet to create a grassroots network across the country, we raised more money in small donors than any Democratic campaign in history. (The movement)...is going to continue to grow and change the country, in the same way the Kennedy/Nixon debate was a harbinger of what television was going to do to change politics. I think the Dean campaign did that with the Internet."

Steve Grossman announced his plans to reach out to John Kerry just before Dean's purported final stand in Wisconsin. To some Deaniacs, it appeared that this further wounded a campaign on life support. Grossman has his own analysis of the campaign.

"When a campaign grows as rapidly as the Dean campaign grows, the momentum can outstrip the infrastructure you put in place. He was a fresh face that energized millions of grassroots activists, giving them a sense that participatory politics matter and political fundraising will never be the same."

The once-extemporaneous Dean read aloud from his resignation speech "I am no longer pursuing the presidency. We will, however, continue to build a new organization using our grassroots effort.'

USA Today's Walter Shapiro had followed all the candidates at the very beginning of their efforts. He chronicled those days in the book, One Car Caravan: On the Road with the 2004 Democrats before America Tunes In. Shapiro is still trying to figure out what happened. In recognition of the limitations of the human sciences, he says "Some things in politics are unknowable." However, he believes that "…after New Hampshire, all Howard Dean had was the movement. Trippi's firing betrayed the movement. All he had left was ashes."

Time will tell, and history will record.

An enduring image of America is of vast prairies, once roamed by buffalo herds that stretched from horizon to horizon. The gently rolling topography of the plains provided a barrier-free surface for fire movement. Prairie plants survived because of deep root systems.

The use of prairie fires is described in a 1970 Cook County Nature Bulletin. "Original Midwestern prairies were actually preserved as such by fires, fires started every spring by the Indians to drive out the game hidden in all that tall thick growth; fires to deprive their enemies of cover through which they might creep unobserved. When it was windy, and the vegetation thick and tall, these became leaping crackling flames that raced faster than a man could run.

"Burning robs the topsoil of its fertility, and increases the growth of troublesome, perennial plants. Many of these have hardy seeds. Burning was also advocated as a means of controlling insect pests. It is now known that burning encourages them by destroying beneficial insects. Fire, admittedly was an ally of the native plants in our original prairies, but only a few remnants of them remain. In their place, we have many worthless pesky weeds and grasses. Fire is their friend. Burning helps spread and replace the valuable plants we need."[3]

Native Americans would use what they called a "ring fire" in their hunting. After the sun had shone on the grass to dry it, the circle would be set around the quarry, except in a passage left to slaughter the targets as they attempted to escape.

Some white men feared uncontrolled prairie fires, calling them the "Messenger of Death." The terrifying roaring of a vast prairie fire would carry on the winds for miles. Knowing it was coming, a search would begin for a natural firebreak, or an effort would begin to make one.

The hand of man rapidly diminished the vast prairies, so that large trees stood stalwart against the forces of nature. Controlled burning is used today, on what remains of the great prairies. Younger seedlings grow, older plants gain new growth, and underbrush is cleared. Nutrients penetrate that could not reach all layers of soil if they were covered by dead vegetation.

Human hair and grass grow from below, rather than from their ends. Prairie plants re-sprout quickly after grass fires. Burns are controlled by firebreaks, just as natural firebreaks like rivers would halt the spread of fires started by Nature. A prairie fire could start by lightning, as if hurled by Mars, the mythical god of war. Or, as Native Americans knew, a prairie fire could start, under the right circumstances, from a small spark.

First impressions count.

My wife and I had never heard of Howard Dean, when he approached us in the Buck and Doe restaurant in Island Pond, Vermont. Island Pond, found in the part of the state called the Northeast Kingdom, where unemployment runs highest, and population density lowest, is classic Vermont quirky. A former railroad town, it now has an odd little religious cult in it, as well as the roar of snowmobiles at least four months a year. Buck and Doe provided what road food connoisseurs Jane and Michael Stern called "...the best food in all of New England... Pea soup soaking up the juices of a ham bone, baseball-sized sticky buns, broiled Gaspe Bay salmon, mile-high banana pie, a fancy wine list (including directions for pronouncing Chateauneuf du Pape and Dom Perignon), apples sizzling in brown sugar, squash glazed with maple syrup..."[4] We were there to eat, not greet.

When Dean told us he was running for lieutenant governor, we said we couldn't vote for him, since we were registered in New Hampshire. Dean said he just liked talking to people, and he stayed with us for quite a while. We talked about Vermont politics, as much as we knew of them. We discussed the sorry state of the nation under George H.W. Bush. We talked about which politicians on the national level seemed promising.

Name dropping, I said that I had asked Pulitzer Prize winning journalist and historian David Halberstam if he thought there were any potential new political heroes on the horizon.

Halberstam had responded that the last chance for a hero had seemed to die with Bobby Kennedy. However, Halberstam had said that he thought Senator Bill Bradley of New Jersey seemed promising. I told Dean the story Halberstam had related, about a deep-pockets supporter going to

Bradley and telling him that the money was there for a presidential run; Bradley just had to say the word. Bradley had walked over to a window and not said anything for a long time. Then he said, "Not now, I'm not ready yet."

We marveled together with Dean at the self-awareness that the story demonstrated. We told him that we looked forward to someday having a chance to support Bradley if he ran for President. Dean said he felt the same way, and that he had been considering sending a letter to Bradley to say that to him. At some point, the food came, but the conversation was good enough that we didn't shoo him away. When he eventually walked away, we looked at one another and said, "He ought to be President."

It is natural to seek affirmation from people you know and trust. **Ray Proulx** is a neighbor by our camp in Northern Vermont. As a superintendent in Essex Township, Vermont, he had first observed Dean as lieutenant governor. Proulx had often found that lieutenant governors were pretty passive. He did not find that with the young physician.

"When he first ran the senate, he ran it with diplomacy, but with authority. You could see in him that there were some real strong convictions that he wasn't there just to slap the gavel down, that he did have a vision, and that he was taking charge. He was a person of conviction and he would lead, but he also understood the political process, and he was very astute to the political machinery.

"I can remember one of his administrative assistants sitting down and talking with him. He (Dean) said to her, 'Someday I will be running for president.' When I spoke with her, she was just kind of joking about it, saying 'Can you imagine?' But I think that deep down, he did have motivation back then that he did want to be President of the United States. I think he is definitely the most skilled politician, in Vermont terms, that I've ever witnessed."

Proulx later lobbied Governor Dean, both in his role as an educator and as a community member looking to bring business to his town. His impression expanded and his positive opinion grew. Ray would go on to contribute money to Dean's campaign—the only presidential candidate he ever supported, other than Jack Kennedy.

George Gladding, a retired general manager of the Barre, Vermont newspaper put me in touch with a former employee of his who is a writer and editor in Montpelier. When I sent an article to the magazine about a caboose we had restored as a bunkhouse, I wrote that I was thinking of working in the Dean presidential campaign, but wanted his opinion of Dean, since politics had long ago made me cynical.

He wrote back that Dean would be a good President, and that if I chose to work for him, I would always be glad I did, regardless of the result.

Kathy Sullivan is the leader of the Democratic Party in New Hampshire. She first met Dean in the spring of 2002. "He had come over to New Hampshire to meet with three individuals who were thinking of running for governor, because he was involved in the Democratic Governors' Association. They make decisions about funding, and financing, and helping out candidates. He had on one of those education ties with the kids on them. We chatted about these individuals who are running for governor. I've always been forthcoming, so I said to him 'Should we plan on seeing a lot more of you in New Hampshire?' He kind of chuckled, and said, 'I think you can plan on maybe seeing me.' I said, 'Do you have aspirations of becoming the Josiah Bartlett, although from Vermont as opposed to NH?' referring to *West Wing*. With (a chuckle and) that expression he has on his face where he smiles a little bit, and his eyes sort of dance, (he) said, 'I'm much more moderate than he is.'"

Dorothy Keville was a lobbyist for the pharmaceutical company that made the first AIDS/HIV treatment. She asked for a meeting with Howard Dean and brought a person from the company with her to Montpelier. They were told they could have twenty minutes. "Howard gave us two hours of his time, because he had a lot of questions, and he wanted to understand what the drug would do. He talked to us like being a doctor, as well as a governor. He cares about public policy. He took the time, and he won my heart, and my support, then."

Steve Grossman first met Dean in 1992, at a regional Democratic Party event.

"We got to know each other quite well when we traveled together in California in 1998, in connection with the election of Gray Davis as governor of California. He was out there helping Davis, and I was out there helping Gray Davis, in my role as chairman of the Democratic National Committee (DNC). We sat down for a dinner one night, Mexican or southwestern food, in Los Angeles. When you sit down with somebody for a few hours, you get to know them pretty well. I was struck by his freshness, his blunt approach, and I was struck by his ease in developing a relationship. I said 'here's a guy who has gotten a lot of things down, and who seems down to earth, who understands some of the things that we as a party need to do to rebuild our brand equity, after having lost the Congress and a lot of other things.'"

For **Jodi Wilgoren**, the 2004 primary season was her first experience covering a presidential candidate. Her interactions with Dean were defined, at least partially, by professional boundaries.

"He doesn't really have real relationships with journalists. I mean, I don't have great evidence of him having many relationships with his staff members - personal relationships. He didn't have them with people who traveled with him, or the reporters.

"…I haven't really found friends. He has a small circle of guys from college who he has very close relationships with. He's not big on developing your basic personal-professional relationship, the kind of relationship you develop with colleagues or the people you interact with, over time. He didn't really have them that I could see. …I think the press covering Dean really loved covering him, because it was such an interesting story. The campaign was the most interesting one around, and it was more interesting than most in history, and we loved that.

"He was a good newsmaker. But, from the very beginning, there were various dynamics working that created a kind of formal press conference interaction, rather than a more conversational one. We were at a constant struggle to get more access to him and to have more conversational interactions, to be able to watch him do things more, to be able to get more press availability.

"I mean, it was a constant battle for us, fighting with them."

Walter Shapiro traveled with Dean long before the first votes were cast, when he was a press entourage of one. "Howard Dean was never warm and cuddly. To some extent, particularly in the early going, the press cuts more slack for candidates who are warm and cuddly, who are accessible, and who care about them. We're all human…we're trying to take the measure of these candidates. Subjective factors invariably seep in, no matter how hard you try to separate out your feelings."

Joe Miller says "In the fall of 2002, I told him that I was going to run for the house. He was very encouraging and said, 'Good for you', and that sort of thing. We didn't become buddies, but he came to know me by sight, and by name. Later, I saw him at a couple of these garden parties, you know, like Carolyn French's. She had one for him."

Ellen Goodman met Howard Dean at *The Boston Globe*. "If he didn't like the question, he'd come back at you, which I think is completely appropriate. But there may have been a lot of people who didn't like that quality… You could probably get a transcript of his editorial board, but you wouldn't get the quality of his exchange… I do think that he did not take fools lightly."

Andrew Smith heads the Survey Center at the University of New Hampshire (UNH).

"My first interaction with him was January or February of 2003, through a professor in the business college here at the Whittemore School. Dean wanted to come and talk with some people from the business school. I went over to that meeting. I was stunned, because he was talking with a group of business people. Granted, most of them are probably Democrats, and sympathetic to him. But he was going on, and talking about the economic downturn and what would you do about the economy.

"He started talking about having New Deal-style economic projects, and having public works projects. Fine, there's a group of people who think that politically that's a good thing to do. But his argument was that government spending on public works projects is a better investment, has better return, has a better economic impact, than tax cuts for businesses, or allowing businesses to invest more. And I'm thinking, *this flies in the face of about sixty years worth of economic data that says that this just is not the case with public works projects.* It's woefully inefficient. Like the Big Dig in Massachusetts, it's incredibly bound up in special interests, and payments, and overpayments...

"I'm thinking, *yes, you can make this sort of an argument, if you are going to a house party, or somebody's house, or talking with some people from the neighborhood. You can't do it in a business school where you've got business professors and economics professors.* I remember hearing him say that, and looking around the room, and I saw a lot of faces of people just looking, not saying anything, not shaking their heads, but just looking and saying 'hmm, I don't know about this.' And to me, that showed arrogance, the arrogance of the doctor. He thinks he's right—he isn't used to having people question him. It seemed to me that he didn't sense that he needed to moderate what he says, given that the audience probably knows a whole lot more about this than he does.

"You certainly don't go into a lion's den and poke the lions. That to me was something that I was surprised at. It was like he knew what was right, he had thought about this, this was what his decision was, and that's it. My sense was that he should have known better than to bring up that topic and talk about it with that group.

"It was also surprising at that event... he was very personable, he led a good meeting, it flowed very well, people had questions. I think he was pretty well received, but we were walking out afterwards... he's walking down the hall with me and down the stairs. He was very, very uncomfortable in what to say in a one-on-one situation, making small talk. He just didn't seem to have that common touch to say, 'Hey, yeah, how are you doing? What's the hockey team going to be like this year?' Any of that... small talk about what's going on in your life.

"My wife's father is a pediatrician. Growing up, obviously, her father's whole social network was doctors. She hadn't really paid much attention to Dean. I think it was in September or so, he was on TV, and she was listening to him talk. She looks at me, and she says, 'What does he do for a living?'

I said, 'He's a doctor.'

She said 'I knew it. He sounds just like my dad's surgeon friends.' And that was not a compliment. It was that sense of, 'this is what I say, don't question me on it, I'm right, why am I even talking to you about this stuff?'"

Rob Werner first met Howard Dean in the fall of 1979, during his freshman year at the University of Vermont, when Dean was just finishing up his residency and he and his wife were just setting up a practice in the late seventies in Shelburne.

"I met him because I was working on the Kennedy campaign. It was the first campaign that I ever really worked on. Howard Dean was working on the Carter campaign, so we were on opposing sides. I became aware of him fairly early on as an activist. Within a short time after that campaign was over, he became the county chairman, in Chittenden County, which is the county that Burlington is in. He befriended a lot of Democrats in the Burlington area.

"Particularly, though, I think he was taken under wing by Esther Sorrell, who is the mother of Bill Sorrell, the current attorney general for the state of Vermont. She was a real mentor to Howard Dean. I took a real liking to him. I thought that he was a very smart guy and somebody who I certainly wanted to keep an eye on.

"He decided to run for state representative from the old North End in Burlington in 1982. By that time I was president of the college Democrats. We were fairly active—we had a good group. He took an active interest in our concerns, as college students and young people, and he sometimes would come to our meetings on campus. We helped him in his initial campaign in 1982, in terms of going door to door with him, and getting stuff out. He won that race, and then went on to become lieutenant governor, and then onto governor, under tragic circumstances.

"Because I had gotten to know him, and certainly trusted him, when I needed primary care as a student, I called him. I had a relationship with his office for my medical needs. So I got to know him in that vein as well."

Jon Finer, who grew up in the Green Mountain State, had watched Dean's growth as a politician, as he himself grew into a career as a journalist. Finer would find himself covering Dean for *The Washington Post*, in the 2004 Democratic primary season.

"The way that the media coverage works, when there are smaller events, or when he does television interviews with the national press corps, he'll give you pool coverage. This means one print reporter will go sit in the room, when he does these interviews, record everything, write up a transcript, and then send it out to everybody else, just so you don't have a room packed with reporters listening to him. Dean won't do that.

"So one time I was pooling Dean while he was doing three hours of satellite TV interviews and local television interviews in other states, somewhere in the Southwest. I had been covering him for two weeks, and hadn't really had a chance to really meet him. I'd asked questions at press availability, but hadn't ever really talked to him. So, in between two of these interviews, I walked over and introduced myself, and said that I was following the campaign, I was from *The Washington Post*, and that I was from Vermont. I thought possibly that telling him that I was from Vermont would start up a conversation about something or another, give us some common ground to talk about. We had maybe a ten-minute break and it was the very beginning of it, he wasn't really doing anything else. But he just sort of said, 'Oh, really?' And that was it. He didn't really follow up, so I went back and sat down. That was basically the sum total of my personal interaction with him.

"There's certainly no obligation on the part of a candidate to engage reporters, to be conversational or friendly to reporters. It's not their job, and it's not our job. But I found it different from other candidates I'd interacted with, given the situation that we were the only two people sitting in a room. Some of these guys will talk your ear off about nothing, and some of them are more private, more reserved. I think Dean certainly falls into the second category, without drawing any conclusions as to why that is, or what effect that may have had on the campaign, if there was one. But I found that to be sort of revelatory in terms of his personality.

"I don't know what the thought process was, or maybe he didn't feel like talking that day, or maybe he had just gotten tired of reporters after a year, I don't know. The thing is, I don't know, because the conversation didn't go any further."

Mathew Gross came to Howard Dean by process of elimination, and over the Internet.

29

"Once Al Gore decided he wasn't going to run, in December of 2002, I instinctively knew that Howard Dean was my guy, because the rest of them were Washington candidates, mealy-mouthed, and had voted for the war. They had just acquiesced to George W. Bush after the inauguration.

"For me, it was Howard Dean. I liked his stances, I liked his moderate position.

"I started blogging about him on *MyDD.com*. Literally, the more I blogged about him and looked at their website... the website was terrible at the time... I thought, *I can really help these guys. I think they should do a blog and everything else... maybe I should go out there, maybe I shouldn't... I don't know.*

"Then I saw the DNC speech, watched it online, and it was just... you could tell the rocket was going off. If I want to do this, now is the time to do it. I hopped on a plane unannounced, showed up at Burlington headquarters, made my way down the hall.

"At the time, it was mid-February... you walked into the office... it was a pretty small room, and there were a bunch of desks and volunteer desks, and there was a hallway going off down the left. No one was looking so I made my way down the hall. Clearly that was the inner sanctum. Clearly the important people were down the hallway, because they weren't out in the reception area with all the volunteers. So...I just made my way down the hall and saw Joe Trippi, and stepped in his doorway and said, 'Hey, you know, I just got here from Utah and I think we need to start...' I sort of stumbled through the explanation and said 'You should do a blog, and here's why.'"

"He sat there and looked at me. I said 'I work for this thing called *MyDD*', and his face just lit up, and he said 'You're hired.'"

Richard Hoefer says "I'd spent a lot of time on line at a place called *smirkingchimp.com*.

"*Smirkingchimp*.com is where Trippi and Matt Gross began the blog. It actually started there. It's a very liberal site, playing off the idea of the chimp—President Bush. It turns out they have an incredible roster of people that are very literate and smart, and they process the news.

"I'd been starting to hear, after the 2002 midterm elections, that there were people like me. There were two camps. You had the die-hard Democrats, who were saying, 'Don't say anything bad about Democrats.' At the same time, you start to hear the people saying '(Forget)…the DLC (Democratic Leadership Council). They don't know what they're doing, all they do is lose, and we need to get rid of that.'

"When 2003 came along, I don't know when I first heard the name 'Howard Dean.' I started to hear that name a little. Then I heard someone mention the concept of a Meetup.

"It was a guy in Chicago. He said, 'I just went to this Meetup, and met this politician, Howard Dean. He's against the war.' It started to sound really interesting. I started hearing more and more about this guy.

"I'm thinking *I'm not politically savvy, so if I haven't heard of him, he doesn't have a chance.* But I'm hearing all these things that are so positive. Then this thread starts, called 'Ask the Dean Campaign.' I didn't know the name of Joe Trippi at all. I was there the day that thread began, and it said 'Ask the Dean Campaign.'

"The first posting was by Matt Gross, and it said, 'Well, you'll never believe it, but my boss handed me a note saying to go start a thread on *Smirkingchimp.com.* So, does anybody here have a question about Howard Dean?' He said it was a first in presidential campaigns.

"In response to that, the people who knew the name Trippi, and Democratic campaigns, were floored. 'This is incredible.' So they started asking questions. Joe would come on, and answer them now and then, but Matt was answering most of them.

"…people's expectations would be raised really high… they'd ask questions, then get angry after five or six questions. 'What's his policy on this?' So it was like once you give people a taste of something, they want more and more.

"I got to be very, very impressed, and then I heard about Meetup, and this guy… went to the one in March, and he reported back really positive things. I said to myself *I want to find out what this guy's all about.* I thought, *because I'm in communications and a filmmaker, I'm sure he's going to be another …(fouled) up looking Democrat, and he will not be electable. He's good, but he won't have the right persona.*

"I went to the website, and he instantly looked presidential.

"And I went 'What the heck, this guy's saying these things and he looks presidential.'

"Then I said to myself, *okay, but what does he sound like?*

"Gore looked presidential, but was boring as could be.

"So this guy 'what does he sound like?'

"I go to the April Meetup, and I was in a room with 130 people in San Francisco, wall to wall people.

"They played the video from the March 15th Sacramento appearance.

"Dean starts with, 'What I want to know is, what the hell are all these Democrats doing coming here, wanting your vote, after they backed a unilateral intervention in Iraq?'

"From the moment he began to speak people were mesmerized.

"When he started saying these things, I thought 'this guy's got guts.'

"It immediately hit my threshold meter that he not only looks presidential, he sounds it.

"He's got the look, he's got the voice, he's got all the TVQ that one needs to win.

"The more I listen to his speech, the more I'm astounded and my jaw just dropped open.

"The thing that nailed it for me right then and there was when he said, 'I'm tired of listening to all the fundamentalist preachers.'

"I just couldn't believe it. I couldn't believe that somebody was saying this.

"In my mind, I said, 'That guy, I'm voting for, and that guy's going to the White House.

"I know that I'm going to work my ass off for him. I knew it right then."

Gwen Graham came to know Dr. Dean through medicine and her father.

"When my dad was going in to have heart surgery, my dad's chief of staff called around to all of the other campaign managers or chiefs of staff of all the candidates and said, 'Please don't make this a political issue.' The only candidate that called back himself was Governor Dean. I think the others had campaign managers, or chiefs of staff, call back. That Governor Dean took the time to call meant a lot to me. It said a lot to me about the person that he is.

"I think that is something that a lot of people didn't really get to see. I feel very fortunate that I did get to see it that. I did get to spend enough time around him so that I got to see him…I remember, one time, we were driving in South Florida to an event. All of a sudden I saw Governor Dean just relax. You know…just relax. He is a genuinely warm, good person. That matters to me. Our leaders, we need that. We need people who have that quality.

"Everybody has a public persona, and a private persona, and I wish more people had gotten to see his out-of-the-limelight, private side. He always made me feel very, very comfortable, and he always listened to me. Being Bob Graham's daughter… I think he really respected what I had to say…as Gwen Graham. That meant a lot to me. He made a comment to me one time when we were talking, and he said, 'Gwen, you've just earned your pay for the month'. He was laughing.

"Those are the back and forths that we had… I knew it was a mutual respect."

William Trezevant explains how he became involved in the campaign. "From January 2002, I was looking around because I wanted to work on a presidential campaign; I was looking at the candidates. I found Howard Dean by going through things, heard that he might be interested, so I went to the State of Vermont governor's website, and I watched the press conference. I thought, *well, this is the guy I want to work for, this is the campaign I want to work on*. Then I started sending letters, even while he was still governor, before he started a campaign. I'd make phone calls. This went on for two years.

"I was disheartened. There is a professor at the graduate school of political management which the Institute is associated with who knew me through my work at the Institute. One day he got a call from the Dean campaign, a person in Vermont that he knew.

"He had been telling them and had sent my resumé to them, not less than five or six different times. I thought I had everything, because, you know, I'm mixed—my father's African-American and my mother's Polish, and I have this long experience. We weren't getting anywhere. Finally this person called and said we have a problem in Washington State.

"They had tried to solve the problem from Vermont, a number of different times doing a number of different things. At its core, I think that there were people in Vermont who just didn't understand campaigns. They had sent multiple people into Washington State and all these people came from the outside. Those people came in, and tried to superimpose, or had a very different notion of what was going on. All that stuff did not work and the state-based campaign was literally about to implode, and there was a very nasty fight that went on.

"This person from Vermont called, and asked this professor, 'Do you have anybody for us?' He said 'I've got one person and one person only, for you, who can go in and fix it.'

"I immediately called the person, then e-mailed them my resumé. They then said 'Set up an interview.' I was dubious…so I said 'We can do it over the phone.' So she set up a phone interview with her, another state director and a high level person from Vermont. That was about twenty minutes. Ten minutes after we got off the phone, I was asked to call the state director who was on a conference call, about what was going on in Washington State. So I call the state director, who says 'Are you still interested?' I said *yes*. At 6 o'clock I got the call, saying 'We want to hire you, we don't' have much money… do you want to take it?' I said *yes*.

"So I took it, in five minutes, and then a week later, I was on a plane to Washington state. Just so you know, I got married in September of 2003. I had to explain to my new wife why I was quitting a stable job. She still lives in Buffalo, New York. Her life's all about stability—she's a special education school teacher. I had to explain to her why, one, I was taking a pay cut, two, why I was quitting this job, and three, why even when I was quitting the job, I wasn't going back to New York, and instead was going across country to Washington state to work on a campaign.

"I think I began it by saying, 'Honey, how do you feel about Thanksgiving in Seattle?' She'd never been to Seattle. 'Well,' she said, 'that's an interesting idea, why would we be going to Seattle?' I said, 'Just to let you know…' She said, 'You've done it already, you've already quit.' And I said, 'no, no, no,'….lying. I said, 'Obviously, I had to talk to you first.' And she said, 'Well, Bill, I support you whatever you want to do.' And so I said, 'I've already taken the job.'

Trevor Haskell's experience was different. "I graduated from UC Berkeley, and raced out to New Hampshire, in hopes that I could be in the most important place at the right time, and got involved in the campaign in June.

"I was originally assumed to be a spy for the Kerry campaign. They wouldn't even let me do a postage stamp for a couple of weeks. This happens at a couple different levels, but when you attend an event, there are a couple of different staffers there who would sign in and passing out position papers and I think that they spread the word up, but the one that actually accused me was Karen Hicks. She said 'You're a Kerry spy, aren't you?'

"That took a while… it was something that had repercussions for some time, because (much later) there were still some people within my employment who still believed I was a spy.

"I started volunteering in Concord, with Alex Lee, stayed with a local family, the Hollowells, in Concord, and it was a fairly good experience."

Hillary Hazan says "I'm 29, almost 30. I'm actually in New York State now, but I lived in Vermont for the past five years. I was there when Howard Dean was Governor. I was there through the whole civil union insanity, and that was what initially drew me to him.

"I was drawn to this man who stood up for civil rights and the rights of others. When I found out that he was running for president, I felt that I needed to throw my hat in the ring and join in also. The spark that propelled me into the office in South Burlington was his announcement speech. I was there on the Marketplace in Burlington, at home, and he hit a chord with the crowd that was really evident.

"It was an incredible amount of energy. It had a lot to do with him, and what he was saying, but also with the way everyone was reacting, the overall energy of it. I was completely overwhelmed, and thought *now is the time to do this*. At that point, I was the grassroots. I've always been involved in grassroots organizing, mostly around feminist and youth issues. I worked with battered women and children, homeless women and children.

"That was my previous experience. I found myself wanting to take it to a national level and feeling that I could inform his policy for issues surrounding women in particular. My initial thought was that I need to get involved in this; I want to be a part of it.

"I knew that the country was not in a place that I was comfortable with, for either myself, or my future children, or my neighbors, or my community. So I just knew that, even if it was just going to be handing out flyers—which I needed to be involved. So I walked into the front door, and I was stuck in front of this computer, answering correspondence.

"We'd get thousands of e-mails every day, and that's what they needed help with. I snuck in the policy department, and found the person who was in charge of women's issues. The energy in the office was so incredible, people were just on fire. And it was absolutely contagious. I was overwhelmed with the amount of energy.

"You just wanted to be there, again, and again, and again."

First impressions last

THE KIDS ARE ALRIGHT

So if you are the big tree, we are the small axe, ready to cut you down.

—*Bob Marley*

Rhodes Cook identifies five stages to the nomination process in *The Elections of 1988.*[6]

The first stage is called the invisible primary (a term Arthur T. Hadley used in his book by that name in 1976), or exhibition season. Hadley said it was the "period of political time between the election of one President and the start of the first state primary to determine the next political candidates."

However, with the advent of cable news around the clock, there was little that was invisible anymore. Just as ESPN had placed obscure sports and meaningless competition before the viewer, now CNN, C-SPAN, and other networks had helped elevate Dean into a nation's consciousness.

In this first stage, candidates concentrate on raising money and recruiting activists. Antiwar sentiment helped the Dean machine acquire many new activists. While some would be older, like me, many had the relentless energy that I've now come to recognize as being the currency of (and, too often, wasted upon) the young. Dante Scala notes: "For a presidential candidate in New Hampshire, grassroots politicking gives a campaign an aura."[7] In 1988, that was eye catching for "…the contributor in Los Angeles, and Dallas, and New York City, for whom New Hampshire is this inexplicable, infuriating place."[8]

In the new millennium, Dean would reach the grassroots by stopping in New Hampshire every time he flew to Washington from Manchester on low budget Southwest Airlines. Dean's fundraising would be largely fueled by the Internet, not traditional contributors in large metropolitan areas. Like most political organizations, he would expand his grassroots campaign through young Americans.

MIT Political Science Professor **Stephen Ansolabehere** comments that "Young people don't vote as much as older people. They're not there yet. Yet, ironically, politics and government are a young person's business; every campaign needs that."

Abi Green was the person who called our house in September 2003 to see if we would be supporting Dean. She ran great house meetings, except that the higher-ups in the campaign told her she needed to sell Dean to the people who would come away saying that they wanted to vote for *her* to be president. Her quick wit led the *New York Times* to coin the word "quippy." She had irately told someone who suggested that Dean house meetings were like Tupperware parties, "We're selling democracy here."

Aswini Anburajan was the organizer for our area who urged us to hold our first house party. We sent out sixty-five personalized invitations to friends and colleagues, and got seven people who showed up. Born of Indian parents, Aswini felt constant pressure from home to give up her idealistic commitment and get a real job, like on Wall Street. Her commitment ran deep. In December, I said to her that my darkest fear was that Dean and the campaign would turn out to be a mirage produced by wishful thinking. From the look on her face, I thought she was going to point at me and scream out, "Blasphemer!"

Like all the people in the office, she was under marching orders to get more one-on-ones and more house parties and not dally too much with issues. That was just as well, since when I tried to get the area organizers to be more conversant with the platform, they had too many demands from the state headquarters to do so.

"Old" Ben was the 23 year-old regional director in charge of the office. An international affairs major at Middlebury College, where he had first had the chance to observe Dean, he put his theater minor to use in staging the elaborate productions when Dean would make appearances in the area. He may have been the youngest of the paid staff, but he had been in politics since he selected a candidate to do leafleting for when he was six.

Garrett Bridgens had come from Oregon, after graduating from college, to serve as an unpaid volunteer. When I berated each of the kids about the horrendously messy workspace, he was initially the one who took responsibility for office hygiene. Even with alcohol wipes, the mess and traffic in the office ultimately made everyone ill. Although Garrett was an enormously fit track athlete from the University of Oregon, he would work himself into the hospital once he got a paying job as an area organizer.

Jim Bentley showed up in Portsmouth, and at our house, in January, 2004. He was on winter break from Bennington College, and was one of the many unpaid volunteers the staff called "winterns," a term which Jim came to feel was demeaning. Jim had gone to school in nearby Newburyport and Portland, in the states on either side of New Hampshire that are linked by the interstate that passes through the truncated Seacoast.

Jim's dad was a minister, and his parents were separated. His character was evident in the story of how he had moved to Portland. When he went to a summer drama program in high school, he knew that his habits and friends in Newburyport were heading him in the wrong direction. After forming a strong bond with the woman instructing the program, he asked her if he could stay with her and go to school in Portland. Her kindness offered him shelter from the storm that is adolescence, and he was successful enough to end up at Bennington.

Jim had great personal skills, but his ability to work with computers pegged him early on as the king of the database in Portsmouth. He would have preferred more human contact, but his ability, coupled with the fact that no one else was eager to do it, kept him chained to a computer in the office. As the constant demands for new lists of voters to call or canvas came in, Jim would generate those.

His days were brutally long. He would get up by eight at the latest, sometimes prodded by our dog, who would push open the door to his room if he hadn't closed it tightly. After a breakfast, which would sometimes be a banana to chase coffee on the way out the door, he would head to the office, occasionally remembering to bring a lunch. Sometimes he got out to be a part of the campaign events, or to do visibility, often in bitter cold. But usually he was to be found hunched over a keyboard, generating yet another list that someone was breathing down his neck for.

Jim typically wouldn't get home until after we went to bed, usually ten or much later. There were nights when he would get home at two or three in the morning, and a few nights when he never left the office. His fatigue grew evident as the day of the primary grew near, and his appearances at our house were usually limited to hours when we were asleep.

One benefit for Jim to being in the office was that he got to be friends with Lizzie. Lizzie Morris was from Carleton College, and was a sweet, genuine, and pretty young woman. When she had arrived in December, she took over the responsibility for housing. That task continued to expand as more volunteers came in as the primary approached.

Lizzie was supposed to go back to school in January, which would allow her to graduate on time. She was torn by a financial need to graduate on time and her commitment to the campaign. As I did for most of the long term staff in the office, I took her out to lunch at the Muddy River Smokehouse, so I could get to know her better.

My goal in such lunches was always three-fold. First, I wanted these kids who were either underpaid or unpaid to have a decent meal, without dipping into what were usually meager funds. Second, I wanted to get to know them so that I could write letters of recommendation for them if they wanted in the future. Third, barbecue is the other major food group, besides chocolate and ice cream.

In my conversation with Lizzie, she talked about the dilemma of having parents back in Houston who wanted her to graduate on time, when she was increasingly committed to the campaign. She inquired at Carleton about getting credit for her campaign work, but was turned down.

So our conversation was about what would mean the most to her as she looked back in the decades ahead. I told her that I was sorry I hadn't worked for Bobby Kennedy, or George McGovern, or Bill Bradley. I told her how this was the first candidate that I felt such a personal commitment towards, and that my work, despite often being menial, was as gratifying as anything I'd done in my life, except for marrying my wife. We talked about ideals, and I gave her a copy of Malcolm X's autobiography, as a book that had profoundly influenced my life since I was her age. When she left for Christmas in Houston, it wasn't clear whether she would return, so her reappearance in the office in the New Year was a blessing for the local effort. Hopefully, it would be for her, also.

Lizzie had a boyfriend when she arrived, but her increasing friendship with Jim coincided with her eventually breaking up with the boyfriend.

On the nights when I would see Jim at home, we would talk about

Lizzie, as I tried to provide him with a scouting report that he could utilize in what seemed like an eminently worthwhile goal.

"New" Ben appeared one day to take on my old hometown of Exeter. The second day he was there, he set up a meeting with me for 8:30 in the morning to give me something to deliver to Exeter. He showed up forty-five minutes late. I chewed him out about being responsive to constituents, and how failing to do so could give the campaign a bad image. What I had seen was Ben's modus operandi. He would be perpetually late to meetings, and "Old" Ben would try to have him fired. Because "New" Ben had been brought on board as a friend of someone in the Manchester office, those efforts at good management were rebuffed.

"New" Ben eventually sank his own ship, when he blew off a meeting in the main office in Manchester, to go to a house meeting that wasn't even his own. It wasn't like he was great at house meetings, either. Area organizers running the meetings were supposed to do a short "story" of no more than five minutes to explain why they were committed to Dean. Reports I got from Exeter indicated that "New" Ben's story ran over an hour, and then he wouldn't follow up on the contacts at the meeting anyway. It was indicative of the management structure in Manchester that "New" Ben's transgressions didn't even cost him his job.

There was much shuffling of responsibilities as "New" Ben finally got banished to the New Hampshire political equivalent of Siberia, the North Country. Abi went to South Carolina, and my home towns of Exeter and Greenland just headed south. Brought in to clean up the mess was the statewide Lesbian-Gay-Bisexual-Transgender (LGBT) coordinator, Wendy Howell, a veteran campaign operative. Unlike the hormonal swings of the younger, politically naïve area organizers, Wendy virtually always had a poker face. She was, however, relentlessly persistent in pursuit of goals. If we needed more calls, another house party, an immediate meeting, she would call until either I got truly angry or she got what she wanted.

This cast surrounded me as I made ID calls and did data entry of the results. Driven crazy by menial work, I carved out a niche by taking over visibility and delivering signs to every person who had requested them, thus becoming statewide volunteer of the week.

The operative definition of "week" was indicative of the bending of the time-space continuum that occurs in a political campaign. I was told I would be on the website, picture and all, within days. It was several weeks before that happened, all the while as the previous "Volunteer of the Week" continued to reign. Still, it was rather gratifying when staffers in Manchester recognized me at events, having seen my picture on the Dean for New Hampshire website.

Even greater glory lay ahead.

WORKING THE SENIOR CIRCUIT

"I wish that I knew what I know now, when I was younger."
Rod Stewart

As a snowy December began, the Dean momentum that had been a growing snowball rolling down a mountain began to level off. In physics, momentum is the product of mass times velocity. The velocity of the campaign certainly was increasing, but the mass of supporters, and the weight of the actual commitment of people being polled, was not increasing as it had been in previous months. The velocity of the campaign had led to mistakes, and the mass media had been right there to document them.

In his 1980 book, *Before the Convention*, John Aldrich notes that "Media attention, along with financial contributions, and standings in the polls, are the three main measures of momentum."[9]

Expanding on this idea, Dante Scala observes that "Often these measures all affect one another in a cyclical manner. A flurry of stories on a candidate boosts name recognition; increased name recognition leads to better standing in the polls; and better showings in the polls prompt more contributors to send funds to the campaign."[10]

The Dean campaign was beginning to see a disruption in the cycle. Intense media scrutiny, far before the first votes would be cast, had started tarnishing a once-golden image. Poll numbers would stay level or begin to drop off in December. The rate at which people signed on to Dean's Internet Express was declining.

I wanted a way to have more direct contact with voters than as an anonymous voice on the phone who identified himself as a neighbor from Greenland. Then Aswini told me that it had been suggested in a strategy session that I should do seniors outreach, which would get me out of the office.

Chaffing at being directed by kids half my age into office chores, I leapt at an opportunity to get out and give presentations that would allow interaction on issues and the platform. Residents of assisted-living and nursing homes represented a wonderful captive audience that would make capturing Dean votes as easy, Wendy would say, "as shooting fish in a barrel." (Notice that all clichés are attributed to someone other than the author.)

I contacted all the area nursing homes by phone, which sometimes required several calls to locate the correct person. I always wrote down the name, correctly spelled, of the people from the facility with whom I worked, so that I might send them personalized thank you notes after the presentation. For people who were particularly helpful, I sent a letter acknowledging that to their superiors.

I learned the best time to make an appearance, and that getting cooperation from the staff was crucial to the nature of the audience I would receive. I also learned one particularly universal and inviolable rule: nothing interrupts Bingo.

I threw myself into producing large print charts highlighting the seniors agenda of the Dean campaign. Fueled by the campaign's idealism and the opportunity to provide a public service, I would explain the new Medicare prescription drug bill. That wasn't exactly easy, and what I found was fairly horrifying. Having been spared by luck in the draft lottery from burning a draft card, my AARP card now looked like a good candidate for kindling.

I sent out press releases, which got printed in all the local papers, and even resulted in a nursing home contacting me to request a presentation.[266] This was going to be great!

The reality of my audience came shuffling home to me at my first presentation. A group of very senior citizens sat gathered around the television, where I would show a Dean video that was immeasurably better than the one Aswini had used at our house meeting. Of course, on an absolute scale, it may not have been that great, but in politics, all things are measured relatively.

A woman in the throes of dementia repeated at regular and short intervals, "I'm going to tell my mother on you!" She was gone by the time I began my first presentation, perhaps in search of a mother well into her second century. She was probably a Dennis Kucinich supporter anyhow.

Another woman asked me three times if *I* was Howard Dean. Apparently dissatisfied with my answer, she would periodically quiz the people around her if they thought I was Dean. If I had been campaigning for Bill Bradley, whom I've always heard I resemble, I at least I could have lied to her.

I began by showing pictures of my mother and father, and the house I had lived in that was in downtown Exeter. Some of the people seemed to recognize the house and one or two knew the name of my Great-uncle Perley, who had raised my mother in that house.

I talked about Perley's devoted friend Bill Lord, who had gone to visit Perley in a nursing home every day for the last twelve years of his life. I emphasized Dean's career as a physician, and how his experience as a doctor made him a type of candidate unlike any choice that preceded him. Then I segued into my presentation on the Medicare "benefits."

Glazed eyes culminated in a total absence of questions at the end. Clearly, I was going to need to change my aim. My goal became giving as simple a presentation as possible, and then identifying potential primary voters, and seeing that they got absentee ballots.

In New Hampshire, voters must be registered as Democrats or Independents by Halloween to vote in the Democratic primary. Unfortunately, the campaign had failed to get that information out effectively.

The Independents were very important. Statistics provided by *washingtonpost.com* state that "The single largest group of registered voters are what we call "undeclared" voters. In 2000 about 39 percent leaned Democratic, and 41 percent, leaned Republican. Only 20 percent insisted they were purely independent.

In the 2004 election, the registration was 37.7% undeclared, 36 percent Republican and the remainder Democrats."[11] (Figure 1, pages 327-339)

So, the routine would be to work my way around the individuals in the room asking the same questions: "What's your name? Are you a Democrat, Independent or Republican?" It became clear to me that New Hampshire Democrats were either living in mansions tended by hordes of servants, or had suffered from short life spans, probably because of the shortcomings of Medicare.

However, one senior brightened my day when she anticipated my questions, without prompting, by identifying herself as "Mindy Gates (not her real name), singer and dancer!" Apparently she was a George Murphy Republican.

The most uplifting moment of my one-person campaign with the seniors came when a member of that day's audience told me the story of a former patient of Dean's. Recently deceased in a Fremont nursing home at 103, the woman had been the proud recipient of regular calls from the then-governor of Vermont, inquiring about her well-being.

I knew then why I was going around to the seniors.

In my initial preparation to speak to seniors, my goal had been to address issues and the Dean platform. First I had thought I would talk about the entire platform, and then I had narrowed it down to senior issues. Ultimately, my presentations would be brief, with a particularly good videotape being the highlight, followed by any questions. While the videotape showed Dean discussing various issues, I would ask the audience to try and read his face as he spoke, to see if they found him to be someone they could trust.

Andrew Smith, the Director of the UNH Survey Center, says that he doesn't believe voters vote on the basis of issue positions. "Voters are looking for leadership qualities, and you won't find that in position papers. It doesn't come across on TV, and you don't get it in the newspaper. You get it by seeing them, by talking to them, and talking with other people who have talked to them. Even in New Hampshire, not that many people meet a candidate, but they probably know somebody who has met that person and will tell them what they're really like. That second wave is very important."[12]

Few of the people in the nursing homes were likely to actually get out and see the candidates. By this point, they would have seen several very different styles. Reporting for *washingtonpost.com*, Leonard Downie, Jr. reflected on the varying stump performers.

"Kerry seemed more relaxed and self-confident as a campaigner than he had earlier. Dean had toned down the volume of his delivery, but still delivered the most hard-edged criticism of the Bush administration, and the competing Democrats. Edwards stayed positive, and continued campaigning like a folksy lawyer. Clark surprised me with his rousing, autobiographic stump speech. Lieberman emphasized that he still thought the Iraq war was justified and that voters should not penalize him for it."[13]

People in the senior crowd seemed to be reacting mostly to me, although they paid polite attention to my efforts to deliver the Dean platform. I guess surrogates are important.

However, follow-through is as important in politics as in golf. I repeatedly urged Ben to select someone from the flood tide of fresh-faced volunteers to go around to the nursing homes after me, to do one-on-one follow-up. Jim was particularly interested in doing this, and had the human skills to get it done. However, having him working constantly in front of a computer screen was deemed more important.

In fact, everything seemed to be more important, as follow-up never occurred, beyond my taking around absentee ballots. In the Portsmouth office, the clientele that I was attempting to engage apparently didn't represent a high priority.

Youth shall be served.

Joe Miller relates an experience working for the Dean campaign. "Well, this was in Rochester or Somersworth. There was an event and he (Dean) couldn't make it, so he was sending this little frail lady, who was his mother. It was a senior citizen place. I said to my wife Betty, 'guess who I'm going to introduce tonight? I'm going to introduce Howard Dean's mother.' I guess they picked me cause I'm a senior citizen too, hoping I'd get half way down to first base.

"I arrived, and there was a bingo game going on. They all had their cards, but it hadn't started yet. I was there to take care of Howard Dean's mother. And apparently they (the campaign) had a driver who didn't know the spot too well. I think it was some kind of Elks club in Somersworth, some place out there.

"She (Dean's mother) arrived with his brother. His brother's name is Jim—younger, a lot younger than Howard. This little lady arrived and she was to speak to this group. We didn't really chat very much. I was very courteous and said, 'I feel so honored Mrs. Dean. I've been a follower and supporter of your son and I certainly hope he'll be our next president.'

"I think she's a Republican.

"So, I went over to whoever was running this bingo game and I said, 'Hi, my name is Representative Miller,' for the occasion to have some clout. 'Mrs. Dean is here. At what point do you want her to speak?' They said, 'oh, it's too late. She was supposed to speak before the start of Bingo.' So I said, 'She's the candidate's mother. Maybe just five minutes.' They said, 'not a chance'.

"It was a terribly rainy night, and she had to get back to Boston to take the train, not a plane, back to New York City, where she lives. So they had a driver and Jim and Mrs. Dean. And so, I made my plea… meanwhile they were calling out, 'B-4.' I walked her out to the car on this rainy night. I talked to Jim a little bit. He was taking care of his Mom, and they had a driver.

"He said to the driver, 'Do you know how to get to Boston?' and he (the driver) said, 'No, but I'll figure it out.' So finally, I got her into the car and said to the driver, 'Are you sure you know how to get onto Route 16 to head for Boston?' because she was taking the Acela train.

"He wasn't from here, he was a driver. I think he was a campaign driver. Jim hopped into the back seat with his mother; this guy was in the front seat. The last thing I said was, 'I hope you know how to get onto Route 16, that's the route to Boston.' Then they drove off into the rain. She was a sweet, little, frail lady. She was supposed to talk before they were to call numbers."

Big Howard's First-born Son

I like to see a man proud of the place in which he lives. I like to see a man live in it so that his place will be proud of him.

—Abraham Lincoln

Dean's road to becoming a presidential candidate could actually have been seen as starting on a bike path. At least, that's what Ben suggested I should open with, in giving a short biography of the governor to seniors. I had viewed it as a suggestion, rather than a directive, much the way Massachusetts drivers view traffic laws.

Since Ben had not read the three books on Dean that I purchased, I was more interested in putting together my own profile of Dean and his platform than having Ben direct me.

I started by looking on the *Dean for America* website, where the area organizers in the office were supposed to direct people, thus avoiding prolonged discussions of issues. From that, I was able to get a better sense of the platform, but the website was actually information overload. The search engine didn't seem to work well, and I found reducing the volumes of material to concise talking points even more difficult than it had been when Judy and I had formulated our presentations at our house meetings.

So I went to the bookstore.

One of the resources that were going unused in the office was a book pulled together in a few months by nine Vermont journalists who had covered Dean. *Howard Dean: A Citizen's Guide to the Man Who Would Be President*, had so much useful information that I reread it and highlighted it so that it could be digested quickly. My wife read the highlighted parts and found it took about half an hour.

The book talked about his record in Vermont, and seemed to be well-balanced journalism, giving voice to people who had been on the opposite side of issues from Dean. It gave me a sense of what actions in his past might be subject to attack, and allowed me to figure how to respond.

I had shown it to each of the staffers. I urged them to read it, and then pass it on to the next person in the office, so everyone could benefit. I think perhaps two people actually did that. For a while, the book had disappeared, but it was eventually located in Aswini's car.

I got tired of waiting for it to be utilized. After a couple of weeks, I took it back, so it wouldn't be lost in the swirling chaos and mess of the office. A second book, *In His Own Words*, was organized by topic, so that you could look up, say, NAFTA, in the table of contents and turn to a page that would have a direct quote from Dean on the topic.

The problem was that the quotes tended to be just a few sentences, so that you were only getting yes/no positions, and not nuanced policy. The pages would have fewer words than the typical Dr. Seuss book, yet no cute illustrations. I kept the book with me for the next two months, but I don't think I referred to it once.

The third book on the market was a campaign autobiography. It gave every indication of having dictated by Dean while he was traveling between events. Although there were some personal touches that were vaguely interesting (i.e. when he went to school in England, the diminutive Dean was, figuratively speaking, huge on the basketball court), there really wasn't anything of value that the *Citizen's Guide* didn't have. When Dean's book disappeared from the lending library I had created in the office, I didn't bother to look for it.

Like George W. Bush, Dean was born into privilege. His father was quite strict, and his kids were clearly not spoiled, earning their spending money with household chores. Young Howard, whose equally small father was known as "Big Howard", was sent off to a boarding school in Rhode Island.

St. George's sits on a hill overlooking Newport, and would like to create the impression it is in Newport, but geographic reality places it in Middletown. It is a beautiful little school, in the tier just below Andover and Exeter in the status-conscious prep school world. When Dean arrived, there were no minority students, although one quarter of the school's population is now from a minority background.

Dean was not a stellar student, but he did participate in many sports, and managed to get into Yale. His prep school background never kept him from a lifetime of being "sartorially challenged," as he would decades later wear the same suit for weeks on end on the national stage.

He is remembered as being brutally direct. "You were either with him or against him, but he wasn't strident or demeaning if you didn't agree. He would never say in an argument, 'You're stupid to think that way,'"[14] recalls classmate Harry Wulsin.

Dean and two friends took summer jobs in 1965 on a hot, dusty, Florida cattle ranch where boarding school French was of no use among the Spanish-speaking workers. In that work and in jobs he held after college, it was clear that he did not shy away from hard physical labor.

Before going to Yale, he spent a year at Felsted, a boarding school in England. Like his father, he was seventeen upon his graduation from prep school. The year abroad was to provide maturity, so he would not be ejected from Yale, as his father had been after two years there.

As the lone American at Felsted, Dean repeatedly was forced to explain the racial strife in the United States, as well as defend American involvement in Vietnam. By the time he got to Yale, he would be "committed, but determinedly non-violent. His hero was Martin Luther King, Jr., not Stokely Carmichael."[15]

During his time abroad, he traveled to visit the family of a schoolmate from Nigeria, as well as venturing behind the Iron Curtain to Turkey. Dean's curiosity about the world outside Park Avenue also led him to request African-American roommates at Yale.

That resonated with me, since I used to hang out with the small black population that UNH recruited when I was in college. (I still remember a son of privilege from Swampscott calling me "nigger lover" in a drunken late night visit to my dorm.)

While Dean was developing his bridge game in late night sessions at Yale, he also was an anomaly in the student body for reading the *New York Times* news section every day, a habit he continues today. He majored in political science, but showed greater dedication to intramural sports and parties.

Like mine, Dean's college transcript was quite unimpressive. However, we were both the product of a time when Vietnam, and the chaos of American society, made it harder to focus on classroom performance. At least, that's my retrospective rationalization. Both Dean and I would marry women who somehow managed to avoid any distractions from academic excellence.

Like me, Dean faced the possibility of going to Vietnam. John Kerry signed up for service and chose to serve on what was, at that time, the Navy's equivalent of John Kennedy's PT boat.

I got a high number in the draft lottery and was never again faced with having to consider Canada, or conscientious objector status, or draft evasion. (The day of the draft lottery, I had raced out to excitedly tell my mother "I'm 285!" My mother turned from her rail-thin son to a friend and said, "He's always trying to gain weight.")

A friend of mine named Mike Cusick studied hard to put together a strong case for conscientious objector status. When he went before the review board of local men, who were grizzled veterans of Korea and World War II, they tried to bait him, to show that he was capable of anger and not a true peacenik. At one point, a vet fired at him, "What would you do if the Communists came over the Western Plain?" He fired back with "and raped my grandmother?"

He envisioned his application going down the tubes as a sacrifice to his impetuousness. However, he got the C.O. status and served for two years, earning next to nothing, in a Minneapolis hospital. Other friends went off to Vietnam, and a different friend named Mike Hathaway went to prison instead of registering for the draft. Like Ali, his conviction resulted in his conviction.

Howard Dean, however, was able to take x-rays of his back to his Army physical, and he was declared medically unfit to serve. His back problem has kept him from ever being able to run any distance, which would be a crucial half of the "fight or flight" instinct every soldier drew on in Vietnam.[17]

However, in a move that would clearly show a total absence of any foresight for a political career, he then spent the year after he was graduated from Yale doing various physically demanding jobs, while he was a ski bum in Aspen. Although he would readily admit to past marijuana use in early debates in 2003, the fact that Aspen was known as "Toot City" in the seventies has never led to questions about cocaine use. Perhaps the unsubstantiated allegations of cocaine use by George W. Bush in his days as a party animal kept the question at bay.

After the hiatus in Aspen, Dean fell in line with his father's expectations and began a career on Wall Street. Although he was apparently successful, he didn't enjoy it. So, unbeknownst to his father, he started taking night school courses at Columbia University that would he would need for medical school. It wasn't without his mother's knowledge. She ran into him on campus one day, when she was working as a volunteer.

At the same time he was studying in night school, he worked as a volunteer in a Manhattan hospital, to determine if he really liked medicine. Dean's friend David Berg recalls his saying that "…he would like to do something, I think his words were 'morally unimpeachable'. That is, something that's a good that everybody can agree makes a contribution to the general welfare."[18]

At about the same time, Dean's younger brother Charlie had become disillusioned after working in the McGovern campaign, and set off to travel the world. In the course of those travels, while he and a friend were on a ferry on the Mekong River, Laotian rebels captured him. The two were held captive for three months, then executed. "Charlie's death, and the agony of his parents as they frantically sought to win their son's release, snapped Howard Dean into focus about his own life. He bore down on the pre-med courses as he'd never done at Yale, aced his exams and won acceptance…"[19] to Albert Einstein School of Medicine in New York.

Dealing with Charlie's death was not as simple as becoming a workaholic, however. Dean resented the anguish his family endured in the aftermath, and sought counseling to deal with his feelings in the 1980s. The stoicism of the physician dissipates when Dean talks about Charlie; he once cried during an interview when talking about his brother.

Yale had led Dean towards liberalism, but friends say that Charlie's death reversed that drift.

Einstein's College of Medicine had a nondiscriminatory admissions policy. This opened the doors to a group that included Dean, which traditionally had a harder time gaining entrance to medical schools: older students who had not been science majors as undergraduates. Dean worked in the poor neighborhoods of the city through Einstein's social medicine program.

Dr. Stephen Goldstone, who double-dated with the Deans at that time, describes Dean's career path. "It was a conscious decision to abandon his career and commit to medicine. He had an exceptional level of commitment and maturity, and he had a calming ability." Goldstone described Dean in terms common to all of Dean's schoolmates. "He was absolutely a straight shooter. There was never a wall around him, nothing phony."[20]

It was at Einstein that he met his future wife, Judith Steinberg, who was also studying to become a doctor. While she was a decidedly better student, they had a natural enough affinity and continued their courtship after he was graduated in 1978 and went into residency in Vermont.

At a time when his career path was diverging from the family tradition on Wall Street, Steinberg represented another divergence. She was Jewish, while the Dean family belonged to a country club that did not allow Jews. Steinberg's residency would take her to Montreal, and they had a weekend relationship until she finished there.

While he was living alone in Vermont, Dean came under the influence of, and into the auspices of, one of the doyens of the Vermont Democratic Party. The Democratic Party in Vermont was not a strong organization at that time. Because Vermont Republicans were moderate, the need for a Democratic Party was not as great. Senator George Aiken had encapsulated that moderation during the Vietnam War when he said the country should "declare victory and get out."

Quirky and outspoken politicians aren't rare in Vermont. Ralph Flanders was the first Senator to denounce Joseph McCarthy on the Senate floor. Former Socialist Bernard Sanders was elected to the House of Representatives with the support of gun owner groups. Fred Tuttle was a retired dairy farmer who played himself in the cult-favorite spoof, "Man with a Plan." In a case of life imitating art, in 1998 Tuttle ran in the Republican primary for Senate against a wealthy former Massachusetts resident who had just moved to his Vermont summer home on a permanent basis. Tuttle's carpet bagging opponent was not as well received in Vermont as Hillary Clinton would be in New York. Tuttle won, and promptly encouraged everyone to vote for the Democrat, Patrick Leahy.

Jim Jeffords departed the Republican Party to become an Independent in 2001, and thereby shifted the balance of power in the Senate. Bumper stickers are still evident throughout Vermont saying "Thank You, Jim." When Jeffords was a young House member in the 1970's, he had saved money by camping out in his office and living in a travel trailer.[21]

Esther Sorrell, whose son William would become Dean's attorney general, was a guiding force in Dean's early political education. The friendship grew over Friday nights, watching the PBS political shows while eating Esther's cookies or brownies. Dean's community involvement began with advocating for a bike path along Lake Champlain. He would do the politicking, going to senior citizens' groups, as well as the manual labor, taking his chainsaw to old railroad ties. The depth of his religious affiliation was shown when he changed churches because he felt his church was not adequately supporting the bike path initiative.[16]

His crusade would continue into his work in the legislature, where he led the repeal of an 1876 law that would have ceded the waterfront land back to the railroads. Subsequent State and Federal Supreme Court rulings on railroad land conversion to bike trails would be at the foundation of the evolving rails-to-trails movement.

His activism on the bike path led him to run as a delegate for Jimmy Carter at the 1980 convention. He had been a hardworking volunteer in the campaign, willing to do the grunt work that every campaign requires. At the convention, he would later describe, he worked for Carter during the days and partied with the Kennedy folks at night. His ability to bridge the two groups paved the way for his becoming county chair for the party afterwards.

When Steinberg finished in Montreal in 1979, she moved into his little apartment, and joined him in the residency program. Their partnership continued in their professional lives, as they shared a practice together after they were married. Their styles were different, but complementary. Much like his style as a governor, Dean was more inclined to move rapidly to results intuitively, whereas she was more process oriented. Both were highly regarded as physicians.

Once he was married, party became a political rather than a recreational verb for Dean. He stopped drinking, because he didn't like the effect it had on him. He eliminated caffeine from his diet. He was renowned in Vermont for his devotion to family and a simple lifestyle.

Biking and canoeing were their idea of fun. He would attend, and sometimes coach, his son's and daughter's youth hockey league games, even receiving a warning from a referee in Quebec for being too aggressive as a fan.[22]

Dean's foray into the political world led him to run for the state legislature. He campaigned on the need for the bike path, and for protecting the waterfront from development. Dean's volunteer work at a low-income medical clinic in Burlington's Old North End gave him a broad demographic appeal that launched his political career in Vermont.

In the legislature, he became minority whip. In running for that position, he had initially faced entrenched power in the form of Ralph Wright. While the position ended up becoming vacant as a Wright crony moved to minority leader, Dean had shown Wright that he did not fear losing, and that he felt "politics is important, but it makes no sense to become attached to the political life or take it too seriously."[23]

Dean next considered running against moderate Republican Jim Jeffords, for Vermont's only seat in the U.S. House. Jeffords, who would go on to become a Senator, hold the longest continuously held Republican seat in American history[24], and then switch to being an Independent, would have been difficult to beat. Although he didn't end up challenging Jeffords, Montpelier lobbyist Bob Sherman saw his consideration of the possibility as a sign that Dean "has high self-esteem, high ambition, and he believes in his intellect. He's aggressive, he's politically astute, and he's lucky."[25] That luck swept Dean into the office as lieutenant governor in 1986, as Democrats were widely victorious in Vermont.

Two years later, his luck continued, as Democrat Madeline Kunin decided not to run for reelection. Popular Republican Richard Snelling decided to come out of retirement to run for governor. Dean wisely did not challenge him, and was reelected as lieutenant governor. All the while he was expanding his political career, Dean was practicing medicine full-time. Lieutenant governor Dean would put in 40-hour weeks as a physician, and another 40 hours as a politician. Then, in a display of frugality that would be a continuing trademark, he would paint his own house, because he didn't want to pay someone else to do it.

Anson Tebbetts describes the two-career Howard Dean: "I've been told from a reporter that had him as a doctor here that he was a good doctor. A woman who was a producer here had him as a doctor and said he was a very good doctor.

"One of his best campaign commercials ever was when he ran for lieutenant governor and he had a woman that was in her 80s. Her line was, 'I'm voting for Howard Dean, he still makes house calls.' After that happened, he would joke, 'Yeah, after that commercial, I still had to make house calls.'"

Tebbetts also describes Dean's unique approach to professional politics.

"At one point, I think he had his former nanny running his campaign. She was a former nanny, turned into a 20 year-old campaign manager. She went into policy later. From babysitting, to campaigns, to being a policy analyst."

Dean learned governmental fiscal conservatism working with Snelling, as Snelling increased taxes and cut budgets to bring Vermont back toward fiscal stability. Then, in August 1991, Dean moved up to the governor's position when Snelling was found lying next to his pool, dead from a heart attack the previous evening. A very youthful-looking Dean finished the physical he was doing, took the oath of office, and never returned to practicing medicine.

As governor, Dean was a pragmatist. In a state where Democrats tend to be very liberal, fellow Democrats viewed Dean with suspicion. Some of his early positions led people to question whether he wasn't actually more of a Republican. Free-spending Democrats found Dean to be most unreceptive. However, his tight reins would make Vermont a rarity when he finally left office in 2003: a state with a budget surplus. When Snelling died, Dean kept on most of the Republicans from Snelling's administration. He retained a bipartisan roundtable of businessmen, and appointed Harlan Sylvester as chairman, a position Sylvester still holds under Dean's successor, Republican Jim Douglas.

Dean sought advice from Republicans such as Bill Gilbert, who has observed that Dean "handled that transition with grace and real sensitivity. He was very thoughtful and generous."[26]

Ray Proulx served on the economic development committee for Essex and Essex Junction. "We went down and talked to him about the circumferential highway, which would serve as a bypass around Burlington. It was a disappointment for some folks that he didn't support it. He didn't talk against it, he just didn't include it in his administration's initiatives.

When it did surface, he did not speak in favor of it. His rationale was that he was hoping that trains would be the way to go. He wanted to put multi-million dollars into the transit system through trains. His view was a broader view, looking at what was best for the state of Vermont. He recognized the importance of IBM, as an economic foundation for the state of Vermont, and he was very supportive of IBM."

A prominent Vermont business leader notes that, "He understood we had to have jobs here. The problem that the liberals have, that they don't understand, is that you have to have jobs in order to create the taxes that generate the revenue that pays for the programs that they want to start or perpetuate." Because of his Wall Street experience and his almost genetic coding for business, Dean "was a pragmatist more than he otherwise would have been. He was not on the left, he was right in the middle." He lured new business to Vermont, such as captive insurance companies that had previously set up offshore, by using tax incentives.

Dean brought on board women from the Kunin administration, including Kate O'Connor, who had worked in a Dean re-election campaign. He angered both environmentalists and human rights advocates when he aligned with power companies in supporting a 25-year deal to purchase power from Hydro-Quebec. The deal would impact both the Canadian wilderness and the Cree Indians of Quebec.

In a state where the environmental standards are equaled only by Oregon's, he infuriated environmentalists by skipping over process to achieve his desired results. However, the results were often seen as win-win, by all but the most extreme. He brokered ski areas' needs for access to water for snowmaking with environmental regulations, and had ski areas transfer mountain lands into state hands in exchange for more land to expand base lodges.

Through such efforts, and a stewardship of the state, almost half a million acres of Vermont, nearly 8% of the state, became public lands while he was governor. While he may have broken the hearts of the most ardent environmentalists, he was a conservationist, in the tradition of Teddy Roosevelt's founding of the national parks system.

He expanded health services, sometimes by combining existing programs to provide greater efficiency at minimal cost and using tobacco funds to partially offset the cost, so that Vermont would be consistently ranked as one of the healthiest states in the nation.

Dean's initial efforts in health care weren't successful. As lieutenant governor, he had worn his physician's hat in testifying on behalf of a Canadian-style single payer system in 1991. After that failed, he embraced the multi payer model as governor. He had Ralph Wright spearhead the effort, which collapsed at about the same time as Hillary Clinton's health care program flat-lined. Wright was not happy with Dean's response to their failure. "I guess this was the one thing I could never understand about Howard Dean. He always seemed so ready to abandon his cause at the first sign of defeat. Maybe it was his medical training that toughened him to the certain failures that awaited us all. Maybe it was an unwillingness to have any cause at all, at least any cause for which he was willing to risk his political skin. It wasn't just causes he was willing to abandon; he was capable of acting the same with people."[27]

However, Dean succeeded in bringing health care to Vermont incrementally.

Dean's personal traits marked his governorship, examples of which are included in *Howard Dean: A Citizen's Guide to the Man Who Would Be President.* "Dean often spoke on an issue before receiving advice from his staff… He could be testy and confrontational when challenged on policy by people he didn't know… He had a reputation for being impulsive and occasionally arrogant… Some of the people who knew Dean best saw him as a governor with a small 'g.' He was aggressively insistent on his own views, but otherwise seemed to think of himself as just an ordinary guy…

(Dean seemed) "…not to need the kind of deference, indeed adulation, that is commonly sought by politicians."[28]

Ray Proulx sent him a letter about the inequality of education in Vermont because of the fiscal inequities. "I was impatient, but he was very quick to respond. In his response he agreed with the necessity for greater equity in the state, but he also was very clear that he couldn't do it by bankrupting the state of Vermont. He was able to articulate, for me at least, his rationale for making the move a little slower. He also said, in a later conversation, that it was also driven by politics, that moving too quickly could have just jeopardized the entire movement. That was something that he certainly was very astute to, and he was absolutely right. If he had moved it too quickly it would have been stopped before it had started. He is definitely the most skilled politician, in Vermont… that I've ever witnessed. He went through some pretty difficult elections and he was just a master at being able to maintain the political support, at the same time that he maintained some pretty difficult public policy positions. He made some very difficult decisions so that the Stowes and other wealthy communities were on his neck, and he just stood tall."

WCAX-TV in Burlington ran a story describing Dean as the most popular elected leader in the world, but that was before Dean's greatest test - civil unions. Although this would become an issue on which he later would portray himself as having been a spearhead, Dean was, in fact, his pragmatic self on gay rights. As with the rulings that led to Vermont's effort to equalize educational funding, the state court system had come down with a ruling no one expected.

The State Supreme Court said that gays must be given equal rights, and that it was up to the state legislature to decide in what form to provide them. Dean had appointed two of the five justices to a State Supreme Court that was viewed as liberal. The ruling was unanimous, including the Republican Chief Justice whom Dean had appointed. Everyone had expected a ruling for or against gay marriage. The options now were marriage, or a form that would provide all the rights without the same title, civil union. Actually, there was a dissent, but Justice Denise Johnson felt the ruling had not gone far enough.

Although the ruling was totally unexpected, within an hour Dean addressed the ruling.

He said he could support a civil union provision, but, like many people, was uncomfortable with allowing gays to marry.

What he did was signal the legislature that he would sign legislation which they would have to craft and pass. They had the courage to proceed, although it would ultimately cost many legislators their seats in the backlash to follow.

All of this was because of a very Republican-like wording of the Vermont constitution about personal liberties. It was old-time Vermont Republican thinking in the Vermont Constitution that provided the phrases they needed to create a court case—not the liberal left politics of Burlington, or Bernard Sanders, or the Greens, or the lingering hippies from the communes.

60

When Dean signed the legislation, he signed it in private, away from the flash of media cameras. Seemingly coining a word, he said a public signing would have been "triumphalist" at a time when the state needed to heal its wounds after a divisive discussion. The media was angry to have been excluded from the signing, yet many in the media wept when Dean later addressed them on his support for the legislation.

While his political finesse, acuity, and low profile on the issue was notable, he would still be a lightning rod for a backlash to follow. Phones rang constantly after a national conservative talk-radio host broadcast Dean's office number and urged listeners to call him.

When Dean ran for reelection, he wore a bullet proof vest at public events because of death threats. His children were threatened. He was publicly cursed and reviled.

Anson Tebbetts describes the civil unions' backlash as witnessed when Dean participated in a Labor Day Parade in Northfield, Vermont: "It was the kick-off for the fall election and that was his last (parade), in 2000. They were worried about him getting pelted with eggs. They had a little extra security for him. At the parade where he (previously) walked, he'd just ride. He'd always walked it. All that stuff about the bulletproof vest that came out long after, during the presidential campaign. We (Vermont journalists) would never report anything like that."

During a fundraising walk in St. Albans, an elderly woman exercised her right to petition the state government by addressing Dean with "You f———, queer-loving son of a bitch."

Dean's self-control was evident in his response. "You should clean up your mouth, lady. You certainly didn't learn to talk like that in Franklin County."

It was also in St. Albans that he held his first session allowing the public to vent its spleen at him. After a period of primal scream therapy, the group was addressed by a man whose brother, as a state senator opposing a gay rights bill a decade earlier, had warned about Vermont turning into a "society of corn-holers."

Harold Howrigan addressed his neighbors with, "You know, I'm not for this civil unions issue either. But this man has done a great job as governor. I think we need to look at him for everything that he's done, and weigh that. When and if you do that, you're going to do what I'm going to do and vote for Howard Dean."

61

Writer **Howard Mosher** captured a common view of Howard Dean: "He's marvelously independent-minded in that New England tradition. Here in the Northeast Kingdom, civil unions are looked at somewhat askance. That issue may have hurt Dean's reputation; I think many of my neighbors were disappointed with his stance on that issue. I admire that he says exactly what he thinks. He's a brilliant man, but he also speaks from the heart."

Things were not always civil within the state capitol.

Anson Tebbetts describes how "when he was governor, it was pretty bad. It was basically Kate O'Connor, and press secretary Sue Allen, versus the rest of the staff. There was sort of an alliance."

Dean's relations with the Vermont media were professional, if not warm. Tebbetts describes how Montpelier was covered: "In Vermont, there're always four to five reporters who cover the statehouse. Dean was always very accessible. To a point, you almost got tired of him. He was always available, if you needed him you could go talk to him at any point, call him up, 'Can we meet somewhere, and can we do it?' He always had some sort of answer, even though sometimes I think he answered the question when he really didn't know the right answer. Then he would send his staff to cover up his tracks. But I think he got pretty good scrutiny. It was never that really confrontational. Some reporters have gotten calls from him, complaining.

"The only time I really got in trouble with him was when there was a flood up in Montgomery. This was like the fifth or sixth flood, or natural disaster, Vermont had in like a two-year stretch, so he'd gotten this routine down where the governor has to visit the area, they fill out the application for federal emergency management money, and they'd do the tour. Well, he flew in a National Guard helicopter, he dropped down, got in a truck, went up, he might have been on the ground for ten minutes, seen the damage, gotten in his helicopter, and took off again. The people of Montgomery were just mad that he only spent a little bit of time there: they wanted him to show them more stuff, they wanted him to pay more attention. He'd sort of gone through the motions; he knew how the process worked. I found a couple of residents who were mad about his short time there, and the way they were treated, so we put them on the air. His staff got very upset with the coverage. That's the only time I've really had confrontational thing with him. Then he went back the next four or five days and got the real tour.

Tebbetts continues: "I think he got a lot of scrutiny here, but it's a little more laid back. The access is better. Here you had weekly press conferences. He was always very good at ten, fifteen people in a crowd, going in off the top of his head. There were lunches he would go to, walk into the room, do it off the top of his head, take a few questions, and walk out. I don't think he ever had notes, except when he did his prepared speeches at the State of the State address, or his budget address. I don't think I remember him ever having notes, at any type of forum when he was governor; he always did it off the top of his head. He's always been his own guy. Sometimes he would get ahead of his staff and he'd make it really difficult when he was governor, because he'd make decisions after a forum or meeting.

Tebbetts recalls a good example of this: "I remember they were fighting about closing rest areas in Vermont. He was determined they were going to close these rest areas because the septic systems were failing, it was going to cost too much. Vermont already had too many of them, but Vermonters really wanted them. He went to this forum up in St. Albans, and people showed up for this great scene at this gazebo on this summer night. He really got blasted by these people. By the time he got to the Georgia rest area, where we were doing the live shot, he had changed his mind and said, 'Okay, we're going to keep these rest areas open.' He had totally changed his mind, right there on the spot, during the time he went from St. Albans to Georgia, a fifteen minute drive. He had been telling his transportation secretary, and his buildings people, 'we're going to close them.' So, of course, they had to go and clean them up and do all that work... he would do that type of thing."

As he listened to fellow Vermonters, Tebbetts also notes that "People tell me he could get pretty upset behind the scenes, at staff meetings, or with lobbyists. I hear he does have a foul mouth. That's the worse I've heard."

Sealed documents from Dean's years as governor produced additional controversy. Tebbetts comments that "One of the things I've heard about the sealed documents that they don't want to release is that there's some of that colorful language in the margins. This first came up during the whole time of the 'anger' issue (during 2003), so they didn't want that extra stuff. Someone was saying that it really wasn't about policy, there wasn't a smoking gun, but there was a lot of colorful language that was written in his hand that might have been embarrassing. But that was just speculation from some folks who apparently had seen some of the stuff when they were on the fifth floor."

A movement calling itself "Take Back Vermont" formed around the woman he had defeated in 1998, Ruth Dwyer. Dwyer had mounted the first opposition representing a serious challenge to Dean. As the election was nearing in 1998, Dwyer had said that it seemed to her Dean was unusually busy going around the state to hand out grants to libraries and local institutions. Dean responded with characteristic pique and an uncharacteristic lack of logic. "I don't run around the state with a big bag of money during election time. I do that all the time."

In 2000, no one seemed too concerned that the slogan "Take Back Vermont" seemed to imply returning the Green Mountain State to the Native Americans who had gotten there first. Nor would anyone have foreseen that Dean would be using the similar slogan that it is "time to take our country back" when campaigning for the Democratic nomination in the 2004 primaries.

In addition to Dwyer, Dean faced a challenge from a Progressive candidate, Anthony Pollina. Pollina undoubtedly drew votes from Dean, who barely got a majority and prevented the election from going into a legislature which, in the civil union backlash, was now controlled by Republicans. Dean's days in Vermont's statehouse seemed to be numbered.

Tebbetts reflects on Dean's ambitions: "When you look back on it, you look at a lot of the things he did as governor, he was thinking about running for the presidency for a long time, probably.

"He didn't sign the civil unions bill in public, there is no picture of that. We all thought it was because he didn't want a picture of it in the gubernatorial race. When I look back on it now, I am convinced it was because he didn't want it because he didn't want it in a national ad. He did that behind closed doors."

The fiscal health that Dean sought for Vermont was more immediately transparent to Tebbetts: "The balanced budget stuff… at the time he was really stressing that the budget was balanced, there wouldn't be a deficit in his last term. They played with the books and made sure they balanced. There was great emphasis, that the headline was that the budget was balanced."

Before Dean ran for his last term, his ambitions were evident to Tebbetts: "In 2000, the word was that Al Gore outed him. Because Al Gore leaked it into the press that Dean was thinking about running for president, and in the polls he dropped a lot here in Vermont, and then he stopped. Then he said he wasn't going to run, but he did it the next time."

Dean was thinking of broader horizons, even if no one else saw them as attainable.

By the end of his last term, the World Trade Center would vanish from the New York skyline. George W. Bush would use that emotional touchstone to wage war in Afghanistan, then Iraq. Opposition to the actions within the United States would be muted by the blizzard of flag-waving after September 11.

Although that patriotism wouldn't translate into greatly-increased voter turnout, as the Republican stranglehold on the nation tightened with the midterm elections, the silenced minority opposing military actions would soon find its voice, in Big Howard's first born son.

THE GREAT DEBATE. OR NOT.

Debate is the death of conversations.

—*Emil Ludwig*

In the year 1858, a comparatively unknown candidate was vaulted in the election process onto the national stage in a series of seven debates between Stephen A. Douglas and Abraham Lincoln. These debates were so significant that phrases from them are still regularly borrowed by pundits today.

The 1858 debates would go on for hours. Almost a century and a half later, the Democratic primary debates would just seem to go on for hours. Instead of two candidates going at each other directly, and at great length, the modern version featured enough onstage participants to field a baseball team. The candidates were given directed, often loaded questions and were expected to answer within one minute.

For Howard Dean, the debate at the University of New Hampshire (UNH) found him on top of the world. Al Gore's endorsement of Dean was front-page news, and it seemed only a matter of time until he became the nominee. In retrospect, however, this period begins to look more like the beginning of the end for the Dean campaign.

The December 9, 2003 debate was held at UNH's snowy campus in Durham. ABC News veteran Ted Koppel would moderate the debate along with Scott Spradling, the political correspondent from the local ABC affiliate station of WMUR Channel 9.

The debate on this night would distinguish itself as the most memorable of a series of rather unmemorable debates. **Ted Koppel** tells us: "I had gone through every one of the debates, I had sat there and skimmed the transcripts, and yeah, they did talk about substance, but oh, boy was it boring."

With so many candidates, differences in positions were marked only by the most miniscule measurements. To avoid the dull business of defining these distinctions, Koppel decided to press the candidates on their political gains, and ask questions aimed at testing the candidates' abilities to think on their feet. Koppel didn't waste any time, either. He opened the debate by taking a quick, informal survey of the candidates. "I would like all of you up here, including you, Governor Dean, to raise your hand if you believe that Governor Dean can beat George W. Bush."

Not surprisingly, Dean was the only candidate to raise his hand.

Koppel then pressed some of the other candidates about why they didn't raise their hands. Senator Kerry said that he believed in his campaign and that the race is not over until the votes have been counted. Representative Gephardt highlighted his experience, after a brief word about unity in ousting Bush. Rev. Sharpton portrayed Al Gore's attempt to direct voters as a form of Bossism. Koppel then asked Senator Lieberman if his chances were hurt by Gore's endorsement of Dean, to which Lieberman strangely replied that his chances were actually increased. Koppel then asked Ambassador Braun and Senator Edwards if voter allegiance could be transferred from one politician to another. Still not satisfied with the talk about endorsements, Koppel asked Gen. Clark if he would accept an endorsement from one of the Clintons.

Clark answered that he had never even considered this, an answer that would later make Koppel say: "Come on, of course you would. That's what I mean about the disingenuity of politics. The suggestion that he wouldn't salivate at the thought of having the endorsement of Bill Clinton is ridiculous."

When Koppel asked Kucinich if anyone else on the stage would have liked to have received the endorsement from Al Gore, Kucinich used the opportunity to chastise Koppel for spending so much attention on the issue. Kucinich chastised Koppel: "To begin this kind of forum with a question about an endorsement, no matter by whom, I think actually trivializes the issues that are before us. . . . And I hope we have a substantive discussion tonight and that we're not going to spend the night talking about endorsements." But this comment from Kucinich did not dissuade Koppel, who immediately turned to Dean and asked him how he felt about the nomination. That was it for Koppel's first round of questions. Then it was Spradling's turn to moderate.

Spradling asked Clark if he was speaking too often on foreign policy and ignoring the voters' more important issues that polls showed to be more important to voters. Spradling asked Gephart whether he'd be too partisan to be an effective president. Spradling asked Kerry if religion would hurt the Democrats, and then he accused Sharpton of only visiting New Hampshire as a presidential candidate once prior to the debate. The WMUR Political Correspondent also brought attention to Braun for the same reason. Spradling invited Edwards to describe why he was the best candidate on the stage. Spradling asked Kucinich to elaborate on his recent shift in stance on abortion, and asked Dean why he seemed to be contradicting himself in specific media appearances. As for Lieberman, Spradling questioned whether his economic package would provide any near-future hope for New Hampshire's manufacturing industry.

For Spradling, the debate "was the scariest moment of my professional career." Spradling explained that the two moderators had had a brief meeting about two hours before the debate began, where they discussed the general layout of the debate. The plan was that Koppel would start the debate by asking each of the nine candidates a question, and then Spradling would ask each candidate a question, and then they would split the third round, with Koppel taking five questions and Spradling taking four. "I remember thinking, 'Ok, he told me he wanted to get them to focus on Al Gore, talk a little bit about it because it was the big news of the moment, and get them going that direction, and talking about Howard Dean'. That was all I knew. When the events unfolded the way that they did, I was both surprised and terrified, because this was my first debate of this magnitude and with this level of exposure. I was nearly sick to my stomach. It was very stressful for me because I had not anticipated that and having to sort of read and react, as I would say, he spent the first fifteen minutes using a stick to poke the hornet's nest, got them all stirred up and then handed the stick to me for my turn."

To Spradling's credit, nearly everyone was unreserved with their praise of his performance that night. Many people noted that, had it not been for the local guy, the entire debate would have been consumed with issues of pure politics. Even so, the most interesting thing about the debate was Koppel's performance. Let's be honest; if it hadn't been for Koppel's unorthodox opening, you probably would have skipped this chapter. In fact, the debate even became known as "the Koppel debate" within certain circles.

But before the first round of the debate was over, Koppel would have five more questions. Koppel asked John Kerry what Howard Dean was doing so right, he asked John Edwards what his campaign was doing so wrong, and he asked Kucinich, Braun, and Sharpton how long it would be before they pulled out. "I really did feel that it was my function as the moderator in this debate to say: Look, there are four or five people up on this stage that have a legitimate chance of becoming the Democratic candidate, and there are three people on this stage who don't have a snowball's chance in hell, who are just sucking up oxygen."

Koppel said about his tactics, "I deliberately did that as a way of shaking up what I had seen as a series of rather dull debates." He also said about his opening salvo, "Frankly, I wanted to rattle the cages of the other candidates a little bit." Koppel certainly appeared to have rattled not only the candidates and his co-moderator, but also many of his colleagues in the media. Many opinion pieces voicing disapproval of Koppel's performance appeared after the debate: Dan Kennedy of the *Boston Phoenix*: "Ted Koppel's opening gambit at Tuesday night's Democratic presidential primary was so inane and disrespectful that at first I didn't realize the proceedings were officially under way. When Koppel asked the candidates to raise their hands if they thought Howard Dean could beat George W. Bush, I assumed he was just warming up the crowd."[29]

William Saletan of the *Washington Post* also thumped Koppel. "This was Ted Koppel's worst performance as a moderator. You can forgive him for experimenting with a couple of questions about the horse race. But when the experiment failed and he persisted, that's on him."[30]

Dick Goodwin comments: "I think that was disgusting of Koppel. He's not running for anything. He's there to present the candidates, and to take over that way, I thought was something that was very unprofessional."

Koppel defended himself by explaining that it was not he who had failed, but the candidates. His opening bid was an invitation for the candidates to say that frankly any of the candidates on the stage could beat George W. Bush, with the help of a united Democratic Party. "They are all terrified at the prospect, as Democrats, not just as rivals, that Howard Dean is going to become the nominee, but they're afraid to go after him in any meaningful sort of way. I wanted to demonstrate that by giving them a chance to say, 'much as we don't like him, he's still better than George W. Bush.' And they wouldn't even say that for him."

And in all fairness, Koppel did ask some good issue-based questions during the second half of the debate. But it was not enough to save the image of the debate.

UNH political scientist **Mark Wrighton** was at the debate, and described the event as offering little enlightenment in terms of issue positions. "I came away thinking that if I'm the voter sitting out there, I didn't really learn much tonight. Granted, they all made it clear that they were against the incumbent president. Beyond that, though, there was nothing for the voter who was looking for the real differences on the issues. I don't think that they were able to get those. And without issues, you rely on candidate characteristics, which is (to say) personality."

Wrighton's colleague, **Andrew Smith**, had a slightly different take on the matter. "The point of not asking about issues but asking about strategy, frankly I don't think that most voters pay much attention to issues. Voters, when it comes down to it, they vote for someone because they either like them or don't like them. I think that is even more the case in New Hampshire, and is I think one of the great values that New Hampshire adds to the campaign cycle… because you get a chance here to evaluate the candidates as people, rather than as resumes, or as lists of issue positions."

Ted Koppel opened up the debate by tossing the candidates a puffball to see who would be able to hit a home run. Instead, they all struck out. The UNH debate was remarkable only in the failure of any of the candidates to really distinguish themselves, except for Sharpton and Kucinich, who had a couple of good one-liners. The candidates were frustratingly similar on the issues, so any nine-way discussion of the issues would be, as Andrew Smith says, "dull as dirt." Perhaps Koppel's attempts shouldn't be criticized too harshly - because if he had stuck to the issues, nobody would have sat through it.

It was at a May 2003 debate in South Carolina where Lieberman argued that voters would reject a candidate "…who sends a message that is other than strength on defense and homeland security." As the Republican wing of the Democratic Party, Lieberman could simultaneously promote his own experience and denigrate the inexperience at the national level of Edwards and Dean. Of course, Lieberman was ignoring the similar absence of national experience that had accompanied Carter, Clinton and Bush into the White House. Furthermore, the October preceding a presidential election is known for surprises that impact the viability of both an incumbent and a challenger. The national security environment that would exist in the Fall of 2004 was as much an unknown to him as the stock market is to investors. His prescient, pre-9/11 report warning of terrorism had led Gary Hart to consider running again for president in 2002. Before November 2004, Al Qaeda was capable of a terrorist attack that could shift the balance yet again. Outspoken Dean advocate, George Soros, was rumored to be plotting to utilize his billions to destabilize the economy and drive Bush from office. Candidates can play on voters' hopes, or their fears.

Howard Shapiro notes: "The choices that voters make are fraught with unimaginable consequences - and they know it. Who in their right mind feels comfortable basing this decision solely on gauzy thirty-second commercials and poll-tested speeches that obedient candidates read off the TelePrompTer? Who can derive lasting insight from newspaper charts dutifully listing the candidates' health-care plans? Rightfully suspicious of media manipulation, and yet supinely dependent on television and the press for information, voters are desperate to cut through the phoniness of a presidential campaign in search of any larger truths about the character of the candidates."[31]

Voters would complain that the candidate's positions seemed to be "eerily alike."

"The candidate's health-care plans can be neatly arranged in newspaper charts by the magnitude of their ambitions. Pardon my refusal to portray these varying approaches... as a titanic struggle for the soul of the Democratic Party. I cling to the stubborn belief that these minor programmatic disputes reveal little about how any of these Democrats would govern as president. ...Instead of zesty policy debates, it brings in the clones."[32]

A major reason was that the candidates openly admitted they tended to utilize the same fonts for wisdom. The head of the DLC, Bruce Reed said: "We provided a number of people with the same lackluster advice. There was a similarity to the arguments they all made, but that probably would have happened even if Gene (Sperling, former White House economic coordinator under Clinton) and I had called in sick that day."[33]

"A leading Democratic consultant put it like this: 'In one way or another, all the candidates are still using some version of the rhetoric that Bill Clinton introduced in 1992. The exception is Howard Dean, who has a very blunt, apolitical way of speaking. Dean has found fresh language and a new way of talking about things that, at least, is different.'"[34]

71

Still, the debate at the University of New Hampshire held the promise of a spectacle - moderated by Ted Koppel, the distinguished journalist of *Nightline*, working in conjunction with the political reporter from the Manchester ABC affiliate, Scott Spradling.

Although this was a year with even more debates than there were candidates, they weren't usually too contentious. They were worth seeing for little details.

UNH Political Science Professor **J. Mark Wrighton** "caught things the TV cameras missed-like the moment when Sen. John Kerry glanced at his watch." Wrighton was reminded of the time when George H.W. Bush looked at his watch during his 1992 debate with Bill Clinton, a gesture widely construed as a lack of engagement and evidence that Bush had lost the debate. A few moments later, however, **Howard Dean** confessed that he had looked at his watch and noticed, with only 12 minutes remaining, that little had been discussed other than Iraq. His comment immediately prompted a shift to domestic issues.

"They both did it, but Dean was able to make something of it,' noted Wrighton."[35]

The UNH debate would prove to be more notable than most, largely thanks to Ted Koppel. "What a disgrace" notes the *Washington Post's* Howard Kurtz. Before the debate, Koppel told him that his goal was to "… 'keep people at home from dozing off.' He accomplished that, but only by tarnishing his own considerable reputation. By focusing on Al Gore's surprise endorsement of Dean, and on the polling, and fundraising shortcomings of the other eight candidates, Koppel actually pulled off the heretofore unimaginable feat of giving Dennis Kucinich a moment in the spotlight."

William Saletan also unloaded on Koppel. "This was Ted Koppel's worst performance as a moderator. You can forgive him for experimenting with a couple of questions about the horse race. But when the experiment failed and he persisted, that's on him. When he asked inside-baseball questions and got substantive answers instead, he chided the candidates for failing to stoop to his level. First he asked John Kerry why Howard Dean couldn't beat President Bush. Kerry talked instead about why he would make the best president. Koppel then turned to Dick Gephardt and said, 'I'm not really asking you — at least, I wasn't then — whether you think you're the better candidate. I was simply asking you whether you thought that Howard Dean could beat George W. Bush.' Later, Koppel asked Carol Moseley Braun whether Al Gore's endorsement of Dean would make blacks loyal to Dean. Braun talked instead about what Democrats should stand for. Koppel then said, 'Sen. Edwards, what I was trying to get to with Ambassador Braun was whether loyalty can, in any way, be transferred by an endorsement.' Edwards wisely ignored the question as well... Kucinich and Kerry chastised Koppel for his obsession with polls, but he wouldn't let up. He derided the poorer candidates and asked John Edwards why he was falling short of 'expectations.' These were the last 90 debating minutes of the year — a crucial opportunity for every candidate other than Dean — and Koppel wasted 30 of those minutes on questions barely worthy of aides in bars."[36]

Howard Dean says "...it was theater, but there wasn't much substance to it. Which is sort of a premonition of what happens in most television shows."[37]

If the debates ended up being more about style than substance, no one was more stylin' than the Reverend Al. Sharpton's wit, both in the debates and on the campaign trail, was an endless source of amusement to the Portsmouth Dean office.

While Walter Shapiro inveighs against Sharpton, Moseley Braun, and Kucinich as vanity-driven candidates, Sharpton's entertainment values were sky high. Shapiro hoped in 2003 that they would each be offered cable TV shows to get them off the campaign trail. By spring 2004, word would be circulating that Sharpton was close to having just such a show.

Sharpton had shown his stuff with comments such as the one before the Democratic National Committee mid-winter meeting when he said that Bush was "...the ultimate beneficiary of a set-aside program—the Supreme Court set aside a whole election." Sharpton suggested at the same time that anyone but Bush could find the still missing Bin Laden because "...he has made more videos than any rock star in Hollywood."

Sharpton's wit was again evident when he characterized Republican economics by saying "We never got the trickle, we just get the down."

Sharpton had utilized fairly bizarre, albeit intriguing, imagery at the debate in May, when the television eye first opened. Ironically, he did it with the anti-establishment rap he shared with Dean: "The way to move a donkey is to slap the donkey. I'm going to slap the donkey 'til the donkey kicks and we kick George Bush out of the White House. I'm going to slap the donkey."

Democrats probably breathed a sigh of relief that Sharpton's menagerie of imagery hadn't veered into corporal punishment and monkeys. Sharpton shared another target with Dean when they each addressed 1,500 abortion-rights activists in Washington. "It's time for the Christian Right to meet the right Christians," echoed Dean's contention that American political dialog needed to stop being about "Guns, God and gays." While Dean had utilized the alliteration popular with ministers, he had begun a trip into the minefield of religious beliefs in which he would encounter a few tripwires.

Preparation for public viewing of the candidate as in a debate is important. **Richard Goodwin** reminds us of other candidates' performances. "Jack Kennedy, before he went out on a Meet the Press program or equivalent, he would prepare for days. The same with Bobby. When Teddy Kennedy was just on Meet the Press, he spent an entire week preparing. I don't think Dean did that kind of thing. These are people who have experience and know how important it is to be able to handle questions and issues that are thrown at you. A lot of that (with Dean)…(is) plain inexperience."

Running for Delegate; No WASPS Need Apply

He knows nothing and he thinks he knows everything. That points clearly to a political career

George Bernard Shaw

Aswini had come over to our house to beseech us to have a house meeting with educators, in order to help Dean get the New Hampshire NEA endorsement. We had insisted that the only way we would do it was if we got to present a summary of Dean's platform. She had been resistant, because the model she was working from was for each person to tell their "story" about why they were there, particularly why they were drawn to the Dean campaign, but not get into issues.

Our feeling was that failure to address his platform, as well as people's specific questions and concerns, represented a very shallow buy-in, not to mention that it was fundamentally disrespectful of the people we were trying to draw into "Dean Nation."

It was only because we would not agree to do the house meeting any other way that she acquiesced. It had occurred to me then that there might be a personal benefit from my upcoming efforts.

The convention was in Boston at the end of July, so I asked her who got picked to be delegates. Aswini was completely unaware of the process, but she was assured that the people who would go would be those who had worked hardest in the campaign. Back in the Portsmouth office, no one, including Ben, the regional director, knew how delegates would be selected. No one ever seemed to make any effort to provide me with details of how the process might actually occur. It would be weeks before someone mentioned the idea of looking at the state party's website. When

I did that, it specified the first date when I could apply. I applied in the first 10 minutes possible.

Even in the last days preceding selection, the Dean campaign was still formulating how delegates would be selected.

Party rules on the selection of delegates were the legacy of the tumultuous campaign of 1968. Insurgent anti-war candidate Eugene McCarthy's 8-point loss in New Hampshire to the incumbent Lyndon Johnson was a factor in Johnson's withdrawing from the race. Johnson had never appeared in the Granite State in 1968, either in person or on the ballot. He had attempted to do what had worked for him in 1964; a write-in campaign.

After Johnson's withdrawal, Vice President Hubert Humphrey stepped forward as the establishment candidate, and Bobby Kennedy joined in as the newest insurgent.

JFK's younger brother Bobby, who had become a Senator from New York after serving his brother, and Johnson, as attorney general, would be assassinated moments after winning the California primary. The anti-war fervor that had driven the insurgencies erupted outside the convention hall into rioting which was broadcast around the world.

The Democratic Party responded to widespread protest to Humphrey's ascension (although he would lose to the man John Kennedy had defeated in 1960, Richard Nixon) by forming a commission that reformed the nomination process. It would be called the McGovern-Fraser Commission, and in 1972, antiwar candidate George McGovern would be the first beneficiary of its changes.

Those changes would help secure McGovern the Democratic nomination. McGovern would lose in a landslide to the incumbent Nixon. The specter of McGovern's loss would be raised over the Dean candidacy 32 years later. The rules modified by McGovern-Fraser on delegate selection would be tweaked many times afterwards.

In 1982, a bloc of "superdelegates" was created. They were unpledged officeholders, assuring the party greater voice in the nomination.[38] National party chair Terry McAuliffe would ultimately prove to have a singularly loud voice in the nomination in 2004. However, like any party chair, there was a high degree of self-interest involved.

The *Washington Post's* Leonard Downie, Jr. has observed that the "Party chairman — whether of the Democrats or the Republicans — is always a precarious job. If the party is doing well, the chairman can bask in glory; if it isn't, off with his or her head."[39]

In 2004, delegates were being selected with specified numbers of each gender required, so I knew I was only running against men. Therefore, I formed a strategic alliance, a la Survivor, with Nancy Beach from Portsmouth. She and her partner had produced the great new videos used across the state in house meetings; surely she'd have juice.

I had been giving out pens with my name on them since before Christmas. The idea had come about from a staff member at a nursing home who said the seniors would love pens. Since the campaign had refused to ante up for pens that would say "*Howard Dean for America*", I decided I could accomplish two goals. So I had pens made up saying "*Dana Dunnan, Dean Democratic Delegate*". When I gave them out at nursing homes, I always made sure they went to registered Democrats.

My eagerness to get into the field was because of my perception that, in early December, the expansion of Dean support seemed to be slowing. Maybe my perception was wrong, because, at the same time, Howard Kurtz's column "Media Notes" in *The Washington Post* described how liberal pundits were clambering on board the Dean bandwagon, even as the stirrings of the "angry man" issue were growing into swells.

Kurtz reflected on the significance of the media movement.

"Here's why it matters. When Al Gore ran (more on him in a moment), I can't think of a single political pontificator who passionately argued his cause. The discussion was all about his wardrobe, and his wife-kissing, and whether he should embrace or distance himself from Bill Clinton - who, by the way, did generate some enthusiasm among columnists, notably Joe Klein, in '92. The lack of media cheerleading for Gore reflected the ambivalence that even many Democrats felt about the man, which in turn was reflected in the photo-finish he failed to win.

"Dean, by contrast, is winning some early liberal converts in the press. Are they a leading indicator of a groundswell of support for the doctor?

Who knows? But so far I see none of the throat-clearing, 'well-he's-better-than-the-other-guy' rationalizations that Gore engendered."

"First up is veteran Texas columnist Molly Ivins:

"It is the bounden duty of bleeding-heart liberals like myself to make our political choices based on purity of heart, nobility of character, depth of compassion, sterling integrity, and generosity of spirit. The concept of actually winning a political race does not, traditionally, influence the bleeding heart liberal one iota - certainly not in the primaries. Over the years, I have proudly voted for a list of losers only a lily-pure liberal could love...In fact, I initially passed on Dean precisely because he looked like one of my usual losers - 2 percent in the polls and the full weight of Vermont behind him ... wow, my kind of guy...

"I went up to Vermont and talked to a bunch of liberals there. They all said Howard Dean is no liberal. Funny, that's what Howard Dean says, too. And indeed, he isn't, but in politics, everything's relative. The conventional wisdom first dismissed Howard Dean (the man has never been to a Washington dinner party!), then condescended to him, then graciously offered him instruction on how he should be running his campaign - which seemed to be going along quite well without their input."[40]

"In *The Nation*, William Greider has a piece called "Why I'm For Dean": While Dean is "… an odd duck, certainly… the man also stands his ground in a fight. When someone jabs him, he jabs back. Pundits describe this quality as dangerous, and no doubt it gets him into trouble sometimes, but what a refreshing departure from the rope-a-dope calculations of the Clinton era... With issues, Dean is pretty much what he says: a middle-of-the-road moderate, neither left nor right, though middle in Vermont is liberal ground."

"Are conservatives worried about Dean? "PLEASE Nominate This Man," screams the cover of the new *National Review*, with a picture of an angry-looking Howard.

"Dean does not specialize in substance, and besides his health-care plan doesn't have much in the way of fleshed-out policy," writes Editor Rich Lowry. "Dean is mostly selling an attitude."

"Not all left-leaning columnists are Deaniacs, either.

"Nicholas Kristof of the *New York Times*, once a young McGovern volunteer, writes that "Mr. McGovern was defeated in a landslide. As Howard Dean will probably be, if the Democrats nominate him."

"Among the problems: "Mr. Dean is smart, but he knows it. America's heartland oozes suspicion of Eastern elitists, and Mr. Dean's cockiness would exacerbate that suspicion...Mr. Dean needs a Berlitz course in self-deprecating folksiness...

"Mr. Dean may be the one Democrat who is even more blue-blooded than Mr. Bush, and who has an even lamer excuse for dodging Vietnam. Mr. Dean grew up on Park Avenue in an old aristocratic family, and after getting his medical deferment from the draft, he moved to Aspen to ski. Unlike other politicians, Mr. Dean doesn't even pretend to be particularly religious, and that's a major political weakness in the battleground states."

"Now for the surprise Gore endorsement. A coup for Dean, no question about it, and a blow to Joe Lieberman that even his former running mate isn't getting behind him. But I'm going to go out on a limb and say this isn't the earth-shattering event that the media will make it out to be over the next few days.

"One, I don't think endorsements matter all that much. It may make some voters feel more comfortable that the former vice president of the United States backs Dean, but I think most will make up their minds based on whether they think he'd be a good leader for the country.

"Two, is there any possibility that Dean, the classic outsider candidate, could lose some of that edge if he is perceived as the candidate of the Democratic Party establishment?

"And who represents that establishment more than Gore?

"But the media stampede is on."

"Dan Balz of *The Washington Post* gets early reaction from a key Gore player:

"'This is huge', said Donna Brazile, Gore's 2000 campaign manager. 'This gives Dean the credibility he's been lacking, from someone from the inside of the party. This will give Dean a tremendous boost in locking down the nomination.'"

"*The Philadelphia Inquirer* notes that "… Gore did not call Lieberman to give him the bad news, according to Lieberman spokesman Jano Cabrera."

"Lieberman may feel betrayed by his ex-running mate's decision," writes *Salon*'s Joe Conason, "but he and Gore simply have very little in common anymore. Agree with Gore or not, his endorsement of Dean is a principled, brave decision by someone with an intimate understanding of what has gone wrong with the political system to which he dedicated his life."[41]

Joe Klein says this will particularly help Dean with black voters and union members, and that the Dean-Gore wing now stands in opposition to the Clinton wing.

National Journal's (National Review Online) Ramesh Ponnuru is not enthralled:

"No word yet from McGovern, Mondale, or Dukakis… Come to think of it, the Ds now have a candidate with McGovern's foreign policy, Mondale's domestic policy, Dukakis's regional background, and Gore's arrogance. How perfect is that?"

In *Slate*, Mickey Kaus asks readers to help draft a Kerry withdrawal statement:

"Democratic Senator John Kerry, once proclaimed the frontrunner in the press, faces not just defeat but utter humiliation in the New Hampshire primary. Is he really going to soldier on to finish in the single digits and get clobbered by both Howard Dean and Wesley Clark, if not one or more other candidates? Shouldn't he save his pride (and possible national political future, if only as a VP candidate) by withdrawing from the race before this harsh popular verdict is rendered?"[42]

Hey, I've got an idea: Why bother with primary voting at all? We just run a virtual campaign and let the prognosticators decide!

ABC's *The Note* strings together some stinging adjectives about Dean:

"The dirtiest little secret of the fight for the Democratic presidential nomination is that the pros running Dean's campaign know full well that the criticisms of The Doctor being made by the press and his opponents are often spot on. They know he is regularly careless, volcanic, dismissive, self-important, mercurial, hypocritical, patronizing, and politically tone-deaf."

The New Republic's Michelle Cottle ruminates on Dean as Angry Man:

"This summer's anti-Dean sentiment seems to have swollen into a barely contained rage, something fit for a Tarantino-style blood bath. Let's call it: Kill Howard. The more Democratic voters to fall under Dean's spell, the more furious—and incoherent—his detractors become. 'He's a paleoliberal. He's a heartless conservative. He's too naïve to beat Bush. He's too politically cynical to trust. He's a Stalinist. He's a neofascist. He kills babies and drinks their blood. And if someone doesn't stop him right this minute, he's going to destroy the entire Democratic Party!!!' Good God. Vermont hasn't unleashed anything this controversial since Ben & Jerry considered coating French vanilla ice cream with chocolate-flavored bullshit and calling them Bush Bars.

"Perhaps the anti-Dean obsession I find most fascinating is whether or not the ex-governor is An Angry Man. Everyone from Gary Hart to Jay Leno has publicly mused about this aspect of the candidate's character, while *The New York Times* has noted that even regular schmoe voters at town hall meetings grill Dean about his reputedly short temper. This, of course, brings to mind all those hours that 2000 presidential phenom John McCain was similarly forced to waste addressing questions about his spicy temper. What gives? If this was 1953, and we expected our politicians to be staid, stoic, ever-reserved avatars of decorum, I could understand such a preoccupation. But in an age where we encourage our pols to crack jokes, make out with their wives, and get all weepy for the TV cameras, why the horror at the idea of a little PDA? (Public Displays of Anger, that is.) ...

"For my money, someone who can competently beat up George W. Bush is just about as inspiring as I could ask for. More broadly, there is a significant difference between a dour, pessimistic political message and a vigorous but legitimately angry one. These days, a lot of voters are themselves angry. Maybe not enough to get Dean elected. But let's not confuse the downward pull of pessimism with the often very motivating oomph of anger. When you think about it, anger-bordering-on-rage actually served Newt Gingrich and Co. pretty well in 1994."[43]

Howard Kurtz notes: "By the way, wonder what the first George Bush ad might look like? It's an online Bush/Cheney video that, while it hasn't hit the airwaves, mocks the Democrats as a bunch of angry men as opposed to the sunny, positive President."[44]

Dean's maiden voyage in national politics had started as an upgrade to ever-better quarters. Now a look out the porthole promised increasingly angry seas ahead.

My running mate and I went together to see the Bradley endorsement speech in early January. I handed out all of the pens and fliers for our candidacy that I had. We left so pumped up that we ordered 250 more pens to give out with our names on them. I printed more of the flyers that I had been handing out urging people to support our candidacies.

Before Christmas, I'd been told that our speeches were going to be 3 to 5 minutes.

I had started thinking about an erudite discourse about the best-known words of Reinhold Niebuhr.

"God give us the grace to accept with serenity the things that cannot be changed, courage to change the things that should be changed, and the wisdom to distinguish the one from the other."

Through variations used by Alcoholics Anonymous and Hallmark cards, among others, this had morphed into The Serenity Prayer. However, Niebuhr, while a theologian, was also a political thinker. He actually was talking about the political process, and firmly-held values. His words were an indictment of the self-righteousness that accompanies ideology, a warning against complacency, and a barrier to the despair that leads people to remove themselves from the political process.

By the time of delegate selection on January 10, there were 60 people running, so we each got 30 seconds. Niebuhr would have to remain the domain of greeting cards and recovering drunks, including the incumbent.

Unfortunately, the results had seemed preordained before the speeches anyhow, when voters were instructed to choose for diversity, diversity, diversity. My running mate and I had turned our middle-class WASP faces to one another and said "We're in big trouble."

I would face similar bias later in January when I was told that I could not attend a rally in Hampton where former Texas governor Ann Richards would be addressing "Women for Dean."

One would think that all those years of being told that I had a woman's name would count for something.

When I was in college, I had been turned away from hearing Stokely Carmichael speak at Northeastern because I was not Black, the same year when young black kids had turned on me and my college roommate as about the only white folks at a Jackson Five concert.

The white man's burden is a heavy one.

Still, I had a great speech - until someone shouting out "What's your name?" interrupted me. I wanted to draw people in with a touching anecdote. Then I would pump them up for Dean. Then, if I had time, I would draw them together. Then I'd tie my candidacy to Nancy's.

I began my speech… "I was making phone calls from the Portsmouth office in September, when I spoke with an older gentleman. He said 'I came here from a Communist country, and my man had the election stolen from him in Florida. And I'm *never* going to vote again."

At that point, two different people shouted out "What's your name?"

I was really annoyed. But I gathered myself, and said in my withering 'I'm in charge of this classroom' voice: "I'm going to tell you."

Precious seconds were slipping away. And, by virtue of my choice to be the first man speaking, I was victimized by the disorganization of the caucus.

We had been told that we would speak alphabetically, starting at a point in the alphabet to be randomly chosen and continuing from there.

Instead, they told us at the last minute to just line up, and then they didn't introduce us, because they probably didn't know our names.

Still, I pressed onward.

"There was a song lyric about Bobby Kennedy that said, 'the darkest hour is always just before the dawn.' We're going to see the light of a new day, in a November to remember, when Howard Dean becomes the *rightfully* elected President of the United States. Because it's *our* turn, it's *our* time, and it's *our* country!"

The last words were stepped on by the person holding the stopwatch saying "Time's up." If they had only done as good a job in running things, and controlling the audience.

I barely got out "My name is Dana Dunnan." I forgot to mention my running mate, because, by now, I was really pissed.

A line which I had already edited out of my speech was originally going to be my 'closer.' I was going to be pedantic and identify the person who first spoke it as Al-Hajj Malik Al-Shabazz. But I had decided that was too many words, simply for showing how knowledgeable I was. So, before I decided I didn't have time for it, I had decided I would identify the speaker as Malcolm X. The line I was going to end with was "One day, may we all meet together, in the light of understanding."

For me, the light of understanding of what was going on with the Dean campaign was starting to brighten.

My running mate's speech consisted of her playing back, over her cell phone, a call she had received from Dean thanking her for the work her company had done in making house meeting videos.

We lost.

The only African-American running was chosen, as were an 18-year-old Jewish woman, an 84-year-old doctor, a female Hispanic doctor, an immigrant from behind the Iron Curtain, and a Greek state representative who, curiously enough, had once been married to Michael King - the former head of the state Democratic Party.

By and large, not the usual suspects.

But in a debate the next night, Al Sharpton would attack Dean for the absence of people of color in his Vermont cabinet, and I understood then that a Diverse Dean Delegation was more important than Dana Dunnan - Dean Democratic Delegate.

In campaigning for delegate, one of the most interesting individuals I met was a 72 year old named Peter Schmidt. Peter is a representative from Dover, in the largest legislative body in the world - the New Hampshire Legislature.

Because the pay is a pittance, and the commitment is large, the legislature tends to skew demographically toward AARP membership. Peter is an outspoken Democrat. I met him at the Merrimack Restaurant at the November Meetup. Judy and I had gotten there very early, particularly by campaign standards, and staked out seats right next to where Dean was going to stand.

We were told an hour later that we needed to move, so the press could have our spot. I indicated that we had long-standing squatter's rights, and that we were particularly unlikely to give up our spot for the media. Peter had come in after that, and worked his way up in front of us, blocking Judy's view, and that of a soaking wet woman in a wheelchair who had ridden three miles in the rain to see Dean. I had asked him to avoid obscuring their view, and he spent the time that followed squatting down uncomfortably.

Afterwards, I thanked him for his willingness to acquiesce, and commiserated on how hard such positions were on older bodies. We exchanged business cards, as I gave him one of the hundreds I would pass out in the course of the campaign. In the previous four years since I had bought them, I had probably used a total of 50.

When I decided to run for delegate, I considered the possibility that I might be facing him, and that, if not, his support might be invaluable. So I called him at his home, and we had an extensive conversation. Peter seems to have a genetic make-up that substituted an extra gene for intelligence, in place of one for brevity.

The conversation probably wound on for an hour and a half. I found out that he was considering running for delegate, but would let me know if he was going to run. He also said he would look into possibly going as a "super delegate", which would mean he wouldn't have to run against me.

In the course of conversation, he described why he felt so strongly that Bush must be defeated, and that Dean was the best person to do that. Part of his antipathy to Bush was tied to 9/11. He talked at length about how it had been the intent of the Bush administration to draw us in to Iraq, and that 9/11 was allowed to happen, to get the public behind an incursion into Iraq. I have often characterized Bush and his cronies as scaly reptilians, but Peter sounded like he thought they actually *were* lizards.

Of course, I am prepared to admit that no matter how paranoid you are, there are still unseen assassins lying in wait, but Peter really seemed to be out there. He talked about how the United States had knowingly allowed the attack on Pearl Harbor to happen, which was an allegation that I knew was grounded in historical fact.

Then he talked about the unlikelihood of four planes being allowed to be hijacked, at nearly the same time, with none of them being intercepted. Peter recommended four books, on 9/11, American foreign policy misadventure, and the history of the Pearl Harbor attack. The one he spoke about most was called *The War on Freedom*. He said it was particularly well written.

Peter reminded me of the crash of the airplane belonging to golfer Payne Stewart, who died during the Clinton administration. Stewart's plane had been unresponsive to radio contact from flight control, after it underwent rapid depressurization soon after takeoff.

Interceptors were there within minutes, and stayed with the plane until it crashed in a cornfield in the upper Midwest, hours later. That is *standard* response, when a plane on radar doesn't respond.

So why had *four* planes gone unescorted, to crash? Particularly when there was significant time between the first and the last crash?

I took the names of the books from Peter, and called the Greenland library to try to get them. The library is in a charming, albeit, small building.

With a limited size to their collection, they had to seek all four books through inter-library loan. Since I didn't hear from the library for a while, and I was knocking myself out on the campaign, I forgot about them. When they came in to the library, I brought them home, and put them down, not looking at them for weeks.

Peter, bright as he was, seemed just a little bit raving.

Until I met Juanita.

In January, house meetings were really starting to ramp up, as the primary drew nearer.

House meetings were part of the grassroots organizing plan that had been drawn up by Marshall Ganz. Ganz is a Harvard lecturer and, curiously, a friend of Karen Hicks. He created the house meeting blueprint, based on his experiences during the social upheaval around Vietnam, civil rights and farm workers rights. The plan did not always work for the Dean campaign, as some voters found themselves besieged by calls and mailings.

I had been going to house meetings, sometimes with Garrett or another area organizer, or sometimes on my own.

It was a very cold Friday night when we went to South Hampton. A colleague of Judy's who was going to be responsible for South Hampton was giving a house meeting, and she called us because she was afraid no one was going to come. I was greatly enjoying leading house meetings by this point, although being recruited to be a part of a small choir to be preached to seemed silly. Still, we skipped a much needed weekend in Vermont to go that night. There would be many weekends in the future, and Beth and Andre were very committed to the campaign.

Beth was right. There was almost no one who chose to come out on a night worthy of a Jack London story. Dan, an area organizer, was there, along with two people that were from Beth and Andre's town. Beth was in excruciating pain, from back trouble that she had been struggling with for months. But she was committed to the cause, so she lay on the floor, shifting uneasily, as we went through the standard individual introductions.

The routine is to have each person explain why they were there. If they were Dean supporters, they would tell what brought them on board. If they were leaning Dean, or just there to be informed, they could say what issues concerned them.

Juanita's story brought me right back to my conversation with Peter.

Juanita had been taking a course, I believe it was in Web design, in August of 2001. In a moment of boredom in class, she had gone into a chatroom. There she saw the exchange of two people vilifying the United States in the most horrid terms. Juanita interjected herself, and stood up for her country. The response she got back was along the lines of "You Americans all deserve to die. It's going to happen soon, you'll see."

It was signed "Atta."

Mohammed Atta was the name of the leader of the 9/11 hijackers.

While Juanita had been disturbed at that time, she was later horrified when 9/11 occurred. In response to the government's pleas for information, she had contacted the FBI, to tell them of her experience. She left a message outlining what had happened.

They never got back to her.

Juanita was at the house meeting because she felt guilty about 9/11, and she felt Dean represented the leadership that could most repudiate George W. Bush's actions, or lack thereof. Maybe Peter was right.

The next week I went to the Unitarian church in Portsmouth, to hear a presentation by Ellen Mariani and her lawyer. Her husband had been killed on one of the planes, and she was refusing a settlement, and suing the government, arguing that there was federal complicity in the crashes. Peter was there, and gave his now-familiar soliloquy about the four books in the course of asking a question.

So I started reading *The War on Freedom*, because it was most current, and was on 9/11. The footnotes were meticulous, the sources unimpeachable. The book left me feeling that *Bush* should be impeached, and tried for conspiracy to murder. I kept reading segments of the book aloud to Judy in the car, ever more incredulous, increasingly nauseous, at what the ideas might represent. People get convicted of murder on circumstantial evidence.

Even if you saw what *The War on Freedom* documented as a colossal mass of coincidence, Bush was guilty. The need for someone to seek the truth, and speak the truth, had never in my life seemed greater. Dean had made reference to allegations of Saudi complicity in 9/11, and gotten hammered for even suggesting it. As far as I was concerned, he should be shouting it.

But, then, shouting is so "unpresidential."

THE IOWA TAR BABY

To keep speech pure, one must not lie, or abuse, or deceive, or indulge in idle talk.

—Buddha

New Hampshire always trumpets its first-in-the-nation primary. The primacy of that claim was reflected in the initial name of a minor league baseball team that was forming in Manchester in 2003 - The Primaries. The name was widely rejected by the public, however, and the team turned to a more traditional sports moniker.

Of increasing importance in recent campaigns is Iowa's system of caucuses. With the newly front-loaded system of primaries and caucuses, the spotlight on Iowa and New Hampshire in 2004 was blinding. The wham-bam, thank you, ma'am, primary season gave primacy to two states with the ethnic diversity of a contra dance, or a snowmobile rally.

Howard Dean was clearly aware of the importance of Iowa.

Walter Shapiro puts it this way: "A prime illustration was the way that Dean precipitously abandoned his lifelong belief in unfettered free trade. His epiphany occurred, conveniently enough, in the middle of a breakfast meeting with Iowa UAW leader David Neil. 'He started talking about the hollowing out of our industrial capacity,' Neil recalled. 'You hear all this rhetoric from people who are (representing) professional interest groups.'

"But the conversation with Neil was somehow different for Dean. 'I understood what this human being was telling me, and it was different from (AFL-CIO president) John Sweeney telling me in Washington or (AFSCME president) Gerry McEntee because it wasn't about (labor) business, it was about people. And all of a sudden, it clicked.' "[45]

This wasn't the only time that he would find himself on the same page of the Iowa hymnbook as the Hawkeye choir. Before 1,500 at the Polk County Convention Complex, Dean would sing the ethanol chorus to add to the labor lyrics. In a theme that would be reflected in a 527 ad in 2004, Dean brought the crowd to its feet by saying "Our industrial capacity is being hollowed out because we are sending jobs to China."

Listening was Iowa Senator Tom Harkin, whose endorsement was widely sought. Although he would eventually endorse Dean, the early state of the courtship was clear that evening, when Harkin referred to him as "John Dean." That would not be the only time on the campaign when someone confused Howard with the canary whose golden-boy looks had compelled him to sing about Watergate, lest he end up keeping house with a burly cellmate somewhere.

Harkin had guaranteed his role by arranging nine forums around the state, to be added to the usual tedium on C-SPAN, where candidates would answer questions directly from voters. Harkin saw himself as "the nine-hundred pound gorilla. I have the best organization. I have the best list. I love (Iowa governor) Tom Vilsack, but he's never done the nuts and bolts of politics."[46]

Vilsack would not end up endorsing anyone before the caucuses, so his wife's endorsement of John Kerry would be trumpeted as carrying great weight. Pundits wouldn't foresee that in 2004, endorsements would start to have the allure of finding the severed head of a horse in your bed.

However, Shapiro adds "… the damning indictment of the caucuses is that they do not inspire in most Iowans anything like the enthusiasm lavished on such heartland curiosities as a life-size sculpture of the Last Supper rendered in creamery butter at the State Fair."[47]

Such heartland hokiness was running up against Iowa's move into modernity, as Des Moines had seen the opening of the state's first Starbucks, in a converted Masonic Hall. (Conspiracy theorists have long cast a wary eye upon the Masons, but a Starbucks/New World Order connection would be a reach for even the most extreme of them.)

Dean would end up wrestling in the Iowa mud with Dick Gephardt. Gephardt had worked with Bush on the final wording of the congressional endorsement of the Iraq invasion, and even appeared on the stage at a White House pep rally supporting passage.

John Edwards had co-sponsored the resolution, but kept his head down in the congressional debate and refused a last-minute invitation to join in the cheer-leading.

Shapiro notes: "Some suspect that Gephardt, who voted against the

1991 Gulf War, had made the calculation that supporting the Iraq war was good politics—and then was chagrined to find himself on the wrong side of the Democratic fault line.

"What was intriguing about both candidates was the dramatically different ways they chose to present their pro-war views to skeptical audiences of Democratic voters. Edwards' and Gephardt's stylistic differences were far more revealing than the intricacies of their foreign policy decision-making. The North Carolina senator consistently presented himself as a determined truth teller, seeking to win plaudits for his honesty, rather than his ideological orientation. You could almost see Edwards calculating: I'm so likable, and so nice, that I can get away with expressing an unpopular viewpoint, as long as no one thinks I'm hiding anything."[48]

"Gephardt needed something more transcendent than just sonorous words to explain why he is seeking the presidency after failing in four successive congressional elections to become Speaker of the House. To a far greater degree than his rivals, Gephardt demands redefinition. But how do you reinvent white bread?"[49]

"Gephardt may have spent half a lifetime in Congress, but his flat, uninflected description of the experience conjures up Bob Dole without the humor, Lyndon Johnson without the earthiness."[50]

Yet this is who Howard Dean would choose to engage in battle in the Hawkeye State.

While skirmishes would be fought on many fronts, the most expensive, and visible, battlefield would be in advertising. Campaign advertising is an area that tends less to science and more towards art, sometimes black art. Science or art, it is expensive, usually exceeding the cost of all other forms of voter contact significantly. In 1992, it helped Ross Perot's candidacy that he was a billionaire, as he ran "infomercials" that were generally quite positive in helping elect Bill Clinton by drawing votes from Republicans.

Advertising can be used by a candidate to define him or herself. The definition created by advertising tends to style more than substance. Studies in 1980 and 1988 showed that voter opinionation about traits exceeded voter awareness of candidate platforms.[51]

Ronald Reagan used "Morning in America"; Bill Clinton used "A Man from Hope."

However, advertising can also be used to define an opponent. George H. W. Bush had defined Michael Dukakis into a colossal landslide in 1988. Bush painted Dukakis as soft on crime by linking him to a black prisoner named Willie Horton, who had raped a white woman while on furlough in Dukakis' state, Massachusetts. Horton was the only furloughed convict ever to commit kidnap and rape, and the program had actually been created under Dukakis' Republican predecessor as governor. Research showed that "the effect of the presidential campaign was to drive blacks and women firmly into the Democratic camp, and suburban voters firmly into the Republican camp."[52]

Because of the furor over the implicit racism in the ads, Bush would tread much more lightly in 1992, when he would lose to a much more vulnerable Bill Clinton. When North Carolina Senator Jesse Helms faced a strong challenge from Harvey Gant, a black state senator, in 1990, he played the race card effectively. Caucasian hands were shown crumpling a rejection letter and dropping it into a wastebasket, while utilizing the loaded phrase "racial quotas" to portray a "victim" of affirmative action. Fourteen years later, Dean would be accusing George W. Bush of similarly playing the race card.

When Dean ran for re-election to his final term as governor, and later for the presidency, he would have to navigate the "lifestyle" battlefield, because of Vermont's adoption of civil union legislation.

When Patrick Buchanan ran against Bush in 1992, he damaged the incumbent by linking him with the National Endowment for the Arts. The Buchanan ad showed scantily-clad men parading down the streets of San Francisco, while the announcer claimed that "...the Bush administration has invested our tax dollars in pornographic and blasphemous art." The ad further tied the NEA to homosexuality and child abuse.

Ironically, the scenes of gay men had been taken from a film the Reagan administration had funded. Since budgets are the result of Congressional acts, Bush's ability to micromanage the NEA was extremely limited. If Bush had vetoed a budget over that one item, it would impact all the other items in the budget, and Congress would still have had the opportunity to override the veto.

Buchanan's ride through the primaries allowed him to trumpet "family values" at the Republican convention. Conservative grandstanding at the convention may have contributed to Bush's defeat in 1992, although he was not helped any by Ross Perot's third party candidacy either.

When Senator Dianne Feinstein ran for governor of California in 1990, she was trailing her opponent badly in the polls. She had even suffered the ignominy of having her campaign manager walk away from the campaign. An advertisement ran that portrayed a calm and collected Feinstein in the aftermath of the assassinations of San Francisco Mayor Moscone and Supervisor Harvey Milk. While witnessing the murder presented a dubious qualification for governor, it cast a positive light on Feinstein, despite the fact that her opponent had been a prosecuting attorney, and was probably more steeped in the underside of human nature than Feinstein. Feinstein rose from eighteen points down to five points ahead. Superficiality, inaccuracy, and the absence of real content did not prevent these ads from being very successful.[53]

For a candidate, an attack ad launched by a group from which you can distance yourself is an ideal weapon. In their book on attack ads, Ansolabehere and Iyengar note: "Organized interests seem to have a unique edge in going negative. Attack advertisements from interest groups convey all of the negatives about the candidate who is attacked, without the risk of a political backlash against the candidate who the group supports."[54]

If a candidate has to launch a negative advertisement, ideally it can be shown a minimum number of times and draw so much attention from the media that it has maximum effect. Lyndon Johnson's campaign portrayed Barry Goldwater as something like the madman of "Dr. Strangelove" in 1964, with a famous ad of a little girl plucking petals from a daisy in a countdown ending with a nuclear explosion. The ad ran exactly once, yet has defined the Goldwater candidacy for history.

Bill Moyers, Johnson's press secretary, reported to the President a week after the airing that "…while we paid for the ad only once on NBC last Monday night, ABC and CBS both ran it on their news shows Friday. So we got it shown on all three networks for the price of one. This particular ad was designed to run only once."[55]

Johnson would win in a landslide, and end up escalating America's involvement in Vietnam. Although nuclear weapons were never used, a joke circulating during the Vietnam War was "I voted for Goldwater, and I got him."

Advertising could also be the source of inadvertent humor. Nelson

Rockefeller had mocked Barry Goldwater's refusal to campaign among liberal Oregonians with billboards that read "He Cared Enough to Come." Given that Rockefeller's life would end in an intimate moment, with a woman other than his wife, he may have written his actual epitaph, even if it wasn't a political one, in 1964.

The Democratic Party would develop a schism over Vietnam that would be evident in the 1968 elections. The loss of discipline and unity in a party that naturally tends to be factional anyways would open the door to the White House for the Republican Party.

Three decades later, Stephen Ansolabehere and Shanto Iyengar would write that "the growing support for independent candidacies, and the growing frustration with negative campaigning, present both a threat and an opportunity for the parties. The threat is that if negative campaigning continues to alienate people, especially nonpartisans, then the parties will lose their legitimate claim to represent the majority will, and any policies they enact while in government will be viewed as a minority's interests imposed upon the majority. The seriousness of the threat, though, opens the doors for party renewal. Facing the wrath of a frustrated and volatile electorate, the parties' leaders now have strong incentives to cooperate and reinvent the rules of political campaigning, so as to foster more positive and responsible electoral behavior. Either that, or let negative candidate-centered campaigns drive one or both of the parties into extinction."[56]

While advertising may aim at assigning a voice to candidates, it is hard for the candidates to be something they are not.

James W. Pennebaker is a psychologist whose linguistic studies have included Nixon, former New York mayor Rudy Giuliani, and George W. Bush. He observes that "Gore was always criticized for being stiff and detached, and you see this in Kerry, too, with the added feature that he's significantly more negative than Gore was. Unlike Edwards and Bush, his language shows he isn't personally connected to his topic or audience, and perhaps to himself."[57]

While Dean may have been a threat to the Democratic Party, his own negative advertising in Iowa was undoubtedly a factor in extinguishing his presidential bid.

Even advertising that was targeted non-specifically against "insiders" and the "establishment" may have been aimed at the wrong audience.

For example, Republicans and Independents distrust their own Congressional representation, and Washington in general, more than Democrats do.[58] Somehow, the decision-makers on advertising in the Dean campaign had overlooked a key fact. Dean, once cast as firmly in the "Republican wing of the Democratic Party in Vermont", was running in the Democratic caucuses, in the Democratic state of Iowa.

Mark Wrighton notes that "...before Iowa, one of the things that the Kerry campaign was able to do was to make, not necessarily character, but personality an issue. They did it, although not terribly overtly. I think that they benefited somewhat from Dean and Gephardt going negative against each other in Iowa, but I think that at the same time the Kerry campaign understood that it was an opportunity to show their candidate in a different light. So we get John Kerry... flying himself in a helicopter, and those images. Then you start hearing the rhetoric of presidentiality coming into John Kerry's remarks. I think that struck an important chord in Iowa."

Gwen Graham says that "...the most touching time on the campaign with Dean people was when we were in Iowa, the day of the Iowa caucus, at something called a blogger's breakfast.

"I saw that this campaign was so much about people connecting with other people, caring about other people, reaching out to their neighbors whether they lived next door, or they lived across the country or they lived across the world. Here we had this room jam-packed with bloggers from around the world. There were even people there from Tokyo.

"I got up and I spoke about my experience on the Dean campaign. I spoke about... how much it meant to me, during the difficult period of my dad getting out of the race, to have these responses, and this outreach towards me, and towards my family. It was just a really, really, human, wonderful life-enriching experience, something that is so much greater than so much of what we do in this world that seems so disconnected with the Internet, in terms of people being on computers. These were people really reaching out to one and other, and humanly touching one another. Those are relationships that remain and will stay. I really did care about this campaign."

Steve Grossman says that "the most important money that a campaign spends early on is to do research on the candidate, to learn what the candidate's weaknesses are, and then deal with those. That NBC news was able to drop that tape describing Caucus participants as extremist and special interests, less than ten days before the Iowa caucus, was a devastating event. There is no excuse for the campaign not having a transcript of that tape and all of the tapes, recognizing the potential damage and getting that behind them in July or August.

"Howard could have very easily said in a speech in a town meeting in July, saying 'folks I have now been to all 99 counties in Iowa, and you have taught me an amazing lesson. I am really humbled by this experience. You know, four years ago, I did an interview on a TV station up in Canada, and I said something really dumb. I said that caucuses were events that were controlled by extremists and special interests. You know how wrong I was? And I want to apologize to the people of Iowa, because you folks understand what participatory politics are, more than any group of Americans that I've met to date. Please accept my apologies.' And then you move on. It's a one day story in July, not a defining moment in January, so that even Tom Harkins' endorsement the next day couldn't save you.

"Saddam, and Osama, and the town meeting, and the tape, all added up. The relentlessly harsh ad campaign that he and Dick Gephardt waged clearly was rejected by the voters of Iowa as negative campaigning that simply went beyond what they hoped would happen."

David Brady says "my mother-in-law's a big Democrat in Iowa.

"She wanted to vote for Dean, but she went for Kerry because the claim was, 'this guy's not electable.' By the way, I think that's a perfectly reasonable claim. I do not think he was electable. In order to energize the base, he was too far out there to win."

John Mercurio points out that "...being in Iowa, and eyeballing the operation, all across the city of Des Moines you saw these bright orange Team Dean hats. It gave the impression of strong organization, high visibility, and, as far as the public perception, it looked as though he still had the momentum, his organization was together. That …perception was definitely not reality. (They) said 'we're a national candidate', when they really knew that in January they were going to have to fight in Iowa, and they were going to have to fight in New Hampshire, and that's where all of their resources were going to be.

"…when it came down to Iowa and New Hampshire, they really weren't organized, in either of those states, enough to compete against Kerry… in the caucus world, it's all about organization, and getting your supporters to leave their houses on a cold Monday night, and go to a caucus. They realized, as everybody did, that there were only 3 tickets out of Iowa and they needed to be one of them. They thought they were going to come in first or second.

"Dean saw Kerry surging in Iowa, and realized he couldn't lose to both Gephart and Kerry in Iowa. Kerry's organization was really underestimated in Iowa. It was underestimated because there were significant changes going on in their organization in Iowa in the four to five weeks prior to the caucuses. They (the Kerry campaign) knew that if they didn't do well in Iowa and New Hampshire that it wouldn't matter how well they'd do in South Carolina."

Game theory earned a Nobel Prize for mathematician John Nash, the subject of the movie "A Beautiful Mind." **Stephen Ansolabehere** describes how game theory impacts upon politics:

"It might be interesting to start with Nash's problem. Nash's problem was an individual trying to make a decision, by just thinking of the odds that something will happen. Then you calculate the expected value of choosing one action or another. The value you get if you take action A, and event one happens, plus the value of taking action A, if event two happens, weights the probability of the value that event one happens and event two happens. That's simple decision theory.

"If I'm gambling (on a football game), I'm taking odds; my decision to gamble doesn't have anything to do with the behavior of the football team. But as soon as you have another person who's also thinking along the same lines about your behavior, then you get into what feels like an infinite regression: 'well, if I do A and they do A, then maybe I'd be better off doing B, but if I do B, then they'll want to do B,' and so on... it doesn't seem like there would be a natural solution.

"A Nash equilibrium is... 'I'm going to assume that you're going to do the best that you can, and given that, I'm going to choose the best thing that I can. You're doing the best for you, I'm doing the best for me.'[59] If people are thinking strategically, then they will come to realize what it is that the other person should do and, therefore, what they (themselves) should do.

"In political campaigns, you're trying to figure out 'what issues should I advertise on, should I attack the other person or should I promote myself?' In the case of attacking and promoting, what turned up in our data (is that) the time when you're most vulnerable is when you're promoting yourself, and the other guy is attacking you. That sort of drives you away from wanting to be in that position.

"It is similar to nuclear warfare: if one goes nuclear, it guarantees that the other will.

"A lot of game theory was developed around the Cold War. The idea of mutually assured destruction (MAD) was that if two super powers have a huge amount of bombs, that will guarantee that nobody will use them.

"In politics, going negative is MAD (mutually assured destruction). In international politics and military strategy, with mutually assured destruction, nobody has actually gone negative. But in national politics, they use it all the time."

With multiple candidates predicting where voters will go is challenging using this theory.

Ansolabehere continues: "In the case where there are two candidates, it's called zero sum. When one guy gains votes, the other guy loses votes. Zero sum is between any two candidates. However, when you have multiple candidates ... the voters aren't switching between any two candidates, they might be going to a third candidate.

"That's... what happened with Dean and Gephart in Iowa. Gephart went after Dean because Dean was leading, and Gephart really needed to win Iowa to be in the game.

"I don't think Gephart appreciated that, by attacking Dean, it didn't mean those voters were going to go to Gephart; in fact they didn't.

"They went to Edwards and Kerry.

"The way to look at it is to look at who people's second choices were.

I now see a number of campaign consultants who've used game theory, and a number of parties who've used it. It did look like Edwards was using it. It looked like Gephart didn't understand it, and Dean couldn't get away from it.

"That's why Iowa was the Tar Baby.

"Theoretically, there wasn't much Dean could do strategically. He had to react to not one, or two, but to six. I think being a frontrunner, at just that moment, put him in a pretty vulnerable position. A lot of the art to advertising, and campaign rhetoric, has to do with choosing what to do right. The Clinton campaign in 1992 and in 1996 was very good at instant response. They understood this. People like Bob Squier understood this. Squier was from the firm of Trippi, McMahon, and Squier, but he died two or three years ago."

Politics is just a game.

I Scream, You Scream, We All Scream, for IA Scream

Technology... is a queer thing. It brings you great gifts with one hand, and it stabs you in the back with the other.
C.P. SNOW, *New York Times*, 15 March 1971

Howard Dean lost the nomenclature war. When his speech became known as the "I have a Scream" speech, or any of the variations that incorporated the word "scream", he lost the ability to define his actions that night. All of the variations reinforced the "angry" temperament that he had been forced to deny for the preceding months. Of course, if you keep calling someone angry long enough, it will become a self-fulfilling prophecy.

It is indicative of the failings of the American educational system that many Americans made the correlation between Dean's decline to seeing media coverage of the Iowa speech. A nation that somehow had found the credentials to psychoanalyze Howard Dean had managed to miss accusing Dean of having a Napoleon complex. Many would make the case that his Waterloo was in Iowa.

The Iowa caucuses were a shock, both to us in the New Hampshire grassroots, and the media itself. David Von Drehle wrote on January 20th, "I sure didn't see it coming. I'm knocked out by what happened in Iowa—24 hours ago, I was still having a hard time believing Kerry's poll numbers. If you had told me even a week ago that John Kerry, who hardly registered a political pulse for the past year, would finish twice as well as Howard Dean, who ran one of the best 'invisible primary' campaigns in history, I would have rolled my eyes.

"The surveys of caucus-goers seem to suggest that people who want to beat President Bush — which surely includes a lot of anti-war voters — moved away from Dean in the final weeks and toward Kerry and Edwards, both of whom supported the Iraq resolution. Dean didn't get nipped, edged or clipped. He got stomped, creamed and walloped.

"So today is the first day I've ever considered Kerry remotely 'electable' because it is the first time he has won diddly in a presidential context. Why it took them a year to get an endorsement from the man whose life Kerry saved is a mystery to me—but surely it helped."[60]

The Dean speech before he left Iowa reverberated with David Von Drehle.

"Really bad speech — he seemed a little bit out of control ... more important, he seemed to misunderstand that he was speaking not to a few hundred friends in the room, but to all the people watching TV — people who had never seen him before. Contrast that speech to the Edwards speech, which was the best post-primary speech I've seen since Clinton's 'Comeback Kid' speech in 1992. Edwards came out early and used his opening minutes to introduce himself and his themes to the wider public."

Robert G. Kaiser saw the speech as a lesser issue for Dean.

"You know, different people react very differently to events of that kind. I am persuaded that a lot of Americans thought Dean made a big mistake that night. But remember, he had just come in a miserable third in a race he was supposed to win, according to polls. That probably hurt his ultimate chances more than the screaming."

Kaiser agreed with an assessment that exit polling on Howard Dean's temperament was "ridiculous, but there is no conspiracy in the big media against Dean."

Kaiser questioned the impact on Dean Nation. "The Dean people are, in many cases, new to politics. Will they be terminally discouraged if their man doesn't win? Don't know."[61]

Now the Gore endorsement, and the forces behind it, began to be questioned.

"I got the impression the party insiders decided the Dean campaign was the best available choice and they wanted to strengthen it and perhaps get inside to offer some advice. That's a calculation that looked pretty sober in December and obviously looks quite different today."[62]

Labor endorsements also looked a lot less valuable since Dean and Gephart had garnered the most labor union support, yet were outmatched by Kerry and Edwards.

Dean supporters' voices were immediately heard online on the blogs.

"Too many of the pundits writing off Dean's innovations are Jurassic fuddy-duddies who never got the Internet and fear it might diminish their status and influence. Let's not throw the baby out with the bathwater in our analysis."

"I liked Dean's speech...He was speaking to his supporters (of whom I am one, although I am ABB all the way, I don't drink the kool-aid coming out of Burlington.) He was quite gracious on the networks in congratulating Edwards and Kerry, he decided to have some fun at an event that was populated with tons of people who had worked their hearts out for him. For cryin' out loud, it seems like people were expecting him to drop out."

Other observers weighed in on Dean and Kerry.

"His wife's appearance and the appearance with Carter in Plains Sunday looked like acts of desperation.

"Kerry on the other hand exuded an air of urgency yet calm deliberation."

Dean's speech drew intense criticism as well.

"I thought he was on drugs."

"Watching Dean's speech last night, I couldn't help but be reminded of the TV anchor from the movie *Network*."

"Dean gave a speech where he sounded even more irrational and nutty than usual."

"My theory about Dean this: that the 'Deanie Babies' did Dean in. I can only imagine what the people of Iowa thought about a crew from Berkeley showing up on their doorstep to tell them how they should vote."

The contrast with the speech of the rising John Edwards was noted.

"I thought it was smart, because virtually no one in the country has ever heard a word the man has said. And a candidate's stump speech should be his or her best introduction. Realizing that he would be speaking to his largest audience so far, he gave his best introduction to his candidacy."

David Von Drehle summarized his reaction to the caucuses.

"When I was jotting a list of winners and losers last night, I put the DLC (the centrist Democratic Leadership Council) on my 'winners' list, because for some party insiders the Dean campaign has been read as an attack on the DLC approach. (This is complicated by the fact that Dean, as governor of Vermont, was a DLCer in good standing ...)

For what it's worth, I had Kerry, Edwards, DLC, and Michael Whouley at the top of my winners list, and Dean, Gephardt, and labor at the top of my losers list."[63]

In the course of cruising for interviews, I saw a trophy catch- Fox News. While I didn't reel him in so that I could personally make them fair and balanced, I did get Major Garrett to tell me about "The Scream Heard 'Round the World".

Garrett had been in the Val Aire ballroom in Iowa, and thought that, given the background noise and the nature of the audience, it seemed rather in context. However, when he got to the TV truck, the technicians, who had watched through television's narrow lens, were going nuts - or at least, they thought Dean was. Dean had joined Chris Wallace in December, when Wallace had his boisterous debut on "Fox News Sunday."

"Wallace was aggressive with Howard Dean, repeatedly interrupting the Democratic candidate while asking eight questions on why he won't unseal his gubernatorial records in Vermont. 'Why not just open them up, Governor?' Wallace demanded. Nor did he shy away from noting that John Kerry had used the F-word in Rolling Stone while criticizing President Bush on Iraq.

"In leading the usually lively roundtable, though, Wallace may have gone a bit far in declaring that 'the conventional wisdom is the Democrats are going off a cliff' if Dean is the nominee. Many political analysts believe that, but others do not. Wallace defended that judgment after the show and said Dean told him during a commercial that the interview had been 'tough but fair.' "[64]

Marshall McLuhan's idea about the power of a medium was perfectly exemplified on Fox. Particularly when Fox replayed the scream more than anyone else did, without the perspective Garrett could provide.

Elsewhere, executive editor Leonard Downie, Jr. defended the Washington Post's coverage. "I think the Post kept its coverage of Dean's performance in Iowa on caucus night in perspective. The question, I guess, is whether it should have been repeated so much on television. It is relevant to voters' perceptions of Dean because it is only the most noticed example of his tendency to say and do things without carefully calibrating their impact beforehand; Dean calls it going with his heart rather than his head.

This may worry some voters and may please others who think other politicians are too calculating, but it is relevant."

Downey also puzzled over the importance of Judith Steinberg's induced role in the campaign. "I just don't (know) the answer. What I think we found out with the Deans is that voters at least want to know who the spouse is — and the Deans answered that with Judy Dean's frequent appearances with her husband over the weekend in New Hampshire." [65]

Overnight, Dean would be more famous for "the Scream" than Edward Munch's painting, which he had done in 1893. Communist propagandists said, "repetition is the mother of reason."[66]

William Blum writes that "Propaganda is to a democracy what violence is to a dictatorship."[67]

Media critic **Noam Chomsky** of MIT says "Fox is like Pravda."

Jon Finer says that "you have an obligation to report what you see, first hand, but that doesn't preclude you from being able to watch it later and develop a different opinion on it in that medium (television), which I think a lot of people did. A comprehensive account would be to explain how the way the sound equipment works created a different experience when viewed on television from how it was viewed in the room.

"In the room, apparently, you could hardly hear what Dean was saying, because the crowd was shouting so loudly. If he was shouting, my guess is that he wasn't losing his mind, as some of the opinion writers seemed to indicate in the days that followed, but that he was trying to be heard.

"The way the microphone system worked, the sound from Dean's microphone was pumped directly into the television audio system, so he sounded clear as a bell on TV. The sound of the cheering crowd was diminished as a result. So, on TV, it really sounded like Dean was screaming his head off, for no apparent reason."

Adrian Walker says that "media is a plural noun. The decisions and actions of Fox should not be applied to all of us. I know they are. They exaggerate everything, they blow up everything: they think that's what makes good television.

"If you go on O'Reilly, I've been on *The O'Reilly Factor*, you have to fight. When I was on, we didn't even disagree, we had to have a fight anyway."

Walker talks about the nature of media, in general: "Everything's different on television than it is in person. I can easily imagine that one might see Dean's speech differently after seeing it in person and then seeing it on television. As far as the pack journalism part of it, I think it is less fear (of your colleagues opinions), as was often characterized, and more of an echo chamber effect.

"You get 20 reporters on a bus, you're together every day, you see each other all the time, and you talk about what's happened all the time, and then something like this happens. I was in my living room watching it and I was like, 'hmm, that was pretty weird, I'll probably be reading about that tomorrow.' But then you talk to all the other reporters, and you talk about it, and talk about it, and talk about it and it becomes a bigger and bigger thing as time goes on.

"It's absolutely more of a subconscious process. It's not like I'm thinking, 'Scott wrote this, my friend Scott Lehigh. Gee, I'd better get with the program.' It's more like, I'll see him, after an event, and I'll say' gee, what'd you think of that scream,' He'll say 'I thought he sounded like a nut.' Maybe I didn't think he sounded like a nut, but I'll start thinking about it, and, suddenly, it will start sounding a little nutty to me too.

"You'll have a reporter on the scene, and they'll call in and file their story, and everyone in the national desk will be going crazy. 'No, no, no, this wasn't a little thing, this was a big thing.' Something like that happens, and people immediately start debating in the newsroom. 'Gee, was it a meltdown, was it not a meltdown, was it a big thing, was it not a big thing?'

"It's not unusual, even in print journalism, to have this sort of warring perceptions between the people who saw it live and the people who saw it on television. I think the effect of the scream has been substantially exaggerated. However, lest we forget, he finished third before the scream. His problems predated it."

Kathy Sullivan says "What was now going to be a very, very competitive nomination process, because of how Kerry and Edwards did in Iowa, really took Governor Dean out - that combination, the Iowa loss, plus the speech. People blame the press. I agree that the press was terrible in the way they played that thing over and over and over. It got to the point where my husband was watching Sports Center on ESPN, and they had a lead-in with Howard Dean doing the speech. They were going to get sports results, from all around the country, and they had Howard Dean going 'we're going to go here, we're going to go there.'

"I didn't see it. I went to bed that night, after I saw Howard Dean on Larry King. It was a fine interview, and I saw John Edwards being interviewed, and Kerry, and I said, 'I'm going to go to bed.' The next morning I got up early, because I thought I would do a trifecta. I'd go see Kerry at the airport in Manchester, then I'd go see Howard Dean at SNHU, and Edwards at the Manchester Library.

"… driving from my house to the airport, which takes about 10 minutes, I hear somebody on the radio saying 'Did you hear Howard Dean last night?' 'Yeah, that was crazy. What was going on?' This was before it had been replayed a thousand times."

Carol Darr feels that "Dean fought the empire, and the empire fought back. That was clearly at play that night, when he did his speech, and it got played 600-1000 times. The thing that Diane Sawyer did, saying 'We were not fair to him,' was played exactly once. They just made him out to be a screaming nut case."

Steve Grossman was sitting with his mother in Palm Beach the night of the Iowa caucuses. "We see Howard start to give his talk, and I looked at my mother. Before he finished, I said, 'This campaign is over.' Because, at that point, not only does he have a devastating defeat in Iowa, but he would have had to come back and win New Hampshire. The only way he could recoup was to come back and stop John Kerry in his tracks, in John Kerry's neighboring state.

"That might have happened without that speech, had he given a vision statement (instead), and looked toward New Hampshire, it might have been a real close race. I think it would have been, but once he gave that speech, for the next five days, it was just a replay of that speech endlessly, so there was no way. It was obvious to anybody watching television that night, when more Americans saw him that night than had ever seen him before. He picked that moment for the wheels to come off the wagon… that was the wheels coming off the wagon, big time."

Jodi Wilgoren observes that "…the guy went out … in the most important speech of his career …and howled. That was a pretty big mistake. He'd have to remember that he'd already come in third in Iowa, and really, basically, had only the slimmest chance of getting revived. But he definitely killed it off with that speech.

"He told me the other day he thought it was the speech of his life. It's one thing to say that the cable news overplayed it, but to not acknowledge that it was an inappropriate speech for that moment is to live in a world of political unreality. To not understand that on the night of the Iowa caucuses, what you're doing is giving a speech to a television camera, is not understanding how politics works.

"I certainly think the idea of small donations is fine, you can do that differently. But a night at the Iowa caucuses is the first time that the rest of the country clues in. All the national networks are going to tape your speech live, and whoever is in the room has heard you speak a gazillion times before. I don't say you ignore them, of course you speak to them. But you are at least 50% speaking to the people in the back of the room…the cameras. To not know that is really missing it.

"I was in the room, I heard all those kids screaming, and I still thought he seemed crazy.

And Tom Harkin…… watch the tape and watch his face."

Richard Hoefer says that "After the scream had been on the web, I submitted another version that put it in context.

"There were 3500 people there screaming at the top of their lungs. The Iowa storm came from all over. They had worked their asses off. The amount of let down was really severe. He was like a football coach giving a pep talk to his troops: 'We're going to come back, it's not over.' They recorded it as you would for television. Then you hear it repeated ad nauseum, over and over, along with the words, 'melting down', 'unelectable', 'he's really nuts.' You repeat that 600 times, which is what they did…and you know you have to be a retard to not have that characterization reinforced."

Hillary Hazan says "I was there for Iowa, the Iowa scream thing. Of course, I didn't know that he had screamed, because you couldn't pick it up at all. I was probably in the back, letting all the grassroots people enjoy being up close. Here we had suffered this huge loss and the energy was still there. I don't know if you can call that incredible or ridiculous. But either way, it worked.

"I really didn't hear the scream. And then, I was driving back from Iowa and I heard the scream played to a James Brown song. And I thought, oh my god that happened! it was played instead of James Brown's scream, at the beginning of the song (I feel good). I was thinking, 'did that happen? Where was I?' The scream made sense when he did it; the crowd was going wild."

Gwen Graham who "had committed to doing some ABC radio, was in the convention center.

"I was not at the party, because they were at the same time. I had just finished doing the radio show, and came out into the press room. They have row after row after row of computers at the little tables. I believe in interacting with media. If you're honest with the media, and develop friendships with them, then it's a respectful relationship. This goes both ways. I talk to them on the record and off the record.

"I was sitting in the midst of all my friends from the media, and Governor Dean came on. I watched it, and I knew instinctively that coming in third was no longer our biggest issue. I knew that this was going to be something …because of the predisposition of the media to cling to the angry Dean angle. Now they not only had an angry Dean angle, but they had a sort of manic Dean angle. That was good drama … that was good TV. I knew instinctively it would be something … difficult to overcome.

"Unfortunately my instincts were right."

MEDIA CULPA

Technology and production can be great benefactors of man, but they are mindless instruments, and if undirected they career along with a momentum of their own. In our country, they pulverize everything in their path — the landscape, the natural environment, history and tradition, the amenities and civilities, the privacy and spaciousness of life, much beauty, and the fragile, slow-growing social structures that bind us together.

CHARLES A. REICH, The Greening of America, 1970

Most readers have probably noticed that when the media runs corrections, they tend to take the form of a whisper, even if they are corrections to what had been a damning shriek. Corrections to front page errors almost never run on the front page. For example, when the *Boston Globe* printed the correction to a front page story that Claiborne Pell was not dead, as they had reported, the correction ran on page two.

After the Iowa speech, Dean was not dead either, although one might have inferred otherwise from most coverage. To the extent that the media would correct itself in the days following, the corrections tended to be microdots by comparison to banner headlines.

The media probably needs no apologists. However, the nature of news dissemination, and the way people digest that news, in a society that has a pace driven ever faster by technology, minimizes time for reflection. The great scientist Neils Bohr was both brilliant and dyslexic. Bohr would anguish for an hour over a single sentence in his writing. Science demands a precision that language may not always allow. Deadlines force an imprecision that journalists probably regret, up until they reach a compromise with reality that is livable.

Consumers of media may see no further than a headline that cannot encapsulate the nuances of the article that follows. The "I Have a Dream" speech, the Gettysburg Address, and Bill Clinton's much ballyhooed address to the Democratic convention in 1988 demonstrate that the power of words tends to have an inverse proportion to their number.

In headlines, that power can be for good or evil, however unintentionally. Channel surfers may listen no further than the opening sentence or paragraph of a television news story that is only a few minutes long, at most. There is enough blame for the shallowness of our culture that it can be spread far beyond the media alone. The nature of the relationship between the media and a candidate bears examination.

Veteran print journalist Walter Shapiro writes that "TV cameras overwhelm the story they are purporting to cover, and print reporters, deprived of access, are reduced to regurgitating self-serving quotes from manipulative press secretaries."[68]

While Gil Scott-Heron sang that "the revolution will not be televised", a line that Joe Trippi posted in the Burlington Dean offices, he probably wasn't anticipating the advent of around-the-clock cable news channels.

The long campaign trail affects reporters as well as candidates. "Cynicism is to political reporters what combat fatigue is to soldiers, an occupational hazard that comes from living too long in the trenches." Shapiro writes of the temptation of "overly facile mockery."[69] Since many reporters are younger than he is, they may not have developed his self-awareness. Shapiro describes the inclination to amateur psychoanalysis as making the political press "forever Jung."

A microscopic examination of issues and platforms is not merely tedious, but sometimes it is misleading. When he covered Clinton for *Time* in 1992, Shapiro did the deep academic analysis of Clinton's pledge to provide health care for all Americans.

"As a result, I and my equally fact driven journalistic counterparts missed the real story, which was the vast policy making powers that were soon to be ceded to an unelected First Lady."[70]

Shapiro points out that "As the self-appointed guardians of the entrance to the Oval Office, reporters are constantly alert for any character trait that smacks of Nixonian weirdness or suggests that maybe this guy shouldn't be entrusted with nuclear weapons."

Probing into a candidate's cultural orientation might provide insight. Maureen Dowd has scoped out this field. She ran a cultural quiz past Bush in 2000, when he called baseball his favorite cultural experience. Bush was a contrast in brevity to Kerry, giving only one answer to each of Dowd's questions. In his interview with Dowd in 2004, when Kerry listed 37 movies, he took as much time on one question as Bush had needed for the whole quiz, at which point aides began to hover around him.

Kerry cited his favorites "National Velvet", "The Deer Hunter", "Men in Black", "Top Gun", "Braveheart", ""The Blues Brothers", "Animal House", "Scaramouch", "Indiana Jones", Adam Sandler, Fellini. But his is not a life lived just through cinema. Musicals like "Phantom of the Opera", and "My Fair Lady", poets including T.S. Eliot, Keats, Yeats, Shelley and Kipling, and music including Elvis, the Stones, the Dead, the Beatles, Buddy Holly, opera and folk music add to a cultural portrait. His reading ranges from Tom, Huck and the Hardy boys to "Trinity", Hemingway, biographies of Lincoln and Roosevelt, and airport mysteries and thrillers.

Unlike the culturally passive incumbent, Kerry likes to write poetry, play classical guitar, and wants to learn to do the dance that appealed to a previous Massachusetts candidate, Mike Dukakis: the sultry tango.[71]

Having so many opinions might well lead to Republican charges that Kerry is indecisive, or too complex, or too smart to be president. At least the Republicans wouldn't face counterattacks on the same grounds.

Walter Shapiro notes that "This time around, the *Boston Globe* tried (unsuccessfully, in my view) to paint John Kerry as two-faced for sometimes failing to contradict the easy assumption that anyone with his last name had to be Irish."[72]

Shapiro continues: "For me, the relevant distinction is between psychology and temperament. No reporter or profile writer knows enough to plumb a politician's inner psyche, but journalists are equipped with the observational skills to describe his personality and draw conclusions from it. It's the difference between unknowable causation and visible effects. But a presidential contender's basic temperament remains an innate and immutable quality that defies the mind-clouding powers of even the most adroit political image makers. Americans want their presidents to be jaunty and optimistic, rather than dark and brooding."[73]

John Kerry's loss of his mother, and bout with prostate cancer in 2003 wasn't enough to keep the *Boston Globe* from revealing in February that the Senator's Jewish-born grandfather had killed himself with a handgun in Boston's Copley Plaza Hotel in 1921. Kerry's paternal lineage wasn't Boston Brahmin, but instead, depression prone Central European Jewish.

"But even as the conversation drifted toward more predictable political topics (Kerry's pique at Howard Dean), the Lincolnesque senator was clearly troubled by the notion that he projects a sad visage. Being aloof was something he could handle; in his February press conference announcing his prostate cancer, Kerry joked that the doctors were planning to remove his 'aloof gland'" Shapiro notes.[74]

The public's need to know had extended into the previously closed world of doctor-client privilege. While John Kennedy's fragile health had been hidden from the public, and might even have impacted his ability to govern, now America knew its politicians most intimately.

"Running for president is to privacy what burlesque is to modesty."[75]

When Ronald Reagan had surgery for polyps, the graphics on dinnertime news left viewers feeling they needed to take showers. The description of Bill Clinton's intimacies with Monica Lewinsky preceded a rise in the incidence of oral sex in adolescents. There seemed to be no limits to where the news would go.

Howard Dean's emotional life was subject to scrutiny long before the speech in Iowa.

"In August 2001, Dean's father, a retired stockbroker also named Howard, died at eighty. That same month, Dean chose not to seek another term as Vermont governor, a decision that soon led to his impetuous bid for the White House. Back in 1974, Howard Dean's younger brother Charlie, possibly a CIA agent, perished under mysterious circumstances in Laos. Subsequently, Dean jettisoned a Wall Street career to attend medical school. Dean, however, denied an overt connection between these deaths and his unorthodox career moves. 'I'd probably have to go into analysis to figure out why,' Dean said, 'but it's not something that conscious... Okay, this is interesting,' he conceded. 'My brother dies, and I switch careers and go to medical school. My father dies, and I take on the big prize. It's an interesting coincidence, worthy of discussion, but no light is likely to be shed on it in five minutes or an hour.' "[76]

Yet journalists regularly attempt to probe the psyche of a candidate, without the years of psychoanalysis that a person might need to understand themselves, let alone someone else. Perhaps it is the youth of many reporters on the campaign trail that gives them the hubris to attempt such analysis. Yet they have less personal experience themselves with life's milestones than the candidates they cover.

When Kerry's mother died, the major political news was that Teddy Kennedy would turn from his protégé John Edwards to back the junior senator from his home state. Reporters pestered Kerry with questions about his prostate and general health, but hardly ventured into the life defining point of losing a parent.

Walter Shapiro asks, "What is the explanation for this unusual degree of journalistic reticence? It's possible that America still commands the last vestige of old-fashioned privacy.... But my own theory, and it is stated tentatively, is simply that most beat reporters are still in their thirties, too young in many cases to personally understand how the mid-life loss of a parent can tilt one's inner world off its axis."[77]

Shapiro continues: "Journalism is not normally considered a 'helping profession,' but those of us in the press pack are as dedicated to inspiring sagas of personal growth as our couch-bound counterparts. What is the point of the endless campaign season, all those bus rides and tarmacs at two in the morning, if we can't chronicle how a politician (a Bobby Kennedy, a John McCain) dramatically changes before our very eyes?"[78]

Shapiro's insightful analysis of his colleagues indicates the power that they hold in their hands, a power to define, refine, and destroy. Power is corrupting, and (speaking from middle age myself) the younger you are, the more easily you can fall victim to the allure of power. "It makes no difference whether the candidate's inner fires radiating external warmth were kindled at birth, or whether the long smoldering embers only began to burn brightly in mid-life. What matters is the glow - and the desire of voters to see their dreams reflected in it."[79]

In the heart of every Deaniac, there lies a belief that their man was a media victim.

The Dean campaign fed that frenzy, for example, when Karen Hicks showed New Hampshire supporters a video that she felt documented the media bias - in the summer of 2003. Dean himself assailed the "established press" and complained of attacks by columnists. On a campaign trail that got rocky in the beginning of 2004, Dean withdrew from the press.

"Many of them got so frustrated one day... that they refused to board the bus until he stopped and talked with them. And, during a series of conversations with *ABC News* last weekend, his advisers threatened to expel the network's producer from his campaign plane, if ABC went forward with plans to report that a Vermont state trooper who Dr. Dean once called 'a wonderful parent' turned out to be a wife abuser.

"Though network and campaign officials said that the threat came in a series of heated arguments, and was never taken seriously - the report ran with no reprisals - the dispute was the most extreme illustration yet of how much Dr. Dean's relationship with the national news media has changed."

"'We failed twice with Dean,' Mark Halperin, political director of *ABC News*, said of the news media in general. 'Dean was able to rise in standing without being held to a high enough standard of scrutiny for months.' But now, Mr. Halperin added, 'he is so overly scrutinized to be beyond fair.' "

"'His own words have gotten him in trouble,' said Chris Lehane, a strategist for Mr. Clark."[80]

"Almost all candidates at some point or another get nasty with the press," the *Boston Globe* quoted *Newsweek* editor Mark Whitaker as saying.

"Andrew Tyndall, who monitors the ABC, CBS, and NBC nightly newscasts, said that in the final quarter of 2003, Dean got more minutes of airtime than the rest of his Democratic rivals combined.

"The Center for Media and Public Affairs, a nonpartisan research organization based in Washington, evaluated network news coverage of the campaign for all of 2003, and found that Dean was the subject of more than twice as many stories as his nearest Democratic competitor for airtime, John F. Kerry.

"'I look at Dean's blog a lot,' says Chuck Todd, editor-in-chief of the *Hotline* political newsletter. 'And the Dean crowd is very skeptical of the major media. It really reminds me of where conservatives thought the mainstream media was four years ago'."

CNN senior political analyst William Schneider says "Movement politics are always 'us versus them.' The press is 'them.' "

While not all of those espousing that theory had strong neural connections, it didn't require a lot of careful reading to provide supporting evidence. Larry Sabato is the director of the University of Virginia's Center for Politics. Sabato says "I talk with a lot of reporters, and they don't like Dean. I can't tell you, over the past six months, how many of them said to me, 'I can't stand him, he's really an asshole, he's nasty to me, he growled at my cameraman.'" [81]

When I contacted Sabato to try to get specifics on this allegation, he sent word through an assistant that he was on his sickbed and couldn't help, but that he never revealed his conversations with reporters anyway. Asked for background direction to any journalists to start with, he refused. That led me to try to find journalists who had covered Dean and who felt so strongly.

Mediachannel.org executive director Timothy Karr feels that the media stereotypes candidates, and had cast Dean as the "unwinnable, crazed outsider."[82] Gaffes by any candidate tend to get reported, although a front-runner who is getting more coverage tends to get the bad with the good. Wesley Clark's fumbling of a standard line into "high leadership" was duly reported.

Kerry was described in behavioral terms by the *New York Times* - as if the commentary on his appearance wasn't enough: "He is alternately on-point or irritable, sometimes misspeaking or sniping at questioners in the audience." A further candidate description includes that "Lieberman has seemed a bit cranky of late. He abruptly shot back 'that's ridiculous' at a man who criticized him for attacking the other candidates. Delivering a staple anecdote, he described the behavior of a woman without health insurance who cannot afford regular medical care for her son and relies on the emergency room as 'stupid.'"[83]

Revelations about Jayson Blair, and his subsequent and widely panned memoir, do raise the issue of residency in glass houses.

Andrew Smith points out that "...as nice a ride that Howard Dean got the months beforehand, he got a rougher ride in that (last) 6 week period. So, it wasn't necessarily evenhanded justice, but I would say it was rough justice in the sense that I think Dean brought a good bit of that on himself. This was not a guy who could stand prosperity."

Ray Proulx says that "... the *Burlington Free Press, Rutland Herald*.... They can all be pretty brutal. When he first announced he was running for the presidency, the *Burlington Free Press* was very positive in all of its articles... (as was) the *Rutland Herald*, but I was seeing that (as being) out of true respect for what he did as governor and his accomplishments. They weren't doing that lightly, they would not have gotten behind him at all... I can think of other candidates in Vermont the Free Press has not gotten behind at all and has been pretty brutal."

Adrian Walker comments that "every campaign I've ever covered, at every level... every losing candidate has blamed the press. I have never covered a campaign where we weren't the reason the loser lost. I don't think we are nearly as powerful as that record would suggest. If you see in the (ABC News) daily newsletter, the *Note*, at some point last summer, you could track this down, that Kerry has received the most negative coverage from the (*Boston*) *Globe* than any presidential candidate has every received by his home town paper."

Anson Tebbetts says "I think that some Vermonters would have a belief that it was a different league, and Dean was in a different league with the press... (national media) are a lot rougher... with cable TV and the deadline's every 15 minutes and the competition between the cable companies to be first, live all the time.

"When everything was going well, I would hear from folks saying that he was getting a free ride from the national media because the national media was creating him, because he was saying things and not afraid to speak his mind."

Tebbetts relates other Vermonter perspectives:

When watching TV news coverage where he was present, Tebbetts recalls Vermonters asking him "'Why didn't he stop to talk to you, you're a Vermonter, he should have talked to you, you're a local guy.?" He adds "... a lot of people were impressed with how far he got but were also just shocked with how fast he fell." Some Vermonters commented to Tebbetts: "'Oh I knew this was going to happen because of his personality'... knowing he would eventually implode because of his personality."

Jodi Wilgoren notes "I work for the...the most prominent news organization or newspaper in the world... Most of the more thoughtful and professional people who were Dean lovers, who I dealt with regularly

and who evaluated my work including Dean himself, thought I was fair...
I think he has a somewhat valid point about the cable news and the Internet overplaying his scream speech. Nobody objective has found anything inappropriate about the coverage of Dean... It's interesting to me that people got so focused on the media.

"I would hope that your discussion of this 'issue' would benefit from interviews with the people I dealt with regularly on the campaign.....Trippi, Jay Carson, Tricia Enright, Doug Thornell, Gina Glantz, Kate, Dean himself, Steve McMahon....because all but Kate and Gina have told me post mortem that they thought I was fair throughout. And I am not sure how the Larry Sabato stuff is being used, but I'm pretty sure I barely ever, if ever, quoted him regarding Dean."

Mark Wrighton comments on the media: "These folks have maybe some knowledge of the political system but they don't necessarily have vast knowledge, so they are coming to people like me to find that out.

"I think more generally, beginning before Iowa, one of the things that the Kerry campaign was able to do was to make... personality an issue. And they did it, not terribly overtly. I think that they benefited somewhat in Iowa from Dean and Gephardt going negative against each other, but I think that at the same time the Kerry campaign understood that it was an opportunity to show their candidate in a different light."

Gwen Graham says "... most of what people know is Dean exclusively from TV. So you believe what you hear, and unfortunately a lot of times it's not the whole picture. It's a part of the picture."

Richard Goodwin says "First of all, he (Dean) got great coverage for a long time...I remember he was on the cover of every news magazine - no one could have asked for more coverage than he was getting...and pretty favorable, on balance. Then he started to make these mistakes - the tide began to turn...that's the way the media are... when they begin to turn on you, they turn on you. The unfortunate thing about the scream is that he did it and it was there on television to be played over and over again.

As unimportant as it may have been substantively, people just saw it again and again."

George Stephanopoulos says the relationship between Dean and the media was "Testy. I think that the relation between him and the media followed the trajectory of his campaign. When things were going well he benefited from the bandwagon. When they were going badly, he crashed pretty quickly, in part because he didn't have that net...safety net...of relationships. But for a long time he felt that having the contentious relationship was working for him politically. They believed that whenever he had an aggressive interview, his supporters would watch it and give more money."

The author said "Let's hearken back to Jimmy Carter, since you were a delegate for him. You may remember Carter had a quote in, of all places, *Playboy*, of having lust in his heart.

"When Paul Tsongas won the New Hampshire primary, NBC's Lisa Myers said to him 'did you ever imagine, a year ago, that you'd win the New Hampshire primary?'

"Tsongas left her speechless with his response, which was 'You have no right to my private thoughts.' "Does the public, or the media, have a right to a candidate's private thoughts?"

Howard Dean says "Some of them. They don't have a right. I don't think anybody has a right to anybody's private thoughts, but I think if you want people to vote for you, they have to have some idea who you are."

Workin' the Media; Cruisin' and Schmoozin' with the News

It troubles me that we are so easily pressured by purveyors of technology into permitting so-called "progress" to alter our lives without attempting to control it — as if technology were an irrepressible force of nature to which we must meekly submit.

HYMAN G. RICKOVER, quoted in The American Land, *1979*

The second stage in the nominating process that Rhodes Cook identified occurs in Iowa and New Hampshire, in the cold month of January. Cook saw this stage as bringing ramped-up media scrutiny. For the Dean campaign, that had occurred much earlier.

The seemingly predatory nature of the media beast was revealed in an observation by Kevin Landrigan of The Nashua Telegram: "I was in New Hampshire while Dean was governor. As far as I could determine, he did not have an 'angry' reputation. He was forceful with state legislators, particularly with Democrats early on while he was trying to balance Vermont's state budget during difficult economic times. Reporters here were looking for Dean to show his temper, as we do all candidates, and he kept himself well in check."[84]

Walter Shapiro ran an anecdote to counter all the anger stories: "Sarah Buxton, who was Dean's personal assistant when he was governor and is now the campaign scheduler, says the only time she saw Dean lose his temper was over rock-chipping. He was angry over the idea of Vermont spending $50,000 on rock chipping to beautify a stone formation after a road was cut through it."[85]

Dante Scala points out: "Iowa and New Hampshire together, plus the media's interpretation of these two contests, winnow the field to a front runner and one or, at most, two or three challengers. Since the modern nomination process was instituted in 1972, no nominee has ever finished out of the money - that is, lower than third place - in either Iowa or New Hampshire. Even before the 2000 cycle, scholars expressed concern over a so-called rush to judgment on candidates once the business of delegate selection actually begins."[86]

MIT ethnologist **Susan Silbey** explains that "Rather than transparent, most of the mechanisms governing the most common and taken-for-granted aspects of our everyday lives are relatively, if not totally opaque to most citizens. As much as we claim to value democracy, and supposedly support the expansion of democracy around the world, the material, technological infrastructure of social relations is less and less participatory or democratic... Our political system, and the operation of the media that tends to form most voter opinion, is opaque to most voters." Such systems "operate almost entirely behind the backs of most people, but nonetheless demand enormous trust, and command almost blind deference. We have transferred our trust from persons that we know or know of (e.g. fathers, priests, the King, the Pope) to 'disembedded' abstract systems- markets, airlines, electrical grids, water and sewer lines, banking, etc... Although people may have a generalized discomfort with the media, politics, or government, they still place a degree of faith in such systems - enough to make them somewhat functional."[87]

By December, the media coverage of Dean had seemed to shift from premature anointment to increasingly critical. "Deaniacs" were up in arms over what they saw as an all-out assault on their hero. While one prick can burst a bubble, Deaniacs saw nearly everyone in the media as culpable.

Howard Kurtz observed "His supporters are passionate. There have even been a couple of obituaries where families ask, in lieu of gifts or flowers, that donations be made to the Dean campaign. Dean might prove to be a weak general-election candidate, if he gets that far, but the pack journalism about him was wrong once before. Maybe it is again.

"Weekly Standard editor Bill Kristol (who backed McCain over Bush last time) offered a contrarian take on this the other day: 'Could Dean really win? Unfortunately, yes. The Democratic presidential candidate has, alas, won the popular presidential vote three times in a row—twice, admittedly, under the guidance of the skilled Bill Clinton, but most recently with the hapless Al Gore at the helm. And demographic trends (particularly the growth in Hispanic voters) tend to favor the Democrats going into 2004...'

"Dean has run a terrific primary campaign, the most impressive since Carter in 1976. It's true that, unlike Carter (and Clinton), Dean is a Northeastern liberal. But he's no Dukakis. Does anyone expect Dean to be a patsy for a Bush assault, as the Massachusetts governor was?

"And how liberal is Dean anyway? He governed as a centrist in Vermont, and will certainly pivot to the center the moment he has the nomination. And one underestimates, at this point when we are all caught up in the primary season, how much of an opportunity the party's nominee has to define or redefine himself once he gets the nomination.

"Kerry is doing his blankety-blank best to attack the front-runner, as *The Boston Globe* reports: 'Howard Dean would be 'eviscerated' by President Bush's re-election team next year if Dean emerges as the Democratic Party's nominee for the White House, chiefly because of the former Vermont governor's 'enormous deficit' of experience in national security and military affairs, Senator John F. Kerry said yesterday.'

"These comments are the strongest Kerry has made in conveying that Dean would lose to Bush, an argument that has become a tacit theme of Kerry's own candidacy as he struggles to surmount Dean's double-digit lead in New Hampshire polls before the primary there Jan. 27."[88]

Since I had taught journalism, had been on television before, and was comfortable, I had been working every media contact that didn't turn and run from me at events.

One of my regular gambits to draw people in would be to divest myself of Dean paraphernalia and pose as an undecided voter. This usually had an effect similar to throwing a steamship round of beef into a pool of ravenous sharks.

New England Cable News even bought it so thoroughly that they interviewed me at several events. I would shape my purported thinking, reflecting how Dean looked better and better as the primary drew nearer. Two days before the primary, I morphed into the "wired" voter that CNN was doing a story on.

"One more thing we know about these super-educated voters. They're super demanding." That was CNN's lead-in to my attempt to undermine support for Clark.

"When I got the chance to address General Clark, his answer to a question I directed at him was not accurate, and so that made me really uncomfortable."[89]

I spoke with a New York Times political reporter who felt the Deaniac response to his coverage of a particular event had bordered on harassment. As a result, he would not allow his name to be used for attribution. His justification for how the "Scream" was reported differently over two days by the *Los Angeles Times* reporter Matea Gold is illustrative. "You take into account other people's experience and how it comes across. TV is the reality, in this day and age."

It appeared that the media were more stenographers than journalists. Television was dictating. Starting in December, polls seemed to show that while the Dean campaign had maintained its mass of core supporters, it was losing the weight of gravitational attraction for many voters, courtesy of a media obscuring the Dean message to the public.

Howard was facing Weapons of Mass Media Destruction.

The power and intent of editorial decisions were never clearer. However, paranoia about the media had long preceded the Dean campaign. A December article in the *Washington Post* reports: "… there are times when the *Washington Post* is not the most popular reading in the West Wing. That was also true more than 30 years ago, as we see in this *Post* account of the latest Nixon tapes. Richard Milhous Nixon had concluded, in those Watergate days, that the real problem is the press. 'Sue the bastards!' he says, pounding his desk audibly. 'Forget the Democrats, sue the media! Sue the *Post*.' He and Haldeman conjure a scenario where [campaign aide Donald] Segretti sues the *Washington Post* for libel.

"'He couldn't win it, of course, and he could drop the suit right after the election, but it would create doubt in the public mind.' Haldeman suggests they could serve *Post* executives with a subpoena during the public dedication of the *Post*'s new building downtown, scheduled for that week. They enjoy the idea but don't appear to take it very seriously. 'The goddamn press can do anything it wants,' Nixon says bitterly.

'It's the damn Eastern Establishment.'"[90]

LETTERS TO THE EDITOR; USING THE PEN TO DEFEND AND ADVOCATE FOR HOWARD

Technology was developed to prevent exhausting labor. It is now dedicated to trivial conveniences.

B.F. SKINNER

In October, I was told at the office that I should write letters to editors. Since this had much more appeal than cold-calling people, I leapt at the opportunity. The first assignment was to write a letter countering a column *The Portsmouth Herald* had run from a Hampton resident. He was complaining at the arrogance of the Dean people in putting up signs on their lawns so far before the primary. I wrote a letter that pointed out that America had a tradition of free speech, and suggested the documentation that had laid that foundation.

Perhaps it was a harbinger of things to come that the *Herald* didn't print it until two months later, when the original column would be long forgotten, and the letter's relevance would be diminished by the appearance of the signs of other candidates.

Still, I loved writing, so I went to the Dean website that was coordinating letters to the editor. There I found that the current suggested topic was Dean's fiscal conservatism in Vermont. I blanketed NH Seacoast papers with variations on that theme. Symptomatic of the absence of coordination in the campaign that was becoming increasingly apparent to me, there would never again be any guidance on what themes might be emphasized in our letters.

I found my own topics in campaign coverage and events along the campaign trail.

Sharpton's attacks on Dean's Confederate flag comment Dean produced a defense. I brought forth Dean's background in medicine. I denigrated Clark as a Democrat-come-lately. I defended Judy Steinberg's right to define herself as a physician and mother, rather than a campaign appendage to her husband.

Repetition of the theme that Dean was an "angry" man seemed endless.

"The whole aim of practical politics is to keep the populace alarmed (and, hence, clamorous to be lead to safety) by menacing it with an endless series of hobgoblins, most of them imaginary."[91]

I wrote that Dean was not angry, but that Americans should be, like the Patriots of the Revolutionary War. Local papers published almost everything, but I could never crack *The Boston Globe*, *New York Times*, *USA Today*, or *Time* magazine. A particular target of mine was *Time* columnist Joe Klein. I wrote that his portrayal of Dean deserved a full palette, not just "Primary Colors." Klein continued to annoy me, and *Time* continued to ignore me.

A political reporter who covered the Dean campaign says "Dean people were hypersensitive to media coverage. The Deaniac counter-offensive was more orchestrated than any ever seen before." One of the divisions of Dean Nation that assaulted the media called itself the Dean Defense Forces.

The *New York Post* ran a column on January 5 by a retired Army officer in which he compared Dean to Hitler, Goebbels, Lenin, Trotsky, and Brezhnev. (Osama was already in play in Iowa, and Stalin had a strong p.r. guy.) The reason for the fusillade? Dean and his legions of darkness "restrict the free speech of others" by attacking their critics on the Internet. (Auschwitz, anti-Semitic propaganda, communism, being attacked in a blog. Which one is not a part of this group?)

A media report upon which the Deaniacs looked askance would result in a blizzard of e-mails to the offending writer or producer. While the impact might have modified behavior on the part of the recipient, the degree of media backlash is not measurable.

Empowerment corrupts.

I guess that described me.

A personal triumph came when I got a call back from the editorial page editor of the state's most widely-circulated paper, the arch-conservative *Manchester Union Leader*. He assured me that my letter would be published on the Sunday before the primary. I probably suckered him with the e-mail lead that said I had been buying the *Union Leader* on my morning walks for three decades. In actuality, I wouldn't use the paper for house breaking a puppy. I never checked to see if the letter actually appeared. It's like I used to tell the kids in the office when they said they had seen one of my letters in print:

I just wrote them. I didn't read them.

Joe McQuaid, the publisher of the *Union Leader*, is described by Howard Kurtz of the *Washington Post* as "crusty." McQuaid's 62,000 circulation paper runs front-page columns describing how to use Thanksgiving leftovers. Still, it is a force in the Granite State.

"For some Democrats, the paper has been a big, fat, juicy target. Ed Muskie famously denounced Loeb on a snowy day in 1972 and appeared to tear up, wounding his candidacy. McQuaid says that Jack Kennedy rallied his troops by doing the same thing in 1960.

"The *Union Leader* had to back out of an agreement to co-sponsor, with ABC and WMUR, the University of New Hampshire debate, after Democratic Party officials objected. "For some reason the Democrats still don't like us, even though we've lost our fangs and the Loebs are gone," McQuaid says.

"McQuaid had dismissed George W. Bush, the 2000 candidate, as 'an empty suit.' When Bush became President, McQuaid told Bush that 'He'd filled out the suit quite nicely.'

"Not that McQuaid is an unabashed fan of Bush, whom he once dubbed 'Governor Smirk. Spending this money when we don't have it is nuts,' he says. 'I fault Bush for that.'

"The *Union Leader* planned to endorse Lieberman. Dean, a denizen of what McQuaid calls the 'left-wing state' of Vermont, could benefit in a perverse way. 'Perhaps having the *Union Leader* say nasty things about you boosts your standing on the left,' says Editorial Page Editor Andrew Cline.

"The publisher was intrigued by Dean, saying: 'He hasn't followed the politically correct script in a lot of ways.' But he also says Dean 'seems like an arrogant guy. I don't like his position on gay unions. Someone' — it was Dick Gephardt — 'accused him of cutting social services to balance the budget. So there's a glimmer of hope there.'"

"McQuaid has little use for John Kerry of neighboring Massachusetts: 'He's a stick — a boring non-personality. He's been in [Ted] Kennedy's shadow for years.'"

"'The union-friendly Gephardt should be doing better', McQuaid says, since 'New Hampshire has lost manufacturing jobs up the wazoo.' And he says that while the congressman is on the dull side, 'if you put him in a room with Kerry he'd light up the room.'

"John Edwards? 'He's in way over his head.'

"Wesley Clark? 'Started off with a whimper, not a bang, and been going downhill ever since.'"[92]

I certainly wasn't preaching to the choir with a letter to the *Union Leader*. It would be more like screaming over a cacophony.

The same computer and internet technology that had raised the tide under the Dean ship made it easy for me, and thousands of other Deaniacs, to flood the media with our support for Howard. Once there was a letter format on a particular topic, it could be slightly modified and sent to most media outlets. That electronic empowerment was euphoric, entrancing.

The "paper of record" was probably the most prominent target for Deaniacs. The *New York Times* reporter Jodi Wilgoren may have been its most prominent target, but the *Times* presented a target-rich opportunity for Dean Nation.

"The *Times* writers were penning inaccurate, misleading and often gratuitously nasty attacks on Howard Dean and his down-to-earth wife, in an effort to drive voters away from him," wrote Aminah Carroll of West Virginia.

"In defending the *Times* against its Deanite critics, you fall back on the naïve notion that what the *Times* does is simply educate the electorate, rather than shape the actual political terrain that candidates and voters must negotiate. Along with the rest of the news media, it does a lot of the latter, as all campaigns know," wrote Brooklyn resident Richard Wells.

The *Times* coverage of Judith Steinberg brought a backlash substantial enough that it published six letters to the editor objecting to the spotlight on her. The front page article had shone the spotlight into a place Dean had sheltered throughout his career.

The *Times* played the role of contrite supplicant as Public Editor Daniel Okrent analyzed the paper's coverage, in the kind of self-analysis Susan Silbey described. He acknowledged Wilgoren's detractors, and mentioned the blog "The Wilgoren Watch." He said "Wilgoren seems to have become the face on the dartboard for Dean supporters... Nearly every time there's a story about Dean in the paper, my in-box fills with complaints from his fans. (Every time there isn't a story providing a précis of a new policy statement from the Dean camp, it's almost the same.) They attack the editors of the *Times*, Wilgoren, national political correspondent Adam Nagourney, and other staff reporters for misrepresenting, ridiculing or attempting to sabotage Howard Dean. They especially object to the *Times* microscopic inspection of their candidate while, many say, the depredations of George W. Bush go unexamined."

Okrent pronounced Wilgoren's description that "Dean smirked his trademark smirk" as "inappropriate" and "columnist's language." He conceded that two headlines might have been done better, one picture was questionable, and that one story had been overplayed.

But "an article detailing what Dean's opponents perceive to be his weaknesses is legitimate news. All the 'on the one hands' and 'on the other hands' you could stuff into such a piece wouldn't dissipate the negative aura it necessarily emits. By my count (I did it quickly, so don't arrest me if I'm off by two or three), from Dec. 1 through this past Friday, the *Times* published 59 major stories or editorials about Dean. Wesley Clark has been up for view 30 times. No other candidate has enjoyed (or suffered) more than 20 appearances in the paper. Carol Moseley Braun got only three shots - and two of those were about her decision to leave the race."[93]

Comedian Stephen Wright used to observe about the instructions on a shampoo bottle, in his deadpan delivery, "Rinse, lather, repeat. I'm afraid if I start, I'll never stop."

Write, copy, paste, send, repeat.

And that had more gratification than washing your hair; sometimes, the letters would actually get published.

THE ONE WAY STREET FROM MANCHESTER TO GREENLAND GRASSROOTS

> I shall do less whenever I shall believe what I am doing hurts the cause, and I shall do more whenever I shall believe doing more will help the cause. I shall try to correct errors when shown to be errors, and I shall adopt new views so fast as they shall appear to true views.
>
> —*Abraham Lincoln*

The itch to take a more active role in the campaign, and perhaps utilize more of what I thought was an impressive skill set, started soon after I began doing grunt work in the office.

When Aswini had asked us to do a house meeting, calling upon our friends in education, she had said that Michael King would come, since the National Education Association- New Hampshire (NEA-NH) endorsement was so important. She wanted us to get at least 20 people. We sent out over 60 invitations, but as the day drew close, it was clear that attendance would be in the single digits. We told her, so that Michael King wouldn't come for a crowd that wasn't worth his time.

King is the former leader of the state Democratic Party, and had been one of the people who rode around with Dean in the early days of his one car caravan. Aswini correctly described him as looking like a character on *Miami Vice*, and she was terrified of him, since she saw him as a bigger boss than Ben.

Although we only got a total of seven friends, Michael King showed up. He was singularly unimpressive. He may have looked *Miami Vice*, but Don Johnson got it done, and he didn't.

But then, much of success in life is determined by whom you know.

So, I decided to take affirmative action and write him a letter laying out my background, and what I felt I could be doing to help the campaign. I could write.

Dean's stump performance would get old.

"Many commentators have suggested various reasons Kerry and Edwards surged in Iowa and in the past week, particularly that their re-tooled stump speeches were vastly improved, whereas, among better-known factors, Dean stuck to his tired speech, which was that of the insurgent he no longer, pre-Iowa, was, rather than that of the front-runner he temporarily was."[94]

When I saw King next, I asked if he had gotten the letter. He said it was still in the pile on his desk. He never responded; in fact it was months before he seemed to know my name.

So the next person I approached was the state director for Dean, Karen Hicks.

I approached her at a Dean event, and she said to send her a letter. Prepared in advance, I handed her the letter on the spot.

When I saw Karen Hicks a week later, I asked if she had read the letter yet. She indicated her desk had the same organizational schemata as King's. Apparently the campaign was only hiring people with identical skills sets.

Actually, that's an unfair representation. She not only did not get back to me, she never learned my name.

The next person I approached was national chair Steve Grossman. Grossman had shocked the person whose Senate campaign he once managed, John Kerry, by signing on with the Dean campaign. I handed Grossman a letter at a Dean Meetup he addressed in Portsmouth. He assured me he would read it and get back to me.

By this time, the unprecedented success of the campaign in fundraising was widely known. In the face of this, I was frustrated at the campaign's allocation of resources. We didn't have any Dean buttons to give to supporters who came to the office, pens for seniors had been deemed too expensive, and the paid staff in the Portsmouth office were getting pathetic wages for 80 hour work weeks.

"Money and organization is only important if it produces delegates, and primary votes are the best way to do that."[95]

Clearly, there was something wrong with the allocation of human resources also, since I couldn't get anyone in Manchester to return my calls. Ben ignored my requests for tickets for a key volunteer in Greenland who wanted tickets to the UNH debate. I called the national office in Burlington twice, the Washington office of the Democratic Party and the Manchester Dean office at least 10 times. The national party office had called back within an hour and told me that Karen Hicks and her assistant, Josh Glasheen, held the tickets.

It wasn't until the day before the debate that I got the call back from Glasheen saying all tickets were already committed. He assured me that they would make it up to me some way before the primary.

Later in the debate cycle, I decided that I wanted to see the spectacle first hand. Calls to Manchester went unreturned again, so Herb Moyer of Exeter and I decided to go without tickets and see if we could crash the event. I had talked to someone who had gone to the UNH debate without tickets and gotten in when someone had walked up and offered a ticket, so I thought we might be similarly lucky.

When milling around the entrance to St. Anselm's College's Dana Center didn't produce any such largesse, we decided to embolden our way in. We got in the line at the door, and when we were asked for our identification at the entrance, said we had tickets set aside by Karen Hicks.

Although we feigned that we were "shocked, I say, shocked," we were rebuffed with minimal prejudice, to return to the hordes demonstrating outside. That gave us a chance to hold signs and chant with other Dean supporters. I sought out media coverage, and got interviewed for Dean TV, whatever that was.

In a theater of the absurd moment, I met Vermin Supreme, a performance artist I had read about in the *Boston Globe* as a frequent denizen of such public events. I shook the great man's hand, and he shook the rooster headdress he wore, and gave me a bumper sticker for his presidential campaign.

The bumper sticker bore the identification that it was a product of the misinformed citizens' bureau. I suspected that Supreme's voter base was siphoning support from Kucinich and LaRouche. Mr. Supreme's chances for election may be less than either of theirs, despite his enlightened platform's advocacy of mandatory dental hygiene. Mr. Supreme also brings outstanding credentials as a journalist. He interviewed John McCain on January 25, 2004, and got McCain to acknowledge the truth behind the destruction of The Old Man of the Mountain. McCain acknowledged, in an interview with Mr. Supreme, that "Karl Rove was responsible for the destruction of the Old Man of the Mountain, to spite the people of New Hampshire" for the shellacking they laid on George W. Bush in the 2000 New Hampshire primary. McCain acknowledged, on camera, that he had sought an investigation from the FBI into the desecration.

The FBI was apparently too busy ignoring Juanita's report that she had been threatened by "Atta" while online in August of 2001.

Unlike most of the young people in Portsmouth office, I was doing the Dean equivalent of "Clean for Gene", I didn't put the sticker on the old pickup that I drove around to campaign events. Vermin's bumper sticker would have to remain a campaign artifact, along with the sticker that said "Somewhere in Texas, a small village is missing its idiot."

My frustration boiled over in mid-January, on a weekend when we were supposed to contact identified supporters in Greenland, re-ID them, and offer to put up new signs in their yards. The weekend was designed to be a dress rehearsal for the Get Out The Vote (GOTV) effort on primary day.

Although my wife had talked me out of resigning in protest a week earlier, I now refused to call the office to report on the progress of our efforts. It may have been a "dress rehearsal," but I decided to send a message to the campaign by not "fully dressing."

Wendy, the new area organizer we were working with, assured me she would get tickets for Katie Drapcho, our newly identified 16-year-old Greenland dynamo, and her mom, so they could go to a dinner to see all the candidates in Nashua.

I also sent an e-mail to Steve Grossman, and Tom Hughes, the state political director, five days before the primary. It was the resignation letter I had drafted earlier, containing all my concerns with the campaign, but without a threat to resign. Grossman called me the same day, to discuss what could be done to strengthen the New Hampshire effort in the precious days remaining. Although I was stunned to actually have seen any responsiveness, since he hadn't responded to my first contact with him, I made a couple of suggestions, which he said he would pass on. He urged me to use his name in bringing my suggestions to NH Director Karen Hicks.

So, the next morning, in a conference call with the Dean pollster Paul Maslin and Hicks, I pointedly mentioned my conversation with Grossman, and one of the remedies I suggested. She assured me she would immediately speak with the political director and have him order all area organizers to follow through immediately.

Never happened.

The pollster had been a late addition to the call, which was supposed to feature Hollywood activist Rob Reiner. Reiner had been astounded at the Dean campaign's initially minimal reaction to the coverage of the by-then infamous Iowa speech. Perhaps he had jumped ship by that point.

Other observers would "feel that the Deaniacs, Dean's campaign workers, were too insular, inexperienced, and inward-looking, to be persuasive in the complex Iowa caucus system, and to them, foreign Iowa culture... (T)he blogs of a number of ordinary Iowa and New Hampshire voters .... said clearly they were annoyed and turned-off by overly-aggressive Dean supporters."[96]

The Iowa caucuses had stunned the campaign, but I had thought the wheels were coming off the cart long before then. In fact, I wasn't ever convinced the cart would make it through state vehicle inspection at any time.

GENERAL ANXIETY

Whosoever diggeth a pit shall fall in it.

—*Bob Marley*

My career as a political operative began at the same time that Wesley Clark emerged as a threat to Howard Dean in New Hampshire. Clark was described by the *Boston Globe's* fervently anti-Dean Scott Lehigh as "… the candidate who has taken a page from the Democrats' winning playbook from 1992. And who clearly has the Dean camp worried."

The *Globe* reported that "A barrage of criticism from his rivals appears to have taken a dramatic toll on Howard Dean's advantage in New Hampshire, and retired General Wesley Clark is benefiting. Clark's support is stronger than Dean's among affluent and older voters….and among those who supported presidential candidate John McCain, Republican of Arizona, in 2000."[97]

Clark's entrance into the Democratic race, following a year of Cuomo-like posturing on the sidelines, had piqued a great deal of interest in the people we were calling and canvassing. Handsome, intelligent, a Rhodes Scholar as well as a four star general, he had a resume that offered a serious threat to a man running as the former governor of a small, rural New England state.

Clark had set the tone for his campaign the day after he finally announced his candidacy. Despite the lengthy practice sessions he had held with aides in September, Clark encircled himself when he was asked the obvious question about how he would have voted on the authorization for the war in Iraq. The leader of a gang that couldn't shoot straight, Clark first said he probably would have, then that he wouldn't have. Having outflanked himself, he then called out to his press secretary: "Mary, help!"

The fact that advertisements hadn't emphasized Dean's previous career as a physician was a drawback that was particularly obvious when people started salivating over a four-star general. As media contract lawyer Leslie Kerman points out, "The quality of the Clark ads was excellent."

Given that much of Dean's early traction had come as an anti-war candidate, it was foolish that his years as a caregiver weren't being emphasized. This missed opportunity was made more glaring when Clark's past statements about the Iraq war made his opposition to Bush's expedition there somewhat ambiguous.

Of course, such ambiguity didn't seem totally surprising from a man who hadn't even registered as a Democrat until after he declared himself a candidate for the nomination. Clark had been quoted as saying that he would have been a Republican if Karl Rove had returned his calls after 9/11. Clark's effusive praise of Bush and his team at a Republican fundraiser in 2001 further cemented his image as a Democrat of convenience. Still, people seemed to be getting blinded by the glare of all that brass, and Dean was going to be in Iowa in the week before the caucuses, while Clark stayed exclusively in New Hampshire.

Joe Lieberman, who Walter Shapiro of USA Today described as "running for the nomination of a party that didn't exist", had encamped his family in a Manchester apartment for his ill-fated siege of the Granite State.

Lieberman had seemed to be the Republican wing of the national Democratic party. He became a hard-line law-and-order guy after his home was twice burglarized in the lawless 1970's in New Haven. Like any humorist, he had appropriated good material in agreeing that he fit the model as a 'conservative being a liberal who had been mugged.'

Lieberman did win the humor primary. Dean had brandished a stethoscope at one of the debates, as a sort of merit badge showing his bona fides in proposing health care for all Americans. Later in the debate, when Dean was under siege from other candidates, Lieberman had said that Dean might need the stethoscope for himself. His comment was both prescient and funny, and the stethoscope made no further appearances in debates.

Walter Shapiro, an avocational standup comedian himself, pronounces Lieberman the funniest of the candidates, but suggests that humor was Lieberman's way of maintaining a comfortable distance from other people, particularly reporters. It also allowed him a distance from certain issues.

The Clinton legacy has brought marital fidelity into the journalistic spotlight. Having been hung by chad with Clinton's running mate, Al Gore, Lieberman felt a need to establish that there were more than two degrees of marital separation between him and the man who had embraced some of John Kennedy's personal legacy. Lieberman self-deprecatingly dismissed such concerns about himself by simply saying "Look at me."

Gore's endorsement of Dean had been mishandled, and Lieberman, who had not thrown his yarmulke into the ring until Gore announced he would not run, had seemed the victim of political insensitivity, if not disloyalty. Gore had not been able to tell Lieberman himself that he would be endorsing Dean before the news was leaked. Joe Trippi may have been the source of the leak in the Dean camp, but the end result would be a debate in December where Ted Koppel would make endorsements, and legitimacy, the initial flashpoint.

Although his campaign would expend 17 million dollars before he would drop out, he never evidenced his self-ascribed Joe-mentum. Inertia is the tendency of an object in motion to remain in motion, or an object at rest to remain at rest. The polls continually showed that Lieberman was going Joe-where.

I felt compelled to defend my home court against the serious challenge Clark seemed to represent.

Ben LaBolt was the 23-year-old regional director for the Seacoast in the Dean campaign. A foreign policy major and theater minor from Middlebury College, Ben had been in politics since he started leafleting for a candidate when he was 6. Ben's theater background was evident when Dean appeared at events on the Seacoast, with carefully chosen speakers to introduce the Governor, music to rev up the crowd, and visuals projected on screens before the Governor would appear from behind the curtain.

LaBolt said he had two political heroes: Joe Trippi and the man whose picture was on his desk, Robert Torricelli. Given Torricellis past history, as well as his connections to John Kerry, I should have figured what was going on sooner. I had told LaBolt on the first day I entered the office that I would confront any dirty politics. From then on, doors would be closed, as the precocious youth plotted strategy. Ironically, I would be accused of being a Kerry spy.

Ben came to me on a morning when Clark was due to appear in the area. He asked if I wanted to go to a Clark gathering to direct a question at the General. Long ago tired of phone calling and data input in the office, I leapt at the chance to do something to challenge the skill set which I was sure I possessed and that was being under-utilized.

Ben showed me five possible questions that had been generated by someone in the Manchester office. He asked me if I wanted to take the top one, which was supposed to be most important.

The difficulty was that the question was worded in such a way that it allowed for a ready escape and non-answer by Clark. Having taught English, I was surprised that the person who generated the question, which was supposed to be asked exactly as written, couldn't see this. Once again, I found myself thinking that the youth and inexperience of the paid staff was detrimental to the campaign.

However, the third question on the list left no room for evasion.

"General, you had the School of the Americas under your command. The history of the school is quite notorious. How can you justify supporting a place that many in Latin America see as a training ground for assassins and dictators?" I was already somewhat aware of the School of the Americas. The left-leaning *Boston Phoenix* had made me aware of such blights on America's international reputation.

When Ben asked me to go to the small town of Epping that night to lob my question at the General, I headed home and went to the Internet to research more on Clark and the school. An internet search led me first to Clark's website. There I found his statement denouncing the human rights crimes committed by graduates of the School of the Americas. Curiously, his lengthy campaign biography did not make it clear whether he himself had had the school under his command, or, of greater interest to me, when he might have been its commander.

Other information from my search turned up that Panamanian dictator Manuel Noriega and Chilean dictator Augustin Pinochet were graduates. There were also hundreds of military graduates who had been accused of war crimes, including the men who had slaughtered a group of nuns in El Salvador in the early Nineties.

In a newspaper article on the school, I read a defense of the now-renamed institution by its commander, who pointed out that less than 1% of its graduates had been accused of war crimes. That seemed like damning with faint praise.

Dean supporter Martin Sheen, who Scott Lehigh lumped with Rob Reiner as "self-important Hollywood glitterati," had been arrested in the annual protests at Fort Benning, Georgia. Kucinich, Gephardt, and Kerry had all co-sponsored or signed bills to shut down the school.

I learned that the federal government had been forced to reveal the curriculum of the school in 1996, and manuals of extortion and assassination had turned up. According to the current head of the school, those manuals were no longer part of the school's curriculum. But I still didn't know when Clark had the school under his command, or if the manuals were being used at that time.

Armed with my newly expanded knowledge, I was eager to question the general. It struck me as odd that Ben hadn't suggested to me that I do research. It was important to me to own the question, and be prepared with facts, if the opportunity arose. And, if I had my way, the opportunity was going to arise.

As I contemplated how I would pose the question for maximum effect, B.F. Skinner arose from the dustbin of my memory. As I remembered it, Skinner was the leading exponent of the idea that humans are not any different than Pavlov's dogs. Skinner, to the chagrin of those who saw humans as higher than other species, felt we were all the products of conditioning. This might show in our response to the environment (dress warmly in winter or you'll get cold- duh) or our interactions with other humans.

A famous story, perhaps apocryphal, described the conditioning of a conference speaker who was denouncing the absence of free will Skinner theorized. As the speaker jabbed the air in emphatic opposition to conditioning theories, Skinner would nod vigorously in apparent agreement. Skinner's reinforcement of the speaker had the effect that, by the end of the harangue, the speaker's watch was flying up and down his forearm as he vigorously gesticulated in reaction to Skinner's reinforcement.

I was quite sure I could get Clark to call on me. Toward the middle of the afternoon, Adele Wick called to say that she was going to see Clark at Fisher Scientific in Hampton at 4 PM. She offered to have me join her and her little daughter Lizzie. Since the Epping event would be much later, and I tend to fade as the afternoon light does in the winter, I jumped at the chance.

Of all the people I had encountered in my little town as I campaigned for Dean, Adele was the smartest. Possessing two degrees in economics, capable of lengthy recitations of Shakespeare, Eliot, Yeats, and Johnson (Ben, not Lyndon), she was married to a physician who was also a classical pianist. Adele had talked about the possibility of holding a house meeting where people could learn more about Dean. That she was interested enough to go see Clark now was significant, and her reaction would be an important barometer of what effect the general would have on the Dean campaign.

She had been kind enough to help me doing calls to Greenland neighbors to identify who they were supporting in the primary, but wasn't ever trying to sell her neighbors on him. Whenever she spoke to someone who had questions about Dean, she would readily admit that she wasn't completely sold on him yet, and turn the caller over to me.

I knew she would continue to evaluate the candidates right up until she cast her vote. My training in science supported the idea of continually trying to add to a database, so I respected her approach.

Having grown more cynical in middle age, I even was willing to jump off the Dean bandwagon myself if I saw something better, or if I was profoundly unhappy with something I found out about Dean or his campaign. If Adele came away from hearing Clark strongly predisposed toward him, I knew we were in serious trouble. Because I had spent the afternoon on the Internet, when Adele called, I had to hurry to shower and dress to be ready when she picked me up.

When we got to Fisher Scientific, it was not what I had expected at all. I was expecting something like a factory floor turning out the equipment I had purchased during my two decades as a science teacher. Instead, we were directed down beautiful wood paneled halls, with portraits of foreboding-looking dead white men hung along them.

Adele had called the Clark headquarters to sign up for the event. I wasn't sure how easily I would get in, but figured I could pass as her guest. No one stopped us as we followed directions to the room where the general would speak. The Clark campaign workers weren't as young as the Dean staff I had encountered.

In contrast to the fervent personal ideological connection that brought young people into the Dean campaign, UNH student Steve Melli had come into the Clark campaign because it was one in which he knew someone.

I was the only person outside of the assembled press horde who didn't have a suit or sport coat. As we stood next to the entryway through which Clark would enter, I shifted uneasily in the fashion faux pas my blue jeans seemed to represent. I was hoping that I could still get Clark to call on me by virtue of the fact that I was in the middle of the room, standing up and in the direct line of his sight.

When he passed through the doorway next to me on the way to the podium, I was struck by his small stature. At a Meetup in Manchester on the first Wednesday in December, I had heard Dean self-deprecatingly refer to himself as vertically challenged, as George Stephanopoulos stood next to me. I had been comfortable with Dean's size, since it seemed like it was part of what contributed to his Trumanesque feistiness. However, I expected a four-star general to be larger than life. I could have eaten soup off Clark's head. Maybe the cameras in his campaign ads would have to shoot up at him from below, like Sylvester Stallone had to do to make himself appear larger in the Rocky movies. Maybe Clark would even have a broader range of expression than Stallone. There are granite formations that could make that claim.

Clark gave a rather standard stump speech. Having heard Dean's a number of times, I knew the kind of themes a candidate had to target. He did tell a touching story about meeting an impoverished man somewhere, perhaps in Haiti, who seemed to look upon him as a sign of hope. However, he undercut the story by saying that he didn't know what had happened to the man after he met him and had not bothered to get the man's name.

Throughout the speech, I kept my eyes directly on Clark. When he made a point, I would nod emphatically. When he left openings for applause, I was an eager cheerleader, with a warm smile on my face. So, when he opened it up for questions, I was the first person he called on.

Sucker.

Knowing that the media was there in force, I opened with a gambit aimed directly at them. "Like many New Hampshire voters, I am undecided right now. However, I come today prepared to be swayed. And I come because I want to believe." At this point, the earnestness was pooling around the cuffs of my blue jeans as it dripped off me.

"However, I do have a concern." Then I launched into the question I had been given.

I watched Clark's eyes as I asked the question. It seemed that he knew this was a setup.

His first response was "Well, you know there are many criminals who have gone to the Harvard Business School." This produced a laugh from all the suits, which I joined, in the spirit of the game. I would later learn that he had been asked about the school before, and this one liner was the standard opening to his response. He then said, "Seriously, I'd be happy to have you go down to Fort Benning to see the school." I responded "as long as you are paying for it." My line got more laughs than his did. If my wit wasn't rapier-like, at least I wasn't a little kid dueling with a stick.

Clark then proceeded to admit that there had been people who had gone to the School of the Americas who had committed war crimes. He mentioned Noriega, and said that there had been dozens of others. I was pleased to have him put Noriega's name into play, although I hoped I would get the opportunity to point out that he was wrong by an order of magnitude in his estimation of numbers of human rights violators. Clark said that the school was our best way to educate people from Latin America about our democracy. He also said he had reviewed the curriculum personally, and found it acceptable.

When he was finished, he didn't ask me if he had answered my question adequately, but I nodded and smiled warmly. He went on to other questions. I looked around at the media, and saw a number of faces looking at me. I suspected that I would get the final word.

When the questions ended, and Clark finished with his closing summary, he exited through the door next to me without making eye contact. Instantaneously, I was in the midst of my own press conference. TV lights came on from two crews, and two print reporters stood in front of me with notebooks poised.

Ron Allen from NBC spoke first. I told him I knew him, and that, as a former journalism teacher, admired his work. He asked if I had been swayed. I said that I had not. When asked why, I said that his answer had been in error, and that I was uncomfortable with Clark as a Democrat-come-lately. Asked to explain, I cited Clark's "oversight" in not registering as a Democrat before declaring his candidacy, as well as having voted for Ronald Reagan, George H.W. Bush, George W. Bush and, most repugnantly, Richard Nixon.

When I mentioned the Nixon vote disparagingly, an older woman interjected herself. To the great and evident annoyance of the other reporters, she said, "He explained that vote. He said because he was in the military, Nixon's strengths in foreign policy swayed him."

The woman reacted to the glares of the other reporters, saying, "I should have brought my notebook." I wasn't sure if she really was a journalist or a Clark apologist - few reporters are going to be easily separated from their notebooks.

I responded that I was about the same age as General Clark, and I had been able as a young man to see Nixon for all he was, not merely for his foreign policy, and Clark's failure to recognize all that Nixon represented was not an acceptable error. I passed out my business cards to the different reporters so they could get the identification correctly. I figured if you make their job easier, they are more likely to use what you have said.

With the media scrum over, I headed down to the reception on the floor below. There, a number of people came up to tell me they thought it was a good question. One said they thought his answer was good, which gave me the opportunity to reiterate why it hadn't satisfied me.

I made a couple of attempts to engage Clark further, but he was usually surrounded by people, and didn't seem that eager to interact anyway.

Go figure.

When Adele, Lizzie, and I left, I learned that Lizzie now wanted Clark to become president since she had seen him in person. This was despite the fact that she had been too shy to shake his hand, as I had suggested. I'm sure if she had actually made that physical contact, she would have been prepared to coronate him.

It seemed to me that, in the very personal politics of the New Hampshire primary, many voters would make decisions with a basis not unlike the one that Lizzie was using.

A story is told of an earnest supporter rushing up to Adlai Stevenson, who lost twice to a general in Presidential elections.

"Any thinking voter will support you, Governor Stevenson," the supporter enthused.

"Well, I'm still going to need a majority," Stevenson replied.

I had talked to enough voters that I had more faith in Lizzie as a bright eight-year old than I did in the average New Hampshire voter. The events of the next week, and the impact of "The Scream Heard around the World", would reinforce my opinion.

Clark would seem to fade as the campaign moved back to New

Hampshire after the Iowa caucuses. He would ultimately make a number of what would be labeled "rookie" mistakes. As an example, his campaign would be suggested as the source of the Kerry –intern rumors that would produce a minor bump in the road for the junior Senator.[98]

While internet "journalist" Matt Drudge had a history dating to his days of pushing the Monica Lewinsky story forward, Clark appeared most unseemly when his campaign would be suggested as the source.

The *Boston Globe's* Peter Canellos offered a critique of Clark's performance.

"His stump speech is loaded with 'values' references, about his personal faith and why he believes education and health care are 'family values' and moral issues. Some analysts feel this style of campaigning plays better in the South and West, and, in any case, is better suited to larger states where there's less 'retail' campaigning. One of Clark's liabilities in New Hampshire was that he was grilled on specifics by a lot of very well-informed voters, and they found him less substantive than Kerry and Dean."[99]

Clark's attraction didn't totally dissipate, however. An MIT professor had offered in December to hold a fundraiser for Dean, once the Fall term was over. She would end up being reluctant to commit to one in late January, however, citing indecision between Dean and Clark.

Steve Grossman says that (Dean) "…wasn't the only one who got himself into trouble, for goodness sake. Wesley Clark practically destroyed his campaign on the first day by that statement to the effect that if he'd been in Congress, he would have voted for the Iraq resolution. The whole rationale for his campaign went down the drain on day one."

PARTYIN' WITH THE MISSUS

"If my heart could do my thinking, and my head could truly feel, I'd look upon the world, and you, and know what's truly real."
From "I forgot that love existed", by Van Morrison

There was a thank you gathering for Dean volunteers in Manchester earlier on Sunday January 25th. My wife and I went, and found a rather stark room on Manchester's main thoroughfare, that was dominated by the union workers who had supported Dean's campaign.

Dean's major union endorsements had been a strong counter to Dick Gephardt's union strength. Dean had been endorsed by an alphabet soup: AFSCME, IUPAT, and SEIU. Dorothy Keville, who had traveled from Massachusetts to participate in the Iowa "Perfect Storm", felt that Ted Kennedy's presence in Iowa had negated the effect of the endorsements.

While Joe Trippi had been credited with brokering the union endorsements, they had come at a time when Dean's fortunes were rising like the tide in the Bay of Fundy. MIT political scientist Stephen Ansolabehere would say that "the labor unions made a number of mistakes. They were followers, and often losers."

Of course, in faulting the union decisions, you have to look at the leadership. Gerald McEntee, the president of AFSCME, would take the unusual step of withdrawing his support while Dean was attempting a final turnaround in Wisconsin. As if that weren't indignity enough, he would follow up the day after Dean's withdrawal by saying "I think he's nuts."[100]

Dean showed how he valued loyalty, praising the two other unions that had endorsed him in his withdrawal speech. McEntee said his union would wait awhile before endorsing anyone else. "I think we need a rest. Maybe in an asylum."[101] For the most loyal Dean followers, there would undoubtedly be a place for McEntee in the Union Leadership Hall of Fame, which is believed to be in the vicinity of the Meadowlands in New Jersey.

Many of the union workers at the Manchester event were from urban areas outside New Hampshire, and the demographics of the crowd took on much more of an ethnic flavor than previous Dean gatherings. I had worn a favorite baseball cap that had the symbol from Spike Lee's movie on Malcolm X on it. As I headed toward the door of the hall, I stopped to talk to an African-American SEIU member who would be heading back to New York on a bus after the celebration. I pointed to my hat and told him that I had mischievously considered asking Kerry if he knew what the X stood for. He said that he doubted Kerry would know, and that I should ask him.

The rally was uplifting, like a Baptist Church service I had attended in Minneapolis when I was in high school. In warming the crowd up, instead of politicians, SEIU members would stand on the stage and lead cheers or chants, with the crowd responding strongly and eagerly.

At one point, a group of kids came up and did a Dean rap, which the crowd loved. Two little girls, one black and one white, joined my wife and me and the others invited up onto the stage. The little girls held hands as they walked up the steps. This was what I wanted to symbolize Dean's support. I told the little girls that I had seen them holding hands on their way up the stairs, and that if they were seen on TV like that, it would be a very good thing.

Caught up in the energy of the crowd, rather as Dean had been in Iowa, I was even persuaded to lead the crowd in a call and response of my own.

"I'm going to ask you three questions," I bellowed.

"That's *three* questions," I reiterated, remembering Richard Pryor's imitation of black preachers.

"Do you want a warrior?"

I should have shaken my head, because some of the crowd said yes, when I had meant the question to repudiate Clark and Kerry.

"Do you want a lawyer?" This time the answer was a loud and unambiguous "No."

"Do you want a care-giver?"

The audience roared its affirmative, as another of the union members led them in the chant "a care-giver, a care-giver, a care-giver."

By the time Dean and his wife arrived, the place was primed. Dan Rather was even lurking around the edge of the stage. Steinberg was

143

greeted with chants of "Judy, Judy, Judy." It seemed that their interview with Diane Sawyer had elevated her above the rock star status that Howard had repudiated in the same interview. As they entered, my wife grasped her hand and whispered "you are a role model to women, and young women, everywhere." Steinberg just nodded.

She seemed poised to define a new role for a candidate's spouse, much as some of her predecessors had. Unfortunately, as **Ellen Goodman** points out "The press turned normalcy into a disease. The fact that she didn't want to talk to the press … the fact that she didn't want to spend her life on the campaign trail, made her agoraphobic? Give me a break!… I think that you have to remember that when he was governor of Vermont, she didn't do any of the state events with him. She thought it was normal… That's parallel… (but) completely the opposite… to Hillary Clinton. When she was first lady of Arkansas the…'two for the price of one' theory developed…and she thought that would wash in a national campaign… I didn't find her shy I found her forthcoming."

Goodman goes on to say, "She (Judy Dean) really truly loves medicine intensely. No doubt about that. Both of her parents are doctors as you know … she did what her Mom had done. So it didn't seem very unusual."

Hazan says 'To me I just felt that he was so proud of her. He was so proud to have her as a partner next to him… There was something so sweet about that."

Howard Dean says "I think she would have been a great First Lady. She would have broken the mold and made it possible for American women to understand that a normal person could be First Lady and still live a reasonably normal life. She would have continued her job, which nobody else has ever done. I think she was somewhat of an inspiration to people, particularly working women, who realize that she could actually be a normal person. It makes politics closer to ordinary people to have people like Judy involved."

Unfortunately, her sudden entrance into the campaign at the urging of Tom Harkin's wife had come in response to the "angry" Dean being portrayed after the Iowa speech. Harkin himself had advised Dean "to lighten up, lest he alienate undecided voters."[102]

Steinberg had a predecessor: Eleanor Roosevelt. Roosevelt had blazed the now well-worn political path through the late night talk shows when she appeared on The Tonight Show, with the now-deceased pioneer of that format, Jack Paar. Asked why, she replied "I want to help Senator Kennedy." She went on to compare "Kennedy's growing rapport with campaign crowds to her husband's experience in 1932 and endorsed him with a simple sincerity seldom seen before or since on late-night TV."[103]

Doris Kearns Goodwin also reminds us of how Eleanor Roosevelt redefined the role of the First Lady. "I think that what happens is that each person who comes into that role as First Lady has their own talents and past and character and temperament that they're bringing into the role that almost has to be redefined each time. It's not like a job that you're going into where the requirements are set. Eleanor at first, when she became First Lady, was incredibly anguished at the thought that all the public and exciting life that she had before…traveling New York State on her husband's behalf and really being an active political force, would be stymied, because at that point, she thought the only thing she could do as First Lady was ceremonial responsibilities. Everything that she had no interest in…to be a hostess in the White House and have parties. There was a real depression that set in when she became First Lady. It was only over time she was able to draw the confidence to realize she could actually transform the role of First Lady, which she really did. She's the first ….

"I really think… Eleanor…over time made it into a powerful position that allowed her to keep fighting for the blacks and the poor, the very things she was doing when he was Governor. And she still could do on an even larger scale as President. So, she was the first one to ever speak in a hearing at Congress, the first one to ever speak at a National convention, the first one to ever hold a press conference. None of this had ever been done. The interesting thing is that when Bess Truman came in after Eleanor, and Eleanor introduced Bess to the press corps… Eleanor had a rule that only women reporters could come to her press conferences, which meant that a whole generation of female journalists got their start, because of Eleanor Roosevelt's press conferences… so she introduces Bess to the press and Bess says 'Oh my god, I've never talked to the press. I don't have to talk to them, do I?' In other words, she was able to become a much less public figure than Eleanor had, and the country was tolerant of it. I honestly believe that the country will allow First Lady with her own

145

definition of… (what) she should (do). Obviously there was resistance to Hillary (Clinton)… (actually no more active than Eleanor had been) … But I guess Hillary coming along at the time of the women's movement was more threatening. Eleanor was just so far ahead of it she just seemed eccentric and they accepted it as Eleanor. But, you know Hillary made her own mark in her own way. Then, Laura Bush came in, people were wondering, will she not be acceptable unless she runs around like Hillary did. She was able to define a much lower key role as First Lady, which I think that Judith Steinberg would have been able to do as well. There would have been enormous tolerance for her (Steinberg) to be what she wanted to be.

"There was increasing respect for what she was trying to do. And when she went on the campaign trail, that smile of hers was so fantastic."

John Dower says "I think that we have these certain myths about America, the other side of which, the mirror image of which is myths about Japan. One of them is of the subordinate, submissive role of women in Japan as compared the United States.

"If you look at one side of that, you look at the number of women who are in the American Congress. The percentage is about the same as the number of women who are in the Japanese Parliament. They're not behind us, and the larger point is that it's a very small number, and, in fact, we are quite hostile to women. I think you really see that hostility to women in the American political scene.

"You can be sure of it, in that Hillary Clinton arouses people because she's strong and opinionated, which are qualities that we think are appropriate for men, but not women. So this country is, in fact, very traditional in its views that a woman's place is standing by her man.

"I thought the Dean thing was pretty remarkable in that a woman who is a real autonomous, interesting individual with…she's a real professional, she's a truly caring person, she cared about him, she cared about her patients, she cared about being a good doctor. That becomes a negative thing and she's forced to go up there and stand by her man.

"It really, in my view, revealed this whole level of mythology about who we are as a nation. We stand for independence and equality, but that doesn't apply to women.

"That gets into the larger thing that I think's interesting about the political scene in America today. We Americans relish the clash of ideas and we really admire the independent voice.

"Everything since 9/11 has highlighted what a consensus conformist society we are. We just are extraordinarily conformist and consensual, so that anyone who criticizes the war immediately becomes called the extreme left. This is incredible concept. Their patriotism is questioned and you can't ask the simplest type of things like Dean was asking, like whether the war was ill-conceived. This doomed him. "If you're someone like me, a Japan specialist, we used to always ask 'why didn't anyone in Japan speak up against the war, why didn't anyone stick out their necks and take a stand, why didn't people say what they really thought?'

"We always had very traditional, peculiar-to-Japan explanations.

"You know, 'confusion, conformist people' and none of that applies.

"Our media has censored itself, our political parties censored themselves. The people within the government censor themselves when speaking publicly. So that when you do have Richard Clark or someone come out and say, 'hey, the war on terror's made worse', 'hey, it was just idiotic', this just becomes a fantastic thing- that somebody actually said in public what they thought in private.

"We know there's loads of people. Look how many resignations there have been. Look how many people really spoken out from inside.

"So, when someone like Dean comes up, he taps that kind of honesty, and in the end you cut him down. And the saying in Japan is 'cut someone off at the legs' or to 'hammer down the nail if it sticks out' and that's always the explanation of traditional Japanese, non-western conformist, consensual societies, when in fact that's exactly what happened to Dean."

Standing next to Howard and Judith as they were being introduced, I whispered to the two of them that Dan Rather was there. They looked at me and said 'thanks.' Steinberg said little, if anything, and Dean's comments were much briefer than any other I had seen, but they left the place with everyone roaring.

I could hardly wait to get home to John Kerry.

DOING THE TANGO WITH "CASH AND KERRY"

"Given the rigorous informality and artless effervescence required by the ceremonies of modern politics, John Kerry's rise to prominence is difficult to explain."

Joe Klein, Time, April 26, 2004

After the stunning results of the Iowa caucuses, the concern was Kerry. Just six weeks earlier I had joked with Ben LaBolt about opening the door to the Kerry office down the street and yelling, "dead man walking" inside. Now Dean seemed to be the one in jeopardy, as the media replayed the Iowa yodel hundreds of times.

Flush with the reinforcement of people who had seen me on CBS, or New England Cable News, or local channels, I plotted how I could give Kerry the same treatment that I had used on Clark. This time, I was ready to act as a free agent, since I didn't want to be operating under the aegis of the campaign.

Dean's third place finish in Iowa had been portrayed as a colossal failure, and a harbinger of ultimate collapse. "The media's expectations are often criticized as arbitrary, especially by candidates who fail to meet them or who feel the media has been too lenient on their opponents."[104]

Reporting that Dean had underperformed in Iowa would only add to Kerry momentum. If I could, single-handedly, get the media to report Kerry's failings, I could help break the cycle.

Of course, they would eventually get there on their own, but it was important that it not come too late for Howard Dean, or for the defeat of George W. Bush. Robert Kaiser would write on the night of the primary, "How well will Kerry survive scrutiny of his record? He is not a popular member of the Senate, and he does not have a long record of legislative accomplishment; I expect we'll be reading lots of critical stories about Kerry and his record in days ahead."[105]

I read the *Boston Globe, New York Times, USA Today,* and *Time* magazine looking for something that could make Kerry's shortcomings media fodder. The media had created the false perception that Dean was "angry." All I wanted to do was have people see the real John Kerry. I was sure that the real Howard Dean would triumph over the real John Kerry, any day.

I had been bothered by what I saw as Kerry's transparent phoniness. Using a four letter word ("I didn't think he could f— it up as much as he did.") in describing Bush's execution of the Iraq war in *Rolling Stone* magazine seemed more a calculated appeal to the magazine's audience than an accidental slip of the tongue. On the F-word controversy, the senator courageously stood his ground. Kerry had said to CNN's Candy Crowley: "Did you ever use a bad word?" "Absolutely," replied Crowley, "but I'm not running for president."

ABC's *The Note* has more on John Kerry's profane description of Bush's Iraq policy:

"En route to a Claremont, N.H. chili feed, Kerry defended his use of the 'F' bomb in a recent *Rolling Stone* article. 'I might have used the word bungled. I might have used the word lied. I might have used the word misled. I might have used the word screwed up or any number of things,' the senator said. 'But then I went to the thesaurus and looked it up. And I think I pretty well described exactly what they did in Iraq, frankly.'"[106]

And to think that he would be running in the national election against an incumbent who believes that the thesauruses died out in the Ice Age.

I'd read weeks earlier in the Boston Globe about Kerry's new image-shaping firehouse chilis. The firefighters union had endorsed Kerry early on. *The Boston Globe* described the chilies as a forum for Kerry to show his informal side. Kerry would ladle out chili, the *Globe* said, as he addressed people as "dude" or "man."

This was apparently meant to be combined in the public mind with his appearance on *The Tonight Show,* where he rode in on his motorcycle (and almost hit a parked car). On the last weekend before the primary, Kerry was going to be back on the Seacoast, including at the Hampton firehouse where he had held his very first chili. I called the Kerry campaign and gave them my name, saying I would like to attend the chili in Hampton. They urged me to show up plenty early for the 5:30 event, with 4 PM the suggested arrival time. I was about to take on a new role.

Figuring I would get chili for supper, I dropped my wife off and headed directly to the Hampton firehouse. When I had told her what my goal was, she had joked about my being confronted by burly fireman. While I wasn't expecting anything as dramatic as a physical confrontation, I did feel I was headed into the enemy camp.

When I got there before the suggested arrival time, I was confused by the absence of activity. Parking was available nearby. Because of the lack of Kerry signs, I asked a fireman if I had the correct station. Told that I did, I entered without being stopped or signed in by anyone.

A stage sat in one bay of the station, with a fire truck parked next to it. I saw a handful of Kerry staffers who were setting up. I went to one and asked for a Kerry button. Once he produced one, I told him I'd be more than happy to help set up the event. He said that they would need help shortly, setting up chairs and hanging signs. I assured him I was eager to help in any way possible.

The press didn't seem to be in evidence yet, so I couldn't work anyone for an interview. I saw one other person who didn't appear to be with the Kerry campaign, so I introduced myself. Jake Lambert was a history major at BU. Because he lived in Massachusetts, he had followed Kerry for years. He was very articulate and knowledgeable, both about American history and Kerry.

We talked about various books we had read on Presidents, and then discussed an article in the Sunday *New York Times* that had pointed out how Kerry's Senate record might raise some issues on which he would be vulnerable.

Warren Harding and Jack Kennedy were the only candidates to move from Capitol Hill to Pennsylvania Avenue since the 19th century; a lengthy voting record was natural ammunition for opponents. MIT's **Ansolabehere** thinks "being a Senator is a liability these days. Having executive office experience, even from a small state like Arkansas or Vermont, makes you an appealing candidate." (History bore worse tidings for Dick Gephardt. The last member of the House to be elected was James Garfield, and his legacy in office would culminate in his assassination.)

I suggested to Jake that we form an alliance to keep a prominent space front and center in the crowd, so we might have the best chance of asking questions. I explained that I expected the event to start very late, and that once the place was packed in, it would be helpful to have a space saver in case the call of nature arrived before the Senator did.

Jake and I worked to help set things up. We repositioned the stage, once the remaining fire truck was moved, set up chairs, moved rope lines. Combining all the Dean events I had gone to as a recognized volunteer, I had not put forth as much effort as I now was as a spook at a Kerry event. Spooks are a common phenomena at town meeting style campaigns to meet the candidate. Surrounded by friendly, enthusiastic supporters, candidates are rarely asked challenging questions. I hoped to have that chance.

I was directed to the stage as a Kerry stand-in, so cameras could set the correct angle for the similarly sized Senator. I stood there for several minutes, reveling in the irony.

All my life I had been told I resembled the last candidate I had given money to support: Dean's endorser, Bill Bradley. My response for the past few years had been that I had fewer chins, more hair, and less jump shot.

We had been directed to put three rows of chairs on each side of the stage. As we worked, we could see the lengthy line forming outside the station, in what was very cold weather. Jake and I congratulated one another on our wisdom in arriving early and working inside. I told him that we should stand, rather than sit, directly between the podium and the press arrayed behind us. By standing, we would be able to make eye contact with Kerry and have a better chance of being called upon.

When the doors were opened to let the crowd in, the seats were supposed to be for those who might have difficulty standing in the lengthy wait that still lay ahead. However, the Kerry staffers failed to communicate this to people as they rushed in, so people of all ages rushed to fill in the seats, leaving many standing that would find it difficult.

Jake and I maintained our positions standing front and center as the crowd surged in around us. I reminded him of how a good basketball rebounder fills space to get in position for a rebound. We commiserated over the Celtics enormous disinclination to do that.

Dispensing chili to a packed room became an impossibility. I saw a couple of people who had bowls, but from the size of the warming pans I had seen, there was no way that more than a few dozen were going to get chili tonight. With the packed house, the likelihood of Kerry serving chili himself to an organized queue of "dudes" and "men" was nil.

As people around us began talking, it was clear that we were surrounded by eager Kerry supporters. However, as Jake and I continued to talk, he allowed little hints to escape that made it increasingly clear that he was not here as a Kerry supporter.

When I mentioned to him how different the rally at Pease Tradeport had been the night Dean flew in from Iowa at 2AM, he whispered, "I know, I was there."

I told him that I had been onstage at Pease, and that his secret was safe with me. He whispered back that mine was also.

During the lengthy wait for Kerry's arrival, various people went on stage to warm up the crowd and/or promote their own political aspirations. One of them was State Senator Burt Cohen, who I had met at a Christmas party given by Nancy Beach. I had identified myself at that time as a Dean supporter, and we had agreed we were unified in a desire to defeat Bush. We had exchanged pleasantries and parted after a few minutes.

Cohen's office was right next to the Portsmouth Dean office in which I had labored since September. After the party, I had gone into his office and left my business card with an aide, saying that I would support him in his run for US Senate. Now, as he stood facing me from the stage, and then addressing the audience, I pulled my baseball cap down and kept looking down in hopes he wouldn't recognize me.

Another Kerry supporter on the stage was a candidate for state senate, Maggie Hassan of Exeter. Her campaign finance manager was Lynda Beck, a wonderful friend from Exeter who had come to our first house meeting for Dean. I also knew Maggie because we had bought a car from her and her husband when we lived in Exeter. As she stood on stage, I tried to avoid her identifying me.

I envisioned Cohen or Hassan alerting Kerry that I was from the Dean camp, and telling him not to call on me. Worse, I feared they might give him the answer to the question I was going to nail him with.

Maggie Hassan attempted to rouse the crowd into a Kerry cheer. In a station with hundreds of people, perhaps a dozen responded, weakly. I whispered to Jake how different the crowd had been from the SEIU people in Manchester earlier in the day.

It was like the difference between Soul Train and the Arthur Murray School for People with Two Left Feet.

Jake agreed, and compared how roused even the quite-white audience at Pease had been. I said, "These folks here just aren't very good at call and response." The Kerry supporter next to Jake interjected "That's because we're leaders, not followers." Not knowing how much of our conversation had been overheard, I just smiled warmly back at him.

Eventually – finally - Kerry arrived.

On stage, Kerry stood in front of the woman he had met at a global warming conference, half-billionairess Theresa Heinz Kerry. The reigning King of Catch-up had taken as his second wife the Queen of Ketchup. Theresa Heinz had ascended to the condiment throne when her first Senator-husband, John Heinz of Pennsylvania, had died in a plane crash. Her new surname was a Rodhamesque campaign appendage.

"Blogs' were becoming a new source of material for journalists who faced deadline pressures or were, if you can imagine it, lazy. *Johnkerry.com* had posted a supporter's comment that "the wife has to look interested and engage the audience."[107] In Hampton, that wasn't happening. This must have been common, as a New York Times article would describe her by saying that she "often wears a pained, or even bored, expression. She says it is merely the look she gets when she is thinking deeply."[108]

The polar opposite of the shy Judy Steinberg, "the most uncontained political spouse in recent memory"[109] was equally non-traditional in the role of candidate's spouse. In an analogy worthy of the SAT's, Walter Shapiro wrote that Heinz Kerry "is to Nancy Reagan as a woodpecker to a cooing dove."[110] *Boston Globe* reporter *Adrian Walker* says that he had also defied traditional definitions; the Mozambique-born heiress described herself as "African-American." Despite her self-definition, she looked to be a representative member of the homogeneous crowd in Hampton.

Heinz Kerry had been portrayed as having something of the potential of a loose cannon. Described as "…uninhibited, cursing in one of her five languages"[111] she was a reporter's dream quote. In machine gun fashion, she could chronicle portrayals of her husband as "Shy? Snobby? Distant? Cut off from people? Arrogant?"[112] while diagnosing his perceived personality as the product of having been sent off to boarding school at an early age.[113] It was hard to tell which role she played best: media source, psychoanalyst, or sadist.

Perhaps it was her own privileged background that kept her from observing, as Michael Tomasky would, "Kerry comes from the sort of stock that was (F. Scott) Fitzgerald's métier."[114] Kerry sometimes had the gift of making Al Gore seem animated, as appearances early in Kerry's campaign had been labeled as "maladroit", "tense, defensive, and curiously tone deaf."[115]

Before seeing Kerry in person, I had joked that he most resembled Cleo, the basset hound on the old black and white TV show called (raise the Irony Curtain here) "The People's Choice." In person, Kerry was the lantern-jawed (a term he used in comparing himself to the host as he made the obligatory Jay Leno appearance), gaunt and Lincolnesque figure one saw on TV and read about in the papers. Shapiro was right on the money when he said that Kerry looked as if he belonged on a Roman coin.

Shapiro expanded upon that, with the perception that he had before he got to know Kerry that the Senator was "a haughty, overly ambitious patrician who is a bit too slick in his eagerness to exploit his heroism in Vietnam." Kerry was almost too easy to caricature as "a heedlessly arrogant and self-important politician." Kerry's attempts to humanize himself with the tired jibe that Massachusetts was an Indian word meaning "land of many Kennedys" fell far short with the urbane Shapiro. However, he found Kerry to have the complexity of superstring theory, when compared to the one-dimensional incumbent. Unfortunately, ignorance is sometimes political bliss, as Kerry's "prolix style" led him to such rhetorical entropy that he had once answered a three word question about Iraq in six painful minutes.[116]

Having Time columnist Joe Klein label Kerry "Lincolnesque"[117] couldn't help but remind one of the story that Abraham Lincoln had grown his beard at the behest of a little girl who was struck by Abe's rather unappealing face. While some portrayed Kerry as Kennedy-like in appearance, his face had deep lines. While the lines would seemingly recede in the next few weeks of the campaign, the Kennedy comparison would haunt him shortly, as stories of his having dated various celebrities and actresses surfaced. As the intern affair allegations would fade, his hair would simultaneously seem to gain new color, even as his campaign denied that he had used Botox. In watching his face carefully, the tissue doesn't seem to move like normal tissue. His visage has a rigidity more like The

Old Man of the Mountain, which in 2003 had cascaded down into the ravine below it. Botox users face the same peril.

Incidentally, the critique of physical appearances is allowed here, since I, myself, am physically perfect.

I attempt the latter jest in an act of self-deprecating liberal guilt. The media steps forward, on the same day I write this, as "the paper of record" chronicles Kerry characterizations as "horsy"[118], "shiny"[119], "creased, droopy-eyed"[120], "a basset hound in a previous life"[121] (Yo, Cleo!) and "French". The latter came from a Bush advisor, not an anthropologist.

Kerry gave a fairly standard stump speech, but kept it short, indicating he wanted to be able to answer questions. It was striking how much he seemed to have co-opted Dean's message, including a now vigorous attack on 'No Child Left Behind', the idea that money spent on prisoners would have been better for education before they became criminals, and the connection between Truman and health care for all Americans. No wonder people said they couldn't tell the candidates apart.

He thanked C-SPAN for being there to cover the event live. I hoped that ultimately I might be more thankful than he would. "'Some people will not stand up and ask a question in an environment of four or five hundred people and fifteen TV cameras in a hall. They don't want to look stupid on C-SPAN,' " Kevin Landrigan of the *Nashua Telegraph* suggested to political scientist Dante Scala. I am not possessed by such fears.

Throughout his stump speech, I did the bobble head doll imitation that I had perfected with Wes Clark. It worked again. Skinner and Pavlov must have been pleased.

I was given the opportunity to ask the first question. I started off speaking loudly, as the crowd quieted to hear my question. "I'm a New Hampshire voter who remains undecided until I hit the voting lever." At that point, someone passed a microphone toward me so my question would be amplified. Better yet, it would be clear on C-SPAN. I whispered to Jake to hold the microphone in front of me, so I could use my pants-in-pockets "regular guy" stance - and in case my hands were shaking.

I continued, "So I come to be swayed, but I am predisposed, since I've followed your career since its beginning in Massachusetts." I gave my most earnest look, trying not to betray the opinion I had formed of him over decades of reading the *Boston Globe*.

"I think you have been unfairly portrayed as a New Englander who cannot appeal to traditional Democratic constituencies." Both sympathy and sincerity oozed from my every pore. Kerry leaned forward towards me; he obviously felt he had found a brother.

"It would be helpful to me if you would say what you see as the significance of the cultural icon I wear on my hat." With that I pointed to the X on the baseball cap.

There was a ten second pause; Kerry assumed the look of the deer in the headlights that Dan Quayle made so popular. Finally he responded, "The Latin, the ten."

I shook my head.

He looked puzzled, and more worried. He suggested "the X man."

I said softly, seemingly disappointed, "No, Malcolm X." I could see the wheels turning in his head as he calculated his answer. At 23 seconds, a continuing banging from overhead heating ducts allowed him to joke "John Ashcroft's here? That's scary. Is that thing going to fly off?"

Fellow Dean supporters who were watching on C-SPAN would tell me that they were rolling on the floor, as Kerry tried to put a wet finger up to test the breeze, only to find a cyclone of indeterminate direction.

Kerry said he had been "profoundly influenced by the autobiography of Malcolm X." He asked me "Your question is, 'what is the significance of the life of Malcolm X?'" He shifted uneasily from foot to foot, looked down to his feet, to the floor on either side of his feet, sighed, and rubbed his nose. Surely the answer was there somewhere. He had bought twenty more seconds to think. He looked as though his internal dialog was similar to the voices of Linda Blair in "The Exorcist".

"I think he represented the anger and the depths of frustration. I think it represented an extreme at that time." At one minute, 45 seconds he said, "My response is this."

He then proceeded to launch into a platform travelogue whose stops included white poverty, Appalachia, Robert Kennedy, the political process, Halliburton, health care, kids, the drug bill, the windfall for drug companies, and the energy bill windfall for oil companies.

Appropriating from John Edwards, he said we needed a "President who knows what's happening in the other America. It's not just African –Americans or Latinos. It's across color, across gender." The comparative absence of people of color, and of hermaphrodites, in Hampton, made this a fairly safe answer.

He then attempted to illustrate this, somehow, by talking about the violence of the Sixties, and a college professor who had talked about "felt needs" and then ended by condemning "crony capitalism." His campaign theme park tour had avoided answering the question for over four and a half minutes.

The profound influence Malcolm X's autobiography wasn't in there anywhere.

He had exercised his platform, without exorcising the demonology of Malcolm X.

Anyone who has read the autobiography knows that its most profound lesson is in the transformation at the end of Al-Hajj Malik Al-Shabazz's life, when he saw all people as brothers and sisters. One can't be aware of his journey without a sense of awe at how, at such a young age, Malcolm had reached a point of such wisdom.

Kerry would later, when asked by a child to name his heroes, first cite his supporter Max Cleland, then Christopher Reeves, and Mother Teresa, all for their inspiration to others in rising above their adversity. As he did so, I was struck by how he was describing my vision of Malcolm X's life. And by the fact that his heroes were all white folks.

Now at a firehouse chili in Hampton NH, one might expect that much of the 99% white crowd wouldn't recognize the X symbol. The first white man I walked up to afterwards, however, did, and said he was surprised Kerry didn't. More significantly, I would bet that more than 90% of African-Americans do recognize the symbol, and many know the story of Malcolm's life.

If Kerry was going to be a man of the people, the people were more likely Brahmins.

Later in the evening, he would try to exhibit his skill in cultural haberdashery by identifying a kid's hat as "an Indiana Jones hat." On his way out, Kerry, wary of another alphabet ambush, asked a man in a York high school baseball hat what the Y stood for.

No point taking any chances.

In describing for you my experience with that question, my fear is that I would suffer from what is known is science as parallax. Things look different when viewed from different angles. That's why the speedometer always looked different to the parent accompanying you as you drove on your learner's permit. It is also why films shoot upward at vertically challenged stars like Paul Newman. Kerry seemed to have some awareness of this, in that he never seemed to miss a photo opportunity after debates where he could drape an arm around the much smaller Dean.

Parallax may be a justification for journalists changing how they reported the Iowa scream, after they saw it through television, or saw how other journalists reported it. That may be at the heart of the "pack journalism" that Timothy Crouse described on in *The Boys on the Bus.*

So, in the interest of avoiding parallax, let me tell you how my question played out for **Gordon Corera** was there covering the event for the BBC. "He gave the worst answer. What I heard, listening to his answer, was how long it was, and it came to no conclusion. I'd seen him a lot in New Hampshire and Iowa back in August, and I remember going to a meeting in either Portsmouth or Dover, and he was terrible. People asked him about civil rights and he waffled for minutes without answering. (At the firehouse in Hampton) I remember thinking that when I started seeing him again at the start of this year that he'd improved. But that answer to your question reminded me of everything he was, kind of reverting to normal, or reverting to the old Kerry.

"To be idealistic, one would say that people should say what they believe. Even if you take a more cynical view, politicians should have an answer in their head, a pat answer on civil rights. A bell should have gone off, 'This is a question about civil rights. I will give my 30 second answer, which will end in an applause line.'"

In recognizing Malcolm X's name, a bell had gone off; Kerry just wasn't playing with a full carillon.

Corera continues "It was just kind of meandering thought. I remember looking around at some of the other journalists and we were like, 'Well, here he goes.' Kerry's been made sharp by Dean and Edwards. As soon as that goes, he risks turning into that kind of flabby, unthinking politician, and that's going to be a disaster for his candidacy." Because no media picked up on Kerry's stumbling answer, that night did not prove to be a disaster for him.

After I finished my question, I told Jake to hold on to the microphone, so he could ask the next question. Kerry called on someone nearby and Jake ceded the microphone to him, whereupon it immediately malfunctioned. I feared Jake was not going to get to ask his question, having given up control of the microphone. However, Kerry did call on him later. Jake asked about how Kerry could reconcile voting to reduce CIA funding in the mid-Nineties with his criticism of the Agency's failures post 9/11, and in Iraq. Kerry gave an answer, which Jake thought was a good one, but which I felt didn't really address his question.

At least Jake had gotten the issue, brought up in the day's *New York Times*, out there. Two months later, the incumbent would be blasting Kerry on exactly the same point, just before Bush left to attend a Texas rodeo. In his closing remarks, Kerry said, "I say what I mean, and I mean what I say." It appeared he had lifted this from Dr. Seuss, who wrote "I meant what I said, and I said what I meant; an elephant is faithful, one hundred percent."

Just another Doctor whose themes seemed worthy of appropriation.

Like comedians, politicians readily appropriate good material from one another.

Dean had seemed to coin a word when he explained that a public signing of the civil unions bill would have been "triumphalism", at a time when Vermont needed to heal the wounds of a divisive battle. In mid-March, Kerry was saying that Bush's "foreign policy of triumphalism fuels the fire of jihadists" in Iraq.

In his quest to be leader of a nation that had gone to war in Iraq without the kind of support Bush I had built, Kerry had burnished his national security credentials with the testosterone-rich phase "bring it on" (Figure 2, pages 327-339). Kerry first used the slogan in Des Moines on November 15. His phrase-appropriation led The New Republic to ask in a cover headline after the Iowa caucuses: *Bring it on? Is John Kerry that much more electable than Dean?* Language maven William Safire points out that "the phrase…adopted the aggressive tone that had been Dean's trademark and helped ignite Kerry's formerly tepid campaign."[122]

On February 22, 2003 John Edwards had brought 350 members of the Democratic National Committee (DNC) to their feet, invoking himself as the antidote to Bush's full-service presidency for insiders.

'Bush ii' himself utilized the phrase in taunting terrorists and Baathists diehards on July 2. The insurgent who gave Bush an early run for Enron's money, John McCain, had used the phrase in 1999 as he faced opposition to his bill to delay litigation that could arise over breakdowns that loomed for Y2K.

And in the millennium year that ended up falling somewhat short of Y2K apocalypse, the phrase "bring it on" had been the title of a movie about high school cheerleaders.

Given the nature of politics, the cross-over from pep rallies to, well, pep rallies, seems only natural.

Just as long as they don't scream.

Before Kerry had arrived, a rather odd audience member had erupted when Burt Cohen spoke disparagingly about spending money to go to Mars. My immediate guess had been that the speaker was a Lyndon LaRouche supporter, probably one who figured that there were other LaRouche supporters and/or relatives on Mars. So, as Kerry wound into his short closing speech, the space explorer interrupted, and verified that he was in fact a staunch LaRouche supporter. (Are there any moderate LaRouche supporters?) Kerry did the politically adept thing and told the audience to stop hooting, booing, and hissing and let the man speak, that "this is America."

In a rambling, agitated discourse, the LaRouche supporter said that Lyndon LaRouche had said that John Kerry was the most Presidential of the Democratic nominees.

I said loudly enough for Kerry to hear "now there's an endorsement for you!"

Kerry looked at me, rolled his eyes, and appeared as if he had eaten some bad chili.

At the end of the question and answer session, Kerry motioned for me to come to the stage. As people surged around him, I weighed getting another shot at him with trying to chase down media interviews.

After I had asked my question, a man standing amidst the reporters and cameras to the side of the stage had motioned for me to come around to the side of the room. I had nodded yes, but lost sight of him over the next few minutes. As the questions went on, I never found him again. I'll never know if he was a reporter on deadline or a firefighter who was going to turn a hose on me in the cold outside.

After ten minutes, I finally handed my hat up to Kerry. He turned to me and asked when I had read the autobiography. I said that I had read it in college. He handed the hat back to me.

My original wise-ass intention had been to tell him that he should keep the hat, as he would need it more than I would. However, not knowing if cameras were recording our interaction, I decided to appear the reasonable man, still a possible supporter, and I took the hat back. It had served its purpose.

Before leaving, Kerry responded in kind to a question posed in French. Like his wife, Kerry speaks five languages[123], which sometimes seems to be five more than the incumbent. As the C-SPAN cameras recorded his exit, he prudently rejected a supporter's gift of a guitar signed by Les Paul, for possibly being over the limit in value of gifts he could accept.

When I looked around me, the media seemed to have packed up and left. I did get to talk to a couple of reporters, and I said that his answer indicated to me that Kerry hadn't finished the autobiography, if he had actually read it. I didn't see any pens go to notebooks, so I figured the C-SPAN coverage was all I could get. However, the next morning, I realized I might as well describe the appearance to some of the dozens of *Boston Globe* columnists who regularly opined about the Democratic nominees. Using the addresses published with their columns in the *Globe*, I sent e-mails to six different columnists. I used variations on the heading "Will African –Americans buy John Kerry?" I even sent the e-mail to Scott Lehigh, whose anti-Dean rants had been infuriating me for months.

The effect was like dropping a pebble into a bottomless well. The *Globe* had early on been very positive in its Dean coverage. However, as he gained presumed front-runner status, their coverage had seemed to turn more negative. In fact, The *Globe* had endorsed Kerry, as its coverage of him had seemed as gentle as the treatment Dean had received months earlier.

Even though I name-dropped that I had taught the daughters of the former editor of the *Globe*, I never heard anything from any of the columnists. Of course, I also had never gotten any of the pro-Dean letters to the editor published in the *Globe* either.

Maybe I wasn't the writer I thought I was. Nah. Just their bias, not my lack of skill.

Of course, my attempt to have Kerry commit a gaffe of the magnitude of Dean's Confederate flag controversy was hindered by the fact that the external symbols in Hampton weren't aligned so that the media could recognize a complete gaffe. If I had been black, surrounded by a black audience in South Carolina, Kerry probably would have fared differently.

Dean's claims that he was the only white candidate talking about race had been somewhat over the top, and indicative of something like hubris. But what Kerry did was try to be another white guy talking about race- he just couldn't figure out how to do it.

Two nights later, at the gathering in Manchester to watch the election results come in, Jake would walk up to me and introduce himself as head of the BU Students for Dean.

Jake's reflections on our initial contact provide another perspective on that evening.

"When we were at the Kerry event, it wasn't just that we were just two guys voting for Dean who went to a Kerry event. We were - two guys supporting Dean at a Kerry event. Our interaction together, while being pleasurable, was significant primarily because we found each other. We spoke about issues, and history, and interacted without overt reference to our Dean support; yet, there was something intangible which made us each suspect the other - almost like a certain energy of attraction. When we both said 'Your secret is safe,' we acknowledged this. However, to someone unfamiliar with the campaign, we may just come off as a couple scheming wanna-be political operatives who think we're clever (though this wouldn't be an entirely false characterization)."

It is wonderful living in New Hampshire, but for one week out of every four years, it is an experience that is worthy of Lewis Carroll.

THE RISING SON OF THE SOUTH

Perhaps the greatest beneficiary of the entanglement of Dean and Gephardt in Iowa was first term North Carolina Senator John Edwards. There is a long lineage of relentless optimists in the Democratic Party, with roots in Al Smith, running through Hubert Humphrey, to the 2004 branch in the Edwards campaign.

Edwards' decision to forego running for re-election to the Senate, so that he could concentrate on the presidential nomination, shows exactly that optimism. When media consultant Tad Devine asked Elizabeth Edwards in 1998 why she had married her husband, she cited his optimism.[124]

The Edwards PAC that had loaned 100 computers to the Iowa Democratic Party and given each state legislative candidate personalized campaign leaflets (which also featured Edwards's picture) was named "New American Optimists." Throughout the primary season, Edwards would be the prince of positivism, so that when Dean's opponents advocated a positive message, they seemed to be driving voters to Edwards.

In the season of 'Anybody but Bush' (ABB), many villagers were lighting torches. Dean led his army toward the castle, seemingly intent on burning it down. Edwards was the torchbearer for upbeat campaigning. While Kerry may have been described as Kennedyesque, Edwards appeared even younger than his fifty years, and his perpetual smile struck a contrast to the images of Dean, Clark and Kerry that were forming in voter's minds.

While Jack Kennedy's fragile health, and even his vigorous appearance, was dependent on a cornucopia of pharmaceuticals, Edwards was the Clemson football recruit whose energy didn't seem to wane until the last few days of his campaign. His sunny outlook never flagged, despite the rigors of a marathon he had initially shown Clark-like reluctance to enter.

Edwards had a natural deep pocket source, as a trial lawyer himself.

While his campaign story emphasized an upbringing that was impoverished in comparison to Dean and Kerry, he did not readily bring forth that he had funded his own 1998 senate campaign, and had a personal wealth of $25 million. Without being as obnoxiously ubiquitous as James Sokolove, he was one good litigator.

His courtroom colleagues made him the headline maker by virtue of his successful fundraising in the first quarter of 2003. Democrats tend to rely on Jews, unions and trial lawyers. Lieberman had natural inroads with the first group, Dean and Gephardt seemed to mine the second group throughout 2003, but Edwards was lifted up on the retainers of his colleagues.

A prominent California Democrat once said that "money is the mother's milk of politics." Edwards made the strategic choice to give Lamaze classes to the American Bar Association, even when it meant ignoring the early caucus and primary states at the beginning of 2003. FEC reports showed that 55% of his donors in the first quarter identified themselves as lawyers. Walter Shapiro suggests that the campaign slogan in those days should have been "Torts 'R' Us."

Edwards' optimism belied a tragedy that was life defining for both John and Elizabeth Edwards. As the death of Dean's brother had occurred when he moved from Wall Street to medical school, the death of the Edwards' sixteen-year-old son, Wade, in a freak auto accident in 1996, had preceded Edwards' move from the courtroom to the senate. Wade's Outward Bound pin remains on the lapel of his father's jacket.

Elizabeth Edwards had told an interviewer in 2001, "The kind of carefree happiness that we had before is gone forever from our lives. We will never have it back." John Edwards was reduced to tears when pressed by a *Washington Post* writer to talk about his late son.[125]

Having faced such loss, Edwards was not likely one to found political defeat threatening. As an insider in his campaign said, "After you have to get up on a table in a medical-examiner's office and hug your son good-bye, there's nothing they can ever do to you."[126]

Edwards had ascended quickly, appearing on Gore's short list for running mates after only two years in the Senate.

On the campaign trail in the 2004 season, Edwards was always considered the most effective at working a room. As Walter Shapiro observed, he "is far more compelling in person than he is in theory." He "never needs to buy a Hallmark card. He is a Hallmark card."[127]

Kathy Sullivan says "From there I went over to the Edwards event…of course they were just really pumped up, happy, and excited because Edwards …I remember I saw Senator Edwards, and I said 'I'm so glad you did so well'…everybody likes John Edwards… everybody just loves John Edwards. In fact, I have a theory about the primary that when people decided to vote, there were really two primaries that day for the Democratic party…there was the Dean-Kerry primary and the Edwards-Clark-Lieberman primary, and Kucinich primary…you either wanted to vote in the Kerry-Dean primary or you wanted to vote in the others.

Tim Fedderman says "Edwards was … The guy was a machine…he knew his message, he repeated it over and over …he said I know who I'm talking to…and that's what I'm doing.

"It's message, message, message."

Howard Dean talks about an issue strangling American courts: "Tort reform is a state issue, not a federal issue. The thing about Ohio is that it's run by Republicans. I think it's not so much a matter of the Republicans vs. the Democratic Party. The Republicans talk about tort reform, but they haven't been able to deliver it.

"I'm not willing to say that it's the Democrats' fault that we haven't had tort reform. The Republicans haven't delivered it either in the same cycle, when they've been in charge. It's a serious issue. Malpractice insurance is a huge problem for physicians. There clearly need to be some changes, but I don't think it's a partisan issue, despite what the Republicans would have you believe."

GETTING POLLED

Technology, while adding daily to our physical ease, throws daily another loop of fine wire around our souls. It contributes hugely to our mobility, which we must not confuse with freedom. The extensions of our senses, which we find so fascinating, are not adding to the discrimination of our minds, since we need increasingly to take the reading of a needle on a dial to discover whether we think something is good or bad, or right or wrong.

ADLAI E. STEVENSON, "My Faith in Democratic Capitalism," in Fortune magazine, October, 1955.

"Too often, polls foster a false sense of certainty, and mask the volatility of the popular mood. National polling about Democratic candidate preferences is virtually worthless months before the primaries, since it measures little more than name recognition and dimly felt and easily changeable impressions of the candidates.

"Iowa is a pollster's nightmare; it is nearly impossible to predict with precision which Democrats will make the major commitment to leave their warm houses on a blustery winter's night to attend the caucuses. And New Hampshire polling is notoriously fickle and unreliable"[128] Andrew Smith reiterated this well known fact when he remembered Karen Hicks showing on her computer program how many one (1) votes or 'strong' supporters Dean had in Manchester.

"The thing about devising a data base like this is you have to think in advance of all the situations that would come up" said **Malcolm Saldanha**. "You get information by doing queries and that's how you narrow the list. The database wasn't organized with the forethought of all the problems that would come up, which usually is the case…when you devise databases." Saldanha continues "there wasn't a uniformity of inputting the data between the regions. The instructions I was given in Manchester with how we enter phone calls were different than the instructions I was given in Claremont or in some of the other regions."

Andrew Smith notes that "One of Walter Shapiro's columns was (about) Karen Hicks, showing… how many votes, how many ones, she had… (that) the Dean folks had in Manchester. I forget the number of ones she had in Manchester's Ward one, which is an elite ward. I thought that (it) was a large number. I wonder what it was like to see all those 1's melt away. A lot of those ones were not ones. Or the story was that a 1, a strong supporter, was turned off by Dean basically by what happened in January."

"Moreover," says **Kathy Sullivan** "the bulk of the voters I talked to were just not sure. So, when the poll numbers were showing these big numbers for Dean and I kept saying to folks, 'I'm not sure how solid this is because people want to vote for the person they think can beat Bush'. I said pretty much the same thing to every reporter who talked to me… Then one day I was sitting in the conference and a reporter came to see me from out of state …things looked so good for Howard Dean at that point…I said, 'I'm going to say something to you I wouldn't say to anybody…I don't think you can stop this guy now.'

"On the day of the primary it was odd…the exit polling in NH was difficult…you get a big vote of … blue collar Democrats voting late…they don't vote early they vote late…so, the exit polling doesn't pick that up… well enough…the people who vote in Manchester and Nashua. The blue collar Democrats vote after work. They also don't pick up sufficiently the fact that (late in the day) turn out in some of the border communities where some of the people commute from Boston. So, even though the polls showed Kerry starting to run away with the thing, the exit polling on primary day showed it to be a lot closer than it turned out to be. I think that's because…they still haven't figured out how to do exit polling in NH…notoriously, exit polling in NH is not right…and so, there were e-mails going around amongst the Dean folks that said 'gee, this is close'. The exit polling is notoriously unreliable in NH. It wasn't totally surprising to me when the results really bore out the polling that had been done immediately, pre-primary. But that was devastating to some of the Dean people.

"Every candidate had access to that same voter file, because they bought it from the state party. We had a program with the DNC. You cannot get a voter file in NH from the secretary of state's office for the entire state or for any town. You have to go town by town, get the voter checklist and get your own voter file. So we did that with the DNC and it's a constant battle to update it and correct it. There are some towns that have better *checklists than others. What each campaign did from there, was up to them, in terms of getting information about voters, identifying their voters, and all the rest. No question that the Dean people did make much better use of the Internet early on to communicate.*"

William Trezevant relates how phone banks and polling was done in Washington State. "I also think was effective was that our phone banks were organized by neighborhood. So, if I lived in Spokane, and I wanted to do phone banking, I got a list of names and numbers of people who were in my precinct and invariably who were on the next block. I think we boiled it down to ... a 5 or 6 block radius. That meant that, (when) I come in and say I want to make phone calls and this is real important to me. I say that's fantastic, here are your neighbors and these are the telephone numbers. Rather than getting a phone call out of some centralized phone bank in Washington DC or a call center in California, and rather than getting a phone call from Spokane Washington into Seattle or into Walla Walla from Seattle, you got a phone call in Seattle from the guy two blocks over. The conversation was very different."

Andrew Smith comments that "most databases are incredibly old... they can't get kept up. And that's one of the problems with distributed responsibility. A lot of these people are doing this on the side. It's volunteer stuff. They might not understand the importance of strict timing."

Aaron Strauss relates his involvement with voter data banks. "I did the voter files for the Dean campaign. There they had a small data base of just their contacts and then they were using a vendor solution through the NH Democrat party to do their file operation. They brought me on so they could have this in-house system that we could keep track of both our contacts and the voter files all in one place... We tried to improve efficiency...because there were so many different pages and so much information going back and forth between the pages of the information... (This) was a slight problem... (we) tried to improve that as best as possible by putting the information they needed on the right pages. You only got 3 solid hours between 6 and 9 PM to call those people and that's not necessarily 3 hours because at 6-6:30 a lot of people are sitting down and eating dinner... if it takes 10 seconds per entry, to call them...that will really make an impact on how many people you can call."

PRIMARY LESSONS - TAKE NOTHING FOR GRANITE

The question is not whether "big is ugly," "small is beautiful," or technology is "appropriate." It is whether technologists will be ready for the demanding, often frustrating task of working with critical laypeople to develop what is needed or whether they will try to remain isolated, a luxury I doubt society will allow any longer.

ROBERT C. COWAN, *Technology Review, February 1980*

The Granite State has worked hard to retain its status as the first primary and its long history of testing candidates. In addition to the national attention, it has some economic benefits. The New Hampshire Political Library report on the economic impact of the primary after the 2000 election showed a total investment in excess of $200 million.

That is smaller than the Boston Marathon.

In 2004, a new focus group had appeared, to join "soccer moms": "NASCAR Dads." NASCAR holds two races in Loudon, NH annually, which generate $200 million in ticket sales alone. The Dads represent a demographic whose wallets speak loudly, even in a state known more for geological formations than blindingly fast aural endangerments

The report concluded that indirect impacts are likely to be far more significant, as the primary media coverage showcases the state as a potential site either for a tourist visit or to locate a business.[129]

New Hampshire's first-in-the-nation primary has a long history of testing candidates.

Actually some candidates never get to the test stage, but remain mired at the quizzical level. Who can forget the perpetually running Lyndon LaRouche and former California governor Jerry Brown, who ran in the primaries in 1976 and 1980. Years ago, Harold Stassen may have been considered a long-running long shot, like Lyndon LaRouche.

Dennis Kucinich's antecedent may have been former California governor Jerry Brown. The bachelor Kucinich had held a contest to find someone to date him. Like the reality television it seemed to parody, it came up with a dizzying array of finalists, including one who was, inconveniently, married.

Kucinich's style of dress and appearance had led to speculation in the Portsmouth office that he had appeared on "Star Trek: The Next Generation." Others in the office speculated that he had appeared in the Lord of the Dance spectaculars.

Jerry Brown, nicknamed "Governor Moonbeam", had dated singer Linda Ronstadt when he was governor. In a 'two degrees of separation' miracle, Ronstadt had performed once in the ballroom in Iowa now made famous by the Dean scream.

The 2004 primary featured two African-Americans. Al Sharpton, a minister who had started preaching while still a child, seemed to be seeking the stage as the leader of African-Americans. Either through his experience in the church, or his pyrotechnical appearance in the spurious Tawana Brawley case, or from his work with entertainer James Brown, Sharpton was perpetually a source of entertainment in the debates. Stephen Colbert, a correspondent for *The Daily Show*, would describe him as having a "face like a Kabuki mask."[130]

Carol Moseley Braun had served as a Senator for only slightly longer than John Edwards, and then as Ambassador to New Zealand. In the debates, she often seemed the calming presence of a grade school teacher, breaking up disputes among the boys on the playground. Her performances clearly seemed to enhance her stature as a national figure.[265]

Sharpton, and Moseley Braun, who dropped out early after defending Dean in the debates, and then endorsing him, had their path made smoother by Jesse Jackson's two runs in 1984 and 1988.

Sometimes, New Hampshire is merely a bump in the road for insurgent candidates. In 1984 Colorado Senator Gary Hart, a former campaign manager for George McGovern, had beaten the rather staid ex-Vice President Walter Mondale in the 1984 primary. Hart's victory was propelled by a grassroots organization that would include future Kerry backer Jeanne Shaheen.

Also in 1984, ex-astronaut John Glenn, still reeling from finishing fifth in the caucuses but first in spending in Iowa, finished third, leading Jesse Jackson. Jesse Jackson essentially tied George McGovern, who was attempting a late career comeback. Finishing sixth was South Carolina Senator Fritz Hollings, who would be a key Kerry endorser in 2004.

The man Dean would engage in the "murder-suicide" in Iowa in 2004, Dick Gephardt, had first had his presidential aspirations curbed when he lost in New Hampshire in 1988.

The man who defeated Gephardt that year was Massachusetts governor Michael Dukakis.

Kerry had once been Dukakis' lieutenant governor. Because Kerry was once Dukakis' lieutenant governor, in 2004 there would be attempts to link Kerry to Dukakis' spectacular failure in the 1988 national election. Peter Canellos of the Boston Globe had some reflections on "Dukakis' lieutenant governor": "There's no question that Kerry has held liberal positions on some social-welfare issues, and that his Massachusetts record probably can be presented as an excess of liberalism. And I'm sure there are some old newspaper quotes that would sound left-of-center right now.

"But is the public really worried about whether the next president will expand SSI or other social programs? Those issues seem so far off the radar screen now that it's hard to imagine the GOP can run on them. And there are other compelling reasons why the GOP wouldn't be able to give Kerry the Dukakis treatment. The one he mentions all the time is his military service. It stands as a rebuttal to the charge that he's 'soft on' anything. And he'll invoke it in ways that might suggest he has more authority on security issues than Bush.

"One example: Bush is already trying to put the Democrats on the spot by pushing for an early reauthorization of the Patriot Act, and Kerry would probably vote no, after which Bush will say they're putting Dukakis-like ACLU concerns ahead of the fight against terrorism. That argument works better against someone who's spent his career in the courtroom… Kerry has been on the battlefield. He's also been a prosecutor with a tough-on-crime reputation."[131]

Coming in third in 1988 in New Hampshire was Illinois Senator Paul Simon (who died during the 2004 primary campaign). He finished ahead of Jesse Jackson, who was making his second run. Behind Jackson was the young Senator from Tennessee, Al Gore. Gore would run as the Democratic nominee in 2000, winning the popular vote, but losing the Supreme Court vote that propelled George W. Bush into the White House, and into Dean's sights.

(Associate Justice Stephen Breyer had dissented, saying the majority decision would be "a wound that may not just harm the court, but the nation.")

Boston Globe columnist Peter Canellos would write that "A nation that still obsesses about conspiracy theories from the Kennedy assassination had little problem accepting an election in which the weak joints and crumbling foundation were obvious to supporters on both sides. The court's reputation survived. The Sept. 11, 2001, attacks conferred a legitimacy on the Bush presidency."[132]

It was a tough campaign against Bush in 2000. Gore was hindered by attempting the Kerry-like multiple positioning of trying to take credit for the prosperity the country enjoyed when he was Vice President, while simultaneously distancing himself from the moral torpor surrounding President Bill Clinton. Gore had distanced Clinton in 2000 by not having him bring his formidable campaign skills to bear. Wary of that double-edged sword, Gore may have severed his own chance at election in 2000.

Another Dean endorsement in 2004 had come from Gore's New Hampshire primary opponent in 2000, former New Jersey Senator Bill Bradley. When Bradley had followed closely upon the Gore endorsement, it was seen by Dean people as a sign that Dean was building bridges with the traditional Democratic establishment. That, in itself, was a double-edged sword for Dean, since he had come to prominence as an outsider, who could build grassroots and raise money outside the traditional party mechanisms. Building bridges within the New Hampshire Democratic party establishment is actually part of the years of groundwork for aspiring candidates. In 2002, John Edwards had the foresight to donate computers to the state Democratic parties in both New Hampshire and Iowa. At that point, Edwards was such a newcomer to the national scene that his act showed both ambition and vision.

Dante Scala identified two major types of candidates in the New Hampshire Democratic primary.[133] One is the Establishment candidate. Gore, Clinton, Gephardt, Mondale, Carter, and Muskie all fit this mold.

The other type of candidate is the Reformer. Reformers are outside of the party mainstream because of non-traditional issues (Figure 3, pages 327-339). Bradley focused a great deal on campaign finance reform in losing New Hampshire to Gore in 2000. Paul Simon was a fiscal reformer, as was another Senator named Paul, Tsongas, who had beaten Clinton in New Hampshire in 1992. In 1984, Gary Hart had cast himself as the champion of "new ideas", before the old impulse of lust brought his campaign to a screeching halt. Arizona Congressman Morris Udall's 1976 campaign focused on environmental protection.

The reformer who actually gained the party nomination as a result of leading party reform, George McGovern, was Dean's antecedent in 1972, when he was the anti-war candidate. Like attempts to link Kerry to Dukakis, opponents of both parties would try to paint Dean as guaranteeing a Republican landslide like the one McGovern suffered to Nixon. Ironically, McGovern endorsed the man cast as the "anti-Dean" in 2004; Wesley Clark.

The way reformist candidates actually earn their label is by insisting that the party, and usually the party leadership, needs new direction. Dean would follow this pattern in assaulting the centrist DNC. In the process, he would be attacking the very heart of what had elected Bill Clinton as the first two-term Democratic president since Franklin Roosevelt. Bill Clinton, and Hillary Rodham Clinton, now a New York Senator, are acknowledged as the royalty of the national Democratic Party.

Peter Canellos recognized the path that led them there. "Bill Clinton learned from the Dukakis campaign that you have to fire back early and often; George H.W. Bush paid dearly for his 1988 tactics in 1992. Whenever he tried to raise legitimate issues about Clinton's record he was accused of engaging in below-the-belt tactics."[134]

The Clintons carefully refrained from endorsing any of the Democrats, although there was speculation that fellow Arkansan Wesley Clark was a stalking horse for a future run by Hillary. The Clintons kept a political distance from Dean. The person who is crying "the king is dead!" is not likely to be chosen as a successor by the still-living king. It can be embarrassing, at a minimum, if you are wrong.

The CEO of the centrist Democratic Leadership Council (DLC) is a staunch Lieberman ally, Al From. In May, a memo bearing the signatures of From and DLC President Bruce Reed stated "What activists like Dean call the Democratic wing of the Democratic Party is an aberration: the McGovern-Mondale wing, defined principally by weakness abroad and elitist interest-group liberalism. That's the wing that lost 49 states in two elections, and transformed Democrats from a strong national party into a much weaker regional one." [135]

It is probably no coincidence that the architect of Clinton's campaigns, James Carville, sent word that he didn't feel he could comment on the Dean campaign for this book. A staffer in Carville's office said Carville felt he didn't know enough about the Dean campaign to comment. Apparently Carville has been sequestered in Shadowland nearly as long as Dick Cheney.

While New Hampshire has an image as a conservative Republican state, shifting demographics have changed the nature of the state's electorate. In 2000, Bush won New Hampshire over Gore by a scant 7,282 votes. Third party candidate Ralph Nader drew 22,156 votes, which probably was the factor in the Bush victory in New Hampshire.

"Exit polling from the 2000 Democratic primary reinforced the profile of New Hampshire Democratic voters as liberal to moderate. An outright majority of Democratic primary voters, 54 percent, identified themselves as liberals, 38 percent as moderates, and just 8 percent as conservative. The primary electorate is also noteworthy for its large number of upscale voters, both well educated and well off financially." [136] (Figure 4, pages 327-339)

Scala describes Democratic territory in New Hampshire as two zones: working class and elite. Contests between reformers and establishment candidates have delineated the differences. Reformers tended to do better in towns where Democrats were well educated and at the upper end of the economic spectrum. University towns like Keene, Durham and the area around Dartmouth College tended to be particularly receptive to reformers.

Working class areas were the bedrock of support for Establishment candidates. Scala cites ten zones in New Hampshire, five of each type. The zones aren't the ten counties in the state, but contiguous communities that can be identified as either elite or working class. [137]

In defining the ten zones, Scala eliminates voting results from communities that are not readily classified into either category. Dean's natural core of support would come from the elite areas. Past trends identified by Scala would show this to be a harbinger of Dean's ultimate demise.

"The more a candidate relied on and appealed to the elite segment of the population, the less likely he would perform well in the remaining primaries. With the exception of McGovern in 1972, *no candidate* (Scala's italics) whose appeal was disproportionately high among the elite went on to win the party nomination. In contrast, candidates who succeeded in appealing to both elite and working class Democrats may not have won New Hampshire, but their balanced performance was more likely to augur success in subsequent primaries."[138]

Clearly, the demographics of Dean's support in New Hampshire represented stormy seas ahead. Scala creates an instructive index, called a candidate's "elite score", to measure their balance in support between the elites and the working class. If the name sounds like a frequent flyer program, that is not altogether incorrect.

On Scala's scale, the ideal number, most predictive of future success, was 1.00, showing a perfect balance between the two groups. For the politicians flying frequently into the Granite State, it promises the ultimate first class upgrade - Air Force One. Scores above one show greater support among elites. Scores below 1.00 show stronger support among the working class.

Johnson, Muskie, and Gephardt would withdraw before the convention, and Mondale and Gore would lose the national election. In winning the nomination, and ultimately, the election, Carter in 1976 had the most balanced score of the top five finishers. Dukakis had a similar path when he scored the most balanced elite index in 1988. In 1992, Clinton pronounced himself the "Comeback Kid" after finishing second to Paul Tsongas from neighboring Massachusetts. Clinton had the most balanced score of the top four finishers in New Hampshire. Al Gore's score in 2000 showed much more balance than Bradley's in New Hampshire. While Bradley would drop out citing money problems, Scala's "elite score" showed that Bradley was in serious trouble against Gore if he chose to continue. (Figure 5, pages 327-339)

Eugene McCarthy became a hero to the liberals of his time, and for years to come, when he rose as the antiwar candidate in 1968. His emergence came at the behest of two progressive activists from Americans for Democratic Action. Ironically, when I was a junior at Phillips Exeter Summer School in 1968, the mock primary that we held selected one of those activists as the person who should be the Democratic nominee. While Allard Lowenstein was not someone I had heard of at that point in my life, by the time he was assassinated, I knew he was a liberal icon.

The McCarthy campaign began using house parties in New Hampshire to draw attention to the candidate just a couple of months before the primary. Celebrities, including Paul Newman in his pre-salad dressing days, would help to draw a crowd, to both homes and the ethnic social clubs that were then popular in Manchester.[139]

McCarthy was shy, aloof, enigmatic and a lazy campaigner. In a characteristic Scala ascribes to numerous insurgent campaigns, his supporters were more enthusiastic than the candidate himself.[140]

"My campaign may not be organized at the top," McCarthy said, "but it is certainly tightly organized at the bottom."[141]

New Hampshire primary campaign advertising was very different in 1968. The Boston television market was very expensive, and had limited penetration into the New Hampshire market. Manchester's Channel 9, WMUR-TV, was, at the time, a weak signal for much of the state. (Later, Republican Steve Forbes would pump so much of his own money into advertising in 1996 and 2000 that WMUR's new facility would be known as "the house that Forbes built.")

So McCarthy's campaign bombarded the state with inexpensive radio ads, at three to five dollars a minute, for twenty to thirty spots each day on each local station. In the last three weeks of the campaign, McCarthy ran 7,200 radio ads at the cost of only $36,000.

McCarthy's campaign was driven by the antiwar movement and propelled by young people.

In an era when the appearance of young people had tended to widen the breech with their elders, McCarthy volunteers, who spent their winter college break in New Hampshire, agreed to be "clean for Gene" if they were in roles contacting voters. New Hampshire governor John King, a Johnson supporter, even showed his backhanded admiration of their impact in calling them "those damned kids."[142]

The young, and the antiwar movement, would propel George McGovern's candidacy four years after McCarthy. McGovern was a hero in World War II, yet he would never utilize his military record as he ran in opposition to the Vietnam War in which John Kerry was distinguishing himself.

McGovern's campaign was grossly under-funded, but he had a commodity that would be much rarer in the compressed primary season of 2004: time. Like Dean, he had months of campaigning before the New Hampshire primary; McGovern announced his candidacy 539 days before the convention. Unlike Dean, he had weeks after the New Hampshire campaign to prepare for the remaining primaries.

McGovern was the only major challenger to the well-financed campaign of Maine Senator Edmund Muskie, who had been Hubert Humphrey's running mate in his 1968 loss to Nixon. "McGovern's campaign was proof that for a national campaign to be successful in New Hampshire, people from New Hampshire should be in charge of resources within the state, and the face of the campaign. Nowadays, presidential primary campaigns are often 'vendorized,' hiring professionals to handle direct mail and phone banks rather than developing a corps of volunteers to handle such tasks."[143]

Five months before the primary, Muskie had held 42 percent in their own campaign poll. He managed to maintain that strength against the McGovern challenge, even as the more centrist Muskie faced attacks from both left and right. At the time, I was in college at the University of New Hampshire. The power and venom of the ultra-conservative publisher of the *Manchester Union Leader*, William Loeb, were infamous. Friends coming to visit from liberal Minnesota were amused and amazed by the right wing lunatics whose letters to the *Union Leader* poured in from all over the country to denounce antiwar protesters, hippies, Democrats, minorities, and all other perceived threats.

Their fascination led me to march into the subscription office at the *Union Leader* to order a mail subscription for them to be sent back to Minnesota. The reaction to the American flag pants my wife had made for me probably kept the office staff from noticing that I had ordered the subscription to be sent to Carl Marx. Perhaps the C threw them off. The subscription would be delivered to an apartment in Minneapolis that my friends would refuse to vacate to make way for a munitions plant. The *Union Leader* editorials and letters to the editor they gleefully posted on the walls would be cited by the prosecution as proof of their abjectly dissolute lifestyle and anti-government agenda.

They got off anyhow.

William Loeb had criticized Johnson in 1968 for not prosecuting the Vietnam War even more severely. In the same election, he labeled Eugene McCarthy a "skunk." In 1972, Loeb's venom was directed more at Muskie than McCarthy. Loeb ran a letter of suspicious origin, and an accompanying front page editorial, that alleged that Muskie had laughed at an aide using the derogatory slang for French Canadian immigrants "Canuck."

(Now there's an NHL team by that name, but American professional sports names have yielded to the winds of political correctness. When the NBA's Washington Bullets realized that Washington had led the nation's murder rate, they changed their name to the Wizards.)

Loeb had also run an article that was less than kind to Muskie's wife. Muskie unleashed a fiery response from the back of a flatbed truck in front of the *Union Leader* building, shortly before the primary. Muskie became emotional, and in a light snowfall, appeared to some to be crying. Jack Driscoll, who would go on to become the executive editor of the *Boston Globe*, was there, and steadfastly maintains that Muskie did not cry. The appearance of unseemly emotion on the campaign trail would be widely reported. Loeb responded that anyone who would get so upset about what a newspaper publisher in New Hampshire said should not have his finger on the nuclear trigger.[144]

Muskie finished slightly better in New Hampshire than his polls of five months earlier. However, he was facing an insurgent, and he had failed to meet or exceed expectations.

"One of his New Hampshire operatives, Maria Carrier, predicted he would at least get 50 percent of the vote. The New Hampshire contest pointed out glaring signs of weakness in Muskie's strategy as an establishment candidate, as his campaign was marked by 'ineptness, mismanagement and over-confidence' that led to an attempt to 'win without a message, plan, or program.'"[145] McGovern finished about ten points behind, and parlayed his better-than expected performance into improved fundraising and, ultimately, the Democratic nomination.

There is a perception that candidates vault to success in New Hampshire by meeting every resident in the state, usually multiple times. "Nothing impresses the pampered voters of New Hampshire more than a candidate who shows up with the frequency of a UPS truck."[146] "The preferred forums for candidates in the state are still town meeting style events in which candidates present themselves to real people and take their questions."[147]

However, media have historically influenced the New Hampshire electorate's choices enormously. "Senator Estes Kefauver of Tennessee, the original grassroots presidential campaigner in 1952, made his name via the televised Senate hearings on corruption."[148]

By 2004, nearly three quarters of the Granite State's adults had Internet access. Delivery brings the *New York Times*, *Boston Globe*, and *USA Today* to most homes, and cable and satellite dishes bring around-the-clock access to news. Over 70,000 New Hampshire residents commute to Massachusetts daily. This means that campaigns must advertise in the Boston media market, which costs about ten times more than New Hampshire television. New Hampshire radio advertising now takes a back seat to television. Still, radio can serve a useful function.

In 1996, Governor Pete Wilson of California was making overtures about running. Another governor already in the race, flannel-shirted Lamar Alexander of Tennessee, saw Wilson as a threat. While television is a warmer climate for sunny visuals, radio proved an apt launching ground for two days of pre-emptive strikes on Wilson. The Wilson campaign never perceivably lifted off. Supporting the contention that political consultants are mercenaries, several workers from the Wilson campaign moved to another struggling candidate. Their new candidate, Boris Yeltsin, was trailing not only his Communist opponent in the polls, but long-dead super tyrant Joseph Stalin.

Yeltsin's daughter was resistant to their suggestions of focus groups, photo opportunities and negative advertising, as "phony American tricks." She did yield to the suggestion that Yeltsin give a speech sober, helpfully suggesting that it might best be scheduled early in the day.[149]

Lamar Alexander's campaign provided an example of the "extreme" campaigning that the New Hampshire winter inevitably requires. UNH graduate Sheridan Brown was a freshman political science major when he volunteered for Alexander. In the midst of a major snowstorm, Brown was assigned to drive a van for the press. "The candidate insisted on going out to meet his supporters. Brown was following Alexander's car in the heavy snow. He remembers sliding around corners, 'and at each stop a few more reporters decided to get out and take a cab back. Alexander pressed on, however, and soon several cars ahead of him spun off the road and into a guardrail. Alexander insisted on checking on the drivers, and gave one overwrought woman a ride home."[150]

Anyone with a driver's license might be a voter, right?

Ads sometimes could have the double benefit of reaching into the news cycle. George H.W. Bush ran ads accusing Senator Bob Dole of straddling on an issue traditionally dear to Granite State voters: taxes. Dole was in the news cycle right up until the primary, fiercely denying the charges. On primary night, Dole, in a fit of pique, snarled at Bush, "Stop lying about my record."[151] What Dole didn't seem to realize was that continuing denials kept the original allegation in the news. Furthermore, continuing denials start to fall into the category of "thou doth protest too much, methinks"

Similarly, if you are alleged to be angry, an emotion Dole clearly showed on primary night, continued efforts afterwards to show that you *aren't* an angry man may give the charge continued life.

On the day before the New Hampshire primary in 2004, Dante Scala would put his perspective on the next day's events. Scala thought Dean could recover from Iowa if liberals shifted back after flirting with Kerry. He saw Dean's strategy, including the Sawyer interview with him and Judith Steinberg, the last debate, and the Letterman Top Ten appearance, as possibly compensating for 72 hours that Dean had lost.

Recalling history, he could not "think of any time when a major non-New Englander had beaten a major New England candidate in a Democratic primary" in the Granite State. He felt that if Edwards or Lieberman picked up 20 percent of the vote and drew from Kerry, that would help. Clark had "gotten jostled around a lot," and people acted as if they were not sold on him, despite his encampment in the Granite State. "Clark had been alone in New Hampshire while the others contested Iowa. And then they moved into New Hampshire with the momentum of their showings in Iowa, taking some of the spotlight away from him."[152]

A good turnout by college kids would favor Dean, and the Dean organization seemed capable of assuring that. A little snow wouldn't hurt, as it would keep away the less-fervent supporters of other candidates. Scala noted that New Hampshire voters were notoriously last minute shoppers, and that the tracking polls might not be good predictors. "Electability" seemed to be a big issue, "in the absence of other clear-cut areas of disagreement on issues of policy."[153]

Washington Post Executive Editor Leonard Downey had similar observations.

"Kerry, Edwards, Clark and Dean — have almost the exact same position on most issues, even though they may have presented those positions somewhat differently to campaign audiences. In some election years, there are big ideological splits among the potential nominees in either party, but that does not seem to be the case this year among the leading Democrats. The most interesting horse race: Dean vs. Clark as the most successful insurgent candidate."[154]

The next morning, Kathy Sullivan, the New Hampshire Democratic Party Chair, had similar observations. "It appears that over the weekend the slide that began in Iowa stopped. I would agree that showing a more human side of Governor Dean was very helpful to his campaign."

A correspondent noted the shortcomings of the tracking polls.

"Zogby, SUSA, ARG, and WMUR all had Kerry and Dean in a statistical dead heat in their most recent dailies (excluding today's Zogby). All the other polls had Dean moving up, and Kerry either flat or down."

Sullivan discounted the polls. "I don't think that most voters here pay attention to the polls. Second, the Zogby poll that showed a statistical dead heat between Senator Kerry and Governor Dean was different from every other poll I saw, so I think there was just something wrong with the Zogby poll yesterday."

Sullivan foreshadowed the importance of New Hampshire to Howard Dean.

"When regional candidates have not done as well as expected, it has set their candidacies back substantially." Sullivan noted the impact of

Kucinich, foreshadowing the role Ralph Nader might play in 2004. "There are several former Nader supporters working as volunteers for other campaigns this year. One of the reasons I am very happy that Dennis Kucinich is in this race is that he has been able to reach out and bring into the Democratic Party process a number of Green Party people or other Nader supporters. I think that we have to build on the effort that Dennis Kucinich has made."[155]

For candidates, the perception of meeting New Hampshire voters face to face, as portrayed through the media, may have become more important than the reality.

The grassroots are still viable in New Hampshire, though. Six months before the Republican primary in 1990, visitors to Patrick Buchanan's offices above the campaign way station Merrimack Restaurant in Manchester would find dozens of volunteers for the conservative, dialing up conservative Republicans.

(Presaging liberal pundit Al Franken's attacks on the right, Mystery Science Theatre 2000 would lampoon Buchanan. After an opening scene to a science fiction movie showed an expanding mushroom cloud, a solemn narrator intones "Patrick Buchanan's first day as president.")

For New Hampshire media, the infestation of national media as the primary nears greatly decreases their access to the candidates. The relationship between reporters and the media becomes more distant and formal. John McCain avoided that pitfall on his Straight Talk Express in 2000, and was generally a media darling because of his accessibility. "McCain succeeded in obtaining the star appeal that made him a candidate that attracted independents, a whole new group of consumers to democracy that don't usually come to the table. This group tends to be less cynical, less ideological, and less interested in politics."[156]

Scala also comments on the Democratic insurgent that same year, Bill Bradley, who did not enjoy similarly warm relations with the media. "Bradley's media relations were 'militant in its operation' (WMUR's Scott) Spradling said, 'the quintessential example of what can go wrong' because the campaign tried to micromanage the media. The Bradley campaign treated the media as an enemy rather than as a means to an end. The Bradley campaign put a premium on controlling media access, an emphasis he (Bradley's national campaign spokesman Eric Hauser) said came from the candidate himself."[157]

"At first, the reporting on the Bradley phenomena in New Hampshire was unaffected by the candidate's discomfort. A story made its way around the press corps about a reporter, newly assigned to the Bradley campaign, being alone in an elevator with the candidate. The reporter introduced himself, but Bradley did not bother to 'really acknowledge' the introduction. Jennifer Donahue of WMUR-TV said 'Bradley didn't warm up to the press, and so they didn't warm up to him. He didn't play the game on the press's terms.

'I think if he had allowed more of that spontaneous side to come out with the media, or allowed some warmth to come out toward the media' he could have countered the perception that he lacked warmth. "[158]

"Bradley, in contrast (to McCain), had plenty of intellectual heft as well as the proper liberal credentials, but was 'boring.' McCain's success at playing both the grassroots game and the media game in New Hampshire catapulted him, for a brief time, into the national political spotlight. Meanwhile, Bill Bradley and his insurgency slipped onto the back pages."[159]

In 2001, historian **David Halberstam** provided an overview of the 2000 insurgents, at the same time as he looked at the Democratic Party and Bradley's past and future. "The role of Bradley was that there was a sense that he could bridge the divisions. The architect of the Vietnam War came from the Democratic Party, as did most of the protesters. In subsequent years, as that battle within the party went on, it was as if there were two teams. There was the Kennedy/McGovern/McCarthy wing, and against it the Lyndon Johnson/Scoop Jackson team. As somebody once said, it was like there were two football teams playing, and in the stands, there were 70,000 people cheering wildly, all of them Republicans."

Shapiro saw the same Democratic conflict between Dean and Kerry. "The quarrel mirrors divisions in the Democratic Party that go all the way back to the anti-war furies of the 1968 primaries. During that tempestuous year, the real cleavage on the left was between the purist partisans of Eugene McCarthy and the pragmatic politics personified by Bobby Kennedy. That Democratic dilemma endures: How do you weigh dewy-eyed idealism against partially flawed electability? In his righteous anger, Dean can be seen as the spiritual descendant of McCarthy, while Kerry never shies away from wrapping himself in the Kennedy myth."[160]

Halberstam described how such a rift might be slow to close. "These cleavages remained. They were there in the Carter administration. You could see it between the Secretary of State, Zbigniew Brzezinski, and the National Security Council. It was a very divided government. There was enough time so it didn't really affect the Clinton administration.

"Bradley seemed, in 1989, that he had the capacity, as Clinton eventually showed, to be able to bridge a chasm, a narrowing chasm, narrowing because the issues had narrowed.

"Vietnam was more in the distance, and it seemed Bradley had the capacity to bridge that.

"I don't see for this moment, now, a great political future for him. He made the run. It didn't work terribly well, to the degree that anybody with a more independent attitude galvanized and captured the imagination of the country, it was really John McCain, for a variety of reasons. I know it was very hard for Bradley to run against a sitting Vice President. We'd had eight years of prosperity. He did, and it just did not work out. I don't know if he has the taste to try it again. It's a brutal thing to run for President, financially and in every other way. He may just think it's not worth it right now."

Media overkill can also devastate a candidate, as Dante Scala suggests. "The advent of the twenty-four-hour news cycle has placed much more pressure on media and campaigns alike to create and control the news. A single miscalculation could cause a five- to fifteen-point decline in the candidate's poll rating over the subsequent forty-eight hours."[161]

For most candidates, as the day of the primary approaches, staged events have largely replaced the house meetings with small groups that were the campaigns initial lifeblood a year or two, earlier. Walter Shapiro suggests that Dean's were actually "over choreographed."[162]

Dante Scala reflects on election campaign activities: "Traditional grassroots activities, such as coffees held in people's homes, are increasingly planned events staged for the benefit of the media. Not just anybody is invited; rather, the invitation list is composed of activists leaning toward the candidate and reporters."[163]

Field operatives try to provide a big turnout for any candidate event, for fear that the media will report poor attendance as a weakening of support.

Spontaneous encounters become increasingly rare, limiting a candidate's vulnerability, but also giving the public less opportunity to know the candidate as a person. Candidates wanted to avoid experiences like Ted Kennedy's in 1980. In a barn in Conway, a participant asked, "Listen, how can I possibly support you when you haven't answered questions about that poor girl that died in the car?"[164]

In the early spotlight, any slipup will be illuminated.

"If a candidate goes ballistic at a press-conference in Iowa or melts under the bright lights of a pre-primary debate, it is a safe bet that he will have problems with recalcitrant congressional committee chairmen, let alone French diplomats."[165]

Reflecting on a frequently mentioned election factor in NH, **Andrew Smith** says "I don't think there's such a thing as a Shaheen Machine, although certainly she and her husband are very well connected, and they pulled out all of the stops for Kerry. And the thing about Shaheen, is that she knows a lot of people in the communities, she's as well connected as any Democrat and most Republicans in the state of New Hampshire."

When talking about Jeanne Shaheen, **Kathy Sullivan** feels that "It's the talent of the people around her."

In addition to reformers and insurgents, there are candidates who appeal to specific factions within the party. This type of candidate has definable effect on the process. **John Zaller** says "Parties, have always had a problem with faction candidates. Faction candidates… (such as) George Wallace in the 1960's… these people who were able to appeal to a part of the party base but were not acceptable to the rest of the party. So you have to try to contain these people. Obviously they'd have to be acceptable to the rest of the party. George Wallace in '72, was the most charismatic candidate out there, by far, but obviously he was also not going to be acceptable to the whole party."

PRIMARY DAY AND DIRTY TRICKS

In the process of gaining our rightful place, we must not be guilty of wrongful deeds.

—Martin Luther King, Jr.

Primary day would be a test for both Dean, and New Hampshire voters. Harvard's Thomas Patterson has written that "The turnout rate in New Hampshire is nearly twice as high as in any other state, and its residents take their role very seriously in other ways.

"One study found they were 100 percent more likely to have particular knowledge of primary election candidates and issues than other Americans."[166]

Frank Sinatra sang that if he couldn't make it in New York, he couldn't make it anywhere. Perhaps New Hampshire would be the same for Howard Dean. Dean had not been helped in Iowa by the revelation of an interview on Canadian TV in which he, as governor of Vermont, had dismissed the Iowa caucuses as captive to special interests.

Ironically, his hero, Harry Truman, had made a similar gaffe about the New Hampshire primary in January 1952. Truman was the product of good old-fashioned Democratic Party machinery, and he had not chosen to face a challenge being mounted by an insurgent Estes Kefauver in New Hampshire. "All these primaries are just eyewash when the convention meets, as you'll find out."[167]

"The ensuing campaign established what became a classic model of a New Hampshire presidential primary: a grassroots insurgency pitted against an establishment candidate supported by party regulars."[168] Truman was absent from New Hampshire; he actually had considered withdrawing his name from the ballot there before being dissuaded by the national party chair. It was 1952 when New Hampshire became the first primary where voters actually voted for a candidate rather than a local delegate whose commitment to a particular candidate was not guaranteed. Kefauver won 54.6% of the popular vote, and Truman withdrew from the race a few weeks later.

Ironically, the Democratic nominee would end up being Adlai Stevenson, who won on the third ballot at the convention, after failing to enter a single primary. Dean had tried to recover from the fallout on his dismissal of the Iowa caucuses by saying that he hadn't understood the caucus process when he made the statement, but the damage from it was undoubtedly part of the currents that had swept him to a third place in Iowa.

In unprecedented and heady days of record-setting fundraising and premature anointment as front-runner, the Dean campaign had boasted of a national campaign with the finances and organization to carry it through primaries in June. In practice, his campaign strategy in December and January moved closer to a model first formulated as early as 1972.

In November 1972, an aide to the governor of a small southern state had formulated a plan to transform himself from obscurity with impressive early showings in Iowa and New Hampshire. That strategy jump-started Jimmy Carter's path to the Presidency in 1976. [169]

Dante Scala notes: "Carter's success in the 1976 primary, starting with Iowa and New Hampshire, codified what had been suspected in the wake of the 1968 and 1972 campaigns: New Hampshire was no longer simply a test of strength for front runner and contender, it now *bestowed* strength on candidates who performed well there and fueled the candidate's efforts in subsequent primaries."[170]

Unfortunately, Dean didn't have the cover of obscurity with which he could rise to prominence in Iowa and New Hampshire. His fundraising and internet success had shone the media spotlight on him months earlier, and that lighting seemed to highlight every blemish, imperfection, and misstep.

New Hampshire is like a wedge between Dean's and Kerry's home states. A primary victory that had seemed a foregone conclusion for Dean a month earlier now was cast as crucial to continuing viability and survival. Whereas smoke filled back rooms had once been the battleground for political supremacy, primaries had opened up the process to those more outside the political power structure.

Scala provides the following insight: "Presidential primaries based on the idea that rank and file members of political parties, rather than party leaders, should be the ones to choose nominees for political office is a fairly new wrinkle in American politics. Over the past two hundred years, America's political parties have lurched in fits and starts toward democratization in choosing a presidential nominee." [171]

Writing about the 1960 presidential election, Theodore White notes, that for Kennedy and Humphrey, "…if they could not at the primaries prove their strength in the hearts of Americans, the Party bosses would cut their hearts out in the back rooms." [172]

New Hampshire wouldn't necessarily be a death struggle for Dean, but it would be another wound that could be perceived or portrayed as mortal. While the campaign seemed to my novitiate eyes to be run along the lines of a Little Rascals "hey kids, let's put on a show!" there were external forces that weren't making things better.

On Halloween, we had a rally at the Pease Tradeport. As I stood at the entrance, I'd watched a large man in full cowboy regalia enter. I had seen him in the same outfit at other events, and, given that it was Halloween, I wasn't surprised to see a young woman in a green lizard outfit enter the room. Her intent was clear once we noticed the hand-lettered banner on a van in the parking lot: "What will chameleon Dean say next?"

We surrounded her at her table, and I gave her my best stern study hall teacher grilling before Dean arrived. Dean people were instructed to stand in front of her to block her view from any photographers. She never did ask any questions, and I saw her pile into the van to leave with a young man I recognized from television as having been onstage at a Kerry event.

Community visibility was a key priority for me. When Megan Garcia, a new staffer from California, had asked me to call from my home to complain about signs other campaigns had put up on public land in the Portsmouth traffic circle, I did so willingly. While the state highway people had said the signs would be taken down as driver distractions, a similar complaint to the city of Portsmouth Public Works department produced the response that while such signs were illegal, they couldn't take them down.

Ever idealistic, I reported this back to Megan, and insisted that although this was absurd, the Dean campaign was going to adhere to the law and not put signs on public property.

Because the kids in the office held some fear of me, following my admonitions about office cleanliness, this was generally upheld. However, another reason was that a Portsmouth police officer appeared in the office twice to instruct them that campaign signs weren't allowed on public property. Which, it turns out, wasn't true.

Although the officer was never identified, the fact that the firefighters union actively supported Kerry led us to suspect the cop's orientation. Maybe it wasn't a cop, but someone who had utilized the same costume shop that had chameleon suits. Or maybe it was one of the Village People. Except that, given Dean's support for civil unions, we felt the Village People would be a natural constituency.

An amazing contributor to the local Dean effort in Greenland was a high school sophomore. Working tirelessly despite the demands of being an outstanding athlete and excellent student, Katie Drapcho did more in a few weeks than anyone else in Greenland, with the possible exceptions of my wife, me, and Carol DeStephano, who had been on board for months.

On primary day, we would hear reports of other suspicious activity. Dean voters had gotten automated calls purporting to be from the Dean campaign, directing them to the wrong polling place. Adam, Katie's brother, who stood holding a sign in the freezing cold outside the polls on primary day, said his answering machine had recorded an automated call that he erased once he heard it was from the Dean campaign. The Dean campaign never made automated calls, preferring to annoy people by overcalling them with live human beings.

The New Hampshire queen of automated calls was former governor Jeanne Shaheen. When she ran a losing Senate campaign in 2002, her automated voice had called our house at least 5 times on Election Day. Despite that loss, the chair of the state's Democratic Party still saw Shaheen as a power broker, with a huge impact on the Kerry campaign. "I think it has helped him immensely. Gov. Shaheen has the best political mind in the state of New Hampshire and she became involved in the campaign when it needed a real shaking up. The campaign has become more focused and more disciplined since her arrival."[173]

The former governor had led the New Hampshire effort in Colorado Senator Gary Hart's insurgent campaign during the George Orwell election year of 1984. (Two decades later, after Dean's withdrawal, Brentwood Dean Leader Roger Goun would fly a bumper sticker reading "Bush-Orwell '04)

In 1984, Hart had seemed mired behind former vice president Walter Mondale and Senator John Glenn. Hart had lost by thirty points to Mondale in Iowa, but had exceeded expectations. Glenn had finished a weak sixth in Iowa. The prototype of an evolving Shaheen machine had led Hart to thrash Mondale a week later in New Hampshire. Hart would go on to be undone by his own peculiar combination of hubris[174] and libido. Mondale's trouncing by the once-insurgent-but-now-incumbent Ronald Reagan led to the formation of the DLC, which Dean would call the "Republican wing of the Democratic Party.".

In 2004, when the specter of McGovern's defeat wasn't being channeled over the Dean campaign, Mondale was available on alternate channels.

Jeanne Shaheen had endorsed Kerry, after her husband became Kerry's campaign manager. The "Shaheen sheen" had been demonstrated in the 2000 primary. Early exit polls had shown Bradley with a lead, so the Shaheens had jump-started their machine, and Bradley went on to lose to Gore. "Gore did a good job, but it's Jeanne and Billy Shaheen who know where to look for votes[175]," said Dante Scala. "Four years later, no asset is more precious.....than the Shaheens. 'Senator Kerry's best shot is probably having them on his side' said Mary Rauh"[176], a Shaheen friend and Clark supporter.

"With Kerry trailing Dean in polls and fundraising" in early January, some Democrats and many political analysts were skeptical that the Shaheens had "enough pull with the heavily liberal primary electorate to bolster Kerry's candidacy and overcome the Dean juggernaut. 'If we had a couple more months, I know we'd win this thing,' "[177] former judge Bill Shaheen had said.

But the Shaheens power also had doubters in early January." 'In presidential primaries, it's always been said that organization is everything,' said Jennifer Duffy, an analyst with the nonpartisan Cook Political Report newsletter in Washington. 'But New Hampshire may prove that to be a big lie.' "[178]

Still, the Shaheen endorsement resonated with some voters. "'I've voted for Jeanne every time, and love her support of kindergarten and working people, and I'm sure her pro-education views will transfer to John

Kerry,' said Audrey Rondo, a Democrat who attended a Milford, New Hampshire chili feed featuring Kerry and Shaheen."[179] From then on, the "Shaheens' fingerprints" were "evident in the recent overhaul of Kerry's message and campaign."

"According to Kerry advisers, both Shaheens supported Kerry's move in November to fire campaign manager Jim Jordan, as a way to attack the growing perception that Kerry was faltering and would lose to Dean. 'Jeanne Shaheen, who had tangled with Jordan during her Senate race, when he worked for a Washington committee that aided Senate Democrats, encouraged the hiring of new manager Mary Beth Cahill,' Bill Shaheen said. 'When you don't have firm leadership at the top, nothing else works.' Shaheen became Kerry's state chairman in January (2003), with his wife coming on as national campaign chair" in the Fall of 2003. Together they "championed Kerry's use of national security as a double-barreled weapon to criticize Bush and point out Dean's deficit of experience."

At campaign events, the Shaheens "coached Kerry to make as much time for as many questions as possible from voters, instead of giving windy answers. "The nice thing about Senator Kerry is that he takes advice well,"[180] Bill Shaheen had observed.

There also were reports of automated calls to voters saying that Dean wasn't Christian enough, since his wife and kids were Jewish. I guess the Christian Coalition deserved as much credit as any group for redefining any line between church and state.

Another report I received, in never-ending calls on the cell phone which the campaign had issued me for the carefully orchestrated primary effort, said that our poll checkers needed to avoid being duped. Our poll checkers would cross off the names of identified Dean supporters as they came to the polls, so we could target supporters who hadn't yet voted to roust them. The report was that a stranger identifying himself as a replacement from the Dean campaign had approached a poll checker in another polling place. The Dean volunteer had then turned over the list of supporters and left.

The list left soon afterwards, along with the mysterious stranger who had procured it.

The morning of the primary, my wife and I had driven around, trying to find addresses in the dark, to drop off GOTV materials at identified Dean supporters' homes. When we had gotten up at 3 AM, we had immediately checked for the earliest of returns in the state. Clark won Dixville Notch and Hart's Location. His hopeful supporters asked if that didn't "legitimize him more then the media gives him credit for. This could change the minds of undecided voters in New Hampshire and carry Clark to a strong second."

Leonard Downie, Jr. of the *Washington Post* wasn't buying it. "As South Carolina Senator Fritz Hollings said, while introducing Kerry at a rally in New Hampshire last week, he won those little, early counting precincts when he ran for president years ago and lost New Hampshire badly. They have little or no effect on other voting."[181]

The cold was bad enough that only a couple of college kids who were friends of Edwards' daughter, and a couple of Clark supporters, joined us Dean supporters at the polls. The Dean contingent numbered up to 5 at one time, in stark contrast to the invisible Kerry supporters who put up signs before the polls opened and never appeared again. A complaint to the telephone company that Kerry signs were up on their poles, which is against company policy, never produced any response. Last time I noticed, those signs were still up.

It was hard to tell how fine the line was between vigilance and paranoia... although there was a history.

Push polling had suggested that McCain's Bangladesh-born daughter was his own, illegitimate black child. Callers would ask McCain supporters if knowledge that McCain had fathered such a child would make them more or less likely to support him.

The smearing of McCain had very old antecedents. In 1884, Republicans had shouted at Grover Cleveland, who had fathered an illegitimate child, "Ma, Ma, Where's my Pa?" When Cleveland was elected, the refrain became "Gone to the White House, ha, ha, ha!"

In his first campaign for congress Nixon had labeled his opponent a Communist, and he labeled his opponent in a later Senate race, the "Pink Lady."

Lee Atwater, George H.W. Bush's top strategist, had raised questions about Mike Dukakis' character in 1988, preceding unsubstantiated rumors that Dukakis had been treated for clinical depression. Reagan, The Great Communicator, had piled on, quipping about Dukakis, "I don't want to pick on an invalid."

"Time and time again, insurgency has been the watchword for the modern New Hampshire Democratic presidential primary. The key question in primary after primary has not been 'who's ahead?', but, rather, 'who's coming from behind?' This is because New Hampshire, time and time again, has been the best, often the last, chance for the 'outs' in the Democratic Party to challenge the 'ins' for the grand prize of the Presidential nomination."[182]

Kerry, the quintessential 'insider', had cast himself as the "Comeback Kerry" after his victory in Iowa. Dean was slowly recovering and gaining ground, over the last week.

In mid-afternoon, another cell phone call from Wendy brought the breathless news that we were within one point of John Kerry. Given that the goal after the stunner in Iowa had been to get a loss within single digits, we were euphoric. After sharing this with the other workers, my cynicism led me to think that this might be a ruse from the Dean campaign, just to rouse our efforts for the rest of a cold day.

My cynicism was misplaced, however.

Robert Kaiser of the *Washington Post* reported "The exit polls of voters after they cast ballots show Kerry beating Dean but not by much. It looks to me as though Dean has survived the first week after the scream; he isn't far behind Kerry, maybe five points or less, maybe a little more. And I have lived through a lot of New Hampshire primaries when the exit polls were misleading. Four years ago we had Bill Bradley ahead of Al Gore in the early exit polls."[183]

Washington Post pollsters Claudia Deane and Richard Morin clarified the situation later.

"The network exit poll left something to be desired. They got the winner right, and they got the order right. It was the margin that was wrong — about half the size it ended up being. This produced initial reporting that the race was close, when it became very clear as soon as votes starting coming in that Kerry had a substantial lead. Dean did well among young people, and among those who made the war their primary voting issue. He won among those who described their own views as 'very liberal', about 15 percent of NH primary voters. But Kerry won among the 'somewhat liberal', moderates and conservatives. He ran roughly even with

Kerry among voters 'angry' with the Bush administration's policies. Other than that, Kerry virtually ran the table.

"Kerry did well among all kinds of issue voters. He lost to Dean among those voters who were voting on Iraq and on national security/terrorism, but only narrowly. He won decisively among voters who rated the economy/ jobs, health care or education as their primary voting issues. We just checked out Kerry's favorability ratings among Dean voters: 55 percent favorable, 41 percent unfavorable (this compared to 72 - 25 overall). Still, he has half and it hard to believe that angry, motivated voters would gravitate to Bush, or sit out this election if it looked like Kerry had a chance.

"It's clear that Democrats ache for a winner, and are willing to compromise on some issues. But in New Hampshire, 57 percent said they voted for the candidate who agreed with them on most of the major issues, and among these voters Dean and Kerry exactly split, 29 - 29. Among the third who said they were voting on electability, Kerry won better than three to one. Dean did do somewhat better among lower income voters. But Kerry performed equally well among the richest and the poorest.

"On the other hand, Dean did do better among those with postgraduate degrees. We don't know the drinking habits of the overeducated, but it does play to stereotypes of Dean supporters as pointy-headed intellectuals. Dean is far from being viewed as a fringe candidate (at least not while Al and Dennis are soldiering on). But he certainly appeals to a specific and fairly narrow segment of the Democratic electorate: very liberal, intensely angry anti-war voters. That's not good news for Dean as he heads south and west. The New Hampshire exit poll did ask about first time primary voters. One out of six voters fell in this category. They gave Kerry 35 percent of their votes, Dean got 29 percent. Kerry won independents by 14 points, he won Democrats by 12. But overall there wasn't a great deal of difference this election between Democrats and independents.

"In 2000, on the other hand, Bradley won decisively among NH independents, while Gore won handily among rank and file Democrats."[184]

Dean would need the same rank and file four years later in 2004.

We also were instructed not to give any information relevant to the campaign to people we did not know, who might be from other campaigns. There were reports that people at other polling sites were being pumped for information by other campaigns. Greenland was Deanland; we would be the best volunteers in the state. When we got the Greenland results a few minutes after the polls closed in Greenland, we had met our target goal of ID'ed Dean voters. However, we had not picked up any of the votes above the goal that a campaign typically expects. Kerry got 265 votes, Dean 147, Edwards 84, Clark 72, and Lieberman 67.

Lieberman was below the Greenland AWACS radar. Statewide, his performance had provoked a wise guy in Brooklyn to observe "Joe Lieberman got 5 percent of Democrat's votes, and 26 percent of Republicans. It begs the question: is he running in the wrong primary?"

A Kansan noted that "29 percent of the Republican 'crossovers' voted for John Kerry as opposed to only 8 percent who voted for Howard Dean." This led to the question "Are Republicans who 'cross over' sincere in their support for a Democratic candidate, or are they simply supporting (what in their minds) would be the easiest candidate to defeat in the general election?" Pollsters Morin and Deane responded "We really don't know who these voters are, and in New Hampshire they made up only 4 percent of the electorate. It could be Dartmouth frat boys having a little fun, or 'undeclared' voters who think of themselves as Republicans but like John Kerry or one of the other candidates."

The pollsters also explained the seemingly invisible nature of exit polls.

"One of us has been voting since 1972 and has never seen a live exit poll interviewer either. In NH, exit poll interviewers were only at 40 randomly selected precincts, and talked to slightly under 2,000 voters. Even in a state as large as California, exit pollsters would only select from 20 - 50 sample precincts. The same laws of statistics operate here as in telephone polls - we talk to about 1,000 people to represent the country. And as long as it's done right, i.e. people are randomly selected, it works. Usually."[185]

Adam Clymer, political director of the National Annenberg Election Survey, explains the polling data in the first two contests: "I think our data showed the same surges for Kerry that other polls showed, but I think what happened there is not something our poll really reflects because we didn't have a great many respondents in Iowa and it is clear that Dean fell off in New Hampshire after losing in Iowa. Our data certainly shows that the New Hampshire voters certainly were paying attention to what happened in Iowa. Our data shows that a majority of people think that the war was worth while. That was down to about an even split in November after the helicopters were shot down, but since Bush's visit to Baghdad and the capture of Saddam Hussein there is not a huge, but a solid majority saying that the war in Iraq was worth while.

"There is no question that media coverage affects people's electoral opinions and candidates count on getting what they call favorable 'free media' - like the reports that boosted Kerry in New Hampshire after he won Iowa. They also worry about negative media - television especially - like Howard Dean's 'unpresidential' (as he put it) reaction to losing Iowa. When our polls showed that 4/5ths of the Democratic voters nationally said they didn't know enough about the candidates to make an informed choice, it was not because there isn't information - if anything there is a surfeit of information. Most people have other things to do with their lives than to check every Website every day."[186]

Al Sharpton was shut out in Greenland. Go figure.
I bet the exit poll predictions on him were dead on.

Kathy Sullivan's take on the NH results are "It was like the bride who shows up at the altar, and the groom comes in the door and says 'Hi' and then drives off in a limo."

Kristin Cooper Rainey relates her experience at the polls. "My husband, Paul, and I were scheduled to do poll checking at the Dover Town Hall for Primary Day. At around 9:30 am, a young man in his 20s approached me saying he was from the Dean campaign and that he was there to take my place. I told him that I would stay with him because we were supposed to have two people doing the poll checking, but he told me that he could do it and that he had been told to relieve me. I was uncertain because I didn't recognize him, but I was new to the campaign and didn't know all the people involved. So after showing him what to do, I left to go check on the situation with my husband who was doing visibility out front. By the time Paul got back upstairs, the young man was gone, and had taken our poll checking information with him.

Donald Mullen, the former Library Director of the Dover Public Library, was responsible for monitoring the door to the polling area. He said that the young man came in and sat down for a minute, and then asked for the men's room. Don pointed out the directions to the rest room, and the young man left. Don noticed that the man was going in the wrong direction, and called after him, but the young man took off down the stairs.

I did not realize anything had gone wrong for quite a while. I came back upstairs about an hour later and Paul told me what had happened. I was shocked and furious. I contacted my area leader and headed down the block to Dean headquarters. I was asked to speak with the lawyer at the Dean office in Manchester, and it was suggested that I walk around with some larger members of the campaign to see if I could recognize the man who had taken our information. I did not do that, but I had stopped in to one of the neighboring campaign offices myself to see if I could find the young man. I also spoke with some Detectives on the Dover Police Force, but did not hear back from them after the initial interview.

Upon thinking back over the morning's events, I recalled another man in his young 30s asking me about the poll checking. I spoke with him briefly and then he went out and was talking to someone on his cell phone. I wondered afterwards if there was some connection.

After the lists were stolen, we heard that the people who took them were calling the potential voters and disseminating incorrect information about voting times and locations.

I am new to the world of politics and got involved because Howard Dean was such an amazing candidate. This incident showed me how naïve I was in the political world, and it was terribly disappointing to realize what other campaigns would do to succeed.

There was difficulty with the entire poll checking situation. We were unable to hear many of the names of the people coming in to vote and it was very frustrating. The town clerk said she was required to provide a space for observers, but she was not obligated to provide a space close enough that we could hear, so our results were inconsistent."

Trevor Haskell's experience working for the Dean campaign was educational. "It was really impressive. There's so much that happens in terms of political science in school…you know there's this idea that the candidate is out there simplifying their message. Reading complex policies and then breaking them down for the voters. And I think that one thing (about) going to NH was realizing that these people not only know what's going on, but they've been volunteering in campaigns for some time and met every presidential candidate on both sides… you're constantly hit over the head that this is a unique place. Something is happening here which is different."

Portents, Premonitions, and Potpourri for $50 million, Alex

–A man's true wealth hereafter is the good he does in this world to his fellow man.

—*Mohammed*

Campaign finance reform has been a goal of various insurgents and progressives for decades. The 2004 election would be impacted by the McCain-Feingold legislation in many ways. Most commonly cited was the doubling of the allowable individual donation in the primaries from $1,000 to $2,000. The potential implications of that were huge. Gore and Bradley had raised two-thirds of their money from contributions of $1000 or more in 2000.

Since many of the 2004 Democrats were reliant on big donors early in the primary season, this meant the amount that could be raised in a fat cat fundraiser was potentially doubled. For those candidates inclined to put all of their "begs in one ask-it"[187], what was supposed to be reform actually meant greater fundraising efficiency. Furthermore, the host of a fundraiser could spend up to $4,000 on food and decorations without it counting as a political donation.

Dean's internet success flew in the face of the big donor windfall, employing a "Big Lots" strategy that raised only 22% of his money in checks of $1,000 or more.[188] Dean's stump speech relentlessly extolled an average donation of $77 dollars per donor. When things were unraveling after New Hampshire, however, Roy Neel held a 40 minute conference call with 100 of Dean's biggest donors, assuring them that staff cuts would be one way to reduce heavy spending.

Of course, donating to a candidate can be done strategically. Hollywood people often gave amounts to all of the major Democratic candidates for the presidency in 2003, hedging their bets against Bush while the field winnowed. The *New York Times* ethicist, Randy Cohen, responded to a question from Republican R.Rothchild of New York about whether it was ethical to donate to the Democrat deemed more beatable. Being a columnist, Cohen had the latitude to snarkily respond that "Were you to reveal to, for example, Howard Dean, your real motive for donating to his campaign, I've every confidence he would still cash your check."[189]

Preliminary estimates of the cost of the drive to the White House predicted a 2003 bill of $15 million per aspirant. (Road conditions weren't quite as perfect as in the test lab, it would turn out.) Dean seemed unaware of that reality early on, when he interviewed Stephanie Schriock for the position of fundraising director. Dean's most expensive re-election campaign had cost one million dollars. Schriock asked Dean in 2002 how much he hoped to raise. Dean probably thought he was setting the bar high when he responded with $10 million.[190] Schriock had responded confidently that raising that little would guarantee a loss, and she was hired on the spot.

Howard Dean's fundraising set records for the Democratic Party, but winning in the money primary wasn't the guarantee of success some envisioned. James Carville had told potential candidate Bob Graham that having the most money in the bank on January 1 guaranteed election.[191]

In Texas, all things are supposed to be super-sized, but the campaigns of John Connally in 1980, and Phil Gramm in 1996, had been contraindications to any Scrooge McDuck political domination theory.

Howard Dean's legendary tight-fistedness was evident early in the campaign, before the money train pulled into Burlington. In December of 2002, Al Gore appeared on *Saturday Night Live* in what was assumed to be a coming-out party for a 2004 run. He followed that with an appearance on *Sixty Minutes* in which he announced he would remain on the sidelines. This meant that staffers who had worked for Gore in 2000 were now coveted free agents. Jano Cabrera talked with Dean by phone about becoming his press secretary, but Dean was nervous about the cost of taking on extra staff, and said he would wait a few months before hiring a spokesperson.[192]

Six months later, at the opening debate in South Carolina, John Kerry had two media consultants, two pollsters, and a horde of press aides. While the numbers would indicate a successful breeding program, the quality of the breeding stock was of paramount importance. Cabrera also talked with Edwards, but ended up with Joe Lieberman. In September 2002, Dean had rejected as "opportunistic" a veteran political operative when the job seeker revealed that he was being sought by the Edwards camp.

Dean's hiring practices were reflected further in his first campaign manager, Rick Ridder. Dean chose the veteran of the Hart and Bradley campaigns in October 2002, having met Ridder while campaigning in Colorado in July of that year. Dean tended to reject Beltway consultants as mercenary, because of the treatment he had received as a client in low budget re-election campaigns in Vermont. His loyalty to the Virginia media firm of Trippi, Squier and McMahon was an exception. When Ridder was shown the door, apparently followed by Kate O'Connor's boot, Joe Trippi would begin his historic role as campaign manager. Cost, past history, and serendipity, rather than personnel planning, tended to determine the players on Dean's Field of Dreams.

Ridder had been prone to caution Dean against creating lasting enmities by attacking the party establishment. Trippi, on the other hand, seemed a perfect messenger for the Dean spleen. Trippi had worked in the Jerry Brown candidacy that tormented Clinton until June of 1992. If Dean was going to scorch the earth, he had found an arsonist.

Courtney O'Donnell had become the seventh paid employee in December 2002 when she presented Ridder with a set of charts that got her the job of deputy communications director, after a few days of volunteering. In February 2003, Matt Gross was hired as director of internet communications for the campaign. Karen Hicks became director of the effort in New Hampshire when Ridder hired her early in 2003. She had worked in Shaheen's failed 2002 Senate bid, and talked with the Kerry, Edwards, and Gephardt campaigns about a post in the Granite State. Hicks had ruled out Lieberman, since he had her arrested in 1993 when she was part of a group of Naderites protesting Lieberman's glacial efforts on health care reform. The Dean camp had been skeptical about hiring someone who had never run a statewide race.

Hicks was equally concerned about Dean's shoot from-the-hip style that perforated the traditions of message discipline. Still, she signed on. In April of 2003, Dean had looked askance at the Cadillac rented at a bargain rate to take him and all of his aides back to Vermont after a late night fundraiser in the Big Apple. Only when told that the day had produced a total in five digits did he shoehorn himself into the car.

One month earlier, the campaign had sent 30,000 supporters a faux "wish you were here in Vermont on vacation" greeting, asking for help in meeting the campaign's goal for the March 30 FEC reporting deadline. The missive asked for $83,000 and yielded more than $400,000 over five days on the Internet.[193]

By the end of January, the Dean campaign finances would seem like the Bay of Fundy. Kerry's campaign spending had narrowed a gap with Dean, as his actual performance in the polling places had eclipsed Dean. (Figures 16 - 24, pages 327-339)

The Dean campaign had a media spokesperson in the caucus state of Maine, and the campaign sent out two expensive mailings weeks preceding the caucus there on February 8th. Metal campaign buttons rained down on Iowa, as his opponents used less expensive paper stickers. The Dean payroll at the end of 2003 had numbered almost 500, double that of his competitors. In a meal fraught with symbolism, the late night charter flight for staff and reporters dined on lobster and shrimp as they fled the Iowa scream.

An analysis of the January 31 Federal Election Commission (FEC) filings indicates differences in spending priorities between the Kerry and Dean campaigns. With resources and time, money could have slowed the momentum that Kerry rode from Iowa. But the front-loaded primary schedule of 2004 had greatly reduced the time to reflect, recover, and rally. By the time the Granite State primary was over, it would turn out that the Dean campaign money was nearly gone.

If you called the Dean headquarters in mid-February, the music you heard when you were put on hold was martial marching music. It was music for a conquering army. History doesn't record what music was played at Waterloo, or Appomattox, or Dunkirk. A more appropriate selection might have been the Beatles song from Dean's and Kerry's youth: "Money can't buy me love".

A request from Dean to supporters over the Internet on February 5th had sought donations for advertising in Wisconsin. The request, for $700,000, produced nearly twice that, as the campaign had raised its goal once the initial target was met. Yet the campaign actually spent only about a sixth of the amount on actual advertising. Dean spokesman Jay Carson was quoted as saying that the campaign had a lot of field expenses, and traveled more than anyone else. Unfortunately, the delegates the spending produced were vastly fewer and costlier than those of Kerry. (Figure 25, pages 327-339)

When discussing the financing campaigns, **Carol Darr** provides an interesting perspective. She explains that she **"...**was a campaign finance lawyer for a long time and ended up feeling like a piano player in a whorehouse. I saw up close the corrosive effect of dirty money and felt like I was effectuating a corrupt system."

Putting up "bats" was an online fundraising strategy employed by the Dean campaign. **Aaron Strauss** says "(In) the third quarter fundraising, there was this huge push to get 50 million dollars.... people were encouraged to give and to get other people to give. So, online you can put up a bat ...so the last day of the fundraising quarter I decided to put up a bat ... (for) $400 and I started to call people and raise money and pretty soon I burst through $400... by the end of the night I had raised $1600 by asking all these people to give."

LET'S DO IT THE
OLD FASHIONED WAY

Impatience of study is the mental disease of the present generation.
—*Samuel Johnson*

The third stage in the nominating process identified by Rhodes Cook in 1988 occurs when a candidate who has triumphed, through the battle plan Hamilton Jordan created for Carter in 1972, breaks away from the pack in the now heavily front-loaded primaries that follow closely behind New Hampshire. Kerry seemed poised to do just that.

Kevin Landrigan observed that "The problem Dean had was Kerry got a much bigger bounce out of his win in Iowa than anyone could have expected."[194] Peter Canellos mused that "...in the polls and the reactions on the stump, Dean started turning things around about Thursday and rescued a second-place finish. But will voters in other states have the opportunity to see the new Dean? Or will their only impression of him be the Iowa film clip?

"In polls, voters have been very comfortable with Dean's stands on the issues and his overall persona, but the 'temperament issue' has become a millstone for him. And, to some extent, people were concerned about his temperament because they wanted to see whether his antiwar stance was a matter of judgment or reflexive antiwar sentiment. In other words, they wanted to know if he were a policymaker or a protester. The Iowa speech made him seem like more of a protester."[195]

Terry McAuliffe had been urging that losing candidates drop out, and in his public pronouncements, he spoke as if Kerry was already selected. In May, McAuliffe told Walter Shapiro that he had said to Sharpton to energize the base, but get out by March 10, if he wasn't the nominee. Ten months earlier, he had met with Dean when Dean indicated that he would fight to the finish, like Jerry Brown in 1976. McAuliffe said, "You will get out, Howard. This isn't about you. It's about beating George Bush."

Dean, whose capacity for bull-headedness has been noted, saw a red cape before his eyes. He told Walter Shapiro two months later, "Sometimes you nominate somebody because he's the favorite…and then you have buyer's remorse. If I don't win, I'm likely to be the Frank Church and Jerry Brown of 2004. I just wanted to give Terry fair notice that this was what was going to happen."[196]

Shapiro's faith in Dean was shaken when he learned that the candidate denied having had such a conversation with McAuliffe while appearing on Larry King, the month before telling him about his "fair notice".

"The DNC wants a nominee chosen early, to avoid any self-inflicted wounds," observed Peter Canellos. "Having a contentious race (had) put the Democrats in the news in a way that they weren't in Washington, where they controlled neither the White House nor either house of Congress.[197]

But McAuliffe was willing to give up that spotlight, for fear of a candidate getting retinal burns that would make the path to election harder to see. "New Democrats" were often under whelmed in their enthusiasm for the front-runner. "Every new Democrat I know is saying 'Dated Dean. Married Kerry…woke up with Bush.' This prompted the question "Did people go for Kerry with their hearts or minds?"

There were exceptions, however. A Washington, D.C. resident who had donated to Dean flew up to Manchester to work the polls for Kerry, after his parents said they feared Dean. "They're comfortable with Kerry. Personally, I'm slightly to the left of Marx, and I'm fine with Kerry. When Howard gets his silver star, we'll go with him."[198]

Kevin Landrigan of the *Nashua Telegraph* wrote that "Most of those voters who went from Dean to Kerry did so with their minds rather than their hearts. Kerry pounded home the argument that Dean's lack of foreign policy and military experience would make him a liability. Of course, former Arkansas Governor Bill Clinton also had neither before becoming President in 1992. Kerry probably could not have won both states without it or he would not have mortgaged his Boston home to generate $6.4 million in cash. Howard Dean learned it only takes one bad-sounding sound byte to change the course of a campaign. In the final analysis, those who loved

Howard Dean the most voted for him, since he doubled poll performance during the last week."[199]

For Edwards and Clark, their hopes lay in the South. Professor Larry Sabato of the University of Virginia has been described by the *Washington Post* as the "Mark McGuire of political analysts." Given one of the new distracters Bush incorporated in his State of the Union speech, this might mean he would be getting tested for steroids soon.

Sabato saw a bleak road ahead for the Democrats. "The only way any of these Democratic candidates will win in November is if the economy is going south and/or Iraq is looking like Vietnam, without the jungle. You may be correct that a more moderate Democrat not tied to Washington would have a better chance, but frankly in this group of Democratic contenders, there just isn't an ideal choice for the Democratic Party. The Democratic nominee, while appearing upbeat and chipper, will have to secretly hope for continued turmoil and disaster. If Edwards ends up fading from the race, he will mainly have Howard Dean and his scream to blame. The now infamous rant—which was greatly overplayed by the press— absorbed the media attention that should by rights have gone to Edwards for his stunning close second place finish in Iowa."

Sabato continues: "Timing is everything in sex and politics, and Kerry's timing has been impeccable. He lost the frontrunner's title before there was too much scrutiny, and he regained it at such a late date that the media are all busy covering the actual primary elections, rather than doing investigative stories. I do not believe that media bias has anything to do with the lack of scrutiny of John Kerry. And I say this as someone who believes that there is a great deal of bias - both left-wing and even some right-wing - in the news media. This is a product of timing, pure and simple.

"As I mentioned earlier, Kerry burst back onto the stage as a winner at exactly the right moment. The resources of the media are completely absorbed in covering the ridiculously frontloaded primary schedule. Don't be concerned: should Kerry lock up the nomination, the press will return to the task it does very well in modern times - a proctoscopic examination of the Democratic nominee.

"Let me also add that the press has been very tough on Howard Dean. The overuse of the 'I Have a Scream' speech was terribly unfair. At the same time, life is unfair and politics is the least fair part of life. It also doesn't help Dean that many members of the national media have a genuine dislike of Dean's personality. Everyone thinks the media are liberal, and in many ways they are, but they are also status quo sticks-in-the-mud. They worship convention and traditions, like Iowa, New Hampshire and South Carolina. There's a gigantic east-coast bias in the establishment media.

"Clark was just a place-holder for the anti-Dean vote. Once two other strong anti-Dean candidates emerged from Iowa, part of the rational for Clark's candidacy disappeared. Plus, Edwards and Kerry actually have political experience, and they have real Democratic pedigrees."[200]

Dean would shift strategies as he shifted key personnel. As Washington, then Michigan, then Wisconsin, came into focus as unattainable goals, the campaign would continue to aim for an unreachable horizon. The goal was purportedly delegates, not just victories.

As Kerry pulled further ahead in the delegate count, victory itself seemed ever more unobtainable. A day of reckoning lay ahead, and some members of the Dean campaign arrived there before the governor himself.

Although the statewide results in New Hampshire ended up with Dean losing to Kerry by only 12 percent, it was widely played in the media as if Dean was now toast, whereas they had once toasted him as front-runner.

Robert G. Kaiser hadn't pronounced last rites, however. "If Dean can win two or three states next week, he'll be in the race."[201] However, the portrayals of Dean as an "angry man" had been given life by the media coverage of his speech in Iowa. After New Hampshire, with Kerry in the front-runner's seat, those portrayals seemed to limit Dean's strategy. Dean, who has the most to gain by attacking, is stuck atoning for his Iowa speech, and risks looking mean if he goes after Kerry."[202]

Dean also became much less accessible to the media, as Dean Nation became more frenzied in seeing him as the victim of a media lynching. While the broad play his misstatements and missteps had received had crippled the campaign, limiting media access for that coverage seemed like a self-serving rationalization.

Having lost Greenland, it was discouraging to lose the state, but it still was clearly a comeback from the third place in Iowa, and the media assault that the Iowa scream had produced. However, worse was to come in the next days.

It was revealed that a campaign that had set Democratic Party records for fundraising, and which had been expending at a lower "burn rate" than the other candidates at the last formal reporting, was now low on money. Where had the money gone, and who was responsible? Perhaps the culprit was Joe Trippi, who had been portrayed as the eccentric but innovative genius of what kept defining itself as a campaign different from anything that had preceded it. Virtually overnight, Trippi was told that Roy Neel would come in to head the campaign. Roy Neel - Al Gore's friend - who had been Gore's campaign manager. Roy Neel, who was described as a *lobbyist*!

Trippi, who supposedly had been calling the shots, resigned, unwilling to stay on as an advisor. Although the media reported his departure as emotional and angry, he would later describe it as "serene."[203] Trippi, who had held the keys to the Internet, was gone.

UCLA Professor **John Zaller** has studied insurgents and says "Dean's use of the Internet weakened insider control, perhaps in a permanent way." But Trippi, the king of the bloggers, was gone. Of course, he didn't disappear for long. Seeming like a hustler, he appeared as an analyst on MSNBC within days. He was on the Don Imus show, which was like Nixon appearing at a legal fundraiser for Daniel Ellsberg.

Trippi's analysis of the campaign's collapse was one that many would share. "You have a party that's tried to make every rule that it can to stop an insurgent. But at the same time - it's not Al Gore's endorsement - what I'm saying is, him endorsing us was a good thing. But at the same time, the unintended consequence of it was that the second Al Gore endorsed Howard Dean, alarms went off in newsrooms and at every other campaign headquarters. At campaign headquarters, they all had meetings and said 'We've got to stop Howard Dean right this second.' That's what the Al Gore endorsement meant. It meant, 'We've got to kill this guy or he's going to be the nominee'."[204]

Trippi's leap from grace was aided by reports that his firm had gotten a huge cut of all the ads for the Dean campaign. I knew that Nancy Beach and Brian Vawter's colossal effort to produce house meeting videos for the campaign anytime Karen Hicks called was earning them nothing.

That made it even less palatable to find out that all the less-than-outstanding Dean ads we were bombarded with in New Hampshire had been putting money in Trippi's pocket. We had grown weary of seeing 5 or 6 Dean ads during prime news time on the main New Hampshire station, WMUR-TV. I understood the idea of ad saturation, but they were so far beyond that as to rival the effect of automated phone calls from Jeanne Shaheen.

Trippi would later defend his role in advertising spending. "There was never a conflict of interest with me, because I never had check-writing authority for the campaign. I wanted that authority, but I never had it. The major media decisions were all made by a group of senior staff. There are three partners in our firm, and the $155,000 that I was paid I would have gotten whether I was golfing or I went sleepless for the entire year or working until 4 in the morning, busting my rear because I believe in Howard Dean."[205] It was even reported that Trippi was held responsible for the Iowa Scream, having whispered a line from a Janis Joplin song to Dean as he headed to the stage: "Freedom is just another word for nothing left to lose."

At that point, I was prepared to see a grainy photo of Trippi on the grassy knoll in Dealey Plaza. Still, as *Washington Post* reporter Jon Finer says, "by the time Trippi left, was anyone controlling the campaign?"

Steve Grossman was cast as receiving a larger role in the vacuum created by Trippi's departure. Grossman had said on the phone to me the weekend before the primary "see you at the celebration in Manchester." I had asked around for him that night, but while he was reported to be in the building, no one knew where. Perhaps he was sequestered in Elvis' dressing room.

Over the next few weeks, Grossman would be quoted much more often in the media. However, his quotes began to look like an exit strategy as Wisconsin approached. If not an exit for Dean, who kept saying he was in a delegate race, then an exit for him, as he said Dean needed to have some primary victories. At the Maine caucuses, Grossman spoke with a friend and indicated he was ready to jump to the Kerry PT boat if Dean's Titanic kept taking on water.

My communications with Manchester had been poor; Grossman's with Dean seemed just as bad, and that was of somewhat more importance to the Governor. At least there should be a clear vision of how the deck chairs were to be rearranged. I took several of the Portsmouth staffers to lunch on the day after the primary. The general tenor was rather like the Last Supper, although their savior was in Burlington strategizing.

The next day, Jim Bentley, the intern from Bennington College who had been living in our house, came home in something like a state of shock. Everyone in the office had been told they were not going to be paid any longer. Megan called Lizzie in tears, Aswini was apparently devastated, and Ben was reported to be headed back home. It seemed like the kids had become the scapegoats on the local level.

The newly-revealed money troubles caused a temporary suspension in salaries. What I had been telling people for months was a national campaign, with a battle plan through June, was suddenly preparing to make a final stand in Wisconsin.

Or not.

Dean changed course on Wisconsin as a make-or-break primary, even as the campaign sent out e-mail asking supporters for more money to be used for ads there. Despite the inconsistent messages from Dean and the campaign, money still poured in, even including our first actual cash donation.

Polls for Wisconsin looked bleak, as Grossman publicly said he would leave the campaign to work for Kerry if Dean did not win Wisconsin. While the impact of that statement may not have been enough to make it a self-fulfilling prophecy, it did result in Grossman's leaving the Dean campaign, even before the Wisconsin primary. Which, of course, Dean lost. Where Trippi's departure had saddened Deaniacs, e-mails about Grossman's departure went so far as to portray him as a Trojan Horse for the Kerry campaign.

Once the Wisconsin primary was over, it was revealed that less than half of the money raised for Wisconsin advertising had actually been used that way. At least when I bought pens, or took staff out to lunch, I knew where my money went.

So many changes had occurred in the top campaign staff since Dean's Odyssey began, and so much money had hemorrhaged out. Dean was now a rider who had changed horses in mid-stream several times, changed saddles as he went from a national to a three-state campaign, and not even clearly held the reins on spending at the end.

George W. Bush, despite his privileged upbringing, was regularly portrayed as a cowboy. Maybe a politician needed a cowboy's skills to get a horse from shore to shore.

The doctor was out. And it looked like he, or his campaign, with some nursing from the media, was guilty of malpractice that would be forever etched in American political history.

WHATALONGSTRANGETRIPPIT'SBEEN.ORG

The electric age ... established a global network that has much the character of our central nervous system.
> MARSHALL McLUHAN, Understanding Media

Joe Trippi is Mercury.

In 2003, he rose to mythological status in American politics. Trippi was the winged messenger of the wired world. He seemed to speak the Esperanto of the Internet, bringing that medium's demographics to the Dean campaign. Like the advocates of Esperanto, the Dean advocates he enlisted were fervent and loyal- sometimes to him as much as the candidate. Personally, he is more the element than the myth.

Rarely found uncombined in nature because of its instability, Mercury beguiles because it offers back a reflection of the viewer. Yet it is unlike other metals, in that it requires a vessel to provide it with form. Extremely dense for such an amorphous substance, its own attraction for itself makes it come back together when it is separated into smaller parts.

Mercury's reactivity makes it potentially lethal. When it is spilled, it creates a toxic environment in the room that makes cleanup colossally expensive. Its toxicity wasn't recognized for a long time, as its allure and utility caused the pathology to be overlooked. In the hat-making industry, workers would rub the felt with their bare hands, to make the hats more stylish and attractive. Mercury acts by tying up the hemoglobin in blood, thus depriving the brain of oxygen. The effect over a lengthy period of exposure makes the victim appear to be mad.

Mad as a hatter.

Joe Trippi was a featured speaker at the Politics Online Conference in March of 2004. The messiah of the new medium, and new message, was to speak, along with the person who might have been Trippi's opposite by that point: George W. Bush's campaign manager, Ken Mehlman.

Despite the spotlight C-SPAN offered by televising the luncheon, Trippi had been slow in confirming for the Institute for Politics and Democracy at George Washington University that he would participate. When he did show up, the opening plenary session had already occurred, and the halls were lightly populated by the few attendees who weren't in the first session of panel presentations. Still, as he was led toward a panel featuring former *Dean for America* Webmaster Nicco Mele, those who didn't come up to greet him turned toward him, affording him rock star recognition.

Trippi was there to recruit Mele and Mathew Gross to join him in the *Change for America* movement he had started on the day when he decided not to accept demotion in the *Dean for America* campaign. Part of the power of Trippi is the same as that of the Internet: validation. When you meet him and tell him that you worked as a volunteer, his acknowledgment that he had read things that you had written bathes you in reflected light.

When you consider further that he probably considers you one of an army of bloggers that you never joined, it makes you more suspicious. Being in his presence is a sensory experience. Part of that is his seemingly constant state of distraction, as his mind races and his eyes dart about. The disheveled appearance that belies a clear reluctance to shave had been evident on the CNN special "True Believers", which aired shortly before the conference.

The sensory experience is heightened by a factor that cannot be captured by television.

It was said that as a young NBA star in the Seventies, Bill Walton took showers, but didn't really lean into them. For Trippi, his appearance on March 19th seemed to support similar conclusions, although his diabetes may have been a factor in knowing that he had arrived before you saw or heard him.

After Nicco's presentation, Trippi greeted him effusively. He told Mele about his appearance on an academic panel a few weeks earlier. When a questioner asked Trippi to give yes or no answers to questions, Trippi had taunted him by doing just that, and then refusing to elaborate further than one-word answers. He laughs with the conspiratorial glee of a kid, at his own description of the experience.

He's not able to set up an interview time with me then, as his distraction seems paramount. After the luncheon, he says he needs to leave, but asks if I will be around the area for the next week. Told that this was a one-day trip, he says he will come to New Hampshire for an interview. This offer leaves me almost speechless, although I quickly realize that it is hard to imagine he will remember this promise, much less follow through on it.

Repeated inquiries to the e-mail address he had provided result in no response. Like the arc of the Dean campaign itself, Trippi had passed through the interviewer's life.

Politics is not professional wrestling. In professional wrestling, a manager sometimes shares the limelight with the star. But professional wrestling has savage verbal abuse, an audience presumed to be simpletons, spectacles staged for the benefit of television, pre-determined outcomes.

Okay, so maybe that wasn't the perfect example for drawing a contrast. Trippi now sees the Dean campaign as a "dot-com miracle, not a dot-com bust." He doesn't feel that the questions raised about his role in the ad campaign are valid. Trippi also never accepted that he was responsible for what Walter Shapiro called "fiscal mismanagement", claiming that he never had such authority.

Joe Trippi's role in the Dean campaign may be illustrative of the difference between strategic and tactical thinking. Given that the Dean campaign rose in opposition to George W. Bush's complete absence of strategic thinking in both counter-terrorism and Iraq, the disconnect Trippi's management style represented for Howard Dean is no small irony.

Trippi was capable of great and entrancing strategic vision. One merely has to listen to Nicco Mele's description of the awe (although not necessarily shock) that swept through the Burlington office in the summer of 2003, when Trippi laid out a strategic internet vision before assembled staffers. Trippi became a messiah to young people like Mele, as the parts of his strategic plan produced record-breaking results.

However, the Internet, by itself, does not equal an entire campaign strategy. Trippi reports his discomfort at Dean's early and eloquent focus on economics and the Iraq war. That song of one or two notes wouldn't be adequate either. A strategy of just Iowa and New Hampshire, or a national strategy that spread resources unwisely or too far, or a vision that shifted between the two reactively or unreflectively, may well have doomed the Dean campaign. Trippi's successes may have made him seem to be a great strategic thinker in the eyes of Howard Dean.

Dean hadn't run for national office before, and had only run one seriously contested race in his political career. Important insights can be gained from losing. For example, Dean describes Clinton as a once-in-a-generation politician for the Democratic Party. Clinton's strategy may have been informed, and his political persona modified, by getting his ass handed to him in a gubernatorial race in Arkansas. Losing tends to test strategy. The ability to be reactive, as well as proactive, defines the strategic capability of a campaign.

The Clinton Rapid Response war room, which included George Stephanopoulos, and elevated James Carville to his current mythic status, proved to be the political equivalent of a successful Strategic Defense Initiative (which isn't technologically possible, by the way).

When it was riding high, the Dean campaign seemed to be guided by a strategic and tactical genius. Anyone working in the offices in Burlington, or Manchester, or Des Moines, had to believe that Trippi had found a new magic, as 2003 headed toward the fourth quarter. The chaos around them, reflected in the unclear command structure, the physical disorder, the shifting and expanding personnel, the tension between the Vermont people and the "outsiders"; these seemed like trappings that might have merely indicated the traditional entropy of campaigns.

But this was a campaign that was defining itself as unlike any before it. The problem was these indicators were also predictors of the campaign's inability to respond strategically to adversity. When things were going well, it didn't matter that the office was a sty, or that Trippi shared an office with Kate O'Connor that had tape on the floor to mark off territory, or that Trippi would have shouting matches with Zephyr Teachout. Relationships are either tempered by adversity, or they collapse.

Trippi's personality engineered a campaign like the Tacoma Narrows Bridge. When that bridge was built in 1940, it was a magnificent technological accomplishment. Unfortunately, the engineers didn't anticipate what effect winds would have on it. Certainly the testing of

215

engineering models wasn't as advanced then as it is now. Because the solid construction of the bridge deck resisted the passage of winds, the bridge would sway when wind came along; bridges and buildings do that anyhow. What the engineers didn't foresee was that the bridge had built into it a natural frequency, which would cause it to resonate in high winds, and then, over a fairly short period of time, tear itself apart.

Because the bridge gyrated dramatically from the date of its completion, the death throes of the bridge four months later are well recorded on film. The winds that brought the end weren't even that high - just 42 miles an hour. Cars were left abandoned on the bridge, but there was enough time that a man even walked out onto the bucking span, perhaps out of curiosity, but perhaps as a scientific observer.

When you watch the bridge finally tear apart, it is breathtaking. You go back and rewind it, over and over again. The film was, at one point, the most requested segment on an old TV show called *You Asked For It*. I never showed the film to my science classes but that they demanded to see it again. And again. And again.

I used to take first dates to the physics library at UNH, where I'd show them the film loop of the collapse. If they didn't show any interest, I knew that we weren't going to be very compatible.

The collapse produced a whole new field of study called bridge aerodynamics. A newer theory would evolve that the bridge's response to stimuli had ultimately caused it to destroy itself, in a process called self-excitation. Innovation, whether in architecture or politics, can advance our understanding of underlying processes to improve outcome.

Sometimes that understanding can only be clear in the wake of a collapse.

When everything was going well for the Dean campaign, Joe Trippi was portrayed as the engineer. A relentless promoter of both himself and the campaign, his eccentricity made him the most colorful figure in a campaign for a candidate who valued normalcy and privacy.

People who encounter Trippi almost always use the word genius. Usually that word is accompanied by a description of the kind of eccentricities that our culture tends to indulge in genius. Those characteristics in Trippi may have insidiously undermined the campaign, at the same time that his genius led to successes.

It is telling that Trippi began to talk of leaving the campaign well before he was demoted. When things are spinning out of control, whether it is in the world around you, or your perceptions of it, you know something is wrong. If you can't put the brakes on either the circumstances or yourself, it is probably natural to look for an external agent to blame.

Trippi blames Dean. Trippi blames O'Connor. Trippi blames the media. Trippi blames the finance guys, and his purported inability to exercise control in that area. Trippi blames the campaign's hiring practices. Trippi never blames the grassroots, because they validated his internet strategy. His exultation of the grassroots gives him the power of anointment. Holding a mirror up to them through the Internet reflects upon him, and allows him to see his own reflection. The mirror-in-a-mirror effect creates a visual echo chamber. And a campaign loses its ability to see, and to hear, and eventually, all ability to react.

But Trippi never blames himself.

Andrew Smith describes how "Joe Trippi came up to the poker table with a big bag of chips. He put all the chips on the table, and said 'match this, fellows.' He was holding a pair of fours. That was the whole strategy. 'You win Iowa, you win New Hampshire, and then that's it.'

"In some ways that makes a certain amount of sense."

A Democratic Party activist commenting on the CNN special "True Believers" says, "I watched part of that documentary. Trippi was wired. It was about Trippi, the whole thing is about Trippi. I had never realized that he was Svengali, because to me, it's the candidate, and the people on the ground. Consultants aren't supposed to be out front like he was. I have been very off put by the way he immediately started doing TV. Michael Whouley (of the Kerry campaign)… people don't even know what Michael Whouley looks like. He's smart, and very good. Marybeth Cahill is, too, but these people aren't out front like Trippi was."

Mathew Gross says that, "Trippi loves the game. One of the things I remember was one time, during the summer, when he brought out that

217

movie, and said 'we gotta watch this, we gotta watch this'. … I was sitting there, I had to finish up an e-mail because a fundraising event was going on. So he sat down, and he set the TV up right next to my desk, and he and Nicco and Zephyr sat there and watched it.

"It was blaring, it was really loud, and I'm sitting there working on the e-mail. I think Joe was fairly mercurial, in a way (and)… As many people have said, he's not the best manager. There were very few people that Joe Trippi treated with a great deal of respect.

It was clear that he really liked people, and the people that he liked, he really liked.

I've sat around tables with women who were talking about how much they love Joe Trippi. He's like a little kid. Women act like mother hens toward him. He's got the big sad eyes, he's kind of a little chaos monster; he needs to be fed, he won't eat."

Gross describes the Trippi 'vision': "Joe believes he's the only guy that gets it. He'll repeat things, even if you understand and say 'ya, I got it.' He repeats it. It's partially an Italian thing. He'll go 'No, no, you don't get it. Here's what it is.' He would read the blog… and the worst thing was if he found something that we had missed. It was like we were idiots for having missed something. There was one time, when the Dean dance mix had been made. I hadn't heard it, but Zephyr had heard it, and Dave had heard it. They had listened to it once or twice, apparently, and sat on it for a couple of days. When Joe discovered that, and realized that people had been listening to it, and hadn't gotten it out there, and put it on the blog, he was just furious. Joe said 'We're running out…we don't have time!' This was… maybe the middle of April (2003)."

Gross continues that "We worked our butts off, we worked around the clock. We worked harder than any other campaign did, and it showed, and that's how we got out in front. On a simple level, it was just the human effort of everyone working their butts off.

"When Trippi left, he was crying. He came in and said 'I'm leaving'. Everybody went out to dinner with him, and then we went to this bar. Everybody just hung out. It was kind of celebratory…it was good."

A volunteer with close ties to Burlington, who spent some time there, says that "Joe is a lot of things, but he's not a manager. His inability to add the discipline necessary to get the campaign across the finish line is a significant contributing factor to a campaign imploding. Ultimately, the responsibility for that falls at Dean's feet. It was not a secret that there was this tension within the campaign. If staffers knew that that was the state of the campaign, then the Governor did, too.

"If he did and he didn't fix it, that's why the campaign failed. If he didn't know about it, and therefore, wasn't in a position to do anything about it, then that's why the campaign failed. But either way, it's his issue. If Joe should have been fired, he should have been fired in November.

"When Kerry fired Jim Jordan last Fall (2003), I said that 'if you can't manage your campaign, you absolutely can't expect to manage the country.'

"When you've got a campaign that is consumed with the negative attacks from Gephart, and everybody else for that matter, and the press, and is not articulating it's own message, when the majority of people are just starting to pay attention - the die hards had already made up their minds - but the people who are just starting to pay attention, all they're hearing is Dean and Gephart yelling."

It is unclear who made the decision to go after Gephart.

"You certainly have to imagine it's a combination of Trippi and Dean. Trippi certainly had some history with Gephart, but I have to imagine it's one or the both of them in concert. I do like that Dean took accountability for the strategy, and the spending by saying 'Look, Trippi was certainly part of many of those decisions, but ultimately it came down to me.'

"Joe could have stepped aside. Joe could have said 'You know, I've built the engine, somebody else has got to drive it the rest of the way'.

Jodi Wilgoren says that Trippi "was the consultant of the cycle. What was interesting about Joe was the media attention, but also grassroots attention. He was a cult figure for a small, narrow band of people. There were no other campaign managers in this cycle who signed autographs, headlined fundraisers, and worked rope lines. It really started in the public, before it got to the press. Joe was a pretty good quote machine, and he was always a good interview.

"But he didn't appear on his first Sunday talk show until December.

"He wasn't as much a media hound as he was a publicity hound."206

Richard Hoefer was unhappy with the campaign advertising: "The work product was crappy. It was amateurish, formulaic, stiff, a product of the 1970's. It had no imagination - it was totally incongruent with the innovation of the Dean campaign.

"I didn't know that there had been any affiliation with Steve MacMahon and Governor Dean. Once I knew that, this made sense. My first instinct was, 'What the hell is the campaign manager doing hiring his own firm?'

"I went to Iowa, specifically to seek testimonials. My intent was to try to get to get to Iowa the last week in December. Because *Dean for America* was so screwed up, nobody (in DFA) was interested. They would not help me do anything that was 'off program'. My goal was to shoot the stuff the last week in December, go home and edit it, and have it available in time to hit the last week in Iowa.

Hoefer continues: "I really am convinced that if had Trippi had organizational skills, had there not been a (fouled) up Iowa operation, had there not been a DLC hit put on Dean, had there not been Dean's candid, admirable response to FCC questions put to him by Chris Matthews about breaking up the conglomerates, he would be president.

"Trippi ...(fouled) up.

"Trippi was just clueless about what the campaign was about.

"He wanted to have some...(kind of) movement.

"He blew this guy's chance to be president."

Michael Silberman says that "I was in the field department and a lot of us were really focused on the grassroots organizing. We were in the lucky position to be in regular contact with some incredible organizers who were optimistic, positive, working their asses off for nothing all day long.

"Joe is certainly one of the most important influences for me in the areas that I worked in, which was trying to mobilize grassroots supporters into action. I remember distinctly my first five interactions with him, like where many other people were being yelled at, because he was frustrated at some sort of incompetence.

"I was fully willing to admit being pretty new to organizing. One of the positives he really brought was having a background as a field organizer from Iowa. Part of his personality that doesn't always shine through, and part of this whole internet story, is that he's an organizer.

"I remember walking into his office, and his asking me specifically about the number of events, or members. I gave him an estimate, and he said 'Don't ever walk into my office without knowing exactly how many new members, how many events, how many whatever.'

"In many ways it's a discipline mentality, which a lot of us grew to have."

Nicco Mele describes how the campaign made decisions that differed from traditional politics: "We ran participatory TV ads in Austin Texas, 100,000 dollars in Austin Texas, nine months before the Texas primary.

"These ads take Bush on, and say 'We're going to take this guy out, stand up to George Bush and you can really participate by going to *Dean for America*.com and signing up or by calling this 800 number.' We spent over $100,000 doing that. We put a bat up on the Internet. This bat's up for 6 or 7 days, because we need to raise a million dollars.

"A million dollars in traditional fundraising would require spending $350,000. On that million, the net would be $650,000. Our way was to put $100,000 up, and net $900,000. Now some guy out there says 'I can't believe they wasted all that money on early television.'

"They never understood what we were really doing. It wasn't early television. No one in their right mind would run $100,000 in Austin Texas nine months before the primary. That wasn't the point. So you have this disconnect, between the folks who are so enmeshed in the standard way to do things, and in what we were trying to do.

"That's how we raised the $50 million. There was method to the madness. I think it's going to be a wave of the future, and I think you're going to see more and more campaigns following our model."

William Finkel describes the genesis of the symbiosis of MeetUp and the Dean campaign: "In early January 2003, I launched topics for Dean, Edwards, and Kerry. I had been looking for topics that would appeal to people and I noticed that all three of them had online representation through blogs.

"Dean's was a little bit more vibrant, but all of them had people getting on board. So I started the topics, and I had reached out to the blogs, and reached out to the campaigns. Dean supporters snatched it right up, through a weblog called *myduediligence*. I had been trying to reach Trippi, and the person who ran that blog talked with Trippi on a fairly regular basis, and he put us in touch.

"Trippi liked the idea, so we met with him at the end of January (2003). While we were in that meeting, he called Sue Allen, and said 'Get a document ready for the Governor, saying that he wants to work with MeetUp.' By the end of the day we had a letter from the Governor, to all our 400 members, saying why MeetUp was important, and why he supported it.

"In the next two weeks we had a linkup on their site, and a month later he attended a Meetup in New York City. There were over 500 people there, with lines around the corner. He was just blown away.

"He said 'Oh, my god, the power of the Internet.

'I think this is going to work.'"

Gwen Graham got involved in the Dean campaign as a result of campaigning for her father. "Along the campaign trail Joe and I would run into each other. I was in Iowa speaking at a pancake breakfast, before the Iowa-Iowa State football game. I'm a Floridian and we take our football really, really seriously down here. Before a Florida-Florida State football game, you'd be lucky to get three people to turn out to anything.

"(Well) there was a huge crowd. It was a political pancake breakfast, there were about 300 people there. John Kerry was there, Joe Trippi was there, and I was there, and they had other surrogates who were speaking for the other candidates.

"I spoke right before Joe. Then I sat down and listened to Joe. (What Joe Trippi said)… really touched me, because it was obvious to me, and I've been in politics all my life, around it all my life, that this was a man to whom it was not just a job.

"As I listened to Joe, I was really touched with how genuinely he spoke and how much emotion he brought to the process. He started to cry. I'm a very empathetic person, and I also happen to be very tactile, so I went up to him afterwards. I gave him a hug, and I told him how much he had touched me, and how I really, really understood that if you don't feel it in your heart, you should probably find something else to do.

"This is so important for our country.

Dwight Morris says "I don't think that you can put Trippi in the same league as James Carville, in the sense that he (Trippi) lost. But you can in the sense of the person getting the press, and getting all the accolades. They set up a campaign that was the 'Gee Whiz' campaign. The press did not pay attention at all, in the beginning, to Howard Dean. The only time they started writing about him, they didn't write about his stands on the issues, they started writing about his internet fundraising, because that was new, and it was cool, and it was a new hook that they could jump on and that's what they began to write about.

Since Joe Trippi was, in large part, the architect of that concept, he was interviewed, and he became almost a media star himself.

"But he didn't win.

"If he had won, he would have absolutely been the next James Carville, and you would have seen him on every talk show, coast to coast."

Jon Finer says that "The real question was whether, by the time Trippi left, anybody was really controlling the campaign. So much of it was decentralized, so much of it was left to state and even substate groups, and all these Dean groups like Doctors for Dean.

All these groups are underneath the campaign umbrella, but not necessarily directly controlled by the campaign and they were making all these decisions.

"I think that's part of the reason why Trippi ended up leaving, or why Dean ended up bringing someone else in to supervise the organization. Dean felt that it had become too decentralized, too, and that nobody was really paying attention, was running the entire ship.

"Trippi is always portrayed, by Dean and others involved in the campaign, as sort of the overarching visionary, the man who came up with the broader strategy of using the Internet, attacking President Bush on core areas of his policy stances, and mobilizing this vast grassroots network.

"That's something that Trippi is credited with. His role in the campaign will be remembered by historians, and other people, for the success of that part."

John Mercurio comments that "Trippi is a pretty conventional consultant. He's worked with Dean throughout the 1990s on his gubernatorial races. He is sort of a Washington insider, inside the Beltway, to be heading up Dean's campaign. That pulls away the myth that Dean was this outsider."

Kathy Sullivan reflects that "At the end of the day, you can have the best organization in the world, but if you haven't gotten the voters convinced, it doesn't matter how good your organization is.

"I met Joe Trippi twice, and I know Trippi gets a lot of credit for everything, but I think you've got to give credit to the candidate, because it's the candidate who inspires everybody. It's the candidate who hires the people, and you got to give credit to the state directors for putting it all together on the ground."

Rick Klau says, "Matt Gross was running the Internet campaign. Matt reached out to me for help in converting the old blog, which was running on Blogger, to get it set up with the new application and get it up and running. So I was the guy who was, remotely, getting a lot of that stuff set up. Especially about something that's going to be public, the last thing to do is to be seen as taking credit for something that a lot of people deserve credit for.

"Trippi should take credit for knowing that it's (the blog) an important thing, and for empowering Matt to build it. Without Matt, I don't think it ever would have gotten off the ground."

Jodi Wilgoren observes that Trippi "… has a very close relationship with his assistant, who's a woman in her mid -twenties. Both his ex-wife, and his current wife, totally adore him. He has a great relationship with his ex-wife.

"He was very close with Tricia, and he's very close with Zephyr. He had both men and women working for him. Among his peers, among people he worked with 20 years ago, that was mostly guys, but that might not be his thing, it might be more that was the way it was.

"There were a lot of young women who idolized him, but there were a lot of young men who idolized him too."

A Staffer in Burlington says that, "Joe Trippi had different relationships with some females he was closer to in the office. Don't misread that, that he had inappropriate relationships, he had joking relationships with many people. He and Zephyr had more of a tense rapport, I thought. They just had natural shouting matches, based on what they believed to be the best decision as an organizing principle or what to do, should they send this e-mail, do we do this with MeetUp or not. That was part of their relationship."

Another perspective on this tension is evident in the following comment from a female campaign worker. "His relationship with Zephyr (Teachout) was that he was really going to put her in her place. He was nasty to Zephyr. Sexism exists in every environment. The Dean campaign was not different in that. I'd like to think that we were. I think that we did great in a lot of ways that we could role model for other campaigns how things should be and how good can come out of things. But, like any other scenario with women, we were not that great."

The staffer sums up Joe Trippi's office relationships this way: "Joe had very different relationships with different people in the office, and he's a jokester as well."

Hillary Hazan provides insight into Joe Trippi's complex nature: "He was a lot of different things to a lot of different people.

"I started off helping to write women's policy. He was really more of a field kind of presence and felt that was the place to start. I tend to be a more academic individual, so I gravitated toward policy. I didn't really have that much interaction with Trippi at all.

"Yet, when I left, I felt so much more attachment for him, even than I did Howard Dean, because he was our leader in the office. He had the vision.

"There were Trippi lovers and there were Trippi haters, there were

225

camps. Regardless of how you felt, when he left, our leader left. For me, that was difficult.

"Everyone said that Trippi was a field guy. They had the whole Iowa Storm. We had the Iowa storm hats, and the Iowa storm bracelets, every volunteer who went to Iowa, became an Iowa Stormer.

"If you go through the blogs, you get a sense of the kind of people who contribute to the blog. People with incredible amounts of energy, they're the people who gave us all of our money, and brought us as far as we went.

"We put this call out to people to come to Iowa.

"We sent them by the thousands, to every single door.

"So, Trippi's vision, with doing something like that, was incredible.

"I have to say, though, that if you put him in front of the camera, I was always really impressed with what he said. In the office, sometimes he was a completely different guy. He would kind of grumble and not be all that articulate at all. He had different ways of expressing himself, at different points, and with different people.

"I've never met another man like Trippi and I doubt I ever will.

"I just appreciated his vision that he was able to bring everyone.

"On the same side, I would jump at the chance to work with Howard Dean again, also."

Women were an integral part of the Dean campaign. **Hillary Hazan** provides the following insight about women in work environments:

"Research shows that… there's so little power for women, in general. (Then) in work environments, the little bit of power that women do get… the more likely they are to hoard that (power) from other women.

"Interestingly enough, women may end up becoming more controlling in the work environment than men do, because there's less power to go around… They become more concerned, perhaps rightfully so, about hanging on to the power that they have, because they know that the power for women is spread less often, and to a lesser extent."

Joe Miller says "I saw Joe Trippi in Hooksett, at a restaurant where they have a big room for gatherings. He had a PowerPoint slide show with the Key states. He had it all figured out. He said 'In Missouri, Ohio, West Virginia, the ball game will be over".

"I came out of that, I came home and told Betty, 'Boy does he have a campaign manager. This guy is sensational. They've had this all figured out for a year. This has all been plotted. The thing is going just the way they planned, and the thing is going to go right to the White House.'"

Michael Goodwin says that, "Trippi's ideology was not Howard Dean's ideology, necessarily. There were places where it conflicted and didn't match. So, all of a sudden, when Trippi left, it became apparent what pieces of the campaign were there because of Trippi.

"I think that Trippi and Dick (Goodwin) really saw eye to eye on a lot of political theory and ideas, much more so than the way the campaign was being run. I remember when Dick came up Joe said that he'd been using Dick's book, *Promises to Keep*, as sort of where he was getting all his ideas about the campaign from.

"Personally I like Joe. I think that his beliefs, and the amount of energy that he had, and the real passion that he had, was huge. While I know that there were a lot of people who felt that he made the office a very divisive place, and that he was bad for the campaign in a lot of ways, that can't cancel out all the incredible amount of energy that he brought to the campaign.

"I don't know if it would have been there otherwise.

"Obviously, he was incredibly busy all the time.

"But there wasn't the interaction one-on-one with people.

"It didn't seem like it was a big priority of his."

Howard Dean, upon Joe Trippi's departure from the campaign: "I am deeply grateful to Joe Trippi, who has decided to leave the campaign. Joe has made enormous contributions, not just to our campaign, but to American politics - revolutionizing the way in which people are brought into the democratic process, and helping hundreds of thousands of people to believe in political change again."

Howard Dean, on his relationship with Joe Trippi, on May 5, 2004: "I don't get into that stuff. The inside the campaign stuff, I've always felt, is private, and should be left inside the campaign. I think the finger-pointing and kiss-and-tell stuff is not something that helps in the long run, so I just haven't done any of it. I think Trippi made an incredibly valuable contribution to the campaign, but I'm not going to get into the who did what to who, and the like.

"It was never true that I was my own campaign manager. You can't run your own campaign. Maybe in the very earliest stages, when you only have three people working for us. It's too large an operation for anybody to be their own campaign manager."

All physicians need diagnostic skills. Dean's were not brought into play, at least not soon enough to save his campaign.

Meet Me in St. Louis, or Burlington, or Seattle, or Cyberspace

Any sufficiently advanced technology is indistinguishable from magic.

ARTHUR C. CLARKE, The Lost Worlds of 2001. *(Dutton)*

In the year when Al Gore had been unfairly accused of claiming to have invented the Internet, the political applications of the medium had first started to take form. By the 2004 caucuses and primaries, that form was beginning to come into focus. While it isn't the final frontier for politics, cyberspace certainly is the next frontier. The Internet is a petri dish of political empowerment. Petri dishes can produce penicillin, but they can also produce biohazards.

For the Dean campaign, Joe Trippi "tried every trick in the Internet book. Some of the ideas flopped, such as sending campaign messages to people's cell phones. Another idea that won't go down in history is Dean-TV, a 24-hour Internet broadcast of Howard Dean's television appearances."[207]

Zephyr Teachout, a former death penalty lawyer who was Director of Online Organizing for the Dean campaign, notes that the learning curve was extraordinary. The candidate web page, internet fund raising, blogging, MoveOn, and Meetups were all key stories in 2004. Their importance may be clearer in historical hindsight, but their impact will only increase with each election. Observers were already measuring the lessons of the Dean candidacy, and framing the future use of the Internet, before the general election race of 2004 even formally began.

While growth of Internet usage has slowed, there are signs that it might be a powerful indicator of the political climate. Research done by *Roper* and at the *Institute for Politics, Democracy, and the Internet* at George Washington University, describes a key role played in American society by individuals they term "influentials." Respondents who rate word of mouth as an important source for ideas and information leapt from 67 percent in 1977 to 93 percent in 2004. (Figure 6, pages 327-339)

Advertising and editorial content had fallen slightly over that period, so that in 2004 these information sources are considered as important only about half as often as word of mouth. In 2004, the Internet expedites and transmits word of mouth for many. The shift to word of mouth over a quarter of a century represents an increased self-reliance on the part of respondents. Self-reliant people are acting as their own filters, as they solicit opinions on topics from restaurants, to retirement, to investments.

Roper's research defines 21 million Americans as "influentials." This group represents the most active and trusted 10% of the public. Roper first identified such a group in the 1940s, and has included that group in Roper Reports since 1973.

The research also defines participation in 11 specific activities as common among influentials. This includes such things as attending meetings, writing or calling politicians, serving on committees or as an officer of a club or organization, and attending a rally or speech. (Figure 7, pages 327-339)

Most influentials are moderately or very interested in news and events and politics. Interest in technology, science, and history is greater among influentials than in the general public. (Figure 8, pages 327-339) They tend to hear about things ahead of others, have well-thought out ideas, and serve as network hubs for many other people. Their impact on others is most profound in the area of politics and government, often being asked their opinions in this area. (Figure 9, pages 327-339)

Between 2000 and 2003, there has been a shift in priorities in the general population and among influentials. Terrorism is now high on the list and the breakdown of the family has become a lower priority. (Figures 10 & 11, pages 327-339)

This group of influential individuals is available to databases using public information. Roper suggests that political campaigns should empower and respect individuals, provide them with input, focus on community and social networks in their effort to target influentials as a group.[208]

The saying that "everyone talks about the weather but nobody does anything about it" has bearing when we consider influentials vs. the general population. While many people talk about politics, the influentials actually do something about it, both through their participation, and through the weight and breadth of their impact on others.

Influentials can also be classified as Online Political Citizens (OPC's) more often than the general public. OPCs are defined as those who have visited a party or candidate site online in the last 2 or 3 months and taken proactive online political action - that is, donated, sent e-mail, blogged, or engaged in other online activity.[209] (Figure 12, pages 327-339) This group is also more actively donating both online and off than the general population.[210] (Figure 13, pages 327-339)

If a democracy reflects the voice of the people, word of mouth has begun to roar in the American political arena.

Traditional media hasn't yet lost, nor have they ignored the Internet challenge. Online newspapers have proliferated, as newsstands close across the country. Still, 54% of respondents to a survey had read only print media in the past week, while 20% became informed through a combination of old and new media. And additional 20% of respondents in this survey reported accessing neither old or new, and only 6% were totally reliant on the Internet.[211]

Trends create industries, although the dotcom bust has shown that the Internet isn't any more of a guarantee of success than opening a restaurant. *CompleteCampaigns.com* provides web tools to campaigns, PACs, and similar organizations. Their most successful clients utilize off-line contacts in conjunction with the Internet.

Direct voter contact is a source of e-mail addresses, and printed materials list campaign websites. Reminders of traditional events can then be communicated both through the website and by targeted e-mails.

Still, "behind every e-mail address is a real person; when campaigns treat them like real people, those addresses become more valuable to those campaigns."[212] Web logs, or blogs, became a place for cyber citizens to become real people. When Gary Hart contemplated resurrecting his presidential ambitions in 2002, he had made history by having the first interactive blog in a presidential campaign.

Joe Trippi learned about "concentric circle organizing" from Hart in the 1980s. "You drop a rock in the water and let the waves ripple out. It occurred to us that the Internet was concentric circle organizing on steroids."[213]

Internet culture is speedy, decentralized, non-hierarchical - even anarchical. That very nature empowers individuals and offers an avenue to political organizing that hadn't previously been on any roadmaps. As with any expedition, there are missteps and wrong turns.

MeetUp.com was also founded on the concept that internet users were real people, with a need for contact and community beyond the glow of the screen. MeetUp.com's growth makes it appear to be a path that will be trod for years to come.

Lee Rainie, director of the Pew Internet and American Life Project says "The Internet is a fantastic social and communication tool, but it doesn't yet give you the pleasure of a true face-to-face meeting. The most important social relationships need to be nurtured in the real world."[214]

The New York Times wrote that "after Richard M. Nixon faced John F. Kennedy in televised debates, people said television had changed campaigns forever. Forty-three years later, some people have begun saying the same thing about MeetUp.com."

One of the founders of MeetUp.com, Scott Heiferman had an epiphany as he waited in line for the opening night for The Fellowship of the Ring – seeing that the various elves and hobbits waiting around him had used the Internet to mobilize. Heiferman saw the Internet as a way to bring together communities of interest - Elvis fans, flashlight aficionados, Texas hockey fans, Chihuahua owners, any group that could get five or more together.

Harold Rheingold wrote "Smart Mobs: The Next Social Revolution." He says, "People want to connect, period, and it's an assumption with anyone who uses the Internet that you can find someone who shares (your) interest."[215]

The Dean campaign utilized Meetups far more successfully than Kerry or Clark, and the growth of the Dean campaign seemed symbiotic with that of MeetUp.com. (Figure 14, pages 327-339)

MeetUp.com provided the Internet organizing tool for like-minded people to meet in bookstores, restaurants, bars, and coffee shops. These businesses pay MeetUp.com to be included as a meeting site, hoping to draw business from the participants. MeetUp.com is "trying to harness the momentum it received from Howard Dean... Liberals embraced *MeetUp.com* first- primarily because the Democrats are having presidential primaries this cycle and the GOP is not - but the company is non-partisan."[216]

The steady growth in enrollments for Dean Meetups parallels the rise of his campaign. (Figure 15, pages 327-339) Even with the Dean campaign over, his supporters continue to gather in impressive numbers on the first Wednesday of every month. The community that was built around him has not scattered to the winds, and Dean's new organization, *Democracy for America*, will be able to continue to draw on their numbers. While people can withdraw their names from the list of Dean Meetup participants quite easily, thereby eliminating the continuing reminders of meetings, 163,395 people remained enrolled in April, almost two months after Dean's withdrawal from the race.

Wes Boyd founded *MoveOn* with his wife five years ago. Their tiny staff uses the Internet to channel thousands of small contributions - and individual ideas - into large, visible actions. On CBS News Sunday Morning, Boyd comments "We said 'We just need $35,000 to do an ad in the *New York Times*'... we sent out this e-mail, and put up the web link for giving money... within 48 hours, $400,000 came in. *MoveOn's* supporters also contribute money for full-page ads in newspapers, stage simultaneous anti-war vigils all over the world and create homemade television ads. And it's all through an average $35 donor, which is revolutionary..."[217]

Several hundred thousand people contacted CBS when the network refused to air a *MoveOn* ad during the Super Bowl.

MoveOn's organizing director, Zack Exley, helped the Dean campaign with internet fundraising, DFA's e-mail list, and increasing the interactivity of the Dean for America website. Exley, who would be hired by Kerry to direct online communications and organizing once the nomination was secured, had offered his services to other campaigns in 2003, but only Dean hired him.

Along with the *Media Fund* and *America Coming Together* (ACT), *MoveOn* represents a new entity under campaign finance, called a 527. Such groups are a conduit for "soft" political contributions, which cannot directly support a candidate, but are able to expend money for a cause, such as opposing a specific candidate. An organization such as this funded the ads in Iowa linking Dean to Bin Laden. Some reform organizations, such as the Campaign Legal Center and the Center for Responsive Politics, have been linked with Republicans who saw the 527's as unacceptable loopholes to campaign finance. The coalition opposing regulating 527's was equally broad, including the Sierra Club and the anti-tax Club for Growth.

One of the authors of campaign finance reform, John McCain, said, "Duh. They're engaged in partisan political activities, so, therefore, they should be regulated." However, regulation of 527's would eliminate the best chance Democrats have of leveling the playing field with the Bush money machine.

While there is a well documented history of dirty politics, there is also a gray area filled with merry pranksters. The Internet would prove a perfect arena for jibbers and jesters.

Long before the Internet, however, the king of political pranksters was a man who may have caused a prone-to-paranoia candidate to ultimately create Watergate.

When Nixon debated Kennedy, viewers on television thought the poorly made-up and sweaty Nixon had lost (although radio listeners felt Nixon had won). Dick Tuck, the aforementioned king, hired an elderly woman to rush out of the crowd and embrace Nixon when he got off his airplane, saying for the benefit of all observers, "Don't worry, son, you'll beat him next time."

On another occasion, Nixon was doing an old-fashioned railroad campaign tour. As Nixon stepped out onto the platform of the last car to begin his campaign speech, Tuck, dressed in a conductor's uniform, waved a lantern, at which point the engineer obediently pulled the train out of the station, to Nixon's chagrin.

The Internet requires no costumes and pranks can be pulled without getting out of your pajamas.

In 2003, a coordinated effort by many websites and bloggers drove the software of search engine giant Google to search its 4.3 billion pages for "miserable failure," and list Bush's official biography at *whitehouse.gov* as the first result. Bush supporters counterattacked, with a search for "great president" that would also link to the biography first.

The Bush-Cheney campaign took notice of the power of the Internet and began its typically well-funded effort to move into that arena. Bush's campaign website, *GeorgeWBush.com* provides a downloadable campaign poster, on which one could place a slogan of one's own choice. The Beltway blog *Wonkette.com* (which had pioneered the Herman Munster-Kerry conspiracy theory by referring to Kerry's "cadaverous hollow visage") posted one with the slogan "But not if you're gay!" appended to the patriotically-themed Bush poster. The editor of the site found through experimentation that the Bush campaign had shrewdly built in blocks to certain key words, including: lying, Hitler, Iraq, evil, prince of darkness, and most expletives. This only slightly reduced the dimensions of the English language, while simultaneously throwing down an irresistible gauntlet. New slogans posted on the Internet included: "Putting the Fun back into Fundamentalism" and "Read my lips. No new jobs." Showing questionable courage under fire, the Bush campaign beat a retreat, eliminating the personalized slogan option.

In April of 2004, law school student Ken Jacobsen, apparently tired of torts, led a movement so a search for "waffles" would link with *johnkerry.com*. The fervor of the reactionaries was not up to the standards of the progressives, as it had only taken five weeks to push "miserable failure" to the top of the charts, whereas Jacobsen projected it would take until Election Day for web searches to be sent to "waffles."

Bill Trezevant's work for Dean in Washington State informed his visionary view of how campaigns should best utilize the wired world.

"What is clear is that the advent, acceptance, integration and continued development of any new innovation begins, continues and ends with people. Over time, only the tools have changed. Campaigns of force moved from fists to clubs to guns, etc. Campaigns of ideas moved from one-on-one discussions to town halls, to TV ads, and now e-mail, websites, and streaming videos.

"What both of these types have in common is a 'top down' model. One person—or a small group of people ('the select class')—sit at the top of the pyramid and run the campaign from the small to the many. Our current political campaign model resulted directly from the inherent limits of past tools. So what has changed? In two words - everything and nothing —yet."

The Internet opened a door for people to "…now instantly 'vote' with their money. Nevertheless, the select class missed this point entirely inasmuch as they continued to operate under a top down campaign model. We focus in on the number of people who got involved in the Dean campaign primarily because it fits within a top down campaign model. Much less time has been spent on how these people, once activated, actually participated outside of voting and giving money.

"In the same fashion that McCain's fundraising facilitated the ability of ordinary people to get involved in a way other than voting, so too did the Dean campaign's appearance of meaningful participation provide a unique opportunity through the use of the Internet. 'You Have the Power' sent the clear message that personal political participation on an unprecedented scale was possible and, with each successive instance of collective action, the supporters believed they occupied a meaningful role in the campaign.

"The problem is that it was not true, except to the extent allowed by the select class at the top. In this regard, the select class was still operating under a top-down approach, with the appendage of an electronic 'suggestion box.' The campaign did not go far enough with a bottom up model and was eventually forced to first admit its usage of the top down model and then succumb to the same.

"The result of this misapplication of models is that it caused unrecoverable problems amongst supporters. By creating the perception that the campaign was bottom up, supporters felt deceived post-Iowa and New Hampshire, particularly after stories' regarding the apparent overnight financial and campaign structural meltdown came to light highlighted by two events: 1. The departure of the campaign manager, and 2. The admission that the campaign had barely a fraction of the record amount of money it collected left in the bank to continue the campaign.

"In short, there must be a new campaign model out there which realizes the benefits of both a top down and bottom up model, and yet retains the necessary structure to operate a national presidential campaign. Some may argue that, in principal, the Dean campaign tried to run an end-to-end campaign enabling supporters to connect independently with one another. But as a practical matter, even though these individuals and groups connected with each other (which I would argue is still the real hidden value of the Internet in campaigns) they sought actual direction from the campaign.

"Unlike a pyramid, traditional or inverted, a campaign organizational structure which has a simplified, linear, hierarchical structure accompanied by an ever expanding linear latitudinal line, with points on the latitudinal line representing areas of campaign responsibility, is the new model for campaigns on the Internet.

"Any attempt to build a national campaign structure over (house parties, discussion groups, campaign blogs, independent blogs, and, most significantly, independent self-initiated non-coordinated and non-web-based action) would simply be Tom Foolery. Such a structure would be financially unfeasible and might possibly implode from the bureaucratic weight alone. Top down has to yield some control, and independent and non-coordinated civic activism has to accept some direction.

"A linear campaign model not only achieves the benefits of the top down model, it also institutionalizes the salient aspects of the bottom up model and in all critical aspects achieves the second prong of the basic proposition, i.e. the institutionalization of the Internet in political life, through the unleashing of human creativity and problem solving in breaking down barriers to active political participation.

"Advocates continue to assume the hegemony of the top down model in modern political life, with the Internet merely as a new toy. What they do not allow for is the possibility that a transformative idea about the Internet is on the horizon, just beyond our sights.

"A new innovation, after it is accepted, survives in ways never before imagined, once individuals grab hold of it and think of ways in which it can facilitate our daily life by breaking down barriers and creating new opportunities for participation.

"To argue otherwise is to be a smart ostrich...a creature that is more advanced than the others but nonetheless continues to bury its head in the sand."[218]

Wired had its own post-mortem of the Dean campaign.

"Sure, Dean flamed out. But so what? Revolutions eat their young; blogs and the Web are now indispensable political tools. The children of the Internet finally have a name for their decentralized, networked, bottom-up philosophy. It's called democracy."[219]

However campaigns utilized technology, they would still be dependent on the interactive technology at the end of the line—the voting machine.

John Dower says "I don't even use e-mail. I'm unwired so I can't talk about that technology. I think that what you can say is that the Internet makes it clear…let me tell you what I do…I tapped into somebody who has devoted his life since September 11th to surveying what's done in the media world wide and putting out a daily report. Things that you can't read in mainstream America.

"I know what's going on out there, but I know because someone else filters it for me, screens it, summarizes it, and I read it every day. I read what's going on around the world, and what opinion is.

"What you cannot get in the mainstream media, whether it's television or print media, including the so-called liberal papers like the *New York Times* and *Boston Globe*, they are so fundamentally conservative that you don't get a sense of what views are going on around the world.

"That's also where the more dissonant voices in America have been doing some of the best reporting on the world since 9/11. You have to tap into alternative sources to get a picture of what people elsewhere in the world are thinking, or what a large number of people in America are thinking.

"Now, in my circles, because I'm academic, and I tend to move around in academic circles, I have never met a Bush supporter. I have never met anyone who isn't appalled by these policies, by the insensitivity to international opinion, the absolute insensitivity to imponderables like something other than the military machine.

"Why is it that these people can come up, and be so ineffective against this fantastic military machine. Any of us who came up against Vietnam and thought seriously about these things, knew that there are things you can do in asymmetrical situations.

"And they simply didn't grasp it.

"There is an anti-intellectualism out there. And Bush is a real wonderful symbol of a kind of visceral pride in being redneck and anti-intellectual. He is a man of no curiosity, no intellectual curiosity.

"Condaleeza Rice, when she's asked about the president, says 'the president doesn't wish to be bothered with details.'

"That's Condaleeza Rice, the president of his fan club.

"We know that the president doesn't like to read anything that isn't canned and presented to him. He takes pride in that. He has to make a positive thing out of the fact that he was a C student.

"A C student is a failing student. He's a man of zero curiosity. He's a man of incredible insularity. You want to do the Japan comparison…we talk about insular people, island mentality…I mean this is a real insular, parochial, mentality.

"So anyone in the US who works with the world, or anyone outside the US who is the rest of the world, is just appalled by the appeal of that this person has, but his electoral base loves him.

"I think the real technology that interests me is military technology. I mean, if you talk about electoral campaign…I think if you look at history, that is the story of modern history. It is extraordinary technological change, exponential technological change.

"We're sitting here today, looking at 150 years of US-Japan relations, and it begins with Commodore Perry 150 years ago. He goes over with these primitive, coal-driven paddle wheel boats.

"Fifty years later you've got the Russo-Japanese war with these gigantic modern navies.

"Forty years later, 90 years after Perry, you've got Hiroshima and Nagasaki.

"Now we're in an age where we can hit someone in an automobile in the desert with a missile sent from someplace hundreds of miles away. And that technology has been constantly associated with violence. "People get hooked on this mirage that 'we're now going to become invincible militarily.' And they always want to try it out…there is always an imperative to use the new technology. You can always predict that there will be a war in which they will get a chance to try out the new technology, and it's always accompanied by hubris…that 'this is going to do it. We've got it.'

"Vietnam, with our technology, we were going to smash them into doing our will.

"It didn't work. But this time it was going to work. We were going to shock them all into absolute compliance. And this administration is mesmerized by the technology, and mesmerized by the personal profits that come from that technology. They're a corrupt administration.

"We have brains at work, doing scientific technology. Scientific technology has been doing great work, but it hasn't brought wisdom with it. I don't' think we have any exponential changes in wisdom. The technology has outstripped our capacity to control it…look at what we're doing today…we're in a situation today where we're more powerful than anyone could have dreamed any nation could be. We're more powerful than the rest of world combined. There's no question that we can smash anyone militarily. We can blow up the world.

"And what are we doing? We'll never have enough money for developing new weapon systems. And if you come up as a politician today and say "hey, can't we move toward real disarmament, can't we cut back on these weapon systems…you will be killed! And Dean was touching those nerves. He was not a fanatic. He was not a man mesmerized by the machine. Dean had a more nuanced sense of the needs of the world. "I think that Dean was a little too independent for America.

"Kerry…I don't think Kerry's gonna win. But, you know, he's safer. Anyone who sticks their neck up in America is always gonna get banged down.

"That's what we always used to say about the Japanese.

"You're (the author) more optimistic than I am. Dean's campaign did tap the power of the Internet, but he got smashed in the end.

"So in the end…I'm not sanguine. In the end, I think these darker forces will prevail, which is man's hubris, his arrogance, his blindness, his insensitivity.

"You go back, some of the people went back recently, and were quoting at length Fulbright's 'arrogance of power.'

"It sounds like it was written today. Absolute power corrupts absolutely. We're going back to Acton. And those things of human nature and power…I don't even mean…it isn't just corruption, in the sense of raking off a lot of money…it's a kind of a corruption of the mind. A moral corruption, corruption of the imagination. Those are things that are still with us.

"Howard Dean wasn't a radical. He's a sensible man, with a clear sense of priorities. Personally we don't think he had the terrible moral failures of Clinton. One of the saddest things , someone that right was just so morally juvenile, immature. That a person like Howard Dean, who was not radical, but was seen as extreme in this country…that's a very sobering lesson about this country."

MEDIA CABAL: A CASE STUDY IN INTERNET CULTURE

It is December 10, 2003, and William Rivers Pitt, journalist, international best--selling author of three books, and managing Editor of *Truthout.org* posts his article "The Trail of John Kerry" to the website.

There are but a few weeks to go before the Iowa caucuses and the New Hampshire primary. Time has grown short. In an effort to galvanize the message Kerry wants to deliver in the time remaining, he convened a powerful roster of journalists and columnists in the New York City apartment of Al Franken last Thursday. The gathering could not properly be called a meeting or a luncheon. It was a trial. The journalists served as prosecuting attorneys, jury and judge. The crowd I joined in Franken's living room was comprised of:

Al Franken and his wife **Franni**;

Rick Hertzberg, senior editor for the *New Yorker*;

David Remnick, editor for the *New Yorker*;

Jim Kelly, managing editor for *Time* Magazine;

Howard Fineman, chief political correspondent for *Newsweek*;

Jeff Greenfield, senior correspondent and analyst for CNN;

Frank Rich, columnist for the *New York Times*;

Eric Alterman, author and columnist for MSNBC and the *Nation*;

Art Spiegelman, Pulitzer Prize winning cartoonist/author of *Maus*;

Richard Cohen, columnist for the *Washington Post*;

Fred Kaplan, columnist for *Slate*;

Jacob Weisberg, editor of *Slate* and author;

Jonathan Alter, senior editor and columnist for *Newsweek*;

Philip Gourevitch, columnist for the *New Yorker*;

Calvin Trillin, freelance writer and author;

Edward Jay Epstein, investigative reporter and author;

Arthur Schlesinger, Jr., who needs no introduction.

We sat in a circle around Kerry and grilled him for two long hours. In an age of retail politicians who avoid substance the way vampires avoid sunlight, in an age when the sitting President flounders like a gaffed fish whenever he must speak to reporters without a script, Kerry's decision to open himself to the slings and arrows of this group was bold and impressive. He was fresh from two remarkable speeches? One lambasting the PATRIOT Act, another outlining his foreign policy ideals while eviscerating the Bush record and had his game face on. He needed it, because Eric Alterman lit into him immediately on the all-important issue of his vote for the Iraq War Resolution. The prosecution had begun.

It receives scant attention by any of the internet media. Several months later, March 21, 2004 specifically, the *New York Times Magazine* publishes Russell Shorto's article *"Al Franken, Seriously So,"* which recounts the same December meeting.

On the Sunday before the nation's first primary in New Hampshire, Russell Shorto is in a rental car with Al Franken driving. Among many topics bantered about during Franken's 2-day swing through the state to meet the candidates, Franken talks about a meeting with John Kerry.

"…I liked Dean," he told me. But Franken was troubled that John Kerry was being written off before a single primary vote had been cast. "I also think Kerry is just a really smart, capable man." "I'd noticed that he was very good in a small gathering, so I thought, what if I invite some opinion makers over to hear him?" On Dec. 4, an impressive collection of the media elite and assorted other notables—Hendrik **Hertzberg** of *The New Yorker*, Frank **Rich** of *The New York Times*, Howard **Fineman** and Jonathan **Alter** of *Newsweek*, Jim **Kelly** of *Time*, Jeff **Greenfield** of CNN, Eric **Alterman** of *The Nation*, Richard **Cohen** of the *Washington Post*, Jacob **Weisbery** of *Slate* and others, —including, as eminence grise, Arthur **Schlesinger** Jr.—responded to his call and had a little powwow with Kerry at the Upper West Side apartment of **Franken** and his wife, **Franni**.

"The whole thing was odd, I would say, because people didn't know why they were there," **Kelly** said. "But I think the idea was to put John Kerry into the belly of the beast. It may have been the actual beginning of the new approach he took –"I'm going to stay in this room and take every question you throw at me." **Alterman** grilled Kerry on his vote on Iraq, and he gave a long tortured answer. Then he was asked about it a second time. "By the third go-round, the answer was getting shorter and more relevant," **Kelly** said.

"It was a really interesting event," **Alter** said. "A lot of these people hadn't actually met Kerry before. Al wanted them to get to know him. It was an example of him playing a sort of intermediary role in the nexus of politics, media and entertainment."

The next time **Franken** saw Kerry was at the rally in Nashua, seven weeks later. Things had changed significantly; Kerry was considered a new and improved candidate and now looked almost unbeatable. The senator took Franken aside, and they talked for a few minutes. "I told [Kerry] I'm taking credit for the turnaround." [Kerry] said, "'I knew you would.'"

Kindled by Fox News Network talk show *O'Reilly Factor*, smoke starts to spread through the Internet. The issue of Kerry and the Franken meeting bursts into flames the same day, when Bill O'Reilly, host of the *O'Reilly Factor*, sparks his listener's attention with a statement that Kerry has met with left-wing reporters to strategize. He posts to the web:

Beware of partisan media - Too many journalists are cheerleading for a favorite candidate. *Commentary by Bill O'Reilly*

<http://www.citizenreviewonline.org/march2004/partisan.htm>

"...Now, this powwow [in December] might have been just an innocent "get to know you" soiree, but there are hints it might have been quite something else. One of the attendees, Jim Kelly, the managing editor of Time magazine, was quoted as saying that Kerry was asked a number of times about his vote on Iraq, and, according to Kelly, "by the third go-round the answer was getting shorter and more relevant."

The "third go-round"? That sounds like coaching to me, but I could be wrong. Maybe the Massachusetts senator simply wasn't making himself clear.

What I'm not wrong about is that more than a few so-called journalists have turned into activists - people who are dedicating themselves to getting a certain party or person elected, and are using their positions in the media to do it.

There is nothing wrong with news organizations endorsing a candidate or a columnist writing about his or her political preferences.

But actively participating in political campaigns by coaching candidates and strategizing with them is absolutely against every journalistic standard, and it is happening - usually under the radar...

But let's face it, with the rise of entertainers like Rush Limbaugh and other radio talk-show people who openly root for the Republicans, those on the left feel they are at a disadvantage.

Thus we now have that vacuum being filled by some opinion journalists who never met a left-wing cause they didn't espouse. Again, fanatical news analysts are allowed, even though they're boring. But crossing the line into actively helping a political campaign cannot be tolerated by any news operation.

The exposure of the liberal journalists who met with Kerry received scant attention from the media. Can you imagine if executives from the Fox News Channel, The Wall Street Journal and The Washington Times had gathered at Camp David for a little slap and tickle with President Bush? And nobody was told about it? And The New York Times found out about it?

Can you say PAGE ONE BOLD FACE HEADLINE...?

(Author's note-Attempts to reach O-Reilly for comment through Fox News Network at oreilly@foxnews.com were not returned.)

In a telephone interview, *Washington Post* columnist Richard **Cohen** said:

"No, it wasn't anything like that," "I don't have the article in front of me, but the mischaracterization is either in the original piece or in the use of it by opponents of Kerry. I remember the mischaracterization along the lines as a meeting called by Kerry. It wasn't. As far as I was concerned, it was yet another meeting with the press, with yet another candidate, a Presidential candidate."

"You sit in somebody's kitchen, or you go into the back room of some restaurant in Washington. This is an opportunity for those guys to get to meet the candidate in an informal setting and for him to relax. Just to get to know them better.

"I think it's become absolutely crucial in this age...from the day the campaign begins, to the day it either ends, or you can't take it any longer and you kill yourself, everything you do is recorded.

"And so, all the campaigns have, what I call these little embedded debs…young women …and the tapes and the cameras going all the time. And so you can't do anything.

"In the old days, …I'm not that old, but I'm old enough to remember when, at the end of the day, the candidate would always come back on the plane or the bus, have a drink and schmooze…it was totally off the record. The advantage was that you got to know the guy a little bit. Nobody would do it now."

"I know the meeting might have seemed odd because Al is not a journalist, and he made it odder by inviting some people I wouldn't have invited if I was doing it. I didn't have a problem with Schlesinger, I didn't have a problem with anybody.

I went to see how he would perform with the rest of the press. And whether or not he was overcoming what I thought was his handicap, of giving very verbose responses to questions. Anyway, I thought it would be interesting and what the hell, it was a cab ride away.

"The list, for the most part, is conventional journalists. It wasn't so much odd, as it was just different, that it was at Al's place. I thought it was very useful.

"What it wasn't, was a secret media meeting designed to help him in his campaign. "

"I got a lot of e-mail because of the article by O'Reilly. His producer called me twice in one day about this meeting and said would I come on the show to defend it. Defend what? What's to defend….I didn't do anything worth defending. But this has taken on a life of it's own out there in cuckoo land."

"O'Reilly, misinterpreted, I'm pretty sure purposely. He has an axe to grind with Al Franken."

Whatever his reason, it suited his purposes to characterize it as a meeting with press in which various people in the press kind of rehearsed Kerry so he would be better prepared with the press from there on in.

What follows is a sampling of internet chatter:

Blog Excerpts from *FreeRepublic.com*

Bill needs to blow this story wide open.
My Favorite Headache, March 22, 2004 7:13PM PST

The shadow DNC.
Peach, March 22, 2004 7:18:16PM PST

What else would one expect with Demotrash? Scum with scum.
AlexW, March 22, 2004 7:20PM PST

Oh Pleeeze involve Franken in this race!! I hear he is on Hillary's speech writing team now too LOL! *Mylife, March 22, 2004 7:20:54 PM PST*

O'Reilly has been harping on the fact the liberal media is out to destroy America as we know it. He is absolutely right on this. My hat off to O'Reilly on this. He is dead right on this.
Uncle Hal, March 22, 2004 7:21:04 PM PST

Do you want a president who injects poison into his skull for vanity?
Mo1, March 22, 2004 7:23:11 PM PST

They weren't there for interviews…it's for a new CBS show. They were gonna call it Left Wing Extremist Home Make-Over, but that was too wordy for the average viewer to comprehend.
Will_Zurmacht, March 22, 2004 7:24:22 PM PST

List of traitors!!
Nopardons, March 22, 2004 7:25:17 PM PST

Can you imagine the reaction if this had been Rush Limbaugh's Apartment?
Mike Darancette, March 22, 2004 7:25:33 PM PST (General - Alien Army of the Right (AAOTR).

How come these "enlightened" liberals had no women in this group? Doesn't that seem a bit strange? This is nothing more than a prep session for their boy.
Rightone, March 22, 2004 7:30:25 PM PST

One thing for certain is that no one will be able to accuse them of not having any Jewish representation.

Varon, March 22, 2004 7:34:02 PM PST (Allegiance to the constitution, always. Allegiance to a political party, never.)

I only thought stuff like this happened in totalitarian countries. These "journalists" put to shame the propaganda organs of the old Soviet Union.

AF68, March 22, 2004 7:34:22 PM PST

Franni Franken??? Sounds like a "Laugh In" skit, doesn't it?

TankerKC, March 22, 2004 7:36:18 Pm PST (Clogged Arteries and Still Smilin'!)

This is a joke right?

isthisnickcool, March 2, 2004 7:36:40 PM PST (Guns!)
End of *FreeRepublic.com* blog

Excerpts from BrothersJudd Blog

Remember the outrage twenty years ago when George Will, a mere columnist, helped Ronald Reagan prepare for a debate with Jimmy Carter? Look at all the freakin' editors on this list.

Orrin Judd at March 22, 2004 10:43 PM

Blog Comments:

Interesting that we are only now hearing about this. Shouldn't these journalists have reported on the meeting? Clearly it wasn't a "trial," it was a supplication/strategy session.

PapayaSF at March 23, 2004 12:34 AM

I'm surprised at several of the names at the meeting; I'd have assumed that they were Dean supporters. The part about the President "flounder[ing] like a gaffed fish", when speaking to reporters without a script, is wickedly funny, when compared to Kerry's recent verbal problems.

Michael, March 23, 2004 01:38 AM

That's quite a "cabal". Did Jim Kelly have to leave the room when they got down to real business.

J.H. at March 23, 2004 09:17 AM

Are you claiming that you would not object to a similar meeting between Bush and Cal Thomas, Charles Krauthammer, George Will, Rush

Limbaugh, Brit Hume, Mort Kondracke, Bob Novak, Matt Drudge, Thomas Sowell, Linda Chavez, Tony Blankney, Jonah Goldberg, etc.? Even to complain that no liberals were invited?
Jim, March 23, 2004 01:16 PM

"Participating in a campaign." How? By asking Kerry questions for two hours, and listening to the answers? I only ask because I have yet encountered no indication that the meeting was anything more than that.
M.Bulger, March 23, 2004 5:45PM

SYSTEM – LORD CLINTON IS A GOD! A GOD CAN DO NO WRONG! AND WE ARE HIS LOYAL JEFFAH!
Ken, at March 24, 2004 01:10PM

No one attending that event has ever had a kind word to say about a Republican (other than John McCain), but the key name on the list is the last one, which I think really is the tipoff as to what it was all about. Schlesinger has spent over 40 years flacking for the Democrats and epitomizes the traditionalist faction of the party; i.e., that which is chiefly concerned with a candidate's "electability." For all the author's talk of a grilling, this likely was little more than a thinly disguised stop-Dean rally. His preference for Kerry shines throughout the article (I love the line about JK's "eyes blazing").
George, March 24, 2004 05.13 PM

George - I think you hit the nail on the head. But the question to ask all of these people is why they didn't just support Howard Dean? He espoused positions all of them have favorably written about or endorsed. Maybe Dean wasn't European enough.
Jim, March 24, 2004 04:52PM
End of BrothersJudd blog

Although there were dozens of Internet news outlets who helped spread the fires of interpretation, the most important message readers might take from these two sites alone is this: Searching for truth in the cyber world of Internet blogs is reminiscent of 14th century poet Dante and his *Divine Comedy*.

Inscribed over his metaphorical gates of hell, he wrote *"Abandon hope, all ye who enter here."*

ICARUS RISING

Our inventions are wont to be pretty toys, which distract our attention from serious things. They are but improved means to an unimproved end.
HENRY DAVID THOREAU, Walden, *"Economy,"* 1854

When you are in the zone, errors turn into victories. Dean appeared with Tim Russert on *Meet the Press* June 22, 2003. Russert grilled Dean on his record, national security and the Iraq war. Dean's performance was generally reviewed as poor in the next day's papers. This sent the "Dean Defense Forces" into action against the offending journalists. Even better, it produced an internet windfall for the campaign. Donations rose on the day of the performance, like Wall Street responding to important news about Greenspan's annual physical.

Dean's travels provided the colors with which he painted a portrait of what America could be. He began with a vision of America as having a sense of community that survival through blustery winters necessitates in Vermont. When he discovered that wasn't so, Dean created a tableau to spread out before voters: the idyllic community that he believes exists in Vermont. That vision, and his anti-war, anti-Bush stance, resonated with those who were paying attention early in the process. Dean's ridicule of the "No Child Left Behind" bill was ahead of that from opponents who were tricked by Bush's bait-and-switch tactics about this bill.

While Walter Shapiro found that the only thing distinctive about Dean was "the unabashed self-confidence in his voice."[220] That voice registered among those who were listening. Dean adopted the suggestion of an early supporter to label the movement *"Dean for America"* without any awareness that this idea borrowed from the television show *The West Wing*.

He traveled America citing his hero, the feisty Harry Truman. "I don't believe you can win by being Bush Lite," the non-drinking Dean said. "If you have a choice between a Republican and a Republican, the Republican is going to win every time." A campaign that began as just Dean with the "over-protective" and "territorial", Kate O'Connor expanded like the universe after the Big Bang. Chartered airplanes replaced early boarding cards on Southwest Airlines.

Dean started traveling with a computer earlier in the year—his own rapid response team. He read the morning papers, dictated a press release by cell phone which then was out in 90 minutes. The speed of the technology may have increased Dean's tendency toward reaction before reflection. His sarcasm was apparent when he claimed that he was "thrilled" to have Kerry echoing his concerns about the war.

A *Los Angeles Times* story on that particular Kerry speech included Dean's reaction, while simultaneously noting that Dean had lobbed one of the first criticisms utilized by any Democratic contender. Dean was establishing himself as the anti-war candidate, a powerful draw that might eventually prove as limiting as it was initially compelling.

On his first trip with the candidate, Joe Trippi reflected that he didn't "know how it would play out."

Dean's opposition to the Iraq war may have been aided by the fact that he had never received one of the intelligence briefings with which Bush had so successfully wagged the dog. Operating in the dark on that issue led to Dean's appearing enlightened.

His disinclination to stay on message further concerned Trippi. "Howard's problem is that he'll get bored with the same spiel, and he goes off in an entirely new direction." Dean warned that looming deficits project a future for America as economically equivalent to Argentina, in decades to come. Trippi felt Dean's prognostication of America becoming a "second-rate nation" might produce voters inclined to shoot the messenger. Trippi advised Dean of his concern, which resulted in a change to "third-rate nation" in Dean's next speech.[221]

In mid-April, after Baghdad had fallen, Dean allowed that Saddam's ouster might be a good thing. That grudging conciliation would be one of many verbal missteps over the invisible primary season. Walter Shapiro was finding Dean "…simultaneously beguiling and exasperating. If Dean were in the White House, Hallmark would probably rush out a new line of Presidential apology cards."[222]

Later that month (April, 2003), Dean was quoted in *Time* magazine, as saying that "…we won't always have the strongest military." While it is impossible to link primacy with infinity, Dean provided fodder for the Kerry camp to paint him as weak militarily.

It was only April, and the stakes in the game were anteed up by Dean's building a lead in the invisible primary. As America engenders resentment, and attacks, because of its dominant position in the world, so Dean was painting a target on himself.

Andrew Smith says "…for eleven months in 2003 it seemed as if Dean could do nothing wrong… then in two months it seemed as if he could do nothing right…"

THE STAFF OF POLITICAL LIFE

The open society, the unrestricted access to knowledge, the unplanned and uninhibited association of men for its furtherance — these are what may make a vast, complex, ever growing, ever changing, ever more specialized and expert technological world, nevertheless a world of human community.

J. ROBERT OPPENHEIMER, *Science and the Common Understanding*, 1953

Politics is a team sport. A candidate can be a manager, and/or a starter, but the number of positions she or he can play is held, by the time/space limitation, to one place at a time.

So, for any candidate, the quality of your teammates is a key determinant in how far you go into the playoffs. (The great sports writer Bob Ryan once joked to me that life is a metaphor for sports, so I'll run with that here.)

In sports as in politics, experience matters. Howard Dean's candidacy brought many young, first time voters into the process. That factor had an invigorating effect on the party. However, without experienced leadership the energy of youth cannot be harnessed to best advantage. William Trezevant arrived in Washington State relatively late in the process to salvage a troubled campaign. His success there may well be due to experience and age. "I'm older than a number of people who are even working in the national office. That became important… because, having been a part of a number of campaigns, on the up side… and the most important thing, having run for office myself… (I bring) a very different view of what campaigns are, what the stresses are, how it impacts people. My job was to translate that experience into an effective way to manage people that were brand new."

Wesley Clark's staff had hastened his demise by leaking a tip that the campaign would be folding. In Vietnam, this would have qualified as "fragging." Similarly, the rumors about Kerry having a relationship with an intern—getting attributed as originating in the Clark camp—produced collateral damage.

In the Dean campaign, some officials revealed to reporters that they were planning to leave the Burlington headquarters, one week before the Wisconsin primary. Dean, who, said the previous week told *Fox News* that he'd stay in through the first Tuesday in March (Super Tuesday), commented about the departures: "Nobody's told me that." Similarly, news that the campaign staff hadn't sought a new air charter contract distributed a script that Dean clearly wasn't reading.

At a time when John Kerry seemed a candidate for political embalming fluid, Kerry made a huge staff change. The timing of this change in his campaign seemed to be too late to rescue it from stagnancy. Internecine warfare dominated to the point where there were two versions of Kerry's announcement speech. Media moved into full vulture mode, and focus groups in New Hampshire were telling pollsters that the country couldn't be led by someone who couldn't lead his own campaign. During a conference call in which Kerry was heard eating supper, he switched campaign managers.

The woman he took on, Mary Beth Cahill, had political bloodlines, and experience that was in sharp contrast to that found inside the Dean campaign. Cahill had run Patrick Leahy's re-election race in 1986, when he defeated four-term Governor Richard Snelling. Leahy has described it as the best-run campaign in Vermont history.

When Cahill graduated from college in 1976, she worked in the Congressional office of Father Robert Drinan, famed for his opposition to the Vietnam War. The Roman Catholic Church ordered all priests out of politics, and Cahill moved to the staff of Drinan's successor, Barney Frank. She went on to do a variety of political jobs, including running EMILY's List, which raises funds for women candidates.

Between the holdovers from her predecessor, and her own hires, Cahill had a Noah's Ark of pollsters, consultants and representatives when she began to revitalize Kerry's campaign. She kept order on the ark because, "…everybody who was around the table was familiar to me." She also ran a tight ship. Michael Whouley, who received much credit for Kerry's success

254

in the Iowa caucuses says, "There is no dissension—zero. There is no second guessing - zero. There is no leaking—zero."

Everything before Iowa was a scrimmage, played by rules that were newly evolved and without any running clock. Iowa wasn't an exhibition game, either; it would prove to be a crucial game that would help define a very short regular season. Cahill says, "We knew that Dean didn't have what he said he did. We knew they did not have on the ground what they said they had. It was never real." Cahill has her eye on the prize, and knows the travails of getting there. "It's the completely unglamorous fundamentals. The thing that is so clear about this election cycle is that you just have to keep on keeping on, because who knows what is going to happen?"[223]

Reflecting on Dean's rise and descent, Adrian Walker remarks that "…it took the other campaigns, particularly the Kerry campaign, a long, long time to come to any decision about whether to attack him (Dean) or not attack him; do we talk about him, do we not talk about him. This was a source of inner turmoil in the Kerry campaign. But eventually, the decision was made that generally, everyone would go after him as he pulled farther and farther ahead… that was a real turning point in the campaign. He was a great underdog, He was not a great frontrunner… being a frontrunner is ten times harder. Being a frontrunner is tough."

A key to Kerry's success would be the not-insignificant effort to keep a candidate prone to the windy pontificating of the senate floor, on message. Kerry stood tallest in a field where the positions were hard to differentiate. "Kerry, on the record, has had mostly conventional things to say about foreign policy. One rarely survives in Washington without going along with the essentials of the conventional 'story' the country tells itself about what is going on in the world, and about what America's role in it should be. One reason Howard Dean failed was that he provoked alarm among the congressional Democratic leadership and Washington media hostility because he seemed to be going 'off' that story as his early lead in opinion polls mounted, and supposedly became unelectable."[224]

As the country watched the rise and fall of the Dean campaign, shadowed by the fall and rise of Kerry's candidacy, the nature of each campaign was reflected in an informal event that took place in New Hampshire. Kathy Sullivan relates this story:

"There was a softball tournament for all of the presidential campaigns over the summer… We had some elimination rounds… (we) had structured it so that it could be a "Dean-Kerry" final. It didn't mean this would necessarily happen. They had to get there (by winning). The final was a great game…Dean vs. Kerry. Dean went way up… was up by several runs.

"Those of us who were neutral were… saying, 'Oh, god, the Dean people can't win.' Not because we didn't like the Dean people… because we knew that if the Dean people lost, they would say, 'OK, we lost, let's go have a beer.' Whereas, if the Kerry people lost they… would have been so angry. At that point, that was the difference in the nature of the campaigns. We were saying, 'Oh, my god, please God, let the Kerry people win,' because we didn't want to deal with it. Then there was this big turnaround, and the Kerry people came back and won the game.

"Just as we had predicted, the Dean people said 'Okay, we lost, let's go have a beer.' "

The nature of Dean staffers and the manifestation of the campaign varied from town to town and state to state. Anyone who believes that all Dean offices applied the same strategies clearly did not spend time in Washington State. Washington is one of two states that Dean won. **William Trezevant** applied the theory of "yes based management" to an operation that had experienced turmoil prior to his arrival. Saying yes to simple requests from staffers and volunteers improved morale and produced a "model candidate" in Flat Howard. Trezevant paints the following picture of this "candidate":

"One of the volunteers came to me and said 'Bill, you know, why don't we get a Flat Howard?' I said, 'What's a Flat Howard?' Flat Howard was a picture of Howard Dean that you could download off the Internet. He showed me … 'This is a Flat Howard.' I looked at it and I said, 'Okay, we'll see,' because that's part of yes-based management.

" 'First, how much does it cost?' 'It's eighty bucks.' 'Fine, I'll approve eighty bucks… if somebody gets mad, I'll take the heat.' Not even knowing what a Flat Howard was, I said 'Just show me what the picture looks like' because if the picture was of Howard Dean with the devil's horns and a mustache, I was going to… (say) 'No, forget it.'

"They showed it to me, and it was a picture of Howard Dean standing in his hundred dollar suit, pointing. They copied it onto a disk, went to a printer, and printed out a full-sized version of this picture of Howard Dean. They then mounted it to dry backer board. It cost another twenty dollars for the mounting materials. Our volunteers put it together. Another volunteer cut it out, so it was a life-size figure. They actually made him taller.

"I had one of our staff people go out and buy a Polaroid camera, one of the instant picture things. Anyone who came into the campaign office got a picture with Flat Howard. (We'd say) 'Hi, welcome, do you want a picture with Flat Howard?' If they wanted a picture for themselves, that was fine, but what we did is say, 'Write your name on it. Do you know why? It's going on our wall of supporters.'

"So when you walked into the campaign headquarters in Seattle, Washington, the very first thing you saw... (was) this cutout of Flat Howard standing in front of you. Sometimes it scared people, other times it'd wake people up.

"It was just a very interesting... watching people's reactions. I think we ended up posting almost seven hundred pictures on the wall. You'd come in, we'd get your name, your e-mail, then we'd ask if you wanted a picture with Flat Howard.

"Somebody brought in the Seattle Super Sonics Rally Monkey. We put a Dean button on the Rally Monkey, and put a Dean sticker on him, hung him around Flat Howard, took a picture of that.

"On the wall we had a section called endorsements. (We had) 'The Rally Monkey endorses Flat Howard', 'Mary with Flat Howard', 'Bill with Flat Howard', 'Kathy with Flat Howard.'

"Everybody signed their names. It had two effects. New people that were coming in could look at this wall and see all these other different people here, whether they knew them or not, no big deal. But then they'd want their picture taken and want their picture up on the wall. The second thing is, it reinforced what we were trying to say about this campaign. That this campaign was about people-to-people - and getting local - and yes based management.

"The kind of campaign model I was running in Washington State, was about the individuals. So, when they walked in, I didn't want them to see a big, huge sign of monolithic *Dean for America* first. I wanted them to see a picture.

"We had a big picture of Howard Dean addressing the crowds in Seattle.

It had Dean off to the side, so the biggest visual you got were a number of people. Next to that were all these individual Flat Howard Polaroid pictures. What subsequently happened is that Flat Howard became so popular, so many people were putting their arms around him, that the cardboard backing began to break down.

"So one of our supporters went out and took flat Howard for a day and a half, and actually laid him down, cut out a 3/8 inch plywood backing for him, put hinges on it, put weights on it, attached it together with bolts. Flat Howard came back sturdy.

"We started calling him Flat, Stiff Howard, because now he was made of wood. The next thing that happened was, when they would do visibility or go to some local function, obviously you couldn't get Howard Dean there, so they would take Flat Howard.

"Then we had a section called 'Flat Howard about town'. Flat Howard at the Pikes Market, Flat Howard at the Seattle Center, Flat Howard at the Space Needle, Flat Howard everywhere. Flat Howard with the Mayor.

"The word got out. It was on our blogs. All of the other offices wanted Flat Howard. So we ended up having six Flat Howards made, and sent out across the state. We had Flat Howard at all these appearances.

"You'd go to a candidate forum, and the Kerry campaign would send their campaign manager, Clark would send his people, etc. Or even local Democratic things, say the 32nd district was having their Christmas party, we'd send our own people, plus Flat Howard.

"When we were at the Washington State Quarterly Democratic Convention, we had Flat Howard at our reception, and we took pictures of people with Flat Howard.

"The thing just took off. It's a small item. Ended up costing one hundred bucks per Flat Howard …plus the cost of film. It sent a very real message and accomplished two things.

"One, when a new person walked into the campaign office, they not only saw the faces of their neighbors, which underscored the people-to-people nature of the campaign. It underscored a sense of community. They then wanted a picture with Flat Howard, they wanted to take something home. Two, they went and they told their friends and other people came. It became a bit of a thing. There was local news coverage about it.

"That clearly wasn't my idea, but it worked."

Politicians have long arisen from graves, dug both by the making of others and by their own misjudgments. Media members sometimes acted as a function of their personalities; they became undertakers because they lacked the charisma to be certified public accountants.

Nixon, whose pallor in a televised debate combined so nicely with his unrestrained enmity toward the media, came back as the "New Nixon": tanned, rested and ready.

John Kerry, who was being cast by many as Herman Munster in the Fall of 2003, was resuscitated, with much of the credit going to wholesale staff changes at a historically late stage of the game.

Time's selection of 100 "influentials" in April of 2004 identified Bush, Kerry, and even the besieged Condoleeza Rice. Wesley Clark rated a mention, albeit by one degree of separation. The former NATO supreme commander ran a campaign where he blurred his most precious commodity —an Eisenhower—like image. Endorsements by Madonna and Michael Moore didn't help develop Clark's self-portrait of a military leader whose bearing was underlaid by his sensibility as a man of peace.

When Time selected the funky men of Outkast as among its 100 most influential people in the world, it cited an endorsement by Clark:

"I don't know much about hip-hop, but I do know Outkast can make you shake it like a Polaroid picture."

While the activities of his fellow Arkansan Bill Clinton had certainly reshaped the world's image of activity in the Oval Office, envisioning Clark in booty meltdown probably did not enhance his electability.

The complete absence of Howard Dean's name anywhere in the same issue, in a magazine which had featured him on the cover so prominently —and so early—seemed to signify that Time had assigned Dean an unmarked political grave.

News cycles are short, and mortal political wounds are rare.

Dean's future will be dependent, at least partially, on his own all-too-rarely shown ability to learn from his mistakes on the national stage. His selection of key staffers for future endeavors will also play a huge role in the mark he would ultimately make on America.

Karen Hicks had cut her teeth with Jeanne Shaheen. In a description of Hicks, Andrew Smith notes: "Karen Hicks struck me as competent, progressive... (she) clearly believed in Dean." Malcolm Saldanha, who worked in Manchester and Claremont New Hampshire feels that "Karen Hicks... (is) charismatic and competent as a leader." Aaron Strauss says "Karen Hicks is the best boss I've ever had. No question ...she's wonderful...in the next presidential cycle or the one after that, when she manages an entire presidential campaign I will drop everything and join her, onto the path of victory." Alex Lee adds his voice on Karen Hicks as a leader "Well, I would say that she's very, very talented—and very, very Machiavellian."

Karen Hicks was reported to be the leading candidate to head *Democracy for America*. Instead, she ended up working for John Kerry.

Many other key people from the Dean campaign left for other jobs, sometimes with 527's like *America Coming Together* (ACT), sometimes with other campaigns or operatives.

Mathew Gross and Nicco Mele allied themselves with Joe Trippi. Zephyr Teachout joined ACT.

Dean's enigmatic hiring practices may well have contributed to his downfall. Carol Darr explains how building a successful campaign really does depend on who you know...and get. "The best operatives want to go with the folks who've got the best chance. If you don't get the money, you don't get the best operatives. If you don't get the money and the operatives, you don't get the endorsements...because...the unions...don't want to waste an endorsement. Then if you don't get the money, don't get the staffers, don't get the endorsements...the political reporters blow you off." Dean's hiring decisions in 2003, whether driven by penuriousness or long-standing loyalty, continue. The person who currently does his scheduling, at a time when he is still in enormous demand, is nineteen years old. While he might be a budding wunderkind, Dean's friends already complain that the young man is not serving Dean's needs.

The well-documented internecine warfare that permeated so much of the campaign staff, even before Dean met his own 'Three Mile Island', would have to be avoided.

If Dean is to avoid consignment to the political scrapheap, he will have to grow, both as a person and as a candidate. The staff he surrounds himself with will be a measure of whether that growth actually occurs.

The staff of his political life.

Hillary Hazan reflects "…the energy of youth is absolutely incredible, and I think, that coupled with the wisdom of some people who had experience, I think we could have been unstoppable. Many great movements have been fueled by youth. I suspect had we had the wisdom to harness our energy in appropriate ways, that we could have gone further. I guess we wouldn't have achieved that success without the youth, but that sword was double edged."

Michael Goodwin enjoyed his experience with the Dean campaign. "One of the reasons I wanted to get involved in the campaign, I was hoping to do some kind of writing. The writing I was doing (for the campaign) was mostly press releases and policy papers for the website. Then also put together some talking points sometimes… that would go to the Governor on specific issues. The bulk of my work was helping to put together position papers. When I first got there I helped out the two people in the Burlington office who were the head environmental advisors there. The position papers were a much lengthier process. I worked on a wetlands piece which I basically started from scratch… and that was probably the piece I had the most fun with when I was working on the campaign. All the other position papers I worked on were based on existing research and existing stands of the Governor, things on his record. But the wetlands… we had no research on it, we had no idea what his position would be, so I researched wetlands issues nationally and worked on developing some type of policy for Howard. There was about a month where I was working on it alone and conferring with a couple of experts here and there. Then… the process of sending it out to experts to look at …then get it back, do a whole other round of revisions, it goes out again, more revisions and it kind of keeps going back and forth."

Garrett Bridgens worked in the Portsmouth, NH office: "With this being my first experience working on a political campaign of any sort, I really didn't know what to expect. Now that it is all over, I don't know if what I experienced was normal for a political campaign.

"Regardless of if it was normal or not, I must say that my experience taught me a lot of things about myself and a lot of things about people in general. It's truly amazing what people will do for a greater cause. The time, effort, and emotion that went into the Dean Campaign from volunteers, interns, and staff members are something that I will never quite understand. It blows my mind.

"For some reason, I kind of have an odd feeling in my stomach when I start to think about what I did during the campaign. The job that was given to me was very tough. It wasn't tough in terms of the hours that I put in, or the computer work that was demanded of us.

'The thing that was tough was going out and meeting potential voters and trying to sell the campaign to them. We couldn't care about any individual. The campaign wanted results. All the campaign cared about was numbers not who the people were.

"At the end of every week I had to prepare a report that went all the way up to Joe Trippi. In this report, I had to state how many one-on-ones I had, how many house meetings I had, how many new one-on-ones came out of those house meetings, how many new house meetings came out of those house meetings.

The job of the Regional Director was to make sure that the Area Organizers were bringing in solid numbers each week. So the Regional Director was constantly putting pressure on the Area Organizers, because he had pressure coming down on him. We, in turn, would go out and just worry about getting new one-on-ones and new house meetings.

"I don't work like that. I care about people, but it wasn't my job to care, my job was to get numbers and results. I hated that.

"The day before Thanksgiving, I was driving down to Massachusetts to have dinner with some friends. On the way down, I had a list of people that I had to call because we were trying to get the NEA—New Hampshire Teachers endorsement.

"Who the hell calls people during holidays? It just made my sick to make those calls. I also made calls two days before Christmas, and on New Year's Eve, and Day. I absolutely regret doing all of that. It was heartless. But when you have a Regional Director barking down your throat for results, you have no choice. It wasn't the Director's fault though; it was just how the campaign worked.

"I met a lot of great people from New Hampshire, and when I think back about what we asked you and others to do during the campaign, I can't help but feel guilt. I know that it was their choice to help the campaign, but the constant nagging we did is what I feel guilty about.

"It seems like every other day I would be going to a supporter's house to ask them to do something new for the campaign. Toward the end of the campaign it got really hard to keep calling the same people over and over again.

"I remember calling one supporter one night to get phone banking results from them, and the person just broke down. The person proceeded to tell how her father was ill, and that some sort of animal had died in the walls of their house over the weekend, and, because the stench was so bad, they had to move out for awhile.

"I had to ask that person if they had a chance to do any phone banking over the weekend. The person apologized to me because they hadn't made any calls.

"I should have been the one apologizing.

"The campaign taught me a lot of things about myself. I learned that I had to grow a really tough skin to make it through the 4 months that I was in New Hampshire.

"I also learned that I really am not cut out for political campaigns. I guess I have too much of a conscience. I care about people too much. I made a lot of great friends that I miss very much, but I am kind of scared to talk to them again, because I feel that they might hold some sort of grudge against me, because I let them down in some way.

"I asked them to do so many things because I said it would be the difference between a win and a loss. They gave me their heart and I didn't deliver for them.

"I don't know if the Dean Campaign was typical of most campaigns, but I do know that what we did almost didn't feel right.

"I enjoyed my time in New Hampshire mainly because of the great people I met, and the great food I ate, but the job, in general, was tough, and it brought me down by the end.

"I was physically and emotionally spent, and I had nothing more that I could give by the end.

"Maybe that is why I was back home in Oregon within 48 hours of the polls closing in New Hampshire.

Melting Wax and
Feathers Flying

Im going to campaign up and down America until we drive the crooks
and communists and those that defend them out of Washington.
—*Richard M. Nixon*

My great uncle used to say "up like a rocket, down like a stick." By
December, the Dean campaign had entered the stick phase. A candidate
once described as Teflon-coated now became a walking advertisement for
Velcro.

Political campaigns are reminiscent of Woody Allen's prescription for
the survival of sharks and relationships. Either they keep moving forward,
or they die. The Dean campaign was beginning to have its fins
contemplated for soup.

In September, Dean had announced a goal of the campaign having
450,000 e-mail addresses by the end of the month. He had also said that
they wanted to have a million by the end of the year. By December, the
expansion of Dean Universe had slowed greatly, and the campaign would
never approach the one million goal. The campaign trail was producing a
Howard Dean that didn't always play positively on television.

Dale Ungerer, a 67 year-old Republican from Iowa criticized Dean for
bashing Bush, without providing alternatives. He called on all Democrats
to "love they neighbor," adding "Please tone down the garbage, the mean-
mouthing, of tearing down your neighbor, and being so pompous." Dean
had sat quietly, but he responded instantly with "George Bush is not my
neighbor." Ungerer started to interrupt, and Dean, clearly annoyed, said,
"You sit down. You had your say, and now I'm going to have my say."

The next day, Dean would be doing damage control. He explained that: "Under the guise of supporting your neighbor, we're all expected not to criticize the president because it's unpatriotic. I think it's unpatriotic to do some of the things this president has done to the country. It is not time to put up any of this 'love thy neighbor.' I tell you, I love my neighbor, but I want that neighbor back in Crawford, Texas, where he belongs."

Ungerer got his rebuttal in a separate interview: "He put me down, definitely, because of who he is."

"The depth of Dean's actual support was embodied in a questioner in Parade magazine stating that he needed to know if Dean was a Yankee or Red Sox fan, as his vote depended upon that allegiance. (This may have been the same gentleman in Seabrook who resolutely assured canvassers that he supported Howard Clark.) A Yankee fan by birth, Dean would change his allegiance to the Sox following unsportsmanlike-like behavior by uber-grunt Roger Clemens. Dean said that he "understood the futility and pain" involved with joining Red Sox nation.

That may have better prepared him for the Iowa ads linking him to Osama bin Laden, which were funded by Yankee owner George Steinbrenner, Kerry fundraiser Robert Torricelli, and others, including some people who had contributed to the Dean campaign who were quite unhappy when they saw how their money was used for that ad.

The group behind the ads, Americans for Jobs& Healthcare (apparently mother and apple pie were already claimed), was run by a pair of former Gephardt supporters and had a spokesman who had worked for Kerry. An irate Dean broke his pledge of a week earlier not to criticize his rivals in an effort to rejuvenate his campaign.

He said Edwards would make a better candidate than Kerry, who he contrasted with Bush as being merely the "lesser of two evils." Dean went on to question Kerry's ethics and electability, and cited phone calls made in Iowa and New Hampshire in questioning Kerry's ethics.

In December, Dean had played a card game with the press that he called "Oh Hell!" In the heated days of January, the cards disappeared. By the middle of February, Dean had come to the card table with the media again.

With the last few sands moving downward in the hourglass, Time's Andrew Sullivan wrote "Why I'm Rooting for Dean": "Dean offers, to purloin a phrase, a choice, not an echo. His pugnacity in defense of his liberal instincts is obviously genuine." Sullivan referred to Kerry's "Hamlet-like anguish and spin", calling him "Gore redux." He cited Dean's telling the *New Yorker* that 'Once you're willing to say whatever it takes to win, you lose.'

In a classic case of "you don't know what you've got 'til it's gone", Sullivan wrote that "the Democrats haven't seen this kind of nerve in a very long time. They will end up with regrets if they throw it away." [225]

The same issue of *Time* featured an article entitled "Howard's End?" It described Joe Trippi first in the article, as "rambling," "frumpy", and "loquacious." The article featured a tearful Trippi describing his departure from the campaign on MSNBC, because the campaign couldn't run with "two captains." It wasn't clear if the other captain he was referring to was Roy Neel, a former lobbyist widely assumed to be leading a campaign in shutting down, or if Trippi had demoted Dean from admiral. "Some advisers to the campaign also complained that Trippi had led the candidate away from himself, turning a pragmatic politician who did not do much shouting into a candidate easily caricatured as a fire-breathing liberal."[226]

Perry Bacon, Jr. wrote of the Dean Web operation posting "hundreds of laudatory farewells within an hour of his departure." However, Bacon also noted "many bloggers said they hoped the reformed campaign would improve its ads, which were designed by Trippi's firm and roundly disliked by the troops for being too negative about the other candidates and too weak in promoting Dean's record. Followers of Dean see themselves, and their connection, as the campaign itself. Trippi may have left Dean's campaign, but his ideas have already been stolen, which guarantees them a life in this political cycle-and probably guarantees him a few lucrative consulting deals."[227]

The official post-mortems on Dean's candidacy were filed after he withdrew from the race on February 19. The BBC contacted me to provide insight into the Dean phenomena for their morning radio show in London.

USA Today said "the same passion and outspokenness that contributed to Dean's downfall also helped focus and energize a race that easily could have seen Democrats continue sleepwalking. He tugged his party leftward from the political center occupied by President Clinton with rousing calls for trade protectionism, tax hikes and costly new programs. His campaign turned out to be a humbling experience for pollsters, pundits and, most of all, himself.

"Joe Trippi… had little control over hiring or spending. Bob Rogan, the deputy campaign manager Dean entrusted with the budget, supplied inaccurate estimates of cash on hand, based on reports from the campaign accounting office.

"Two holdovers from the Vermont governor's office - Rogan, hired by Dean to handle money and personnel, and travel aide Kate O'Connor, who filtered Dean's contacts and information - saw their job as protecting Dean. They clashed with Dean's national political advisers, who felt thwarted in trying to improve the campaign.

"He refused to get coaching to ready himself for presidential-level speeches and debates. He rarely read debate preparation books. Over aides' protests, he penciled into a foreign policy speech the line that America was not safer after the capture of Saddam Hussein. He tossed his talking points in Iowa and the result was his shouted 'concession' speech.

"Tom Harkin, a supporter, advised him to tell stories about his medical practice, his family or people he met on the campaign trail. But Dean didn't.

"The outer circle, Dean's national advisers," …"wanted to get Dean's wife more involved. As far back as Labor Day, they wanted new hires to bring order to the chaotic operations at headquarters. Some sensed the Iowa campaign was flagging and recommended fundamental changes. All their suggestions were ignored or rejected. 'Every campaign running against them had more opposition research (on Dean) than they did,' said Anita Dunn, a party strategist. Steve McMahon, a senior adviser, said, 'Every major strategic and financial decision was made collectively. If mistakes were made, they belong to all of us.' 'The candidate needed to rise to another level. The campaign needed to rise to another level,' Dunn says. But neither did."[228]

The *New York Times* quoted former radical Tom Hayden as saying that Dean "never got a chance to completely enunciate a positive message." The *Times'* own analysis provided a historic perspective that would mirror that of David Halberstam. "The Democrats' shattering divisions in 1968 led to reforms in both major parties that emphasized grassroots power over party insiders, and paved the way for Mr. McGovern's nomination in 1972. In 1976, Jimmy Carter and Ronald Reagan both surged to prominence as outsiders, and four years later, Mr. Reagan and his conservative backers took over the Republican Party with effects that remain obvious today.

"But those three candidates were riding historical forces—opposition to a years-old, stalemated war; the corruption of Watergate, and the sense that liberals had forsaken middle-class America-that, at least in hindsight, seem more powerful than the anti-Bush backlash that propelled Dr. Dean.

"There is reason to believe that Dr. Dean's clear power to press his party to the left this year might turn out to be…transitory, rather than transformative. Cass R. Sunstein, author of *Republic.com*, a study of the social impact of the Internet, agreed in part (with Trippi, who described a dot-com miracle). 'One thing that might be exploited,' he said, 'is that if you get like-minded people in constant touch with each other, then they get more energized and committed, and more outraged and extreme. You can create a cult," he said, "but long term political change requires more than that."[229]

Jodi Wilgoren added her analysis in the *Times*: "His vaunted decentralized movement of political newcomers lacked experience and agility, failing to quickly make, or clearly communicate critical decisions. The campaign became obsessed with itself, focusing less on the issues and more on the number of supporters signed up on its Website, on letters written to voters, on house parties in New Hampshire or volunteers canvassing Iowa in orange hats.

"Not taking time for intense policy briefings to layer substance under the lines of Dr. Dean's stump speech; having a one-note schedule of rallies and forums rather than a range of activities to build a three-dimensional profile: ignoring brewing problems in the Iowa field operation as early as last summer.

"Energetic 20-somethings were put in charge of critical realms like field organizing and politics, and the staff failed to exploit the experience of endorsers. The longtime campaign manager, Joe Trippi, according to several of his acolytes, was an inspirational but dysfunctional leader, who held authority close to his messy office, left problems to fester and never built a close enough relationship with Dr. Dean.

"Some supporters fretted over advice ignored, and help rebuffed, by an organization more likely to adopt ideas from the blather on its Web log than from people on the payroll. Mr. Trippi insisted it was a myth that he was running the campaign. Now, critics say he was right - nobody was running things at all."[230]

The *Times* also ran an op-ed piece by Jon Margolis, who had been one of the writers of *Howard Dean: A Citizen's Guide to the Man Who Would Be President.* Margolis wrote of "the apparent transformation of a campaign clod into a fiery orator who inspired a movement. In Vermont, Dr. Dean was never a very good politician. He was quite a good governor. On the campaign trail, though, Dr. Dean was a dud. Here was a man with neither a thirst for the political jugular nor a sense of timing.

"Dr. Dean actually had to campaign against Ms. Dwyer (in 2000), and met her and the Progressive Party candidate, Anthony Pollina, in debates. Mr. Pollina won them all. Dr. Dean was almost always stiff. But he did not react well to adversity, perhaps because he had known so little of it. The experienced national political reporters wondered why he blew it. Up here, no one was surprised."[231]

Molly Ivins weighted in on "my man Howard Dean."

"Life is not fair, but I still think a whole lot of people who should have known better freaked out over Dean, treating a mostly mild-mannered, perfectly sensible and quite cheerful fellow as some kind of anti-establishment antichrist. I mean he was governor of Vermont for 10 years (sic), not Lenin.

"But he did tap into some real political anger, and look how many people turn out to be just scared to death of that. Could it be because he (and some very bright young people who worked with him) found this way to raise real money in small amounts from regular people, and that just threatened the hell out of a lot of big corporate special interests? And out of an entire political establishment that is entirely too comfortable with the incestuous relationship between big money and politics?"[232]

Richard Davis, of Thornton, New Hampshire, wrote to the *Boston Globe* that Dean defined "real leadership." He cited the failed candidacy of Adlai Stevenson, "still remembered by many as a pivotal progressive candidate of the 20th century."

Robert Kuttner wrote in the *Globe* that: "New generations of naturally idealistic young keep being born. Dean was the hero of this one. Despite his rebirth as a populist in the campaign, neither his policies nor his temperament suggested a man of the people. The entire machinery of meet-ups and viral enlistment of activists was the raw material of a new-style campaign, but something short of a campaign.

"One recalls the old tongue-in-cheek line, 'We anarchists have to get organized.' Dean didn't. If Dean had been sandbagged by the Democratic Party establishment, you would have thousands of the most energetic of Democratic foot soldiers going away angry - and with justification. But Steve Grossman's exodus speaks for the entire Dean campaign."[233]

The *Globe* analyzed: "History will probably record his role in the 2004 presidential race as that of message-maker. 10-way candidate forums transformed into focused attacks on Dean. He never re-grouped, in part because of the punishing pace of a front-loaded primary and caucus schedule that his party created to produce an early nominee. Dean's sudden fall is a subject of immense sadness for supporters and glee for his detractors.

"The day after New Hampshire" it emerged that "no longer would he wage a promised 50-state campaign; he would instead compete selectively. The *Globe* quoted William Schneider, an analyst at the American Enterprise Institute in Washington: "The other factor is that they just don't like him. Voting for president is the most personal choice people make, and they just haven't warmed up to his personality, and that was way before 'The Scream.' "

Time wrote that Dean "served the dual purpose of channeling the anger of the Democratic base while letting the other candidates sound almost measured in comparison."[234]

When Dean left his Milwaukee headquarters in mid-April, he received a T-shirt from the reporters who had been with the campaign for the entire ride. The shirt mockingly read "Establishment Media: We have the Power."

Andrew Smith suggests: "They (Dean campaign) weren't able to make that difficult transition from being an insurgent to being a frontrunner. Democrats flocked to him early. Or at least were intrigued by him because they were all angry Bush, and they've been angry at Bush going back to 2000, and Dean was angry too... I think what happened was Democratic voters... (moved) on from that anger. But Howard Dean never did, so they got out of sync. He was another insurgent who couldn't take a punch..."

Adrian Walker reflects that "Dean didn't collapse so much as he stopped growing. And part of that lack of growth was not connecting with that traditional, mainstream, urban, Democratic audience. Which, again never seemed to know quite what to make of him."

Steve Grossman speaks about his mistake in Wisconsin. "I called him after I did it, to apologize to him, because, in retrospect, it was a mistake. What I did was a mistake. "But you learn."

Carol Darr says "(Dean) overplayed the antiwar...he had 3 messages...I want my party back, I want my country back, and this particular war was a really bad idea. And it resonated with a whole lot of people.

"He saw that the Democratic Party was just the Republican Party lite, taking money from the same lobbyists, and the people were just fed up with it. I think that was what resonated as much as the anti war stuff. He took on the empire."

Malcolm Saldanha states that "towards the end after the Dean scream speech, they decided to make 100,000 copies of the interview with Diane Sawyer and send it out so we were told on our canvassing trips to offer copies of the tape. That to me seemed like kind of a stunt. I take a dim view on celebrity interviews, like Diane Sawyer, Barbara Walters, because I think .... they become as important as the people they are interviewing. I think that we put these people on a pedestal in terms of the deference they get from the public or people ...just in general I think we make too much of their positions."

Jodi Wilgoren says that "the campaign ended up having... more heat than light... there was always more activity on the Internet than there was any votes.

"I think there are a bunch of things that brought down the campaign. Chief among them was Howard Dean's failure to grow as a candidate. He was a very good insurgent. They had a strategy that brought him an incredible amount of success and he never really grew in response to that."

Mark Wrighton comments on how quickly things can shift in a campaign: "…the anger is what was working for Gov. Dean. In a heartbeat, the double-edged sword switched, and it slashed him. That's politics."

Andrew Smith suggests that "… (a) level of hubris, it really was there. And voters in NH, they see that and they don't like it."

Gwen Graham notes that "… the sealing of his records became a real issue. What's in those records? What you don't know always seems to be the most enticing…you always want to know what you're not supposed to know."

Richard Goodwin comments that "What did him in were his gaffs and his mistakes, none of which, I'm sure were written (in prepared speeches).Some of that was pretty… badly timed…I think it hurt his candidacy badly."

George Stephanopoulos describes his comment to the author in December, when he said he thought the campaign would be a short one: "Either he was going to run the table or the table was going to get run on him. Actually, I thought at that point that Dean was going to do it, but the way it was set up meant that if he won early he would be almost impossible to stop and if he fell early it would almost impossible for him to come back ."

Howard Dean says "I'm sure there are a half a dozen strategic decisions we would have made that are different. If I could control things I couldn't control, I'd peak in December instead of August. But I learned a lot from the run for the Presidency. It's a great country, with bad leadership. The problem is not the people of America, the problem is what's in Washington. I learned I'm a lot tougher than I realized I was.

"The only really bad moments that the public doesn't really know about are the times that I was on the road for a long time. I like being home with my wife and my son; my daughter's in college, of course. I really missed being home when I was on the road.

"Being separated from your family is one of the really tough things in campaigning. But there are a lot of things you've got to do if you want to change the country. And changing is not easy, and we're not nearly done yet. It also has to be sustained, it can't just be a one year of two year effort."

"The rest of the bad ones the public knows about.

"The great moments were meeting people… there are a bunch of really great moments, but one of the greatest was a woman who was on SSI Disability, who'd saved fifty dollars of quarters over the years, and gave me that as a campaign contribution. I just about cried… I could hardly get through it… because she really wanted a different America."

"Presidential campaigns are a whole different matter than practicing medicine. It's very much in the moment, very hard work, very intense. Decisions have to be made very, very quickly."

"It was obviously very frustrating. It's been more frustrating recently. I realize now, that if California had gone first, we would have won. But, I've watched over a thousand hockey games in my life, because both my son and daughter played youth hockey, and complaining about results like that is just, woulda, coulda, shoulda. The referee may make a bad call, and you lose, too bad. That's the way… that's part of the game. So I think that you just have to roll with the punches. Politics is a tough business."

THE SUM OF ALL FEARS

There is unquestionably a contradiction between an efficient technological machine and the flowering of human nature, of the human personality.

ARTHUR MILLER

The *Washington Post* ran a lengthy article by Howard Kurtz that seems to answer many questions about the inner workings of the Dean campaign. Its apparent confirmation of our worst apprehensions had the effect of making us nauseous as we read it. Walter Shapiro has written that "all campaigns are different, though the unhappy ones always provide the best stories." Kurtz seemingly found a great story.

Many people either don't have, or don't take, the time to read past a headline.

The headline read:

"Divide and Bicker; The Dean Campaign's Hip, High-Tech Image Hid a Nasty Civil War." The article featured a number of voices.[235]

Most prominent, and conspicuous in its absence, was that of Howard Dean. While Dean gains voice through the words of others, the article never actually quotes him directly on his campaign.

"Dean did not really want to be president, according to several people who worked with him.

"Dean said at the peak of his popularity late last year that he never expected to rise so high, that he didn't like the intense scrutiny, that he had just wanted to make a difference. 'I don't care about being president,' he said. Months earlier, as his candidacy was taking off, he told a colleague: 'The problem is, I'm now afraid I might win.'

"Dean was swallowed by the bubble that envelops every major candidate, he allowed his campaign to sink into a nasty civil war that crippled decision-making and devastated morale.

274

"In the end, say some of those who uprooted their lives for him, these tensions hastened the implosion that brought Dean down.

"Over the next six weeks (after the Gore endorsement), Dean's rivals escalated their attacks on his fitness for the White House, and he was hit by an avalanche of negative headlines. 'Every media organization and reporter went after us because, you know, take down the front-runner,' he told CNN.

"Dean did not respond to an interview request."

The predominant voice in the article was that of Joe Trippi.

Nature abhors a vacuum. Joe Trippi's human nature appeared to lead him to rush in to fill the vacuum created in the absence of Dean's voice.

His side of the purported "civil war" was laid out in the greatest detail. Trippi seemed to wear union colors, trying to do whatever possible to hold the Dean machine together.

"The polarization revolved around two people: Joe Trippi, the rumpled, passionate, sometimes headstrong campaign manager who drew rock-star coverage in the press, and Kate O'Connor, the quiet, shrewd, low-profile Vermont confidante who never left Dean's side.

"Trippi, 47, said it was 'hard for a campaign manager to function' amid the 'infighting' when he was constantly being undermined. He said O'Connor was trying to help Dean, 'but there were two worldviews of what was best for him, and those two worlds kept colliding.'

'We would have served the governor better if it hadn't existed, but it did, and it did play a role in our not making it. Those differences were a disservice to him. But he is the candidate and had a lot of say.'

"In October, as much of the media and political establishment began to view the former governor as unstoppable, Trippi was so frustrated by the mounting strife that he threatened to resign, he and other officials confirmed.

"Trippi asked his campaign allies to join an 'intervention' with Dean to get things changed, but they told him he was being unrealistic. Trippi's partner in a consulting firm, Steve McMahon, and Trippi's wife, Kathy Lash, a campaign aide, talked him out of quitting. But he made a pact with his wife that, win or lose, he would quit the day after the New Hampshire primary.

"Even when there were just a handful of staffers, Dean and Trippi had trouble seeing eye to eye. Trippi complained to others that the candidate — and O'Connor, who was always by his side — didn't trust him.

"On a plane ride that spring, Dean asked Trippi about working out a contract for his salary and for his consulting firm to handle the advertising.

"As Trippi has recounted to several colleagues, he told Dean to deal with his partner McMahon because he didn't want a salary and wasn't doing this for the money.

"Dean's response, according to these accounts, was to tell another staffer that he would not give Trippi financial control of the campaign because 'he doesn't care about money and I don't want anyone who doesn't care about money managing the money.'

"When Trippi, who worked from a messy office with a beat-up couch in the Burlington, VT, headquarters, had trouble reaching Dean on the road, he became convinced that O'Connor wasn't giving him the messages.

"As fundraising surged and the campaign was rapidly expanding, Trippi tried to hire several seasoned pros but told colleagues that O'Connor had blocked his efforts.

(Regarding a Newsweek report on Dean campaign finances that O'Connor reportedly got Dean agitated over just before an Iowa debate) "Trippi told Dean by phone that the piece was tame.

"Trippi said that 'people like Trish Enright, who thought we should give more access to reporters, were seen as somehow soft on protecting the governor. You got a bad mark next to your name. . . . That created a schism. This was an overly protective group of people who thought they were protecting the governor but were hurting him.'

"While Trippi constantly bantered with reporters, he could lose his temper as well. When the Washington Post's Jim VandeHei wrote a story on Dean's misstatements — filed on the night that he and Trippi had dinner and drinks — Trippi sent word through an aide that neither he nor Dean would speak to him again.

"The strains of the campaign, meanwhile, were exacerbating Trippi's diabetes. On a June visit to California, his blood sugar level got so high that he lost his vision for several hours. But he disregarded medical advice and kept working around the clock. "Trippi, who said he regrets some of the early spending on television ads, tried to stop what he saw as marginal expenses, such as the hiring of a communications director in Maine, the 11th state to vote. Trippi openly grumbled about Dean giving the financial authority to deputy campaign manager Rogan. He and two other senior officials said they were mystified that the amounts they were told they had in the bank would abruptly shrink by millions of dollars after spending decisions had been made.

'With 20/20 hindsight, the biggest mistake I made was not to demand ironclad authority over the budget and check-writing,' Trippi said. 'Bob Rogan is a really good person, one of the best I've met in politics, but he had never run a presidential campaign before and it made no sense to put him in that position.'

"Trippi made the cover of the New Republic, and the Howard Dean phenomenon was taking the country by storm. Trippi seemed to be engaging in false modesty when he kept telling reporters, 'The biggest myth in American politics is that Joe Trippi is running the Dean campaign.' Few grasped at the time that he was sending a veiled message, and that he felt the campaign ship might soon hit an iceberg.

"While he was talked out of quitting in October, Trippi clearly had never bonded with Dean.

'We talked a lot on the phone, but we never became best buds,' Trippi said. 'I respect him a lot more than I liked him. I think he respected me a lot more than he liked me.'

"It was early December, and Dean and Gore had agreed to keep quiet about the former vice president's plan to announce his support within days, fearing a premature leak. Trippi grew suspicious when staffers were asked to charter a large plane to Cedar Rapids, Iowa. He asked Dean, who said someone would be endorsing him but he couldn't tell Trippi who it was. Trippi reminded him that he was the campaign manager. But Dean wouldn't budge.

(After finishing third in the Iowa caucuses) "Trippi told him the front-runner's weight Dean had complained about, because it was forcing him to measure every word, had been lifted from his shoulders, according to accounts from colleagues. Trippi said Dean should tell his supporters that he'd only just begun to fight.

"The warfare continued over Dean's message, the outsider-against-Washington-special-interests pitch that Trippi had developed in a PowerPoint presentation, tested in polls and, despite O'Connor's concerns, used to sell the candidate to major labor unions.

"But Trippi argued that John Kerry and John Edwards had beaten them in Iowa by stealing the message.

Trippi, who had been courting former Gore aide Roy Neel as an addition to the team, started hearing rumors that Neel might replace him. He told O'Connor and Rogan that he was prepared to leave and there was no need for whispered meetings about his future. They assured him there was no effort to dump him.

"On Jan. 28, the day after Dean lost New Hampshire, Trippi had his bags packed, ready to quit. Kathy Lash says she confronted O'Connor and Rogan in

277

their office, saying that they had lied to her husband for days and that this was no way to treat him after all he had done.

"When Dean delivered the news that Neel was getting the top job, Trippi declined an offer to stay on in a secondary role. McMahon repeatedly told Dean he was making a mistake, but Trippi told him to sit down, that he didn't want to make things harder for the governor. When Trippi and his wife left the building, they were surrounded by photographers and concluded the story had been leaked.

"Trippi returned to his farm on Maryland's Eastern Shore, having earned $165,000 through his consulting firm, and signed on as an MSNBC pundit. When Dean bowed out from the presidential race on Feb. 18, Trippi was driving to Washington and could only hear the speech on Rush Limbaugh's radio show, fuming as Limbaugh made disparaging remarks. Afterward, he fought back tears.

'I wouldn't have done it for anybody else,' Trippi said. 'He really did inspire me. . . But it came to a point where I realized I couldn't make a difference in his campaign anymore.'"

Trippi's main opponent in the civil war seemed to be Kate O'Connor. O'Connor seemed to be flying the flag of a confederacy from which Trippi felt excluded.

"O'Connor, 39, joking about her 'evil' reputation, said that 'my mind boggles at some of this stuff. . . . You don't manage Howard Dean, and that was a problem for some people who came in and wanted to manage him. I understood that. Other people just didn't understand that. . . . You learn who the loyal people are. You learn who your friends are.'

"O'Connor, according to a staffer who saw the e-mail, wrote a friend that she wanted to get rid of Trippi and that she felt like quitting herself except that she needed to protect Dean. This followed a clash in which Trippi and other top political advisers helped craft a major Boston speech in which Dean was to denounce special interests — only to have him toss out most of the speech after O'Connor expressed her opposition.

"O'Connor, who said she had 'possibly' sent the e-mail but did not recall it, said Dean felt the speech wasn't suitable for a large rally. But she confirmed that she was "uncomfortable" with the campaign's move toward 'harping on the special interests. . . . I thought it was not a message that was true to who Howard Dean was.' While she offered her opinions, 'the thought that I could manipulate *him is just absurd.'*

"O'Connor does not believe the disagreements damaged Dean's effort. 'Maybe I'm just naive,' she said. 'Maybe it did and I'm oblivious to the fact that it hurt the campaign.'

"Back in 2002, there was just Howard Dean, an obscure small-state governor, and Kate O'Connor, who had managed his Vermont campaigns and was running the presidential effort out of her house.

"Even when there were just a handful of staffers, Dean and Trippi had trouble seeing eye to eye. Trippi complained to others that the candidate — and O'Connor, who was always by his side — didn't trust him.

"O'Connor dismissed that complaint, saying, 'Nobody who wanted to talk to the governor couldn't get to him.'

'Completely false,' said O'Connor. 'I didn't meddle in hiring.' She said Trippi refused to hire some people suggested by Dean, which Trippi confirmed.

"O'Connor said it wasn't her job to decide which journalists got on the plane. But she acknowledged her frustration with the coverage. 'I stopped reading newspapers and watching television,' she said, because many stories were 'completely false.'

("We won't always have the strongest military.") "According to an official who heard the discussions, Dean and O'Connor told Trippi, who was worried about damage control, that the candidate had never used those words and Trippi should explain that to the press. It turned out the Time reporter had recorded Dean's comment.

"O'Connor called the matter 'petty,' saying she could not have disputed the quote because she wasn't there.

"Kate O'Connor knew about the Al Gore endorsement (but Trippi didn't).

"O'Connor said she was simply doing what Dean and Gore wanted.

"Still, she said, 'he didn't expect to be there' as the front-runner, and they were surprised at the intensity of the media barrage. 'We never anticipated the constant getting beaten up over something every single day,' O'Connor said.

(After the Iowa concession speech) "In the days that followed, O'Connor minimized the impact of that moment.

'We didn't get to see television because we were on the road all the time,' she said. 'We had absolutely no idea it was being played all the time.'

"O'Connor insisted she knew nothing until Dean and Neel sealed the deal *that morning. 'There was no 'Get Joe out of here.' I know people don't believe that,' she said.*

"O'Connor thanked her longtime boss at an emotional staff meeting that day. 'I came into this campaign not because I wanted to work in the White House or be a television commentator or write a book,' she said. 'I did it because Howard asked me to help him. My loyalty is to Howard.'

The chorus in the play included many voices, some for attribution, some who would be the ubiquitous "unnamed sources" that are a staple in journalism.

"Interviews with more than a dozen Dean advisers — portions of which were not for attribution because many did not want to be viewed as disloyal to their former boss — produced a picture far different from the public image of a hip, high-tech operation of dedicated Deaniacs.

"Bob Rogan, the deputy campaign manager and, like O'Connor, a longtime Vermont aide to Dean, believes the criticism is overblown.

'While it's easy to blame the Vermonters, I'm not going to participate in the blame game," Rogan said. "It's ridiculous to think that Kate, Howard and I ran this into the mountain on our own.'

"Even the highest-ranking advisers found Dean resistant to changing his approach. Dean strategists say campaign chairman Steve Grossman repeatedly urged the candidate to talk about treating patients as a physician and expressed frustration that Dean never took the advice.

'Unfortunately Howard never took advantage of that unique quality and experience he had, that of being a doctor,' Grossman said. Had Dean used more 'personal examples' involving patients, it 'would have humanized him and created more of an emotional link between him and the voters.'

"Trippi dispatched various aides to accompany Dean and O'Connor on the road, but problems developed each time. One said he was viewed as 'Trippi's spy.' Another said O'Connor would 'kill' people she viewed as insufficiently loyal. A third said staffers were frightened of 'the wrath of Kate.'

'If Washington people wanted to change a position, Kate would be the first one to say no, because she knows how long and how adamantly the governor held a particular position,' said Sue Allen, Dean's longtime Vermont spokeswoman.

'She had the thankless job of keeping him on message. He's the kind of guy

who will chat with somebody and change his opinion. She would control access, and that angers people. . . . She's a handy scapegoat.'

David Bender, the New York senior deputy campaign director, said that when O'Connor complained about exhaustion and he suggested some time off, 'she looked at me with a ferocity in her manner and voice and said: 'I know they want to get rid of me. . . . I will do this job if I have to do it from a hospital bed hooked up to an IV because I'm the only one who protects Howard. Everyone else wants something from him.'

"Dean's often testy relations with journalists were exacerbated, several officials said, by what one who spent time on the trail called O'Connor's 'contemptuous attitude toward the press.'

"When Dean was to fly from New York to Detroit and back on a small charter, O'Connor turned down a request by New York Times correspondent Jodi Wilgoren to ride along, a campaign official said. At a luncheon, Wilgoren slipped Dean a note saying the staff's decision would prevent her from covering the Detroit event. Dean overruled the staff and allowed her on the plane.

'Kate didn't speak to me for a couple of weeks because I'd gone around her,' Wilgoren said.

"Several officials say O'Connor helped stoke Dean's anger about articles viewed as negative, sometimes before public events. She 'got him very worked up' about a Newsweek report on his finances before an Iowa debate, said one staffer who saw her read it on her laptop.

"Dean sometimes pressed Tricia Enright, the communications director, to complain to editors about negative stories by their reporters and say Dean would no longer deal with those reporters — calls that Enright usually declined to make, two officials said.

"Enright said she tried 'to develop relations with the media.'

"Even Trippi's admirers dubbed him the "mad scientist," a fast-talking, frenetic salesman who worked the phones all day and spent the wee hours answering bloggers on the campaign's Website. But his detractors said he wasn't attending to the nuts and bolts of staffing and scheduling.

'Joe was a brilliant strategist, but he wasn't a manager,' said an official sympathetic to O'Connor. 'We all tried to fill in for Joe's shortcomings.'

"Enright's press operation also drew some internal flak, with detractors saying she held no morning message meeting and was slow in getting back to reporters. National spokesman Jay Carson said the campaign 'got so big so fast *that we weren't ready for a lot of the stuff that came down the pike.'*

"Enright said her small staff, which she couldn't get permission to expand, was deluged with hundreds of calls a day. 'We did the best we could with the resources we had,' she said. 'A lot of times it was triage.'

'Everyone worked their heart out,' McMahon said, 'whether they had been around Howard a long time or a short time. The system that Howard set up and Howard liked was a lot of different people giving him a lot of different advice simultaneously. That's not necessarily the best way to run a presidential campaign, but it was the way he was comfortable with.'

"Said Rogan: 'The revisionist historians are hard at work. Together we made some mistakes, all of us. What I managed was the checkbook, not the spending decisions. . . . It's preposterous to suggest I was the one making those decisions unilaterally.' He said Dean, Trippi, McMahon and pollster Paul Maslin were all involved, a point confirmed by McMahon.

"It was during this period that some senior officials became convinced that Dean wasn't serious about doing what it takes to win the White House, especially when he refused repeated requests to ask his wife, Judith Steinberg Dean, to make even an occasional campaign appearance.

"But others felt the campaign should have been better prepared to play defense and that this contributed to the daily drip of damaging stories.

"Senior officials, for instance, said they had never been able to gain access to the boxes of Dean records in O'Connor's garage or the files kept in her car trunk. Enright had reviewed tapes of Dean's appearances on a Canadian talk show from 1996 to 2002, but there was one tape she never got — and NBC triggered a flap by reporting that Dean on that tape had disparaged the Iowa caucuses as 'dominated by the special interests.' "The staff blamed O'Connor, who said she had never seen that tape and that the material in her Ford Focus was just news clips from Dean's gubernatorial days.

"Campaign officials said they also tried to get O'Connor to dig out old National Rifle Association questionnaires completed by Dean. Enright was blindsided when the New York Times obtained one from a rival campaign, showing that Dean had opposed restrictions on owning assault weapons — a contradiction of his current position.

"When Dean, despite raising $40 million, finished third in Iowa on Jan. 19, he ripped up his prepared remarks and started yelling on his campaign bus, officials said, proclaiming that the message of taking on Washington's entrenched *interests hadn't worked, that the grassroots were a mirage and had let him down.*

"Returning to Vermont, O'Connor maintained in a meeting with Hollywood activist Rob Reiner, who had flown in to advise Dean, that people were overreacting to the high-decibel speech and voters didn't care. "Reiner was flabbergasted at this attitude — he wondered whether the staff was 'crazy' — and expressed amazement that they hadn't moved faster to neutralize the issue, two participants said.

"Dean's policy director, Jeremy Ben-Ami, declared in an e-mail: 'The message of the campaign is simply no longer our campaign vs. the special interests. This is not what the governor wants to be saying — or frankly what he ever really wanted to be saying.'

"Joe Drymala, the chief speechwriter who received the e-mail, resigned in protest. 'I refused to believe it because I didn't want to,' he said. 'To believe that was to believe that Howard Dean was a fraud.'

"Ben-Ami said he was explaining that Dean 'wanted his message to be at least equally focused on solutions and his record.'

"Rogan said he had known for a couple of days that Dean was courting Neel but that 'the governor was hoping Joe could accept he needed some help with his management skills and would see it as a positive.'"

Howard Dean talks about campaigns: "I think there's infighting in every campaign and I think it has relatively little to do with the results of the campaign. Anytime you get a large number of talented people together there are going to be some people who are pretty insistent on their own points of view."

Between the time of his demotion/resignation and Dean's withdrawal, Trippi maintained a high profile. After Dean's withdrawal and before his announcement of his new plans on March 18, Dean was nearly silent in the media, while Trippi seemed omnipresent.

Following the withdrawal, Trippi analyzed Dean's campaign and its legacy.

"I think the first thing is that both candidates sound a lot more like

Dean in message and tone. Particularly when you look at how they both voted for the war and No Child Left Behind — They have moved.

"One of the things I think that people don't realize about the Dean campaign is the dramatic difference this movement will make in 10 years. A lot of the young and new people who have been brought in may not realize it today, but many of them will be members of Congress, state Representatives, Senators and one of them will be President of the United States. Few campaigns create change over successive election cycles. The Dean campaign has already done that. There are people who are leaders in Meetups or took leadership at local Dean efforts who will run for office, who will become members of Congress, who will become Senators, who will become the President of the United States — that is the legacy of the Dean campaign. The Dean campaign lit a match and the fire will not go out.

"Every frontrunner goes through intense scrutiny once they become the presumptive nominee. It is the course of politics. It happened with Jimmy Carter in '76. It happened with Clinton in '92, but for the first time in history, it happened to a candidate before a single vote was cast. In other words, what usually happens is a candidate comes out of nowhere after winning a few states — the Dean campaign was the first campaign to emerge as strong as it did before a vote was cast. What that means is that all the other campaigns decided right after Al Gore endorsed us that they had to kill Dean and his campaign right there. The press, now alerted to the front-running nature of the Dean campaign, decided they had to put Howard Dean through the kind of intensive scrutiny that all presumptive nominees must go though with the press. There was no grand conspiracy, it was just two gigantic forces honing down on Dean at the worst time — three weeks before a vote had been cast. The one thing I think people have lost sight of was that our strategy had worked. We had run all the other candidates to the ground. Kerry was literally at that moment a dead man walking — out of money, nowhere in the polls, a campaign that was laying flat on the ground. The other campaigns weren't doing a lot better. The biggest thing that happened at that moment was that John Kerry wrote himself a $6.4 million check. And he deserves credit for that — he looked into the abyss and said "Hell no, I am going to fight, put my own money in and go to Iowa." Now I am not saying that if Kerry had not written that check that Dean would have survived the hits and won Iowa, but I am saying that if you look at the fact that Kerry got 34 percent and Edwards got 32 percent, that that $6.2 million was more than a 2 percent bump. The case could be made that without that money Edwards could have won Iowa. And New Hampshire would have become an Edwards vs. Dean race and the Dean campaign and the nomination fight would be in a much different place today than it is. What you had were these two forces bearing down, while the Gephardt campaign admitted it had engaged in a "murder-suicide pact" in which they decided they had to kill Howard Dean at the risk of killing themselves if they were to have any shot at the nomination. They accomplished both. At the same time Kerry wrote himself a check breathing life into his campaign at just the right moment.

"The fact is that I made about $165,000 working on the Dean campaign over a 13 month period. While $165,000 is a lot of money, it is not $7 million. I never worked on any political campaign for money. I specifically, after being out of presidential politics since 1988, came back to run the Dean campaign because Dean inspired me to continue to make a difference, and that was my motivation. What I found most rewarding is not money, but the people across the county who are now involved.

"The real issue is why do they want to make you think I made $7 million instead of $165,000? How do you stop a movement for change? To make everyone think that the whole thing was a scheme to make Joe Trippi rich instead of believing that it is about changing the country. And believe me, there are a lot of people out there with an interest in stopping a movement devoted to changing the country, but I intend to stay in this fight.

"I think there are several people in the race Dean genuinely liked and considered friends.

"I think Sen. Graham was one, who had also been governor of Florida. I think since they had both been governors they had worked together and found a mutual respect. Carol Moseley Braun and Dean really did connect from the days when he was the underdog. That is probably one of the reasons Braun endorsed Dean just before Iowa.

"Dick Gephardt was another candidate who Gov. Dean had a lot of respect for and again they knew each other because of the battles they fought over healthcare over the years and because in 1988 Gov. Dean supported Dick Gephardt for president and spoke on his behalf across the country.

"On Kerry and Edwards — I think with many of the other candidates it wasn't a question of like or dislike. I think that because they were Senators and their paths never crossed Dean didn't have much of a relationship with either that I am aware of, so I think it would be unfair of me to comment on his feeling of any one.

"Dean led the way in turning the Democratic Party into a true opposition party that would stand up to the president when he was wrong and say so loudly. That is one of the reasons we are finally having a debate about where the WMD are. It is responsible for why Bush's numbers and favorable ratings have fallen so low that Kerry and Edwards now lead the president by over 10 points in the latest Gallup poll. And lest you console yourself with the fact that we are months away from the general election and the polls don't matter let me remind you that at this point in 1992 Bill Clinton was 20 points behind George H. W. Bush.

"Second, Dean built a grassroots movement that has energized the party and brought in new voters. He took a party that believed no one could beat Bush and energized it, mobilized new voters into the party, and the entire party today is filled with energy. He also proved that this party could raise millions from small amounts from thousands of Americans. I believe before this cycle is out millions of Americans will contribute in small amounts to defeat Bush and they will do it because Dean showed how to.

"Third, George Bush opted out of the public funding system. You can thank Howard Dean for the fact that John Kerry also opted out because the Kerry campaign stated that the only way they were going to opt out was if Howard Dean did it. The Dean campaign forced John Kerry to opt out as well. That fact means that if John Kerry is the nominee he will be able to compete dollar for dollar against George Bush. Even that is a direct result of Howard Dean's campaign.

"I think there are a lot of threats to grassroots organization. One of the things I can say after working so hard with the Dean campaign — it is unbelievable what the Federal Election Commission's impediments are to local grassroots organizers. The fact that if 20 or 30 people in a town who get together and print leaflets to pass out, once they raise or spend $5000, have to file with the commission, make quarterly reports, etc. is ridiculous.

"The rules were all created in a media age where campaigns were raising lots of money to buy TV ads. They meant to regulate three or four wealthy contributors putting together a committee and spending hundreds of thousands of dollars. Yet the same rules apply to a small group printing leaflets at Kinko's. After this election cycle I would like to make the case to the FCC that they have to change their regulations. The American people's involvement in the process needs to be encouraged not impeded.

"I believe the Dean campaign really did light a match of change and started a brushfire within the grassroots."[236]

Howard Kurtz' "Media Notes" in the *Washington Post* analyzed the media's shortcomings in the campaign.

"It's time for political reporters to swear off some long-standing habits. For decades, they have built their campaign narratives around four bedrock pillars: money, organization, polls and endorsements. But much of that has crumbled in the shifting sands of the 2004 race, most recently when John Edwards surged to a surprising second-place finish in the Wisconsin primary.

"The missteps were magnified by a prediction-obsessed culture in which many pundits and journalists were all but writing off candidates as the voting began and constantly trying to push the narrative to the next phase and get on with the general election.

"It's hard to fault correspondents for relying on what has usually worked in the past. But like generals fighting the last war, they wound up using muskets and cannonballs in an age of laser-guided missiles.

"Any political reporter whose humility level has not at least quintupled based on the events of this cycle should probably find something else to do in four years," says Mark Halperin, ABC's political director.

"The usual indices are 'a crutch because there are so few other ways to measure,'" says *Philadelphia Inquirer* reporter Dick Polman.

"In the case of Howard Dean," he says, "when the tech stock was rising we had no way of knowing how it was going to trade on the open market, when voters actually got involved.

"At the beginning of the year, *USA Today* rated the Democrats by bestowing donkeys. Dean got four donkeys ("good odds") and Dick Gephardt three ("some chance"), with two apiece ("long shot") for John Kerry and Edwards. Oops.

"The standard measurements of campaign progress remain "good yardsticks," says *USA Today* reporter Jill Lawrence. "Perhaps what we underemphasized was this really strong sentiment among Democrats to pick the candidate they thought could best beat Bush. And perhaps what we over-relied on in the conventional wisdom is the capacity for lightning-quick changes at the last minute."

"Reporters love to write pieces about ground troops, phone banks and get-out-the-vote drives, fueled by the belief that this is what wins elections. Dean and Gephardt were favored in Iowa in part because they were seen as having the strongest field operations. But they finished well behind Kerry and Edwards

"Al Gore's endorsement of Dean was trumpeted as a political earthquake but did little to help him. Nor did the backing of former senator Bill Bradley or Iowa Senator Tom Harkin. Popular South Carolina congressman Jim Clyburn supported Kerry, who still lost the state to Edwards.

"The problem with all these ironclad rules set out by the 4,000 people who pay attention in the year before the election is that we don't have a very long history in the modern era," Halperin says. "A vibrant democracy can produce things that even the minds of Howard Fineman and Adam Nagourney can't fathom," he says, referring to the *Newsweek* and *New York Times* correspondents.

"There's a cognitive dissonance between the reporters who live with this every single day and a general public that's barely thinking about it" until each state votes, Polman says. "We need to get away from the traditional indicators and talk to people more."

"MSNBC anchor Laurie Jennings was conducting a routine interview with Bob Dole last week when she asked about Vice President Cheney and his former company, Halliburton.

"He hasn't been in Halliburton for years. . . . I don't think most Americans buy that, despite the liberal media's efforts, like MSNBC, to push it every day," the former Republican senator said. When Jennings protested that MSNBC was trying to be fair, Dole retorted: "Keep trying. You're a long way from it, but keep trying. . . . Don't slant it." Dole then trotted out Fox News's trademark phrase, saying coverage should be "fair and balanced." "[237]

MIT linguistics professor **Noam Chomsky** describes himself as a critic of the "elite media." Chomsky saw the *Washington Post* article in a different light.

"Journalists are often perfectly competent. But infighting is common in organizations. There's infighting on the board of directors at General Motors, or any other corporation.

"The Sixties are portrayed the same way as the Dean campaign. 'Kids going crazy, breaking windows, smoking pot.' That portrayal obscures the fact that the Sixties produced civil rights, women's rights, environmental awareness, etc.

"I was struck that commentators more liberal than Dean hated him with a passion. The only reason I can think of is that he was bringing about a democracy by involving so many young people.

"The countries with the most freedom can't control people with force, so they have to use the media.

"The reaction to the Dean scream was a way of expressing fear and hatred of the possibility of democracy.

"Compare the reaction to Dean to that with Eugene McCarthy. It's a perfect counterpoint to the Dean phenomena.

"McCarthy, the liberals' hero, was a total fraud, a total cynic, one of the worst frauds in American history. When his supporters were beaten bloody at the Chicago convention by police, he didn't scream.

"When he lost the nomination, McCarthy went off and wrote poetry, wrote about baseball.

"What they hate about Dean is that Dean is saying 'let's go on.' And that's unacceptable. McCarthy just went away. Dean kept at it. Therefore, he's a devil."

John Dower says "Chomsky has been regarded as beyond the fringe. The sign of changing times, though, is that, I think, until the last year or so, Chomsky was never on mainstream anything. He was never in the mainstream media, never picked up on mainstream television, or even cable very much. He was a real, real fringe element. He's always listed as extremist and he's always listed as ferociously anti-American. Whereas what he's doing is saying 'I have an ideal for this country, and it is not living up to it." It's only in the last year or so that he's starting to be on C-span, CNN. They're starting to say 'he was right on many things.'

"And he's not a wild-eyed flaming guy, he marshalls a lot of facts. You can disagree with him, but he's got a lot of interesting things to say. His marginalization…I think that what's very interesting is that a man who speaks out…what Dean was saying would have been absolutely centrist throughout the rest of the world. What Chomsky's saying…he's probably the most translated American in the world. And certainly probably the best known name in the world. Anything that we call extreme left in this country is centrist in almost any other country in the world. Because we have become a very conformist, very conservative country."

Satanic images weren't strictly the province of Noam Chomsky, however.

Helen Thomas is arguably the dean of White House correspondents. Under the George W. Bush administration, she has been treated as a "non-person," to use Stalinist terms.

Thomas' view of what happened to Dean is quite like Chomsky's:

"I do believe he was demonized; I have never seen such a pile on against a candidate in one's own party.

"I do think the establishment had already picked Kerry, and were determined not to allow an upstart take over.

"Who determines electability, anyway?

"Dean was the spark plug and put some life into Kerry, et alia."

Kerry's resurrection came in the same year as a film about Christ inflamed public opinion while drawing huge box office numbers, and a remake of a film about zombies, *Dawn of the Dead*, brought the undead into theaters everywhere. Perhaps apropos of Kerry's DLC support, the fabulously wealthy Republican Bob Hope had defined zombies in 1940. Hope's character in *The Ghost Breakers* was told "A zombie has no will of his own. You see them walking around blindly with dead eyes, following orders, not knowing what they do, not caring."

Hope's response was "You mean like Democrats?"

Kerry's poll numbers remained stagnant after he had been anointed. McAuliffe had declared on February 20th that "people are turning out in record numbers." However, Curtis Gans, of the nonpartisan Committee for the Study of the American Electorate, noted that the Democratic turnout in primaries was generally low, the third lowest on record, in aggregate. Only New Hampshire and Wisconsin had shown impressive increases, according to Gans. The numbers in Iowa doubled from 2000, but were equal to those of 1988. New York State reached a record low on March 2.

That led the powers that be within the Democratic Party to urge their reluctant nominee to announce John Edwards as his running mate. Polling showed Edwards adding from 5 to 7 percent to the ticket. Media speculation had Kerry considering John McCain as a running mate. McCain had worked with his fellow vet Kerry to normalize relations with Vietnam. When asked if he would cross party lines to run with Kerry, McCain had said "Obviously I would entertain it." McCain's chief of staff was backtracking and denying such a possibility within the same day.

Hillary Clinton ruled out running for the position being elusively occupied by Dick Cheney in mid-March. Former Clinton adviser Dick Morris, who had been tabloid fodder himself, had written that Kerry should choose the Senator from New York or risk a "schism" in the Democratic Party.

Kerry had never ignited people himself. Polling data in early 2004 from the Ray C. Bliss Institute of Applied Politics had placed Dean at 86 and Bush at 12 on a "feeling thermometer". Kerry had come in at a lukewarm 56, a temperature that probably would cause alarm in a Board of Health restaurant inspection.

An electorate that is either polarized or disinterested might be prime territory for another Nader candidacy. Nader had indicated that he probably would not run if the Democrats choose Dean.

Princeton professor Sean Wilentz hosed down the embers of a Nader movement with a column in the *New York Times*: "Historians and pundits like to cite the rise of Abraham Lincoln's Republican Party as the exception to the rule about the small influence of third parties and candidates in American presidential politics. Ralph Nader, with his announcement that he will try to challenge what he calls a 'duopoly' that makes Washington 'a corporate-occupied territory,' seems to think that he can replicate the original Republicans' spectacular success.

"But Nader will never be a Lincoln - for we are not living in the latter-day equivalent of the 1850s. After four years of the corporate-dominated

Bush administration, the Democrats are more united and outspoken in their goals than they have been for many years.

"Nader offers little to differentiate himself from liberal Democrats besides tarter slogans about corporate greed and domination. On 'Meet the Press,' Nader contemptuously dismissed critics who have called him a spoiler, charging that such complaints would never arise in Western Europe or Canada. Third parties can only be goads or spoilers (now). Nader has committed himself to performing the second (role) in living out his grandiose delusions about destroying the Democratic Party. If Nader could magically rewrite the United States Constitution and replace it with Italy's, his continuing efforts might gain plausibility. They would at least qualify as rational.

"He is destined for political oblivion. He may leave behind as his most striking achievement the re-election of George W. Bush-a man who stands aggressively for everything Nader claims is most corrupt about America."[238]

The author asked "If you were crossing a parking lot right now and you ran into Ralph Nader, what would you say to him?

Howard Dean responded "I'll tell you what I said privately to him... I think this is not the right year for a third party candidate. The stakes are too great for America."

Dean endorsed Kerry by the end of March, and Kerry's fundraising had begun to climb sharply in April. Kerry would need it, as $40 million dollars spilled out of the overflowing Bush coffers in March, with $30 million going towards advertising that targeted Kerry.

Kerry had taken a vacation from the campaign trail, and produced the kind of personality analysis that had been Dean's domain for so long, when he cursed at a Secret Service agent after colliding with him on the toney slopes of Sun Valley.

Kerry's cabinet was also subject to media speculation. Kerry's advisers Sandy Berger, Richard Holbrooke, Joe Biden, and George Mitchell were all considered to be possibilities for the hot seat of National Security adviser occupied by Condoleezza Rice.

Rice, the reluctant public witness on the Administration's anti-terror efforts preceding 9/11, was portrayed on John Kerry's favorite TV show, *Saturday Night Live*, by another fading star, Janet Jackson.

Jackson had suffered a very public costume malfunction at the Super Bowl, when Justin Timberlake ripped off the covering to one of her breasts. This had led to a terribly retro clamor for decency on the airwaves, so that viewers besotted with the violence of football would not be subjected to any more graphic portrayals of the human body than were routinely exposed by the Dallas Cowboy Cheerleaders. The afore-mentioned cheerleaders had first caught the nation's leering eye, more than a quarter century earlier. This was before C-SPAN was available to distract from more titillating issues; a CBS Sports producer had said "the audience deserves a little sex with its violence."

On SNL, a character portraying Cheney had successfully urged Jackson, portraying Rice, to flash a pixilated breast to distract 9/11 questioners. Joe Klein commented on American culture: "We are addicted to the explicit, and then quickly inured to it.

"In this campaign we have already been buffeted by exceedingly powerful social and political images... Janet Jackson's exposed breast... Howard Dean screaming.

"It is also possible that a public besotted with the sensational will be unable to engage in a substantive argument - and instead be deflected into periphery. In 2004, the quality of the debate may be the election's most important question: Are we going to be serious about this or not? Democratic voters, a perversely serious minority of whom rejected the passionate Howard Dean in favor of John Kerry, a candidate nuanced to the point of paralysis."[239]

Klein's take on Dean had seemed to change once he was out of the race: "With Howard Dean gone from the race, the last traces of passion - and, I fear, conviction - have been leached from the electorate. Unfortunately, without Dean, the Democratic primaries are lapsing into a synthetic and unsatisfying beauty pageant.

"Edwards is not a particularly sharp candidate. He is a slick speaker, but lacks the crackle and candor of Dean's plain talk. Indeed, Edwards gives the same speech, platitude for platitude, every time.

"Kerry has a flannel-mouthed inability to utter a simple sentence, but his orotundities also serve to reinforce the notion that the Senator is a patrician stiff, too smug to speak in a manner decipherable by ordinary

Americans. There was a real sense last week that Kerry, assuming victory, had lapsed into flabby aristocratic entitlement, a persona he inhabits when not in mortal combat."[240]

Charles Barkley is a TNT NBA commentator, a millionaire, and a Republican who has threatened to run for governor of Alabama. His commentary on American culture is equally astute: "America is a funny place. Should she have done it? Probably not. But it's not like she started a war or something, just to make money. I wish people were more irate with the Bush administration for starting a war for profit than they were with Janet Jackson for showing her breast. But that's America - we don't know what's important and what's not important."

The Internet search engine Lycos had recorded that the number of searches for Jackson had tied the record set by 9/11 related searches on and just after 9/11. Aaron Schatz, a columnist on the Lycos top 50 site wrote "That a single breast received as much attention as the first attack on United States soil in 50 years is beyond belief."

Kerry advisers again floated McCain's name, this time as a possible Secretary of Defense. Battle lines were definitively drawn. George W. Bush's Gallup Poll approval ratings showed members of the two parties polarized by a vastly greater amount than any president back through Harry Truman.

In Iraq, things kept on getting worse, because you can't kill ideas with guns, and American ideology just wasn't taking root the way the Bush seed catalog had promised. As marching lines of Redcoats had seen in the American Revolution, insurgents learn how to succeed, whatever the odds.

It would be the measure of Howard Dean, whether or not he would be an insurgent who learned.

For the members of Dean Nation, it was both the best and worst of times.

It was the best, in that they had lifted an obscurity, an asterisk, to national prominence, where he could influence the Democratic discourse. They had raised record amounts of money, and participated in ways unimagined before the development of the Internet, and blogs, and Meetups. By mid-April, *Democracy for America* had identified over 500 candidates drawn into local and state-wide races across the country by the activism the Dean campaign had spurred.

It was the worst of times, in that when Dean's victory had seemed inevitable, the tide had reversed, leaving them high and dry. It was also, for many in Dean Nation, a tale of two cities. The campaign had risen from national headquarters in the very small city of Burlington, Vermont. Eminently livable, the college town looked out upon Lake Champlain, which Vermont Senator Patrick Leahy had once tried to have labeled a new Great Lake. On the other side of town ran the mountains (Verdes Montes, Green Mountains in Latin) from which Vermont got its name.

A campaign based on the technology that empowered Dean Nation had arisen from the idealists who truly believed in Howard Dean, and in the messengers who were the link between the campaign's leadership and the grassroots.

The other city was Washington. The entrenched political establishment of the Democratic Party made its home there. While the media might come under varied headings that implied their bases were elsewhere, the messengers that the Nation saw as having delivered Dean to the altar of political sacrifice were all *Washington* reporters.

It is said that the pioneers get the arrows, and the settlers get the land. Kerry had appropriated the message of Dean, without the microscopic examination Dean had endured. Kerry would have a shot at the land on Pennsylvania Avenue, while Dean would remain in his rather plain little home in Burlington.

Kerry's ability to deliver the message is a continuing source of concern. In March, his summary of the legislative process in the Senate provided fodder for anyone who wanted to see him as a "waffler." Kerry explained his Iraq stance with "I actually did vote for the $87 billion, before I voted against it." Viewed outside of the context in which bills are modified in the Senate, it sound-bit him in the ass.

Kerry's opposition, having successfully questioned the patriotic qualifications of Max Cleland, who had merely lost three limbs for his country, was aiming squarely at Kerry's patriotism. Kerry's ancestry in France was a subject of regular news coverage. The man who had skippered one of Kerry's swift boats before Kerry was quoted as saying "I had a dislike for the man as soon as I met him. He was not a genuine type of guy." The validity of Kerry's Purple Hearts, the first of which had been initially rejected by Kerry's commander until he "acquiesced" after receiving "some correspondence", was now media fodder.

One of the crew members on Kerry's first swift boat was inspired to speak out against Kerry, after he heard Rush Limbaugh question Kerry's war credentials. Kerry's campaign considered legal action against what they called lies and slander on the Wild West electronic frontier. Kerry had been called "baby killer" on the Internet.

The fact was, in the heat of battle, Kerry's crew did kill a baby, by mistake. Swift boat commanders had wide latitude in Vietnam in "free-fire" zones to shoot first. Kerry was inclined toward caution, for which he was, of course criticized by at least one former fellow warrior.

It is worth saying that those who go to battle are damned if they do, damned if they don't, and really, damned to and by their experience. Kerry is remembered as having told crew members under his command to call him "John" on the river and "sir" back at the base. As far as being overly cautious, Kerry had spent his first tour on a guided-missile frigate, which would be largely out of harms way, before he signed up for a swift boat tour. On the second tour, he would see men around him wounded, and watch someone carrying a human being in two halves.

If the 25 year-old Kerry saw a war around him that seemed to be of dubious merit, and unproductive savagery, and he found three Purple Hearts bought him a ticket Stateside, it can be seen as in service to conscience as much as to self-interest. The crewmember who volunteered to appear in Iowa, Jim Rassmann, is a Republican. His commitment to the man who saved his life is clearly not out of political expedience.

Politics is a dirty game.

George W. Bush, a man whose moral compass could serve as a ceiling fan, knows this.

War is hell.

John Kerry knows this.

A stated goal in writing this book was, in addition to relating an intense personal experience, to provide objective journalism that would explain the arc of the Dean campaign.

That is simply not possible.

In the early years of modern atomic theory, it seemed that the electron might be the smallest particle in nature. Attempts to pinpoint the electron, and, therefore, define the parameters of the atom, seemed doomed to failure. This led German physicist Walter Heisenberg, who would ultimately lead the Nazi effort to make an atomic bomb, to formulate The Uncertainty Principle. Generally speaking, it said that the electron could not be fully knowable, that the act of measuring one parameter would change another.

A similar case could be made philosophically about any measurement. The act of measuring changes that which is being measured.

Journalism, even at its most objective and professional, has attempted to measure and define the Dean campaign. In the process it traced and propelled the very arc of the campaign.

Journalists are always faced with a semantic black hole. Eskimos are said to have dozens of words to describe snow. That ever-expanding vocabulary indicates an inadequacy in the process of describing something so fundamental to their culture. Every time a journalist chooses a word, or a picture, or a video image, an uncertainty principle kicks in.

In the evolution of this book from a tale of personal experience to one of analysis, I initially thought, condescendingly and rather paternalistically, that I could provide readers an explanation of what happened. I don't want to pretend to be capable of doing that. There are many limitations, to both my own capabilities, and to semantics.

For the reader seeking conclusive answers, the best source of understanding may have been in Howard Dean's response to a supporter during his withdrawal speech.

By the time the speech came around, I had begun working to remove myself emotionally from the topic of the book.

But hearing that exchange broke through that distance and flooded me with emotion.

During his speech, a supporter called out, "We believe in you!"

Dean's answer was firm and instantaneous.

"Believe in yourself."

HOWIE, WE HARDLY KNEW YE

For a successful technology, reality must take precedence over public relations, for Nature cannot be fooled.
RICHARD P. FEYNMAN, What Do You Care What Other People Think?

"If you bring forth that which is inside you, what you bring forth will save you. If you do not bring forth that which is inside you, what you do not bring forth will destroy you."

Gospel of St. Thomas

The anger of Dean Nation, with the media and the Establishment, reflected a dissonance between the man they felt they knew and the one that was portrayed before them.

To them, he was the good doctor. However, not everyone sees the culture of doctors as good.

USA Today reports that "He (Dean) readily volunteers that his medical background has helped him and hurt him in politics... 'When he first became governor, he acted like a doctor,' says Jeanne Keller, a health-care policy analyst who was president of a statewide employer coalition on health during most of Dean's tenure. 'Accept our word for it. We know the answer.' It was like 'take this legislation and call me in the morning.' He developed the humility that non-doctors have later on.' ...Humility hasn't been Dean's hallmark in the race.

"'I know there's always another patient,' he says. 'So I tend not to be process-oriented. There are lots of stories about how abrupt I can be with legislators. That's not helpful in politics."[241]

"For at least the last three decades, the talk and the style of Washington have been dominated by a permanent corps of successful political operatives, lobbyists and journalists... Dean criticizes (them), sometimes harshly, sometimes with a touch of the snide. The establishment tribe does not approve of these manners especially when exhibited by Democrats."[242]

Stephen Ansolabehere and Shanto Iyengar had seen the very Party Dean was often attacking as the key to the campaign reform that the Dean movement seemed to promise. Since it was in the Democratic Party's vested interest to keep participation high and pull in the non-partisans, a stronger Party was their remedy for reversing voter apathy. Dean's prescription for campaign success targeted the same groups, but he was simultaneously attacking the Party that shared his goals.

Vermont journalist Jon Margolis had foreseen the troubles resulting from Dean's personality. "What no one can predict is whether Dean will beat himself - which he is totally capable of doing. For example, he can be prickly."[243]

Prickly or not, Dean is a private man, a man apart. He always showed an unwillingness to have the laundry of his personal life aired in public. Even if he had, it was spotless by the standards of the 21st century, so the media would have to look elsewhere.

Dean, who rejected labels in what he saw as a pragmatic approach to issues, had embraced the role of liberal, and been damned with a capital "L". Dean had come into politics as a supporter of Jimmy Carter, who had faced a challenge from the left in the form of Teddy Kennedy. "Worse, from the liberal perspective, is the fact that a combination of conservative cleverness and liberal obtuseness has created the impression that a liberal is someone who is not tough enough."[244]

His future in politics as a candidate is unclear. In late October, a statewide poll in Vermont had given Dean a 40 percent unfavorable rating, with 49 percent favorable. Forty-one (41) percent of likely voters also said they disapproved of Dean's seeking the presidency. Six months later, these figures remained statistically unchanged, despite Dean's expenditure of over 50 million dollars.

Vermont voters' memories of Dean's governorship hadn't been glowing either: in June 2002, 47 percent of respondents identifying themselves as likely voters had rated Dean's time as governor as either fair or poor. In April 2004, a majority of Vermonters surveyed opposed the idea of John Kerry selecting Dean as a running mate. Despite Dean's victory in the Vermont primary, only 40% of Vermonters surveyed indicated that they would have preferred Dean as the Democratic nominee.

Thirty-one (31) percent of Vermonters surveyed in April felt that Dean had lost due to his own faults, 23 % blamed the media, and 27% felt Dean shared the blame with the media.[245]

Dean's New York roots might bode better for another run at the Presidency than his residence in Vermont. The only two native Vermonters to serve in the White House -Chester Arthur and Calvin Coolidge - ascended to the office after the deaths of Garfield and Harding. Perhaps that was why Dean's name never came up in discussion of a running mate for Kerry.

Dean's responses to the media had not helped his cause.

"With few exceptions, Vermont's journalists tend to be gentle. That's what Dean was used to. Dean, though no charlatan, was at first less than nimble, denying, for instance, that he had ever spoken favorably about the idea of raising the Social Security age. He must have thought he was in Vermont, where reporters were less likely to check old transcripts."[246]

Dean's lack of agility was shown when he told a New Mexico audience that the United States should not "take sides" in the dispute between Palestinians and Israelis. "Not to 'take sides' sounded a little like being 'even-handed,' an old phrase that once meant granting bona fides even to the Palestinian hard-liners who seek nothing less than Israel's dissolution. Dean, whose wife and children are Jewish, meant nothing of the sort."[247]

Dean's efforts to reveal a warmer side had been too little, too late. The 125,000 copies of the interview he and his wife did with Diane Sawyer had smacked somewhat of desperation.

It must be hard to have a dream slip away, when you've held it in your hands.

Kathy Sullivan says, "Since the whole thing collapsed, I've said to some folks that I just don't how you deal with that. Because here is a man who must have seen the path to the White House. It was there - it was before him. And then, pffft, it's gone. It's just gone…His followers were looking at him as all things to all people. I remember meeting Howard Dean back at the office in Concord. The more moderate guy. Part of that is, as Democrats… we let them (the Republicans) get away with defining us. To be opposed to the war in Iraq meant you suddenly became some sort of left wing, whereas to me, it's common sense. I hope everybody's anti-war. Nobody should be pro-war.

"I defended Howard Dean because the DLC really went after him. I think most people in America are moderate. But the DLC, it was just offensive to me. They were just attacking the guy. I was on their mailing list and I would get their weekly faxes with their talking points and their position papers and I finally said, 'Don't even send me your stuff anymore.' I just didn't want to read it. I had never really had any issues with the DLC, but I had just got so fed up with what I thought was this unfair attempt to characterize Howard Dean as this major threat to the Democratic Party. Somebody from the DLC called me up about it, and I said, 'You know, the DLC should just shut up.' I said, 'Anybody who attacks a Democrat should not do it, and the DLC should just shut up.' A guy from the DLC e-mailed me (in response) and I mailed it to the *Concord Monitor*... Sometimes you have to speak out. I got this letter from somebody at the DLC saying 'You don't know what you're talking about.' I said, 'Listen, as Democrats we should not be beating up on each other.' Then one of the DLC people in New Hampshire issued a press release blasting me, and I just said, 'whatever.'

"I thought they'd gone over the top.

"Then there was that group that ran the ad with Osama. I said to somebody, 'that's wrong. That should not happen in our party.' I saw Governor Dean that day, and he said ' I want to thank you for defending me.' I said, 'I'd do it for anybody. It's just not right.'

"Richard Nixon proved that no one ever totally kills their future unless you do something criminal.

"I liked Governor Dean. But he is not a warm and fuzzy guy, like Bill Clinton is. He's not going to have nicknames for everybody and pat you on the back like George W. Bush. As State Party chair, candidates see…(me) and they say, 'Oh Kathy, how are you?'… they give (me) the hug and kiss (me) on the cheek. I'm a very traditional Irish-American, and a New Englander. I've got my space. It's one of those things I tolerate. I don't really love it when people I don't know very well feel the need to kiss me or hug me. Howard Dean was not like that. I always appreciated the fact that (he) may shake your hand, but he never felt this overwhelming need to come over and kiss me and hug me."

Further discussing the physical greetings that can occur, Sullivan notes,

"I love John Edwards. When John Edwards came back from Iowa, I hugged John Edwards, because I like John Edwards. He was such a good person, I consider him to be a friend. The other people, they're not really my buddies. Howard Dean, maybe because he's a New Englander, too, he's not that touchy, feely, huggy, person.

"I also think that because he's a doctor, and he's very smart, that can be something that people don't like. If you think this person thinks he's smarter than you are that can be off-putting. I do believe that Howard Dean is probably smarter than me. But if you find that somewhat offensive, that may be part of … (people's dislike). I never experienced or saw negative aspects of the Dean personality. I'm not sure where that (feeling) came from."

George Stephanopoulos describes Howard Dean's personality: "It's contentious. The plus side of that is that he's candid, he's frank, (and) he's good copy. The down side of it is that he can be testy, and, at times, condescending. When things were going well, that worked for him. When they started to go poorly, it turned on him."

Dorothy Keville says that "this is a guy who, at one of his inaugurals… when all of the men were in black tie, came in a suit, Judy was in a granny dress, and the two kids had sneakers on. I thought, 'This is my kind of guy. He's a doctor, he cares about people, and materialism doesn't matter to him that much, and he's fiscally conservative, so what more could I ask for in a political candidate and my president?' "

Mathew Gross says, "He's very serious. That's not quite the right word. He has that gruff voice. I mean, he's a governor, you can tell the man's been a governor for 11 years. Anybody who's done that, and also the doctor thing, takes on a certain authority. He's very good at treating everybody with respect."

As an insurgent candidate, Howard Dean attracted comparisons between his candidacy and earlier Democratic presidential contenders.

Joe Miller compares Dean with Bill Bradley in 2000. "I saw Bill Bradley as someone who came from a somewhat more humble background than Dean, and who followed his star by fulfilling what was his talent in basketball. Yet it was not a wasted talent, from a societal point of view, because it enabled him to associate with blacks and come to the field with two issues that resonate very deeply with me: poverty and racism. He comes at these issues, not in a rabid way, but in a very deeply thoughtful way.

"Howard Dean feels deeply about these issues, but he never really enunciated them as clearly. He got carried away by the Iraq situation, perhaps rightfully so for the times. And, also, in his vicious attach on George Bush regarding economic and tax issues. They were appropriate ways to attack Bush, but I felt that he became a 1½ issue candidate, with the 1 being Iraq and terrorism and the ½ being his economic views.

"I just feel that that ultimately led to the scream. I think he would have lost even without the scream. It turned out to be the wrong noise, at the wrong time. The energy of Dean has its good side, but could have a down side as well."

Dante Scala comments on Bradley as a candidate and compares Dean to Paul Tsongas (1992). "I'm from New Jersey originally. I introduced myself, in 1999 or 2000, to Bill Bradley. It was like, 'Wow, it's Bill Bradley.' I said, 'I'm from Somerset County, New Jersey.' He walked by, and said 'Oh, really?' and then he walked off.

"What Dean reminded me of, more than anything, was Paul Tsongas, back in '92. I thought, now here's a guy, if he gets up there and starts talking about balancing budgets and so forth, he could have an appeal in New Hampshire. You know, gay civil unions and all that would actually play well here. I thought, 'Well, Dean might be someone to watch as a dark horse, someone like a Tsongas.'

"They (the Dean campaign) seized upon the issue of the war, and used that to become the anti-Bush candidate. It was almost as if their whole campaign, including Dean himself, was put on steroids. It was all about becoming the anti-establishment candidate. It wasn't so much about the issues anymore, because they've got this tiger by the tail, all of this anti-war, anti-Bush anger. And that's all it became about. And then when that started to dissipate, it was almost as if a fever had passed.

"Dean didn't have a second act, so there wasn't anything to pull back on. It wasn't just the scream that sent his campaign into a ditch, although that certainly didn't help, but it wasn't clear who he was. Once it was clear that rank and file Democratic primary voters weren't interested in a crusade with this Don Quixote-like character, there wasn't a second act for him. It was like the steroids were gone, the campaign drops thirty pounds, and what's left? There just wasn't anything left of the original Howard Dean that existed before he became this larger than life thing."

John Zaller adds the perspective provided by another insurgent candidate, Ross Perot. "Howard Dean was running within the party, and Perot (1992) was running outside the party. I guess they were similar in the sense that they (both) inspired… large numbers of people to come into the system. Dean did it through the Internet, while Perot tied into some pre-existing network of people suspicious of government. Perot utilized his pre-existing reputation as a no-nonsense guy."

When asked to reflect on Dean as a New Englander seeking the White House, **Ellen Goodman** reminds us of another such candidate, Michael Dukakis (1988). "Mike Dukakis always wanted to be governor. He never really, in my view, wanted to be President of the United States. He was still being governor while he was running for President of the United States. When he lost, he felt terrible, in the sense that he thought he screwed up in various things, but he's the most centered human being. He's just out there, the same Mike Dukakis as before he ran, and the same Mike Dukakis from before he lost."

Eugene McCarthy (1968) and George McGovern's (1972) presidential bids are often mentioned nostalgically by some Dean supporters. **Richard Goodwin**, whose political involvement reaches back to those early years observes: "The closest comparison (to Dean) that I can think of right now is McCarthy, because McCarthy came out of nowhere. He did put together a grassroots movement, with student volunteers, and he did energize people. What he did was energize the whole anti-war movement, in the same way that Dean helped energize the Democratic base. To some extent, he helped provoke Bobby Kennedy into the race, and that was a lasting contribution.

"I wrote the peace plank of the Democratic convention in 1968, and went back after Bobby was killed… I stayed and worked with McCarthy at the convention. He wasn't going to be nominated… after that I was very surprised how he then faded away. After the thing was over, McCarthy didn't really follow up. He didn't start a committee, which he was going to do, he didn't continue his work—he just sort of retired. But the fact is that he'd really made his contribution. He wasn't going to go any farther anyway.

"None of the other candidates were talking as toughly about Bush as Dean did. But they all began to, and that had a lot to do with energizing and solidifying the Democratic Party base for our candidate.

"That was a real contribution, and McCarthy made a somewhat similar contribution.

"McGovern never succeeded in doing that, although I loved the guy."

Anson Tebbetts has spent years covering the Vermont political scene has observed Howard Dean both professionally and personally. He reflects that "The whole money thing is what's surprising to me. Dean was so close to the money here. That's the amazing part, that he didn't have a grasp of that (in his campaign). I'm shocked about it, because he really is a cheap guy. I suppose it got so big, so fast, it was so out of hand that there was no control of what the hell was going on.

"A lot of (Dean campaign) people I've talked to since the campaign stopped, (have said) they got tired of the finger pointing, they got tired of the in your face type.

"Some people thought he was angry, but, in the beginning, I think he tried to over-compensate for his sort of style. He was not used to being energetic, in that kind of rip-roaring, crowd-pleasing stuff, which just doesn't happen in Vermont. He had more people behind him (on stage), on those primary and caucus nights, than he would have in his entire crowd in Vermont on election night. In Vermont, he'd be lucky if he got 200 people, and that included all the other candidates. At all those rallies, it seemed like he was always serving up red meat to the people in the audience.

He never took the opportunity to talk to someone who might be watching... at home. It seemed like he had to please the people that were in the audience.

"He may not have been equipped for that much scrutiny, even though he kept saying that he was ready for it. He had repeatedly talked about the opposition's research, how it works, how they feed it to the press, so he was well aware of that stuff, he even talked about it publicly.

"I was kind of surprised he didn't move to the center quicker.

"If you talk to people, they think he doesn't have much of a future here (in Vermont), but a lot of people think he may run for US Senate, if Jeffords retires."

The press traveling with Howard Dean was afforded a view of the politician and the person that adds further contrast in the portrait of this presidential. *New York Times* reporter **Jodi Wilgoren** says, "I did not think the part about Dean not wanting to be president was true at all. If you spent five minutes with Dean, you'd know he desperately wanted to be president. When he set out, he didn't think he would have anywhere near the shot that he seems to have had. He never believed he could be president until quite late in the game."

"I've traveled with him for a long time, and I traveled with the other 8 or 10 people who really covered him full time....I've never asked them, but I don't think anybody really does (think he's a jerk). I would constantly get e-mail, and stuff would be on these blogs that would say my hatred for him, or my contempt for him, was so visible. I don't hate him, and I don't have contempt for him. If someone had written that my love for him was on display, it would be equally false. I don't have any feelings about him, about liking or disliking him. I have more evaluative thoughts about him. I most definitely wouldn't say he was a jerk overall. I thought he was surprisingly disinterested, and unnecessarily private, and unnecessarily hostile at times.

"Frankly, the time I thought he most acted like a jerk, it wasn't about me, it was about his supporters. I thought, when he, in the last couple of weeks in Wisconsin, was ignoring everything that was happening in the process, and saying he was going to stay, I thought he was being a jerk to his staff, and a jerk to his supporters. But, that doesn't have anything to do with me."

Having access to the "numbers" provides an additional lens through which to view the candidate. **Andrew Smith** of the University of New Hampshire Survey Center says that "You get elected by telling people why they should vote for you. And you have to have a positive message. He (Dean) came out of, essentially, nowhere looking for a hook. He found his hook by being the only person who was willing to come out against the Iraq war early on. Everyone else, because they were in Washington, had to take political votes on it, to take political positions to position themselves. He had a free field there. I think the other campaigns ignored him for a while. I mean, 'Who is he, the governor of Vermont? Are you kidding?' They ignored him for a while.

"But the people who paid attention to politics early, and particularly in a state like New Hampshire, are upper-income, highly educated, more liberal voters, the same people that Bill Bradley got in 2000. The arcs of the two campaigns are very similar. You get the people who are really interested in politics and they are really mad with George Bush. You've got them on an issue like the Iraq War, which is a catalytic issue, people focus their anger with Bush through that issue. So the people who are really concerned about it, and exercised about it, they're vocal, they've got money, time, they've got political abilities, they are used to touching and interacting with the political system. That's why he took off early on. He knew who was out there paying attention early on, and he did a good job of touching them.

"His message was a negative message. It was negative against Bush, certainly, but it was also negative about the other people running. 'These people are afraid to do this, and I'm the only one willing to come out and take this stand.' He had very much an anti-message that was harnessing the anger on the part of the Democrats… they were very upset with Bush. But coming towards the election in the fall, he never translated that into a positive reason as to why people should vote for him. You've got to give people an optimistic message of why they should vote for you—what you are going to do to make their lives better. Even that message, 'Take your country back' is a negative message. Take it back from whom? Or from what? It's still not saying what I (Dean) am going to do to make things better.

"I don't buy that any government can necessarily make things better. The three biggest lies are, 'The check's in the mail', 'I'll respect you in the morning', and 'Hi, I'm here from the government, I'm here to help you.'

"But (as a candidate) you have to present… (a) vision.

"The speech in Iowa certainly hurt him here, but it was because it clarified for people a lot of the fears that they had about Dean. As a metaphor… (Consider) Dean on a platform held up by a lot of wooden pegs… he is still essentially an unknown commodity to most people. They recognize his name, they know that he is leading in the polls, but people here in New Hampshire didn't know anything else about him. Put yourself in the position of a Dean supporter, and you're at a cocktail party. There's maybe a Kerry supporter who is a friend of yours, and you're having a discussion about politics. And they start bringing… (issues) up. Well, if there's two or three, you can explain it, and say 'what about these things that your guy has said?' But when you get to eight, nine, ten, eleven, you've got a serious problem.

"So, back to that platform (metaphor), every time you hear one of those statements, a peg of credibility gets knocked out. Another one gets knocked out, another one gets knocked out. By the time that you get to that Iowa speech, that platform's getting a little bit wobbly. There are not that many pegs left. That speech caused the last of the pegs to come out and drop. So it looks like there was this gradual loss of support for Dean, but it wasn't gradual. It was one day, just off the cliff.

"He was not campaigning like a typical candidate, particularly not like a typical candidate who spent a lot of time in Washington. I think their brains (Washington politicians) automatically refocus their words to make them come out bereft of all emotion or anything that might offend anybody. Dean was plainspoken. The problem… is, that's when you make mistakes.

"A good candidate is a guy who can go out and give the same speech 50 times a day, identically each time, and do it each time with the same level of enthusiasm. That's why John Edwards was so good. He had the motions down exactly the same and the pauses.

"I ran into, not only journalists, but people who move in the political circles in New Hampshire. Their sense was that, the more time that they spent with the Dean campaign, the less they liked them. I heard that from journalists, but also from people who had actually known Dean for years back in Vermont and were considering going with him. He didn't wear well, which is different than most candidates. Usually the more time that you spend with a candidate, the more that you... like them.

"When you're in a small state like Vermont, the political class is very small. The journalistic class is very small. You are talking with the same people for years and years and years. You are going to see everyone on the good days and the bad days, warts and everything. It's like small town politics. You've got to live with these people. You are not going to come out and say terrible things about the people that you live with. It may not matter that Dean's not going to be governor, or run for office in Vermont anymore, but a lot of his friends are going to be people that you've still got to work with (as a journalist). Your editor might be one of his friends. It is very difficult to get people to go on record to speak about specific things. That's just not the kind of stuff that you want to talk about. You don't want to recall the time that you were berated and called names by somebody. It happens in any sort of business.

"I bet you could go to any state and find that the governor has a reputation for chewing people out. Clinton did it all the time. He had a notoriously bad temper, but it doesn't come out that often in the books that were written about him. It is mentioned but it doesn't go into a lot of detail.

"That was the impression that I had about Dean, as governor of Vermont, before he even announced that he was running for President."

Gwen Graham, who has long standing experience in politics, through family campaigns and as a Dean supporter, says "It's about 'anybody but Bush', more than it is about any one particular candidate

"Governor Dean speaks freely and he's not governed by focus groups and I respect that.

"I'm not going to name the candidate, but there was a candidate running for president this time that was asked a question by my father. The candidate said, 'Well, Bob, I'll get back to you on that, but I've got to do a focus group on that before I can figure out what my answer is.'

"You've got to respect a man that has the courage to say what he feels. Governor Dean apologized a couple of times that I know of for things that he had said. We all once in a while say things we regret."

Hillary Hazan worked in the Burlington headquarters of *Dean for America* and says, "I didn't run for president. But I would imagine that when one runs for President, one can't be running the (campaign) office, he's got to be running for president. He's got to be on the campaign trail.

"I imagine when you become president that you need to surround yourself with a group of advisors who are going to push you in the right direction. And at a certain point, you can't question every last thing. You put them there because you trust their decision-making.

"His record in Vermont for women was phenomenal. I jumped on as someone who wanted to represent them. If I'm going to say I represent Howard Dean, and his stands for women, I have to really believe it, because that's my community. So I really believed it."

When talking about endorsements, Hazan notes: "We were very concerned with courting politicians, which is interesting in my opinion. Here we are, a grassroots campaign, and we're not courting grassroots organizations, besides labor. There are a lot of women's organizations that I feel we could have courted and didn't. I feel that Howard Dean, the man, was really supportive of women.

"Howard Dean went to a Lifetime for Women event, which was a forum for women in NH. There was a gathering afterwards of the people who put it together... supporters and representatives from each campaign." Campaign staffers invited Hazan to attend the event at the last minute. "Afterwards, all the other women who were actually traveling with Howard Dean that day, who briefed him about what he was going to say, went on the bus with him, instead of staying after and schmoozing with the heads of these women's organizations. I think that a lot of the people schmooze the candidate instead of the people."

"How much of the campaign was about Howard Dean and how much of the campaign was about the energy of the grassroots and not about Howard Dean at all? Howard Dean, as a name, may have provided the forum for people." Hazan describes a friend's visual representation of this concept as "...a pixilated picture of Howard Dean that's created... (from) pictures of other people."

"Howard Dean is great, and I was drawn to him for a reason, but this movement was about people. Trippi didn't like us to use the word movement because it took away from Howard. A lot of us in this country were ready to start that fire and he (Dean) gave us a forum to do that.

"I think in the end, we weren't supposed to create a president, we were supposed to create a movement. I think that was the purpose here."

Richard Goodwin says that, "Dean's mistakes indicate total inexperience. Presidential politics… is very different from politics at any other level. Once he got out front there, he just was not aware of the impact some of these gaffs would have, or of the enormous attention that would be given to them. Very few people are really successful running for president the first time anyway." Regarding a candidate's personality or temperament Goodwin notes, "We've elected arrogant people. He seemed to have plenty faith in himself, and confidence, maybe too much. Maybe he just thought he could wing it, and he couldn't." Commenting on Dean's future, Goodwin suggests, "What happens now really depends on Dean. First of all, you've got to have issues. He had issues this time. If it's going to happen again, there's going to have to be another set of issues, or maybe the same ones, although I doubt it. There is a lot of potential in his organization, but it has to be mobilized again around causes, issues, and not just around the fact that it's Howard Dean's organization."

Dr. Joe Miller provides another perspective on the Dean temperament with the following story: "In the spring of 2003, there was an event that was supposed to take place in front of the Capital Grill, right in front of the State House in Concord. There he (Dean) was, standing by himself. He was just knocking around, without many people around him, which was very rare at that time, and very undesirable on his part. I came up to him and said, 'Hello, Governor. I don't know if you remember me, my name is Joe Miller. We met in Durham, with Iris Estabrook, whose husband was a doctor with you at UVM.' I said, 'I have been very active in the campaign, and I think you're doing great, but if you don't mind a suggestion from someone who's very fond of you and your candidacy, I would like to make a comment that I hope won't offend you. I think you're great, you're fiery, you really get the mob going, but if you don't mind my saying so, I think you come over some times a little bit feisty, and I hope that it won't hurt you ultimately in the campaign. Some people want a softer sell. From my point of view, I think it's great. I love when you stir people up, and talk about coming from the Democratic side of the Democratic Party, which means a lot to me.' He said 'Well, I guess you're right. I've been told that before. I suppose I do come over that way. I realize that it sometimes may not be the most attractive side of me. I realize that I'm going to have to calm it down and control it as the campaign progresses. I am working on that and hope it will soften things up as the campaign progresses.' I said, 'it's nice that you're thinking about it that way, because it's meant constructively and not critically.'"

Access to Howard Dean by campaign staffers at the Burlington headquarters varied. Working in that office, **Michael Goodwin** provides his perspective on Dean: "I didn't have too much interaction with Howard Dean. I saw him whenever he'd come into the office. I'd say hello. I never once talked to him about anything policy related, or anything that I was working on, not even for a second. That did seem odd, especially when I was trying to develop it from scratch... building it up. You would think that he'd be interested in it, to the degree of at least wanting to talk about it a little bit. I never talked specifically with him.

"I talked to him in Iowa a couple of times briefly, and at that point I wasn't even sure that he knew who I was. I had introduced myself a couple of times, but he meets so many people. I remember out there, in Iowa, he looked at me, and called me by my name, and said 'Thanks for the good work.' I thought 'at least he does know who I am.' Then, the night of the Vermont primary, I was downtown at this bar Nectars, where all the Meetups were held. He came down, and there were probably about 50-60 people in there. He came in and out, in about 10 minutes. I was leaving as he was leaving, and we were both walking out on the street together. He was interviewed by a television station, and then he was just walking down the street by himself, getting into his car, and I was walking next to him. It was just a funny experience, because all of a sudden, with everything being over, it was two guys walking on the street. I sort of talked to him then. It was a very relaxed conversation. I just said, 'I'll see you soon.' And he said, 'Of course, I'll see you soon.' Then he gets in his car and drives off, with no cameras following him around, driving himself.

"It was a pretty neat moment."

Howard Dean suggests the issues he would be introducing to the country right now, if he were in John Kerry's shoes: "I have made a practice of not giving Senator Kerry advice in public since I am giving him some in private.

"Healthcare and a sense of community. Bringing back America, the kind of America we had when we were growing up, when we were all in it together. Getting rid of the divisive politics of the Republican right."

"I'm going to support Kerry vigorously. There's no question in my mind that John Kerry would make a far better President than George Bush. In terms of the environment, in terms of balancing the budget, in terms of health care, in terms of foreign policy, which gives us our rightful leadership role. I hope that every single one of my supporters will vote for John Kerry. I know that they won't all work for him, but there's lots to be done, and many great candidates, and I hope that those who won't work for him will work for other Democratic candidates, because it's all going to the same place. It's all about changing the country."

"Under this President, we've lost our moral leadership, which we held from World War I until the day we thumbed our nose at the UN and went into Iraq. We need to get that back. We also need to treat each other with respect. The President talks about that, but of course he's the President of the 2% who have everything, not the President of the 90% who are struggling. We need to put together a real community where ordinary people are going to be respected again."

Dean talks about his sense of mortality. The author said "If I, myself, were to choose to have a gravestone, the epitaph I would want on my gravestone, and this is in reference to my own wife, would be "He loved Judy". What would you want your epitaph to be?" **Dean** responded "That sounds like a good start, but I'm not there yet. Well, I haven't thought about epitaphs, to be honest with you."

Regrowth at the Grassroots?

"The front-loading of the breakaway stage has left the *mop-up stage*, which includes contests held from mid-March to mid-June, increasingly irrelevant. Since 1976, the candidate with the most delegates by mid-March has won the party's nomination."[248]

In 2004, Dean wouldn't even get to the cruelest month. His hopes would lie in retaining influence at the final stage in Cook's road map to the nomination, the convention.

"*Conventions*, once the place where nominations were decided among party bosses, have become rubber stamps of the primary process, as well as made-for-television venues where the party presents its message for the general election season."[249]

Dean had not joined the small state governor, Carter, or McGovern, the antiwar candidate who benefited from party campaign reform that he himself had helped shape. It remained to be seen whether Dean was on the outside looking in.

A week after his withdrawal speech on February 18, Dean was seeking money from his donors to eliminate a half million dollars in campaign debt. His campaign had raised over fifty million dollars, in record time for a Democrat, and it was all gone. Dean's withdrawal speech had actually been written down, and he had stumbled over a word as he read it. He still had some of the rhetorical flourishes he had gained as he ran for president, but reading the speech brought back memories of when he would read two speeches a year to Vermont legislators. The lawmakers used to joke that they would count the light bulbs out in the ceiling as he gave his speech.

In 2002, Dean was a "confident public speaker, but not dynamic, not charismatic. When you change the tone as many times as Howard Dean has changed his tone, people look at you and say 'I'm not sure who you are, and whether I trust you.'"[250]

Now, the finger-pointing that had made him seem angry to predisposed viewers wasn't in evidence, nor were whoops or screams. Dean looked truly weary. He had said earlier in the campaign "I encourage people on my staff to take time off, but that's not easy to do on a campaign. We could run a reasonable schedule. But we don't."[251]

The kids from the Portsmouth office were scattered all over. Some had continued in the campaign and would now have to find a new direction after the end of the crusade they had joined.

I had given corsages to Aswini and Wendy on the day after the primary. For the last time, I passed around chocolate-covered apricots from The Chocolatier in Exeter. I gave Ben LaBolt an autographed Halberstam book. I said goodbye to most of the kids I'd taken out to lunch, and counseled over the past months. Garrett was still out sick. Wendy, Garrett, Lizzie, and Jim were the only ones I ever heard from again.

Ben LaBolt, whose wisdom the day after the primary was "always sleep with a finger on the trigger," went on to other states.

Aswini and **Joe** went to Maine.

Garrett Bridgens went back to Oregon.

Lizzie Morris went home to Texas.

Wendy Howell, whose observation had been that she was trained that 10% of all people are crazy "and in this campaign, I met them all," went to Kentucky to work for a Congressional candidate.

The power of endorsement seemed headed for the scrapheap of political history, at least for candidates who started out as reformers. It appeared the Gore and Bradley endorsements, combined with a stunningly large sum of change, might buy a latte at Starbucks.

"It did appear in New Hampshire that those endorsements failed to help, and, in fact, may have peeled away some support for Dean among those who saw him as a 'non-politician' who would shake up the party establishment. Gore and Bradley were not in the state since Iowa. Given what happened out at the caucus, I'm not sure Dean would have wanted them to campaign.

"Bradley came to make his endorsement here, but Gore never came to New Hampshire for Dean, before or after Iowa."[252]

Dorothy Keville was still in charge of the Massachusetts for Dean office, near Central Square in Cambridge. She had hoped Dean would still get enough votes in Massachusetts to pick up delegates for the convention, and perhaps she could be one. Steve Grossman had called her to respond to her angry letter over his actions preceding the Wisconsin primary. She cried as she accepted his apology, and gave her forgiveness.

Grossman had offered his services to the Kerry campaign. He was not welcomed with open arms. By his own admission, he was rather like the protagonist in the story "The Man without a Country" politically adrift and hoping to be welcomed back ashore. Grossman attended a fundraiser for Hillary Clinton's Senate re-election campaign. He also held conference calls with fundraisers to finalize plans to raise several million dollars. Many of the 16 donors are Jewish, and were lobbying Kerry to select Pennsylvania Governor Edward Rendell, who is Jewish, as his running mate. John Kerry seemed to be headed for the nomination. The *New York Times* editorial page endorsed Kerry for the Democratic nomination.[253]

John Edwards seemed to hold the only possible chance of delaying or preventing Kerry's ascension. Edwards lavishly praised Howard Dean as his friend, for whom he had "great affection, respect and admiration."[254] If he could get Dean's supporters, he might have a chance. Dean and Edwards were in communication, but Dean remained noncommittal.

While Kerry had less than a third of the delegates needed for nomination, Terry McAuliffe was clearly trying to hold the coronation as early as possible, the better to focus his war hero on a President once again struggling to explain his truncated National Guard experience. Kerry seemed to be the greatest beneficiary of Bush's ill-advised "mission accomplished" appearance on an aircraft carrier.

Michael Tomasky, the executive editor of the liberal magazine *The American Prospect*, reviewed historian Douglas Brinkley's book on Kerry, *Tour of Duty*. "It is a campaign book" in the "long tradition going back at least to Nathaniel Hawthorne's quickie biography of his old college chum Franklin Pierce. The odor of salesmanship notwithstanding, Kerry's story is impressive. It convincingly shows us a man driven from an early age by a sense of destiny—and almost obsessed with risk.

'Risk' might not be a word that would spring to the minds of students of John Kerry's Senate career."[255]

The up, down, and up again ride of Kerry's candidacy seemed to have passed the point where he would take any risks on the road to the nomination. Senior Senator Bob Graham of Florida endorsed John Kerry. Graham had first revealed his own ambitions for the White House to a child calling in to a Haitian-American radio show. Graham had then been the first of the ten Democratic candidates to drop out, when he had cardiac problems. When Dean seemed headed for the nomination, there had been talk that Graham was under consideration as his running mate.

Graham had seemed well aligned with Dean's targets. Graham had cited the Bush administration's "Nixonian stench of secrecy." He had even called for impeachment in July, citing the Republican standards for such actions as based on nothing more than "a personal, consensual relationship" when they were applied to Clinton.

Graham's hallmark in Florida has been his "work days", when he takes the jobs of constituents, ranging from mixing mortar to grooming circus animals. He was willing to do the figurative stable-cleaning associated with Blair House to be a heartbeat away from the White House.

That conjecture was partly fueled by the fact that his eldest daughter, Gwen Graham Logan, had played a key role in the Dean campaign. In endorsing Kerry, Graham admitted he would be open to consideration as Kerry's running mate. Graham would later skirt the issue, as he assured reporters on the Kerry campaign plane "I would do anything within reason —I will not sacrifice one of my grandchildren, for example - to elect John Kerry."[256]

Should Graham end up opposing Cheney for the vice presidency, Americans would have a choice of two hearts with recent problems, a heartbeat from the White House.

In the Green Mountain State, John Bauer urged Vermonters to cast their Super Tuesday ballots for Dean. "It's a way to say thanks to Howard Dean for all he has done as governor and for all the ways he has changed Presidential politics. Where else, but Vermont?"[257]

On Super Tuesday, the first Tuesday in March, when 10 states had joined in to produce half the delegates needed for nomination, Kerry won every state, except for the Green Mountain State. Vermonters remained loyal to their former governor, as he won 58% of their votes.

It used to be said that "as goes Maine, so goes the nation." After a particularly disastrous landslide, that had morphed into "as goes Maine, so goes New Hampshire."

It seemed unlikely that a victory in the land that produced Ben and Jerry's ice cream would yield a new phrase of "as goes Vermont, so goes the convention."

John Edwards, whose turnout and stump performances had diminished in the preceding days, would announce he was withdrawing. Only Dennis Kucinich and Al Sharpton remained standing, ants before the Kerry steamroller. In the middle of March, Sharpton conceded, and Kerry would claim Sharpton's endorsement, although Sharpton had never used that word. Kucinich would continue to vow that his candidacy would remain in play through the convention in July.

New Hampshire primary expert Dante Scala of St. Anselm's College in Manchester had written in his book *Stormy Weather*, "For all the candidates who ventured to New Hampshire for the Democratic primary in hopes of unseating the front runner, no candidate has succeeded in duplicating the unexpected successes of Carter or McGovern."[258]

When the Dean campaign had been in its ascendancy, it was widely reported that the Internet had changed politics. With the free fall of the campaign, it became less clear how great that impact had been.

Historian and Pulitzer Prize-winning journalist **David Halberstam** wrote *The Powers That Be*, a book that defined how print media, radio, and television had a symbiotic relationship with the Presidency. "The Internet is clearly something new, and a new use of technology. But it is not as politically powerful and transforming as television. Television changed the cosmetics of politics, it changed access, it was the most profound change in all aspects of our society in the last fifty or sixty years.

"The Internet is an instrument that is enabling and gives access to a lot of people who felt outside of the political system and were looking for some form of community. Not just political community. It gave connection to people who did not otherwise know how to be connected. So it was perfect for an outsider coming in, like Dean."

To the most fervent members of Dean Nation, the Internet had built Dean up, and the traditional media had worked with the political establishment to bring him back down.

Adlai Stevenson said that, in a democracy, the voters get what they deserve.

The community they had formed remained alive on the Internet; they felt they deserved better than traditional politics had offered them. It would be seen whether or not they would remain inside the political world.

Dean had said in an e-mail to supporters that he would announce on March 18th the formation of a grassroots organization to carry forward his political message. That organization, which would be born one month after Dean's withdrawal, would allow supporters to organize locally, as well as supporting progressive candidates. During his own campaign, Dean had urged supporters to donate to the campaign of Leonard Boswell in a key Iowa congressional district, even though Boswell hadn't endorsed Dean (and later endorsed Kerry). The outpouring from Dean Nation had greatly expanded Boswell's campaign war chest. Ever the loyalist, Dean would later urge supporters to contribute to politicians who had supported him, including Jesse Jackson Jr. and Patrick Leahy.

Dean's "estranged"[259] campaign manager had started a website called Change for America, "a group with goals similar to those expected in Dean's organization. Trippi's organization will be a 'national organization that unites progressive communities and sets an agenda for meaningful reform.'"[260] "Dean spokesmen said Dean and Trippi are going their separate ways."[261]

George W. Bush had proven antithetical to his own campaign promise of "being a uniter, not a divider."

Trippi seemed to be following a similar path.

After the fierce partisanship of working in the Dean campaign, I sat at a laptop, in our log cabin in Vermont, struggling to find journalistic objectivity.

Howard Dean talks about his new organization: "*Dean for America* was made up of moderate Republicans, Democrats, independents, and Greens. We are interested in working with all those groups. We will be allied with groups such as 21st Century Democrats, which also does grassroots organizing.

"I don't consider myself to have been marginalized. American political history is full of examples of so-called mainstream politics being pulled by reformers and even third party candidates, such as Robert LaFollette and Theodore Roosevelt. I doubt there is a conspiracy, but there is an enormous amount of confusion and incompetence in mainstream media... The enormous support for *Dean for America* essentially helped craft the Democratic Party platform. I don't think I did that. Only by standing up for what we believe can Democrats win elections again."

"The campaign is part of a continuum, and it's not stopping. Democracy for America is going to continue many of the themes of the campaign… towards ordinary people, trying to rekindle the Democratic Party, trying to get some straight talk back in Washington. But trying to set up a mechanism so that when Washington does its thing, which is to shut everybody else out and forget about ordinary Americans, we need a feedback mechanism that's strong enough to punch through that. That's what grassroots politics is all about and that's what the Internet was all about. So, hopefully, whatever I might say about the campaign, I'd like to be able to say it was a start… it was the start of a change in the political process, but I guess we'll have to see over the next two years if that was true or not."

"I think the administration is like Pravda. They have not presented a believable case for an awful lot of the things they've done. The tax cut did very little for ordinary Americans and middle class people. Sixty percent of the people in this country got a $304 tax cut on average. We're in a war in Iraq, and we've lost over 700 soldiers. None of the reasons the President told us we were going turned out to be true. There is a peculiar quality in this administration… they seem to have an aversion to the truth."

Mark Wrighton notes "I think the party's goal was met. The goal of getting an early nominee, starting a general election campaign very early, with an effective nominee, was met. I think there has to be some effort by the campaign to keep the momentum going up until the convention in order to keep people excited, on board."

Andrew Smith says ", in the campaign it was anybody but Bush, but then there was anybody but Dean, an Anti-Dean movement that lined up not just for reasons of electability but also for cultural reasons."

Aaron Strauss comments on his experience "…at the end when we were going through the positives of the campaign… that you really can be inspired in politics and work for something you really believe in and even if you lose, you come out with a very positive feeling and positive experience."

Gwen Graham exemplifies one of the outcomes Dean had envisioned: "I think I will run for office in the future."

THE RECKONING AND THE FINAL WORD

When a man dies, the people ask what property has he left behind? But the angels, as they bend over his grave inquire what good deeds hast thou sent on before thee?

—*Mohammed*

At a time when the world is focused on a new American quagmire in Iraq, **Howard Dean** admits "that the arc of the myth of Icarus is pretty accurate" in describing his campaign.

Because the mixed blessing of technology produced an unprecedented quantity of media, his historic humiliation is etched in history forever. The lessons of that experience could shape Howard Dean, and move him further toward his enormous potential. The issue is whether Dean himself is prepared to learn from a reckoning that he had sought.

When Japan sifted through the rubble of a once-proud nation after World War II, it turned to an American, one who embodied attributes that the Japanese associated with Americans. W. Edwards Deming was spiritual, rather than materialistic. Yet his values shaped a new field - quality control - in the eminently material world of manufacturing. Deming was a man who listened more than he talked.

Deming had little tolerance for fools, particularly those whose currency was lip service to his principles. He was a prophet without honor in his own land, but revered in Japan.

Deming saw that the success of an organization depended on its people. His system, ostensibly about quality control, allowed a nation whose material resources were still smoldering to draw upon its greatest resource - legions of committed people.

Although a mathematically based model, at its heart lay a core of group participation.

David Halberstam described Deming: "True quality demanded a totality of commitment that began at the very top; if top management was committed to the idea of quality, and if executive promotions were tied to quality, then the priority would seep down into the middle and lower levels of management, and thus inevitably to the workers. It could not, as so many American companies seemed to expect, be imposed at the bottom. American companies could not appoint some medium-level executive, usually one whom no division of the company particularly wanted, and, for lack of something better to do with him, put him in charge of something called quality. The first thing an executive like that would do, Deming said, and quite possibly the only thing, was come up with slogans, and display them on banners."

Halberstam continues to describe Deming's views: "'What is the motivation and purpose of men like this?' he would say with contempt. 'Do they even know what they do anymore?' All they knew about was numbers, not product. All they thought about was maximum profit, not excellence of product. The numbers, of course, he added, always lied. 'They know all the visible numbers, but the visible numbers tell them so little. They know nothing of the invisible numbers. Who can put a price on a satisfied customer, and who can figure out the cost of a dissatisfied customer?"[262]

Deming felt that the engineers of a company should not be isolated in offices, but out on the floor with the workers, upon whom a revolution would be built. He was elevated to unparalleled status in post-war Japan. In touching upon the souls of a people striving for change, for improvement, for recognition, Deming harnessed a nation that was readily prepared to forgo individual glory for the common good.

Deming believed in the grassroots.

Sara Lawrence-Lightfoot wrote a wonderful book entitled *Respect*. Her book encompasses the nature of human communication, spirituality, harassment, societal values, and so many other things that it is best just to suggest that you read it.[263]

Lightfoot talks about her dad's secret… he gained respect by giving it. She talks about passion, commitment, and empowerment.

Sara Lawrence-Lightfoot is an artist whose writing draws compelling portraits. One person drawn through her powerful writing (which she refers to as portraiture) is a physician, Dr. Johnye Ballenger. This physician talks about the expectation people have that doctors are perfect. For herself, Dr. Johnye Ballenger uses prayer, and asks God to make her an instrument of healing. Ballenger talks about the importance of doing her best, not because she could be perfect, but because she must avoid doing harm. She works to be respectful of her patients, and their families, and her profession, and herself. She knows she cannot be perfect, and seeks to do good, with humility and a clear sense of purpose.

Another Lightfoot portrait is of Kay Cottle, a teacher, a field Howard Dean once tried, and one in which he felt he failed. Kay Cottle shared her innermost self with her students: she revealed a dream to them from her adolescence. In revealing her human imperfections, she treated her students as peers. She told them her story.

A third portrait is of a photographer, Dawoud Bey. He is a professor whose respect for the subjects of his photography is predicated upon establishing reciprocal relationships with his subjects. Bey wanted relationships with his subjects that were symmetric and respectful.

In early cultures, taking a photograph without the permission of the person was sometimes viewed as stealing the soul. Journalists tried to establish relationships with Howard Dean, but he never wanted them to steal his soul. He may not have found it himself.

In describing a community activist and midwife whose skills were called upon by so many others, Lightfoot explains how Jennifer Dohrn established "clearer boundaries and protecting moments of solitude" to sustain herself. Dohrn was drawn to Buddhism, and meditates daily, in finding spiritual replenishment. Dohrn says that serving as a midwife allows her "to become more me."

Howard Dean changed churches when the one he belonged to did not support his initiative to build a bike path.

In the classic *Invisible Man*, Ralph Ellison wrote "it is as though I have been surrounded by mirrors of hard, distorting glass. When they approach me, they see only my surroundings, themselves, or figments of their imagination - indeed, everything and anything except me."

What some people project as arrogance actually belies enormous insecurity. Joan Didion wrote an essay on self-respect in which she said: "To have that sense of one's own intrinsic worth which constitutes self-respect is potentially to have everything: the ability to discriminate, to love, and to remain indifferent. To lack it is to be locked within oneself, paradoxically capable of either love or indifference."

Lightfoot describes Bill Wallace as "a man who exudes both intensity and calm." Wallace works with AIDS patients, and says that therapists and healers need to "be involved in ongoing supervision, critique, and self scrutiny." He refers to mutuality, a deep, selfless love that expects nothing in return, and comes without being sought after, or expected.

In her book, Lightfoot also describes the work of Jean Miller Baker, who wrote a paper entitled "Connections, Disconnections and Violations." Baker identified five characteristics in mutually empowering relationships: the relationships are energizing, both parties are active participants, both parties gain clarity and knowledge, both have their self-worth enhanced, and the relationships enhance connection, which creates a desire for more connection.

The relationships between Dean and many of the key figures in his campaign have become disconnected, sometimes at his choice, sometimes mutually, sometimes by the person, who decided to reject Dean himself.

When Howard Dean suddenly found religion on the campaign trail, he cited his favorite book in the New Testament as Job. He may have been working on a bike path when his church discussed the fact that Job is in the Old Testament. Still, Dean's choice is rich with irony.

Job was a most prosperous and happy man, whose faith was tested by Satan, with God's permission. Satan destroyed all that Job owned, killed his children, and covered him with sores from head to toe. False friends of Job urged him to abandon his Lord, but Job, even in absolute misery, would not curse the Lord. God rewarded Job's faith by healing him, and "gave him twice as much as he had before."

Job is associated with patience.

Howard Dean is not.

The Bible has many lessons. This book has but a few. As with any lesson, learning it requires a willing, or better, an eager recipient. What you take from this book will be determined by how hard you choose to examine the ideas, and, thereby, yourself.

We live in a society where technology advances faster than the human soul (which is probably static anyway). Technology drives people at a pace that eliminates self reflection and guarantees an ever increasing distance from the soul. Although we condemn the shallowness of media coverage, our tendency is towards the expedient, or the familiar, or the affirming.

While I would rather have root canal work than listen to Rush Limbaugh, I realize I should listen to him. When I was in college, I had a subscription to *The Socialist Worker*, just because I wanted to see that end of the spectrum. I could no more embrace it than I can Rush Limbaugh today. But that doesn't mean I cannot learn from every perspective, or from seeing through the eyes of others.

In earlier incarnations of this book, I had promised not to direct the reader towards the specific lessons I found in my journey - or Joe Trippi's - or Howard Dean's. However, I believe that Walter Shapiro was right, when I spoke to him months ago. There is a lesson here that can be summarized in a single word - hubris.

I felt insecure about trying to draw any lessons in this book, because it is about that most complex of organisms, human beings. Emotions and attitudes are generally seen as outside the quantifiable realm.

However, consider the story I told Howard Dean about Bill Bradley, when Dean met with me and my wife in 1989. Bradley, when approached by supporters ready to open up the cash cow for him to run for the presidency, took a long time to respond. Unfortunately, there is no recording of that discussion, which would have allowed for the quantification of Bradley's self-reflection. It is worth noting that he came to the conclusion that he was not ready, at that time.

When my wife and I interviewed Howard Dean, on May 5, 2004, I thought I had come away with nothing that was indicative of the true Howard Dean. It was only upon listening to the tape again that I recognized how well he had quantified the very attitudes and emotions which Jodi Wilgoren was pilloried for trying to capture in her writing.

I said to him, well into an interview he cut short after twenty minutes (as if there was another patient waiting), "Walter Shapiro told me, as a hypothesis (and he's still forming it) that he thinks your campaign was undone by hubris. He has compared the arc of the campaign to the myth of Icarus. What are the political mythologies of your campaign and what are the political realities?"

In contrast to the reflection Bill Bradley demonstrated in my previous anecdote, Dean's response was immediate, and an uncategorical rejection of the premise. "I certainly don't think the campaign was undone by hubris, I think it was undone by a concentrated effort on the part of five capable opponents and the media. But I think that the arc of the myth of Icarus is pretty accurate."

Dean's silent reflection before responding lasted exactly 1.21 seconds. *Hubris.*

Yet, hope is always on the horizon, for those who remember "that is it never too late to be what you might have been. "[264]

FIGURES

Figure 1

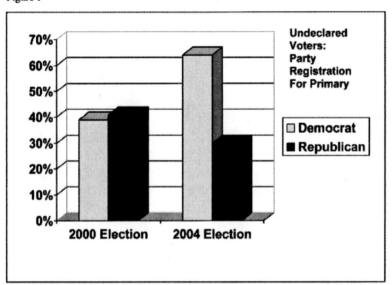

Source: Leonard Downie, Jr., "Election 2004: New Hampshire", washingtonpost.com, January 27, 2004.

Figure 2

Use of the phrase "Bring it On!"

Date	Speaker	Context	Impact
1999	John McCain	Y2K litigation bill	Attempt to delay litigation that might result from Y2K glitches
2000	Movie Title	Cheerleaders	Another drop in a polluted cultural pool
2003	John Edwards	DNC	Invoking himself as the antidote to Bush ii's full service presidency for insiders
2003	George W. Bush	Speech about Baathists and terrorists	taunting
2003	John Kerry	Des Moines, Iowa	The New Republic writes an article questioning Kerry's electability over Dean

Figure 3

Reform Candidates

Year	Candidate	Reform
1972	George McGovern	Party reform
1976	Morris Udall	Environmental protection
1984	Gary Hart	"New ideas"
1992	Paul Tsongas	Fiscal reform
1992	Paul Simon	Fiscal reform
2000	Bill Bradley	Campaign finance reform
2004	Howard Dean	Party reform

Figure 4

2000 Democratic Primary Voters

Liberals	Moderates	Conservatives
54%	38%	8%

Source: Dante Scala, <u>Stormy Weather: The New Hampshire Primary and Presidential Politics</u>. Palgrave Macmillen: New York, 2003, pg. 52.

US Personnel Killed in Iraq

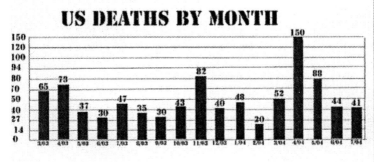

MONTH TOTAL	
MAR-03	65
APR-03	73
MAY03	37
JUN-03	30
JUL-03	47
AUG-03	35
SEO-03	30
OCT-03	43
NOV-03	82
DEC-03	40
JAN-04	48
FEB-04	20
MAR-04	52
APR-04	150
MAY-04	88
JUN-04	44
JUL-04	41
AUG-04	31 *
TOTAL	956

* AS OF AUGUST 16, 2004

Figure 5

Elite Scores

	Strong Elite Support	Score	Strong Working Class Support		

Year/ Candidate		Score		Nomination	Election
		1.0			
1968	Eugene McCarthy	-1.62-			Lost
	Lyndon Johnson		.62		Withdrew
1972	Edmund Muskie		.81		Lost
	George McGovern	-1.57-		WON	Lost
1976	Jimmy Carter		.82	WON	WON
	Morris Udall	-2.26-			Lost
1980	Jerry Brown	-1.64-			Lost
1984	Walter Mondale		.69	WON	Lost
	Jesse Jackson	-2.29-			Lost
	George McGovern	-2.29-			Lost
1988	Michael Dukakis	-1.04-		WON	Lost
	Dick Gephart		.69		Lost
	Jesse Jackson	-1.50-			Lost
	Paul Simon	-1.43-			Lost
1992	Bill Clinton		.78	WON	WON
	Paul Tsongas	-1.80-			Lost
2000	Al Gore		.76	WON	WON/Lost
	Bill Bradley	-1.56-			Lost
2004	Howard Dean	-1.20-			Lost
	John Kerry		.9	WON	??
	John Edwards		.8		Lost
	John Kucinich	-1.40-			Lost

Source: Dante Scala, Stormy Weather: The New Hampshire Primary and Presidential Politics. Palgrave Macmillen: New York, 2003, pg. 52.

Figure 6

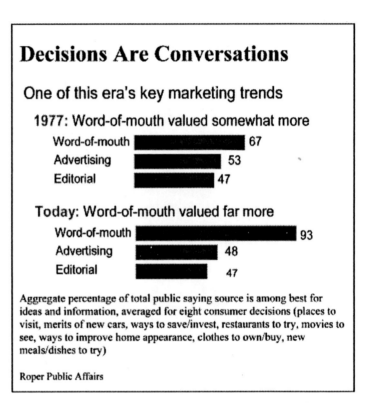

Decisions Are Conversations

One of this era's key marketing trends

1977: Word-of-mouth valued somewhat more

Word-of-mouth 67
Advertising 53
Editorial 47

Today: Word-of-mouth valued far more

Word-of-mouth 93
Advertising 48
Editorial 47

Aggregate percentage of total public saying source is among best for ideas and information, averaged for eight consumer decisions (places to visit, merits of new cars, ways to save/invest, restaurants to try, movies to see, ways to improve home appearance, clothes to own/buy, new meals/dishes to try)

Roper Public Affairs

Source: Ed Keller & John Berry, <u>Politics Online Conference</u>, March 19, 2004.

Figure 7

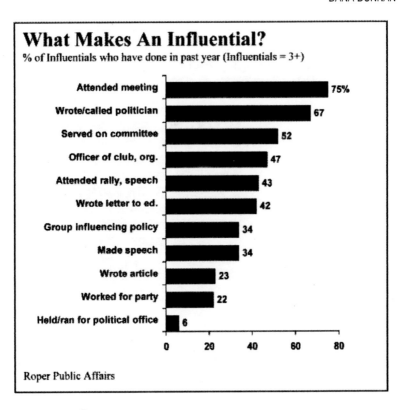

What Makes An Influential?
% of Influentials who have done in past year (Influentials = 3+)

Roper Public Affairs

Figure 8

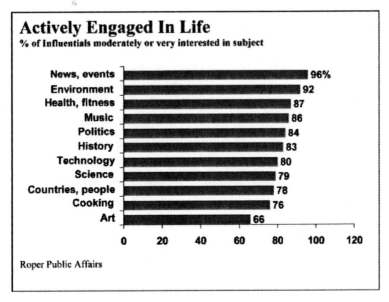

Actively Engaged In Life
% of Influentials moderately or very interested in subject

Roper Public Affairs

Source: Ed Keller & John Berry, <u>Politics Online Conference</u>, March 19, 2004.

331

Figure 9

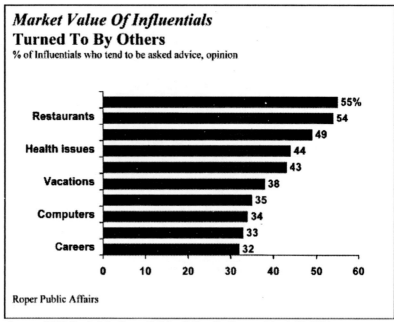

Source: Ed Keller & John Berry, Politics Online Conference, March 19, 2004.

Figure 10

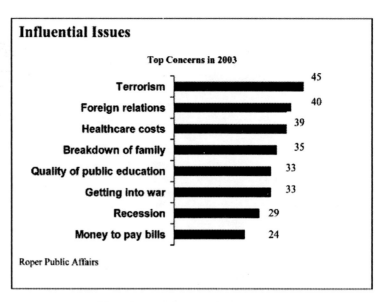

Source: Brad Fay, Politics Online Conference, March 19, 2004.

Figure 11

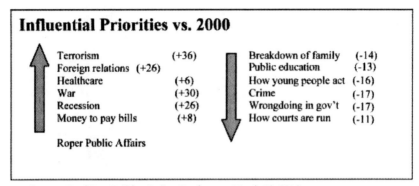

Source: Brad Fay, <u>Politics Online Conference</u>, March 19, 2004.

Figure 12

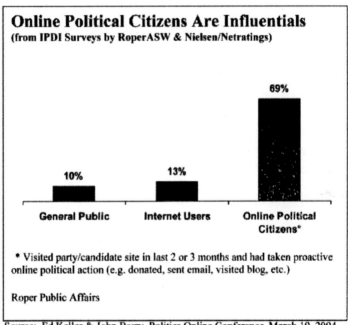

Source: Ed Keller & John Berry, <u>Politics Online Conference</u>, March 19, 2004.

Figure 13

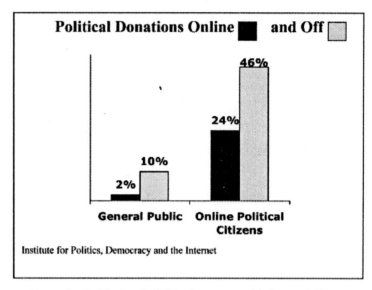

Source: Joe Graf, Institute for Politics, Democracy and the Internet, _Politics Online Conference_, March 19, 2004

Figure 14

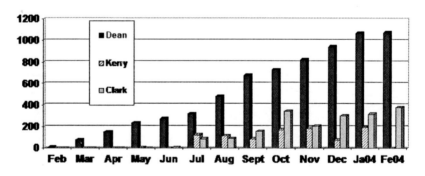

Comparison of actual Meetups by month (2003-2004) across 3 candidates. From data provided by Michael Silberman, Dean for America.

Figure 15

Total DFA MeetUp Membership by Month

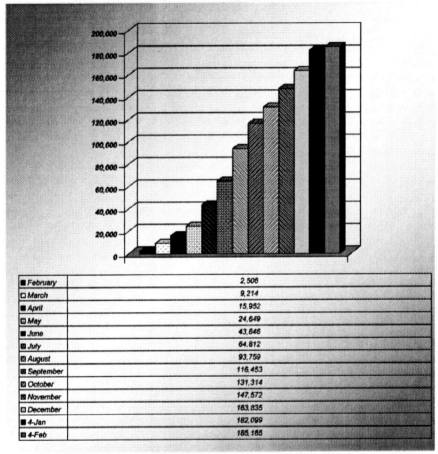

■ February	2,506
□ March	9,214
■ April	15,952
□ May	24,649
■ June	43,646
▨ July	64,812
▨ August	93,759
▨ September	116,453
▨ October	131,314
▨ November	147,572
□ December	163,835
■ 4-Jan	182,099
▨ 4-Feb	185,165

DFA Meetup information provided by MeetUp.com

Figure 16

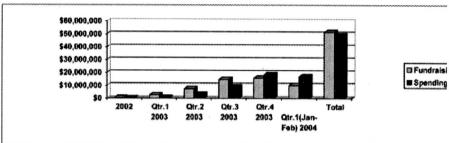

CNN information on Dean fundraising

Figure 17

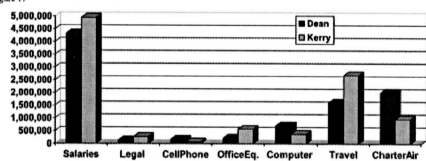

Comparison of Dean and Kerry campaign spending for selected "Overhead" items through January 31, 2004, from data provided by Dwight Morris (http://www.dwightlmorrisandassociates.com)

Figure 18

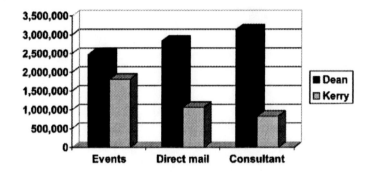

Comparison of Dean and Kerry spending for fundraising by selected items through January 31, 2004, from data provided by Dwight Morris (http://www.dwightlmorrisandassociates.com)

Figures 19 & 20

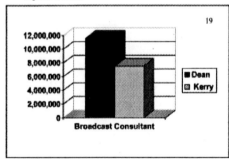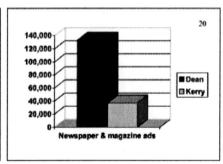

Comparison of Dean and Kerry spending for advertising by selected items through January 31, 2004, from data provided by Dwight Morris (http://www.dwightlmorrisandassociates.com)

Figures 21, 22, 23

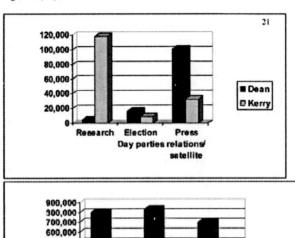

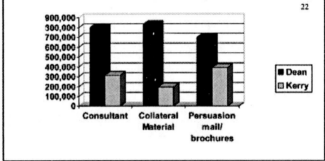

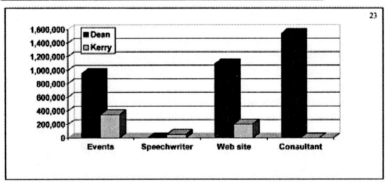

Comparison of Dean and Kerry spending for traditional campaigning by selected items through January 31, 2004, from data provided by Dwight Morris (http://www.dwightlmorrisandassociates.com)

Figure 24

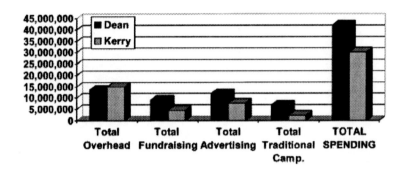

Comparison of Dean and Kerry campaign spending totals for selected categories and grand total through January 31, 2004, from data provided by Dwight Morris (http://www.dwightlmorrisandassociates.com)

Figure 25

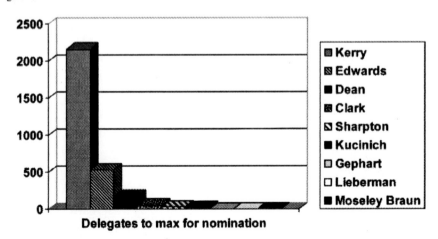

CNN Delegates Scorecard from CNN.com 2004 Primaries

ACKNOWLEDGEMENTS

Writing this book has been a great adventure. No adventure can be fully enjoyed without traveling companions.

Many of my companions are listed among the cast of characters that follows, as well as being listed on the website *www.burningatthegrassroots.com*. That cast of characters also includes a stunning array of people who were kind enough to impart their wisdom to me. It is simultaneously humbling and elevating when people of the level of accomplishment indicated by the bios that accompany their names freely offer their time to you.

One of the profound lessons of the Dean campaign, and my experience within it, is the immutable value of time.

***

It was the first week in January, and the primary was starting to bear down on us.

I had just finished railing at Wendy Howell about how the young people in the campaign needed to see the big picture of people's lives, beyond their own intense focus on their crusade.

I left that conversation fully confident that I myself had a perfectly internalized sense of the value of time. The call that came after my lecture to Wendy said that my beloved brother-in-law George was hospitalized with strep A. His chance of survival at age 69 was not far from zero.

I was torn between staying in New Hampshire and fulfilling my commitment to the campaign, and heading to Pennsylvania to be at his side. George had nursed my older sister through decades of ill health. When her health finally improved, she got the flu, and died, of what the courts found to be malpractice. George spent years before he found Diane, whom he married last August.

So they had 5 months together.

I chose to stay in New Hampshire through the primary, as conflicted as I've ever been in my life. Every day was a reminder of what is important in life.

And George lived.

I never prayed for the Dean campaign to win.

Priorities.

As I've written this book, my priorities have been on the people I worked with in producing it.

Walter Shapiro's ready gift of his time and insight early on inspired this effort to heights it would otherwise have never reached.

Having **Noam Chomsky** respond so immediately to an interview request made it clear to me that this was an important project.

The response, interest, cooperation, and support that I got from so many of the people I interviewed for this book compelled me to make this the best effort my human limitations would allow. It should not go without noting that the two least responsive, and, generally, least forthcoming, of the interviewees were **Joe Trippi** and **Howard Dean**.

My co-authors' commitment to various chapters, as well as the project as a whole, made this a vastly better book.

Adam Drapcho's chapter on the debate at UNH shows his training in anthology, as well as an array of human skills that are equally broad in his sister Katie, who worked as a research associate.

John Hlinko's insights into the parallel universe of the Clark campaign greatly informed the chapter on the General. John's listing of political website resources is a great addition to our effort. Some people might see John's inclusion of the website he runs himself as self-serving. To such people, I would point out that their consumption of oxygen is self-serving. Get over it.

Eleanor Bonsaint's personal support, along with that of **Ron Latanision,** has put me in the position to do this book to the best of my ability. Eleanor's chapter on Internet culture encapsulates the empowerment, fervor, and fever, of Dean Nation that she and I were too often caught up in.

But most of all, there is the person whose support allowed me to do this, the defining work in my life.

I am the moon to my wife's sun. Whatever shine I have is a product of the light she gives off. She is why I rise every day, filled with the newness of morning.

CAST OF CHARACTERS

When I took office, only high energy physicists had ever heard of what is called the Worldwide Web.... Now even my cat has its own page.
President william m. clinton, during announcement of Next Generation Internet initiative, 1996.

Howard Dean is a physician who served in the Vermont legislature, then was elected as lieutenant governor under both Democratic and Republican governors. When Governor Richard Snelling died in 1991, Dean left the medical practice he shared with his wife, Judith Steinberg, to serve as governor of Vermont for 11 years. His tenure as governor brought fiscal stability, health care, education reform, land conservation, and civil unions to Vermont. In 2001, when George W. Bush seemed invincible in the wake of the 9/11 tragedy, Dean chose to run for President. Like another small state governor who had run against George H.W. Bush when he seemed unbeatable, his quest initially appeared to be one for Don Quixote. By the end of 2003, he had convinced the Democratic Party that Bush was beatable, and had been anointed the front-runner himself. Utilizing the Internet, he raised, and then spent, historic amounts of money, as his campaign reflected the mythology of Icarus.

Nancy Beach and **Brian Vawter** operate *Atlantic Media Services* in Portsmouth, NH. They produced videos and DVDs used at house meetings in NH at no cost to the Dean campaign. Nancy ran as a delegate for Governor Dean in the First Congressional District in partnership with the author. Atlantic Media is an award winning full service film and video production company.

Marlowe Bergendoff is a resident of Exeter, NH who volunteered in the Dean campaign. She attended the delegate selection caucus to support the failed candidacy of the author. A highly regarded editor, she worked as an editor on Burning at the Grassroots.

Garrett Bridgens was an area organizer in the New Hampshire Seacoast, for the Dean campaign. A 2003 graduate of the University of Oregon, he came to the campaign as an unpaid volunteer, and was hired to organize the small towns of Newmarket and Newfields.

Katie Drapcho is a sophomore at Portsmouth (N.H.) High School whose efforts to organize and Get Out The Vote (GOTV) in Greenland and Portsmouth had an enormous impact. She did poll checking and visibility in Greenland on primary day.

Adam Drapcho is an anthropology student at the University of New Hampshire. He worked at the polls in Greenland on primary day. He is considering running for office in the largest elective body in the world: the New Hampshire State House of Representatives.

Charles Friou was born in Brooklyn, NY on September 11, 1926. He attended the New York (Brooklyn) public schools, graduated from Bard College with a bachelor's degree in 1946, and Yale University with a Master's in Divinity in 1949. He also did graduate studies at MIT. His has experience as a Refugee Camp Administrator, with the American Friends Service Committee, in Gaza 1949-50. Mr. Friou was ordained a Congregational Minister of the Gospel in 1951, and served Congregational churches in Flushing, NY and Chester, NJ, followed by an urban ministry in the District of Columbia 1956-69, serving a congregation tens blocks east of the US Capitol. He was significantly involved in the Civil Rights movement as a Pastor and Officer of the Council of Churches of Greater Washington and was supportive of Clergy and Laity Against the War (Vietnam). He participated in task force and staff positions with the US Office of Economic Opportunity, in both the Boston and Philadelphia headquarters. He is now retired.

Gwen Graham Logan was the head of the Dean campaign in the South. She was born into a political family. Her father is Florida senator and former presidential candidate Bob Graham, and the late Katherine Graham of the Washington Post was her aunt.

Mathew Gross was director of Internet communications for the Dean campaign. He started the weblog for the Dean campaign in March of 2003.

Steve Grossman served as national chair of the Dean campaign before leaving just prior to the Wisconsin primary. He has served as chair for John

Kerry when he ran for Senate, chair of the state and national Democratic Party, and has run for governor of Massachusetts.

Andrew Hanauer is a Dartmouth student who worked in the press office in Manchester, NH. He had worked in Jeanne Shaheen's campaign for the Senate in 2002.

Richard Hoefer is a media consultant in San Francisco. He specializes in strategic media analysis, PC-TV video convergence, communication design, and influence messaging. He created *deanport.com*. He also created *Cut, Cropped & Out of Context*, which was a finalist for a Golden Dot award for best breakout or impact Internet moment, at the Politics Online conference held in March 2004 at the Institute for Politics, Democracy, and the Internet.

Wendy Howell is a veteran political operative whose work for the Dean campaign belies her youth. A resident of Vermont who grew up in New York, she was in charge of the LGBT outreach in New Hampshire before she was sent in to clean up someone else's mess in Exeter and Greenland.

Paul Johnson is a 48-year-old small business owner in Nashua, with a five person Internet applications service provider/software firm. His proudest moment was when his son, who had no interest in politics through high school, came home from college for Christmas break, cast an absentee ballot for Dean, and then convinced some of his friends to do the same. A few weeks Paul's son forwarded an e-mail to Paul from Moveon.org about an issue he cared about.

Dorothy Keville was the head of the *Massachusetts for Dean organization*. A former lobbyist for the pharmaceutical industry, she first met Dean when he was the governor of Vermont, and the firm she represented was marketing the first HIV/AIDS drugs.

Rick Klau is an attorney and author who is one of the most distinctive and articulate voices of the Dean for America weblog. Klau helped head the Dean effort in Illinois, and traveled to Vermont for a week at Dean headquarters.

Jake Lambert is a Dean campaign volunteer, a student at Boston University, and was active in Mass for Dean in Boston, MA. He is also known as the "Duke of URL".

Nicco Mele was the webmaster for *Dean for America*. He was the first webmaster for Common Cause. Mele produced streaming webcasts from the 2000 presidential election cycle. In December 2003, he was named one of the "best and the brightest" by Esquire magazine.

Howard Frank Mosher , like Howard Dean, grew up in New York State and moved to Vermont as an adult. His works of both fiction and non-fiction provide portraiture of Vermonters that is unequaled. Two of his six novels have been turned into movies. *A Stranger in the Kingdom* starred Dean supporter Martin Sheen, and *Where the Rivers Flow North* starred Rip Torn. A resident of Irasburg, Vermont, he gains grudging acceptance from true Vermonters with each passing decade, despite being a flatlander.

Ray Proulx is a retired superintendent of schools in Vermont. He first observed Dean in the legislature, and then lobbied him on issues concerning education and business in Vermont.

Kristen Cooper-Rainey is the librarian in Madbury, New Hampshire. She worked, along with her husband, as a volunteer in the Dean campaign in Strafford County. On primary day, she was serving as a poll checker as part of the Dean GOTV effort, when she had the list of Dean supporters taken from her under false pretenses, by a stranger claiming to be from the Dean campaign.

Michael Silberman worked as the National Meetup Director for Governor Howard Dean's presidential campaign and managed grassroots field organizing and leadership development programs for Dean's activist base. Leading a team of four others, he oversaw the successful growth of Dean's monthly "Meetup" program, national grassroots actions, and the creation of online field organizing tools and resources. He also implemented a multi-faceted communication strategy that kept over 2,000 grassroots leaders engaged and directly connected to the national headquarters. As a field organizer, Michael co-lead campus GOTV operations in the Iowa, Michigan, and Wisconsin caucus and primaries, organizing a series of grassroots organizing summits across the country. Prior to joining the Dean campaign, Michael gained valuable organizing and political experience at the Union of Concerned Scientists (UCS) and in the Clinton White House at the Council of Environmental Quality (CEQ). Silberman is an alumnus of Middlebury College, where he earned his bachelor's degree in political science and environmental studies.

Malcolm Saldanha was a volunteer in the New Hampshire Dean campaign. He did LGBT outreach, as well as the all-purpose work of all Dean volunteers, first in Manchester, then in Claremont, New Hampshire.

E. William Stetson III, a film producer and environmental consultant, served as an advisor for the HBO movie "Earth and the American Dream", and co-produced "Citizen Suits", a PSA starring Alec Baldwin and Robert F. Kennedy, Jr. He co-executive produced Nora Jacobson's award winning, independent feature film "My Mother's Early Lovers", which follows the true story of a New England family for half a century. Bill also co-produced the recent AIDS documentary, "A Closer Walk", directed by Academy Award nominee Robert Billheimer, and narrated by Glenn Close and Will Smith. The film was recently featured on OPRAH. For over twenty years, Mr. Stetson has co-produced Dartmouth College Radio's "Environmental Insight", the nation's longest running, radio talk show on the subject of the environment. For nearly 15 years, Bill has advised Governor Howard Dean on environmental issues, and he served as an advisor and executive committee member in his bid for the White House. He has served as a national advisor to three other presidential campaigns, and served on the National Political Committee of the Sierra Club. Bill has volunteered in many New England political races over the past 30 years- all were exhilarating, some even successful. For eight years, Bill served as CEO of Fairhill Oil Ltd. in Calgary, Alberta, Canada. He transformed the company from a floundering oil concern to a successful natural gas exploration firm, and an example of environmental sensitivity in the extractive energy field. In 2001, he co-founded the energy and environmental think tank, Foundation For Our Future, based at Shelburne Farms (Shelburne, VT), becoming its first chairman. Bill Stetson's board service includes that of River Watch Network, which he co-founded in Vermont and helped to merge with River Network, the Washington, DC and Portland, OR based rivers advocacy organization. He is currently president of the Boatwright Foundation, and serves as a trustee of the Smith Richardson Foundation. In 1997, Bill helped found the Vermont Film Commission, and he served as its first president. The Film Commission, dedicated to encouraging film and television production in Vermont, also initiated the Vermont Public Television series, Reel Independents and developed the Vermont Filmmakers Fund, to aid independent filmmakers. In 2001, Mr. Stetson was appointed to the prestigious board of the Center for the Environment at Harvard University, where he received a bachelor's degree and subsequently studied at the Graduate School of Arts and Sciences and the John F. Kennedy School of Government.

Aaron Strauss is an MIT graduate student in political science. He worked in the Dean campaign and designed the vaunted voter database.

Zephyr Teachout was director of Online Organizing for the Dean campaign. She is a Vermont native, and a former lawyer, who auctioned her belongings to work on the Dean campaign.

William Trezevant was deputy director of Washington State *Dean for America*. He handled day to day management in the state, which produced the highest percentage of Dean voters outside of Vermont. Trezevant has over 15 years experience running and managing local and regional campaigns. He has served as deputy director of the Institute for Politics, Democracy and the Internet.

Joe Trippi served as campaign manager of *Dean for America*. He worked in campaigns for Mondale, Hart, Gephardt, and Ted Kennedy. He is recognized as a guiding force behind the historic success of the Dean Internet effort. He is a partner of the media firm *Trippi, McMahon and Squier*.

Peter Welch is a Vermont lawyer and state legislator who has advised Howard Dean for many years. In Dean's debate preparations, Welch played the role of Joseph Lieberman.

MEET THE PRESS

Gordon Corera is the US analyst and world affairs editor for the British Broadcasting Corporation. He followed the Democratic primary campaigns in 2004.

Jon Finer is a Boston-based reporter for the *Washington Post*. Finer grew up in Vermont when Dean was governor, and then ended up covering him on the 2004 campaign trail.

Melinda Gipson is Electronic Media Director of the *Newspaper Association of America*. She covered the White House and Capital Hill as an award-winning journalist and founded the newsletter Multimedia Daily.

Ellen Goodman is a nationally syndicated, Pulitzer Prize-winning columnist. Goodman did the first interview in the national media with Judith Steinberg Dean. The best selling author's latest book, *Paper Trail*, is available on *Amazon.com*. She has also written *I Know Just What You Mean: The Power of Friendship in Women's Lives*. Her insight and common sense commentary on American culture and politics is seen in major newspapers across the country.

David Halberstam is a Pulitzer Prize-winning journalist and historian. His book, *The Powers That Be*, defined the relationship between the Presidency and what is now called the traditional media. Vanity Fair called Halberstam "The Moses of American journalism" for his style and epic treatment of events. Vanity Fair said Halberstam "isn't afraid to draw straightforward morals."

Ted Koppel is the anchor of the ABC program *Nightline*. He moderated the debate at UNH, and was criticized for his role in that debate. Koppel has won every major broadcasting award, including 37 Emmy Awards, six George Foster Peabody Awards, 10 DuPont-Columbia Awards, nine Overseas Press Club Awards, two George Polk Awards and two Sigma Delta Chi Awards, the highest honor bestowed for public service by the Society of Professional Journalists.

Kit Seelye is a political reporter for the *New York Times*. She covered the Gore campaign in 2000, and was credited with reporting that Al Gore claimed to have invented the Internet, and that he and his wife had been the models for the main characters in Love Story. As a prominent writer for the "paper of record", she was subject to the intense media criticism that was common to some provinces of Dean Nation.

Walter Shapiro is a political columnist for *USA Today*. In 30 years covering politics, he has worked for Time, Newsweek, The Washington Post, and Washington Monthly. His book *One Car Caravan: On the Road with the 2004 Democrats before America Tunes In* (New York, Public Affairs, 2003) describes his interactions with the candidates and his observations of the campaign trail in 2002 and 2003.

Scott Spradling is the political reporter for *WMUR-TV* in Manchester, New Hampshire. Spradling currently anchors WMUR News 9 at 5:00, and covers New Hampshire politics throughout the year. Scott holds the distinction of being the first TV reporter to interview President Bush in the Oval Office after he was inaugurated in 2001. His responsibilities stretched from the State House hallways to the campaign trail and all the way through election night. He worked with Ted Koppel to moderate the primary debate at the University of New Hampshire

George Stephanopoulos is a political commentator for ABC. Stephanopoulos was widely praised for his role as moderator of the first Democratic Presidential Debate in Columbia, S.C., on May 3. Stephanopoulos has also conducted several interviews with presidential candidates including Sen. Bob Graham, Sen. John Kerry, and Gov. Howard Dean. Stephanopoulos is the author of *All Too Human*, a No. 1 *New York Times* best seller on President Clinton's first term and the 1992 and 1996 Clinton/Gore campaigns. Prior to joining ABCNEWS, Stephanopoulos served in the Clinton administration as the senior advisor to the president for policy and strategy. He was a key strategist in both Clinton presidential campaigns and was involved in the development of virtually all major policy initiatives during Clinton's first term in office. During the 1992 presidential election, Stephanopoulos served on the Clinton/Gore campaign as the deputy campaign manager and director of communications. He oversaw polling, policy, scheduling, press relations and media operations. Before joining Clinton's campaign, Stephanopoulos was executive floor manager to House Majority Leader Richard A. Gephardt.

Anson Tebbetts has covered Howard Dean since Dean was in the Vermont legislature. Tebbetts is an award-winning political reporter for *WCAX-TV*, the leading news station in Vermont. Tebbetts is a Vermont native, whose journalistic career has been spent in the Green Mountain State.

Adrian Walker is a political columnist for the *Boston Globe*. He has observed John Kerry for many years, and is an astute commentator on urban politics.

Jodi Wilgoren covered the Dean campaign for The New York Times. It was her first national presidential campaign as a reporter. Her front page article raised the issue of the absence of Judith Steinberg from the campaign trail. Because of her coverage, she was the subject of "The Wilgoren Watch" by Dean supporters monitoring media coverage.

EXPERTS IN A SOFT SCIENCE

Stephen Ansolabehere is a Professor of Political Science at MIT. Professor Ansolabehere studies elections, democracy, and the mass media. He is coauthor (with Shanto Iyengar) of *The Media Game* (Macmillan, 1993) and of *Going Negative: How Political Advertising Alienates and Polarizes the American Electorate* (The Free Press, 1996). His articles have appeared in The American Political Science Review, The British Journal of Politics, The Journal of Politics, Legislative Studies Quarterly, Public Opinion Quarterly, The Quill, and Chance. His current research projects include campaign finance, congressional elections, and party politics.

Bill Bicket is the director of Venue partnerships for *MeetUp.com*. *MeetUp.com* and the Dean campaign grew symbiotically during 2003, as over 180,000 people eventually signed up for Dean Meetups, meeting in nearly one thousand locations, on the first Wednesday of each month.

David Brady is a senior fellow and associate director for research at the Hoover Institution at Stanford University. He is also the Bowen H. and Janice Arthur McCoy Professor of Political Science and Ethics in the Stanford Graduate School of Business and professor of political science in the School of Humanities and Sciences at the university. His current research focuses on the political history of the U.S. Congress, the history of U.S. election results, and public policy processes in general. His recent publications include, with John Cogan, "Out of Step, Out of Office," American Political Science Review, March 2001; with John Cogan and Morris Fiorina, and Revolving Gridlock: Politics and Policy from Carter to Clinton (Westview Press, 1999); with John Cogan and Doug Rivers. In 1992 he received the Dinkelspiel Award for Excellence in Undergraduate Teaching from Stanford University, and in 1993 he received the Phi Beta Kappa Award for best teacher at Stanford University. He is a member of the American Academy of Arts and Sciences.

Charles Buchwalter is vice president of client analytics for *Nielsen/ NetRatings*. He is an expert in online advertising and the politics of the Internet.

Noam Chomsky is an Institute Professor at MIT. Professor Chomsky has received honorary degrees from University of London, University of Chicago, Loyola University of Chicago, Swarthmore College, Delhi University, Bard College, University of Massachusetts, University of Pennsylvania, Georgetown University, Amherst College, Cambridge University, University of Buenos Aires, McGill University, Universitat Rovira I Virgili, Tarragona, Columbia University, University of Connecticut, Scuola Normale Superiore, Pisa, University of Western Ontario, University of Toronto, Harvard University, University of Calcutta, and Universidad Nacional De Colombia. He is a Fellow of the American Academy of Arts and Sciences and the National Academy of Science. In addition, he is a member of other professional and learned societies in the United States and abroad, and is a recipient of the Distinguished Scientific Contribution Award of the American Psychological Association, the Kyoto Prize in Basic Sciences, the Helmholtz Medal, the Dorothy Eldridge Peacemaker Award, the Ben Franklin Medal in Computer and Cognitive Science, and others. Chomsky has written and lectured widely on linguistics, philosophy, intellectual history, contemporary issues, international affairs and U.S. foreign policy. His works include: *American Power and the New Mandarins; At War with Asia; For Reasons of State; Peace in the Middle East?; The Political Economy of Human Rights*, Vol. I and II (with E.S. Herman); *Rules and Representations; Lectures on Government and Binding; Towards a New Cold War; Radical Priorities; Fateful Triangle; Turning the Tide; Pirates and Emperors; On Power and Ideology; The Culture of Terrorism; Manufacturing Consent* (with E.S. Herman); *Necessary Illusions; Deterring Democracy; Year 501; Rethinking Camelot: JFK, the Vietnam War and US Political Culture; Letters from Lexington; World Orders, Old and New; The Minimalist Program; Powers and Prospects; The Common Good; Profit*

Over People; *The New Military Humanism*; *Rogue States*; *A New Generation Draws the Line*; *9-11*; and *Understanding Power*.

Carol Darr is the director of the Institute for Politics, Democracy, and the Internet at George Washington University in Washington, DC (*http://www.ipdi.org*). She was a campaign finance lawyer and worked in the Dukakis campaign in 1988. Darr served in the Clinton-Gore administration, as well as serving as counsel to the Carter campaign in 1980, and as general counsel to the Democratic National Committee in 1992.

Rick Farmer is a Fellow of the Bliss Institute of Applied Politics at the University of Akron. He has been a local and state party official, managed a successful congressional campaign, and is an expert in Internet campaigning, campaign financing and advertising.

Tim Fedderson is Wendell Hobbs Professor of Managerial Economics and Decision Sciences at Northwestern University. He is a Professor in the department of Political Science and the Kellogg School of Management.

Richard N. Goodwin graduated summa cum laude from Tufts University in 1953. He went on to study law at Harvard University, graduated summa cum laude in 1958 and joined the Massachusetts State bar the same year. After clerking for Supreme Court Justice Felix Frankfurter in 1958, Goodwin came to Senator John F. Kennedy's attention in 1959 while working as special counsel to the Legislative Oversight Subcommittee of the U.S. House of Representatives. Goodwin joined Kennedy's speech writing staff in 1959, and after Kennedy's successful presidential bid, served as assistant special counsel to the President in 1961. Goodwin was also a member of Kennedy's Task Force on Latin American Affairs and in 1961, was appointed Deputy Assistant Secretary of State for Inter-American Affairs, a position he held until 1963. As one of Kennedy's specialists in Latin-American affairs, Goodwin helped develop the Alliance for Progress, an economic development program for Latin America. From 1963 to 1964, Goodwin served as secretary-general of the International Peace Corps and in 1964 became special assistant to President Lyndon Johnson. Goodwin left government service in 1965, though returned briefly in 1968 to write speeches for presidential candidates Robert Kennedy, Eugene McCarthy and Edmund Muskie. After leaving government, Goodwin served as a fellow at the Center for Advanced Studies at Wesleyan University in Middletown, Connecticut from 1965 to 1967 and as a visiting professor of public affairs at the Massachusetts Institute of Technology in 1968. Along with acting as a contributor to *Rolling Stone* and the *New Yorker*, Goodwin has published numerous books, articles and plays. Goodwin is married to Doris Kearns Goodwin, author of *The Fitzgeralds and the Kennedys* (Simon and Schuster, 1986).

Doris Kearns first came to the attention of President Lyndon Johnson when she co-wrote a very critical article on Johnson for the *New Republic* magazine. Several months later, when they met in person at the White House, Johnson asked her to work with him in the White House. He soon asked her to help write his memoirs. During and after Johnson's Presidency, Kearns visited Johnson many times, and, three years after his death, published her first book, *Lyndon Johnson & the American Dream*. She drew on the friendship and conversations with Johnson, supplemented by careful research and critical analysis, to present a picture of his accomplishments, failures and motivations. She married Richard Goodwin in 1975. Her husband, an advisor to John and Robert Kennedy as well as a writer, helped her to gain access to people and papers for her story on the Kennedy family, begun in 1977 and finished ten years later. This book, too, was acclaimed critically, and was made into a television movie. In 1995 Doris Kearns Goodwin was awarded a Pulitzer Prize for her biography of Franklin and Eleanor Roosevelt, *No Ordinary Time*. She then turned to writing a memoir of her own, about growing up as a Brooklyn Dodgers fan, *Wait Till Next Year*. She is a regular political commentator for television and radio.

John Hlinko was co-founder "*DraftWesleyClark.com*", a web-centered movement that generated nearly $2 million in pledges for a Clark candidacy, engaged tens of thousands of volunteers, earned massive coverage in national and international print, television, and online media, and prompted General Wesley Clark to run for President. As a youngster, John Hlinko never dreamed he'd grow up to be the stand-in for Riverdance star Michael Flatley. And, indeed, it never happened. But Hlinko has been an investment banker, campaign manager, published economist, dotcom marketing director, professional comedy writer, and "Buzz Tsar" for a range of grassroots/guerilla campaigns.

Jesse Jackson ran for President in 1984 and 1988. Reverend Jackson's *Rainbow Coalition* changed Democratic Party politics and opened the door for the candidacies of Carol Moseley Braun and Al Sharpton, as well as illuminating the way for other insurgent candidates, including Howard Dean. Although Jackson did not endorse any of the candidates for the Democratic nomination, his son, Jesse Jackson, Jr. endorsed Howard Dean.

Ed Keller is the CEO of *Roper ASW*. A highly acclaimed author, he is recognized as an authority on consumer trends. His book, The Influentials, profiles the 10% of Americans who profoundly influence the decisions of the other 90%.

Kathleen Kendall is a Visiting Professor in the Department of Communication at the University of Maryland. She traveled in New Hampshire during the 2004 campaign to analyze the communications skills of the various candidates. Kendall, an expert in presidential primaries, has written Communication in the Presidential Primaries: Candidates and the Media, 1912-2000.

Leslie Kerman is a media contract lawyer. She negotiated the media contract for the 2004 Wesley Clark campaign. Campaign consultants have previously made their fees by acting as the agents who buy the television time for the campaigns, usually at 15 per cent of the total fee paid. Clark and his campaign chief Eli Segal (who helped run Clinton's 1992 campaign) changed all that, instead offering Clark's ad maker Joe Slade White a fee of $75,000 a month. Kerman reckons it saved the campaign over $1m. James Carville says he would have never accepted such a deal. "I'll just tell 'em that the Clark campaign shows you get what you pay for."

John Mercurio is a veteran political reporter at CNN. He serves as Political Editor, and is based in Washington. His writing appears regularly on *CNN.com*.

Dwight L. Morris has served as President of the Campaign Study Group, Editor For Special Investigations at the Los Angeles Times Washington bureau, Assistant Managing Editor of the Atlanta Journal-Constitution, Vice President of Telecommunications and Media Research at Opinion Research Corporation, Vice President of Telecommunications Research at Louis Harris & Associates, and Special Projects Director at The New York Times.

Phil Noble is the founder of *Politics Online*, the premier international company providing fundraising and Internet tools for politics. In 1997, he was recognized as the International Political Consultant of the Year. His politics and public affairs consulting firm have offices in South Carolina, Washington and Stockholm.

Samuel L. Popkin has published in unusually diverse areas. His most recent book is *The Reasoning Voter: Communication and Persuasion in Presidential Campaigns*. Earlier he co-authored *Issues and Strategies: The Computer Simulation of Presidential Campaigns*. He co-edited *Chief of Staff: Twenty-Five Years of Managing the Presidency*. He is equally well known for his work on peasant society, with particular reference to East and Southeast Asia, including *The Rational Peasant: The Political Economy of Rural Society in Vietnam*. Popkin has also been a consulting analyst in presidential campaigns, serving as consultant to the Clinton campaign on polling and strategy, to the CBS News election units from 1983 to 1990 on survey design and analysis, and more recently to the Gore campaign. He has also served as a consultant to political parties in Canada and Europe and to the Departments of State and Defense. His current research focuses on presidential campaigns and the relationship of public opinion to foreign policy.

Dante Scala is a leading Scholar of the New Hampshire primary. His book, *Stormy Weather: The New Hampshire Primary and Presidential Politics*, New York, (Palgrave MacMillen, 2003), tells the history of the Granite State's first-in-the-nation primary. He is an Associate Professor of politics and a Fellow at the New Hampshire Institute of Politics at St. Anselm's College in Manchester, where primary debates are held every four years.

Susan Silbey is a professor of sociology and anthropology at MIT (insert link). In 1998, she published *The Common Place of Law: Stories from Everyday Life*, describing the ways in which Americans imagine, use, and construct the rule of law. Professor Silbey is Past President of the Law & Society Association, and a fellow of the American Academy of Political and Social Science.

Alan Skorski is a political media consultant at *Interactive Political Media*. The primarily Republican clientele of his firm may explain their Washington address- 1700 Pennsylvania Avenue.

Andrew Smith is the Director of the *UNH Survey Center*. The UNH Survey Center is one of the most technically advanced polling facilities in the Northeast. Private companies, media organizations, government agencies, and non-profit groups utilize their services. A special focus of the Survey Center is on developing innovative uses for e-mail and the Internet in social surveys.

Kathy Sullivan is the Chair of the *New Hampshire Democratic Party*. An attorney in Manchester, she has observed Democratic presidential candidates in New Hampshire over many campaigns.

Steven C. Weiss is communications director for the *Center for Responsive Politics*. The Center for Responsive Politics is a non-partisan, non-profit research group based in Washington, D.C. that tracks money in politics, and its effect on elections and public policy. The Center conducts computer-based research on campaign finance issues for the news media, academics, activists, and the public at large. The Center's work is aimed at creating a more educated voter, an involved citizenry, and a more responsive government.

Christine Williams is a professor of government at Bentley College. She has worked in conjunction with *MeetUp.com* to survey the *role of MeetUps in the 2004 election*.

J. Mark Wrighton is an Assistant Professor of Political Science at the University of New Hampshire. He co-taught a course on the Presidential primaries in 2003. He is co-writing an article with Lara Brown on the 2004 Democratic nomination process.

John Zaller specializes in public opinion and the mass media. His principal publications are *Nature and Origins of Mass Opinion* (Cambridge, 1992), and *Politics As Usual: Ross Perot and the Mass Media* (Chicago, 1997). He has written numerous articles and has co-authored *American Ethos: Public Attitude Toward Capitalism and Democracy* with Herbert McClosky (Harvard, 1984).

CAMPAIGN TIMELINE

· February 18, 2004—Officially ends his candidacy
· February 17, 2004—Finishes third in Wisconsin with 18% of the vote.
· February 5, 2004—E-mail to supporters says Wisconsin is a must win or he is out.
· February 3, 2004—Seven more states go to the polls; fails to get more than 16% in any state.
· January 28, 2004—Dean names Roy Neel as CEO; Joe Trippi resigns.
· January 27, 2004—New Hampshire primary; finishes second.
· January 19, 2004—Iowa caucuses; comes in third; "The Scream" concession speech
· January 18, 2004—Judith Steinberg Dean joins the Governor on the campaign trail for the first time.
· January 11, 2004—In an Iowa debate Rev. Sharpton confronts Dean over the number of minorities in his cabinet as Vermont governor.
· December 31, 2003—Campaign says it raised over $40 million in 2003, the most of all the Democrats, must of it over the Internet and from small donations.
· December 15, 2003—Dean says in a Los Angeles speech, "The capture of Saddam Hussein has not made America safer."
· December 9, 2003—Al Gore endorses Dean.
· August 4, 2003—Dean appears on the covers of both *Time* and *Newsweek*.
· July 15, 2003—Dean finishes first among the Democrats in 2nd Quarter fundraising, bringing in $7.6 million.
· June 23, 2003—Dean officially announces his campaign in Burlington.
· April 2, 2003—Campaign announces first-quarter fundraising will exceed $2.6 million.
· March 29, 2003—Campaign announces Rick Ridder leaving as campaign manager, effective April 15, 2003.
· March 3, 2003—Joe Trippi becomes campaign director, freeing campaign manager Rick Ridder to focus on traveling and building the campaign organization in key states.
· February 21, 2003—Dean's speech at the DNC Winter Meeting.
· February 14, 2003—Dean names Karen Hicks and New Hampshire State Director.
· January 2003—Rapid growth as many new staff come on board in Burlington.
· November 20, 2002—Dean names Rick Ridder as his campaign manager, to start January 2003.
· November 11, 2002—Dean announces that Steve Grossman, who served as national chairman of the Democratic National Committee from 1997-99, and ran for governor of Massachusetts in 2002 (withdrawing from the five man race in July 2002) has signed on, with his role yet to be determined.
· June 22, 2002—Dean holds his first *Dean for America* fundraiser on Fire Island in New York.
· May 30, 2002—Dean mails FEC papers establishing *Dean for America*.

INDEX

ENDNOTES

[1] Never met the man. I just wanted to see if you are actually reading the footnotes.

[2] David Paul Kuhn, chief political writer, CBSNews.com

[3] Nature Bulletin No.377-A April 11, 1970 Forest Preserve District of Cook County

[4] Jane and Michael Stern, Goodfood, (Alfred A. Knopf, New York, 1983), p.55

[5] A clarification from Jodi Wilgoren- "This year is, indeed, my first covering a presidential candidate fulltime as a body person. But if you're going to mention that, it seems to me you might want a little more background on my bio. I covered LA City Hall for two years for the LA Times, including the 1997 mayoral campaign; spent a year as a Washington correspondent for the LA Times; covered Paul Wellstone's death and the subsequent Coleman-Mondale campaign for the NYT; wrote numerous stories for the NYT in the 2002 cycle on various Senate and gubernatorial races; did a project called "Ground Zero" for the last two weeks of the 2000 campaign; and spent a week with McCain in NH in January, 2000. Before doing this campaign I spent two years as the NYT's Chicago bureau chief and another two as a national education correspondent. The blind quote you have in your text is, I believe, the first time anyone has raised my experience as a reporter in this context; yes, it is my first — and last — time being a candidate reporter for a presidential, but that is incredibly common."

[6] "The Nominating Process," The Elections of 1988 (Washington, D.C.: Congressional Quarterly, 1989) The other four stages are described at later points in this book.

[7] Dante Scala, Stormy Weather, The New Hampshire Primary and Presidential Politics, Palgrave Macmillen: New York, 2003, p. 27

[8] Dayton Duncan, Grassroots

[9] John Aldrich, Before the Convention (Chicago, University of Chicago Press,1980)

[10] Dante Scala, Stormy Weather, The New Hampshire Primary and Presidential Politics, Palgrave Macmillen: New York, 2003, p. 21

[11] "Election 2004: New Hampshire", washingtonpostcom, January 27, 2004

[12] "Only in New Hampshire", p.24, University of New Hampshire Magazine, Winter 2004

[13] Leonard Downie Jr., "Election 2004: New Hampshire", washingtonpostcom, January 27, 2004

[14]Dirk Van Susteren, Ed. Howard Dean: A Citizen's Guide to the Man Who Would Be President, Steerforth Press: South Royalton, 2003, p. 37-38

[15] Ibid,p.44

[16] It has been suggested that Dean currently worships at the Church of the Sunday New York Times.

[17] "My back bothers me a lot more now that it ever has since I was in High School. I think that riding in the car… it bothers me a lot. Running bothers me a great deal." (from a Howard Dean interview with the author)

[18]Dirk Van Susteren, Ed Howard Dean: A Citizen's Guide to the Man Who Would Be President, Steerforth Press: South Royalton, 2003, p. 50.

[19] Ibid,p.52-53

[20]Ibid, p.54-55

[21] Ibid,p.169.

[22] When his son Paul was caught by police in 2003 driving a car while waiting for some hockey buddies who were breaking in to the Burlington Country Club in search of alcohol, Dean took two days off the campaign trail to return home. Perhaps remembering his own wilder youth, as well as Big Howard's stern parenting, he said "Children do stupid things, and this is one of them. I'm cutting short my next two days on the campaign trail to deal with a family problem that I consider to be a serious problem."

[23] Dirk Van Susteren, Ed. Howard Dean: A Citizen's Guide to the Man Who Would Be President, , Steerforth Press: South Royalton, 2003, p.68

[24] Vermont historically is the most Republican state in America. FDR never carried it once, nor Maine. Maine started to elect Democrats years before Vermont. The urban area of Portland, Maine helped. Vermont was mainly just rural villages. The Burlington population was 36,000 and less for many years. Up until 1965, Vermont had more cows than people. The last town (Victory) did not get electricity until 1966.

[25] Dirk Van Susteren, Ed. Howard Dean: A Citizen's Guide to the Man Who Would Be President, , Steerforth Press: South Royalton, 2003, p.69

[26] Ibid ,p.81

[27] Ibid, p.98-99

[28] Ibid, p131-133

[29] "Only in New Hampshire", p.24, University of New Hampshire Magazine, Winter 2004

[30] "Is Dean Doomed?", WashingtonPost, December 12 2003

[31] Walter Shapiro, One Car Caravan: On the Road with the 2004 Democrats Before America Tunes In, Public Affairs:New York, 2003, p.178

[32] Ibid, p. 166-167

[33] Ibid, p.169

[34] Ibid

[35] "Only in New Hampshire", p. 24, University of New Hampshire Magazine, Winter 2004

[36] "Is Dean Doomed?", WashingtonPost, December 12, 2003

[37] In May, Dean would go to Hollywood, to discuss the possibility of having his own talk show, with the producer of "Judge Judy."

[38] Dante Scala, Stormy Weather, The New Hampshire Primary and Presidential Politics, Palgrave Macmillen: New York, 2003,p. 14-15

[39] "Election 2004: New Hampshire", washingtonpost.com, January 27, 2004

[40] "Howard Dean Looks Like a Winner", Molly Ivins, Creators Syndicate, December 16, 2003

[41] Joe Conason's Journal, Salon, December 8, 2003

[42] "Kerry Withdrawal Contest", Mickey Kaus, Slate, December 5, 2003

[43] Micelle Cottle, "All the Rage", New Republic Online, December 5, 2003.

[44] Howard Kurtz, Media Notes, Washington Post, December 9, 2003.

[45] Walter Shapiro, One Car Caravan: On the Road with the 2004 Democrats Before America Tunes In, Public Affairs: New York, 2003, p.108-109.

[46] Ibid, p.104

[47] Ibid, p.115

[48] Ibid, p.137-138

[49] Ibid, p.152-153

[50] Ibid, p.155

[51] Stephen Ansolabehere and Shanto Iyengar, Going Negative: How Attack Ads Shrink and Polarize the Electorate, The Free Press :New York, 1995, p.218.

[52]Ibid, p.220

[53] Ibid,p.4-7,39

[54] Ibid, p.128

[55] Ibid, p.133

[56] Ibid, p.158

[57] John Tierney, Political Points, New York Times, February 29, 2004

[58] E.J. Dionne, Why Americans Hate Politics. Simon and Schuster: New York, 1991.

[59] Ansolabehere further explains "One very famous game is called a prisoner's dilemma. There are two people the police have apprehended. They take the two people into separate rooms and interrogate them.

"The payoffs are roughly these…if both of you say nothing to the police, then you're let off. That's your best payoff.

"If you say nothing and the other guy confesses and says that you were part of it, then he cuts a deal such that his confession lets him off with a one year of prison, but you get four years of prison.

"The same thing's true of him.

"If you both confess, then maybe you both get two years.

"So, it turns out that if you think about what's the best thing, given that the other person is thinking, what's the best action for him that you both can do, it turns out that you'll both confess.

"An equilibrium is any pair of actions such that nobody has an incentive to unilaterally change their actions.

"So if we both confessed, I have no incentive to change from confessing to not confessing, because if I change from confessing to not confessing, I end up with four years in prison, not two.

"That is an equilibrium. That's a point that's stable, nobody will want to move away from it.

"If we both cooperated with each other, if we both decided to keep silent, then there's an incentive to actually confess. In the prisoner's dilemma case there is an incentive to actually move away from cooperation."

[60] "Election 2004: Iowa Caucus", David Von Drehle, Washington Post Staff Writer, washingtonpost.com, January 20, 2004.

[61] "Instant Analysis: New Hampshire Primary", washingtonpost.com, January 27, 2004.

[62] Ibid

[63] "Election 2004: Iowa Caucus", David Von Drehle, Washington Post Staff Writer, washingtonpost.com, January 20, 2004.

[64] Howard Kurtz, Media Notes, Washington Post, December 8, 2003.

[65] "Election 2004:New Hampshire", washingtonpost.com, January 27, 2004.

[66] Nafeez Mosaddeq Ahmed, The War on Freedom. Media Monitors Network: Brighton, UK, 2002.

[67] William Blum, Rogue State, , Common Courage Press: Monroe, 2000.

[68] Walter Shapiro, One Car Caravan: On the Road with the 2004 Democrats Before America Tunes In, Public Affairs: New York, 2003, p.6-7.

[69] Ibid,p.27

[70] Ibid, p.202

[71] "J.F.K., Marilyn, 'Camelot' ", New York Times, March 7, 2004.

[72] Walter Shapiro, One Car Caravan: On the Road with the 2004 Democrats Before America Tunes In, Public Affairs: New York, 2003, p.179.

[73] Ibid, p.180

[74] Ibid, p.186

[75] Ibid, p.187

[76] Walter Shapiro, One Car Caravan: On the Road with the 2004 Democrats Before America Tunes In, Public Affairs: New York, 2003, p.188-189.

[77] Ibid, p.189-190

[78] Ibid, p.192-193

[79] Ibid, p.194

[80] "A Sometimes-Rocky Relationship Between Dean and Press", New York Times, January 17, 2004.

[81] "The plot shifts", The Boston Phoenix, February 6,2004.

[82] Ibid

[83] "An Excess of Foot-in-Mouth Is Linked to a Lack of Shut-Eye", New York Times, January 18, 2004.

[84] "Election 2004: New Hampshire Outcome", washingtonpost.com, January 28, 2004.

[85] Walter Shapiro, USA Today, January 16, 2004.

[86] Dante Scala, Stormy Weather, The New Hampshire Primary and Presidential Politics, Palgrave Macmillen: New York, 2003,p. 29.

[87] Susan Silbey, Forecasting U.S. Supreme Court Decisions. Unpublished Paper.

[88] "Is Dean Doomed?", Washington Post, December 12, 2003.

[89] CNN, January 25, 2004

[90] "Is Dean Doomed?", Washington Post, December 12, 2003

[91] H.L.Mencken, 1922

[92] Howard Kurtz, Media notes, Washington Post, December 8, 2003.

[93] "Dr. Dean Assumes His Place on the Examining Table", New York Times, January 18, 2004.

[94] "Instant Analysis: New Hampshire Primary", washingtonpost.com, January 27, 2004.

[95] Ibid

[96] Ibid

[97] "Dean slips, Clark gains in N.H.", Boston Globe, January 16, 2004.

[98] The Boston Phoenix, February 20,2004.

[99] "Election 2004: New Hampshire", washingtonpost.com, January 28, 2004.

[100] New York Times, February 22, 2004

[101] "A Top Labor Supporter Says Dean Ignored His Entreaties to Quit Race", New York Times, February 20, 2004.

[102] "After Long Hike, Dean Watches His Step", New York Times, January 18, 2004.

[103] New York Times, February 22, 2004

[104] Dante Scala, Stormy Weather, The New Hampshire Primary and Presidential Politics, Palgrave Macmillen: New York, 2003, p. 21.

[105] "Instant Analysis: New Hampshire Primary", washingtonpost.com, January 27, 2004.

[106] "Is Dean Doomed?", Washington Post, December 12, 2003.

[107] Time Magazine, February 23, 2004.

[108] New York Times, February 22, 2004.

[109] Walter Shapiro, One Car Caravan: On the Road with the 2004 Democrats Before America Tunes In, Public Affairs: New York, 2003, p.51.

[110] Ibid, p.50

[111] New York Times, February 22, 2004.

[112] Ibid

[113] Ibid

[114] New York Times Book Review, February 22, 2004.

[115] Walter Shapiro, One Car Caravan: On the Road with the 2004 Democrats Before America Tunes In, Public Affairs: New York, 2003, p.59.

[116] Ibid, p.15-17,19,132

[117] Time Magazine, February 2, 2004.

[118] William Safire, New York Times Magazine, February 4, 2004.

[119] New York Times, February 22, 2004.

[120] The Daily News, January 27, 2004.

[121] Dana Carvey, February 19, 2004.

[122] William Safire, "On Language", New York Times Magazine, February 29, 2004.

[123] Time Magazine, March 15, 2004.

[124] Walter Shapiro, One Car Caravan: On the Road with the 2004 Democrats Before America Tunes In, Public Affairs: New York, 2003, p.182.

[125] Ibid, p.184

[126] Ibid, p.44

[127] Ibid, p.213-214

[128] Walter Shapiro, One Car Caravan: On the Road with the 2004 Democrats Before America Tunes In, Public Affairs: New York, 2003, p.xiii.

[129] "Election 2004: New Hampshire Outcome", washingtonpost.com, January 28, 2004.

[130] "Election 2004: The Daily Show", washingtonpost.com, January 28, 2004.

[131] "Election 2004: New Hampshire", washingtonpost.com, January 28, 2004.

[132] "Stirrings in Florida bespeak 2000 dispute", Boston Globe, March 16,2004.

[133] Dante Scala, Stormy Weather, The New Hampshire Primary and Presidential Politics, Palgrave Macmillen: New York, 2003.

[134] "Election 2004: New Hampshire", washingtonpost.com, January 28, 2004

[135] Walter Shapiro, One Car Caravan: On the Road with the 2004 Democrats Before America Tunes In, Public Affairs: New York, 2003.

[136] Dante Scala, Stormy Weather, The New Hampshire Primary and Presidential Politics, Palgrave Macmillen: New York, 2003, p. 52.

[137] Some counties do seem to be better predictors than others. Since 1952, only two Democrats have won the primary without winning Strafford County.

[138] Dante Scala, Stormy Weather, The New Hampshire Primary and Presidential Politics, Palgrave Macmillen: New York, 2003p. 69.

[139] Ibid, p. 77

[140] Ibid, p. 78

[141] David C Hoeh, 1968, McCarthy, New Hampshire, Lone Oak Press: Rochester, 1994, p. 336.

[142] Ibid, p. 335

[143] Dante Scala, Stormy Weather, The New Hampshire Primary and Presidential Politics, Palgrave Macmillen: New York, 2003p. 83.

[144] Ibid, p. 84

[145] Ibid, p. 85

[146] Walter Shapiro, One Car Caravan: On the Road with the 2004 Democrats Before America Tunes In, Public Affairs: New York, 2003, p.101.

[147] "Election 2004: New Hampshire Primary", washingtonpost.com, January 27, 2004.

[148] Dante Scala, Stormy Weather, The New Hampshire Primary and Presidential Politics, Palgrave Macmillen: New York, 2003, p. 168.

[149] "Moscow on the Hustings", Time Magazine, March 15, 2004.

[150] "Only in New Hampshire", p. 25, University of New Hampshire Magazine, Winter 2004.

[151] Dante Scala, Stormy Weather, The New Hampshire Primary and Presidential Politics, Palgrave Macmillen: New York, 2003,p.173-174.

[152] Leonard Downie, "Election 2004: New Hampshire", washingtonpost.com, January 27, 2004.

[153] "Election 2004: The New Hampshire Primary, washingtonpost.com, January 26, 2004.

[154] "Election 2004: The New Hampshire Primary, washingtonpost.com, January 27, 2004.

[155] Ibid

[156] Dante Scala, Stormy Weather, The New Hampshire Primary and Presidential Politics, Palgrave Macmillen: New York, 2003, p. 191.

[157] Ibid, p. 188-189

[158] Ibid, p. 189

[159] Ibid, p. 192

[160] Walter Shapiro, One Car Caravan: On the Road with the 2004 Democrats Before America Tunes In, Public Affairs: New York, 2003, p.122.

[161] Dante Scala, Stormy Weather, The New Hampshire Primary and Presidential Politics, Palgrave Macmillen: New York, 2003, p. 179.

[162] Walter Shapiro, USA Today, January 16, 2004

[163] Dante Scala, Stormy Weather, The New Hampshire Primary and Presidential Politics, Palgrave Macmillen: New York, 2003, p. 179.

[164] Ibid, p. 179

[165] Walter Shapiro, One Car Caravan: On the Road with the 2004 Democrats Before America Tunes In, Public Affairs: New York, 2003, p.84.

[166] "Only in New Hampshire", p. 23-24, University of New Hampshire Magazine, Winter 2004.

[167] Charles Brereton, First in the Nation: New Hampshire and the Premier Presidential Primary. Peter E. Randal: Portsmouth, 1987, p.3.

[168] Dante Scala, Stormy Weather, The New Hampshire Primary and Presidential Politics, Palgrave Macmillen: New York, 2003, p. 11.

[169] Dante Scala, Stormy Weather, The New Hampshire Primary and Presidential Politics, Palgrave Macmillen: New York, 2003, p. 17-18.

[170] Ibid, p. 19

[171] Ibid, p. 6

[172] Theodore H. White, The Making of the President 1960. Anthaneum: New York, 1961, p. 79-80.

[173] "Election 2004: New Hampshire Primary", washingtonpost.com, January 27, 2004.

[174] Walter Shapiro was part of the press posse that hunted this down. See Walter Shapiro, One Car Caravan: On the Road with the 2004

Democrats Before America Tunes In., Public Affairs: New York, 2003, p.165.

[175] "Granite State's Shaheens put weight behind Kerry", Boston Globe, January 4, 2004.

[176] Ibid

[177] Ibid

[178] Ibid

[179] "Granite State's Shaheens put weight behind Kerry", Boston Globe, January 4, 2004.

[180] Ibid

[181] "Election 2004: New Hampshire", washingtonpost.com, January 27, 2004.

[182] Dante Scala, Stormy Weather, The New Hampshire Primary and Presidential Politics, Palgrave Macmillen: New York, 2003, p. 4.

[183] "Instant Analysis: New Hampshire Primary", washingtonpost.com, January 27, 2004.

[184] "Election 2004: New Hampshire Polls", washingtonpost.com, January 28, 2004.

[185] Ibid

[186] "Election 2004: Voter Trends", washingtonpost.com, January 29, 2004.

[187] Walter Shapiro, One Car Caravan: On the Road with the 2004 Democrats Before America Tunes In, Public Affairs:New York, 2003, p.63.

[188] Campaign Finance Institute (non-partisan), as of 2003 filings

[189] "The Ethicist", New York Times Magazine, February 1, 2004.

[190] Walter Shapiro, One Car Caravan: On the Road with the 2004 Democrats Before America Tunes In, Public Affairs:New York, 2003, p.69.

[191] Ibid, p.55

[192] Ibid, p.81,83

[193] Walter Shapiro, One Car Caravan: On the Road with the 2004 Democrats Before America Tunes In. Public Affairs:New York, 2003, p.69-71.

[194] "Election 2004: New Hampshire Outcome", washingtonpost.com, January 28, 2004.

[195] Ibid

[196] Walter Shapiro, One Car Caravan: On the Road with the 2004 Democrats Before America Tunes In, Public Affairs:New York, 2003, p.145-150.

[197] "Election 2004: New Hampshire", washingtonpost.com, January 28, 2004.

[198] Ibid

[199] Ibid

[200] "Election 2004: Analysis", washingtonpost.com, January 30, 2004.

[201] "Instant Analysis: New Hampshire Primary", washingtonpost.com, January 27, 2004.

[202] "Election 2004: New Hampshire", washingtonpost.com, January 28, 2004.

[203] New York Times Magazine, February 22, 2004.

[204] Ibid

[205] Ibid

[206] Jodi Wilgoren re: Trippi and women: "I have categorically said that I have no information or reason to believe he has any issues or problems with women, and if you include anything from our interview in a section of your book that questions this, it would be completely unethical of you not to include that."

[207] "Digitizing Democracy", CBS News Sunday Morning, March 7, 2004.

[208] Brad Fay, Managing Director, Roper ASW, Politics Online presentation, March 19, 2004.

[209] Ed Keller, CEO Roper ASW, Politics Online presentation, March 19, 2004.

[210] Joe Graf, Institute for Politics, Democracy and the Internet, Politics Online Conference, March 19, 2004.

[211] MORI Research, "Power Users 2004", cited by Melinda Gipson, Electronic Media Director, Newspaper Association of America, Politics Online presentation, March 19, 2004.

[212] Benjamin Katz, CompleteCampaigns.com president, Politics Online presentation, March 19, 2004.

[213] Dirk Van Susteran, ed., Howard Dean: A Citizen's Guide to the Man Who Would Be President. Steerforth Press: South Royalton, 2003, p.205-206.

[214] "Internet meets real life using Meetup.com site", Associated Press, November 9, 2003.

[215] "Online Friends 'MeetUp' in the Real World", Fox News channel, February 11, 2004.

[216] "Meetup.com working to become a force in local, state politics", Chris Gray, Philadelphia Inquirer, February 8, 2004.

[217] "Digitizing Democracy", CBS News Sunday Morning, March 7, 2004.

[218] "The New Model of Campaigns: Innovations in 2004 and Beyond", William Trezevant, Politics Online Conference, March 19, 2004.

[219] Adam Rogers, "For Electrifying the Grassroots", Wired, April 2004.

[220] Walter Shapiro, One Car Caravan: On the Road with the 2004 Democrats Before America Tunes In. Public Affairs:New York, 2003, p.31.

[221] Ibid, p.124

[222] Ibid, p.213

[223] Time Magazine, March 8, 2004.

[224] William Pfaff,"How Kerry differs on foreign policy", Boston Globe, March 8, 2004.

[225] Time Magazine, February 9, 2004.

[226] Ibid

[227] Ibid

[228] "Staffers fill in details of the decline of Dean", USA Today, February 19, 2004.

[229] "So What Was That All About? The Impact of Dr. Dean", New York Times, February 22, 2004.

[230] "Dean Makes his Exit From Campaign but Vows, 'We Are Not Going Away' ", New York Times, February 19, 2004.

[231] "Howard's End", New YorkTimes, February 19, 2004.

[232] "A face-off on the issues", Boston Globe, February 20, 2004.

[233] "Dean's chance to be a hero", Boston Globe, February 18, 2004.

[234] Time Magazine, February 16, 2004.

[235] "Divide and Bicker", by Howard Kurtz, appeared in the Washington Post on February 29, 2004. I have deconstructed the article here into four sections. In each section (all italicized), I have kept the material in the order that it appeared in the original article. The parenthetical insertions I made are to provide the kind of continuity that every ninth grade English

teacher urges writers to use to assure the flow of paragraphs. Kurtz did not respond to repeated requests for an interview.

[236] "Election 2004: The Dean Campaign", washingtonpost.com, February 19, 2004.

[237] "Dean Defeats Truman! Why Political Analysts Keep Getting It Wrong", Washington Post, February 23, 2004.

[238] "The Third Man", New York Times, March 7, 2004.

[239] "The Culture War is really a Culture Circus", Time Magazine, March 8, 2004.

[240] "Beware flannel Mouth Disease!", Time Magazine, March 1, 2004.

[241] "Dean's medical training has helped him-and hurt him-in politics", USA Today, January 13, 2004.

[242] Dirk Van Susteren, Ed,.Howard Dean: A Citizen's Guide to the Man Who Would Be President, Steerforth Press: South Royalton, 2003, p. 13-14.

[243] Ibid, p. 25

[244] Ibid, p. 15-16

[245] WCAX poll of 400 likely Vermont voters. Conducted by Research 2000 of Rockville, Maryland by telephone between April 28 and April 30, 2004. Margin of error plus or minus 5% percentage points.

[246] Dirk Van Susteren, Ed,.Howard Dean: A Citizen's Guide to the Man Who Would Be President, Steerforth Press: South Royalton, 2003, p. 21.

[247]Ibid, p.22

[248] Dante Scala, Stormy Weather, The New Hampshire Primary and Presidential Politics, Palgrave Macmillen: New York, 2003, p. 30.

[249] Ibid

[250] University of Vermont Professor Alfred Snyder, who teaches a class on Presidential rhethoric, on WCAX-TV "You Can Quote Me", February 22, 2004.

[251] "Political Points", New York Times, February 22, 2004.

[252] "Election 2004: New Hampshire Outcome", washingtonpost.com, January 28, 2004.

[253] New York Times, February 25, 2004.

[254] Burlington Free Press, February 22, 2004.

[255] The New York Times Book Review, February 22, 2004.

[256] Boston Globe, March 4, 2004.

[257] WCAX-TV news, February 27, 2004

[258] Dante Scala, Stormy Weather, The New Hampshire Primary and Presidential Politics, Palgrave Macmillen: New York, 2003, p. 32.

[259] WCAX-TV news, February 27, 2004

[260] Ibid

[261] Ibid

[262] David Halberstam, The Reckoning. William Morrow and Company: New York, 1986, p. 312-317.

[263] Sara Lawrence-Lightfoot, Respect. Perseus Books: Reading, 1999.

[264] 19th century English novelist, George Eliot

[265] Lincoln must come from within each of us. However, as a specific leader, Lincoln may once again come from Illinois. Either Carol Moseley Braun or Barrack Obama could be the next Lincoln.

[266] I was perplexed when Ben chastised me for sending out the press release without clearing it; I had more years in writing and journalism than the people who might clear it had on Earth.

With my own ability I cannot succeed, without the sustenance of Divine Providence, and of the free, happy and intelligent people. Without these I cannot hope to succeed; with them, I cannot fail.

PHOTOS

Howard & Judy Dean

Howard Dean supported businesses in his eleven years as Vermont's governor. Dean is on the left, Senator Jim Jeffords on the right, as Paul Johnston, the head of AgriMark, addresses an audience at the opening of a new facility. (Photo courtesy of Jacqui Johnston.)

The bandstand was the center of the small New Hampshire town of Exeter. Candidates would speak, and the town band would play on warm summer nights. (Photo from Dunnan family archives)

Exeter residents would watch candidates at the bandstand from the steps of Perley Gardner's house. (Photo from Dunnan family archives.)

Al-Hajj Malik Al-Shabazz

Drawing by Melissa Parra

Bill Bradley endorsed Dean when the campaign seemed to have all of the momentum. Here he addresses a group of organizations gathered to talk about Meetup.com's potential to spread their message. (Photo by Adam Drapcho)

Scott Heiferman is the co-founder of Meetup.com. While Meetup.com is non-partisan, and brings like-minded people together on issues from chihuhuas to knitting, the organization's early growth occurred at the same time as the expansion of Dean Meetups. Dean Meetups continue, on the first Wednesday of each month. (Photo by Adam Drapcho)

Larry and Mary Nunes with Authors

On the campaign trail.

Joe, Anita and Dana on the caboose steps.

A middle-aged bachelor lawyer, Perley Gardner adopted his niece when her mother was going to put her in an orphanage. (Photo from Dunnan family archives)

Ray Proulx

"It is for us the living, rather, to be dedicated here to the unfinished work which they who fought here have thus far so nobly advanced. It is rather for us to be here dedicated to the great task remaining before us—that from these honored dead we take increased devotion to that cause for which they gave the last full measure of devotion—that we here highly resolve that these dead shall not have died in vain—that this nation, under God, shall have a new birth of freedom—and that government of the people, by the people, for the people, shall not perish from the earth. *--Abraham Lincoln from his 1863 Gettysburg Address*

"I stand here knowing that my story is part of the larger American story, that I owe a debt to all of who came before me, and that, in no other country on earth, is my story even possible.

"There is not a liberal America and a conservative America — there is the United States of America. There is not a Black America and a White America and Latino America and Asian America — there's the United States of America." *—Barack Obama from his keynote speech at the 2004 Democratic National Convention*

The official portrait of Howard Dean hangs in the Vermont State Capitol in Montpelier. The artist was Carroll M. Jones. Picture courtesy of Lillian Zuber, The Art Gallery, Stow, Vermont.

To George Hall, and Dona + Judy Dunnam,

     Thank you for your support of the Republican National Committee. Grassroots leaders like you are the key to building a better, stronger, more secure future for our nation and all Americans.

               Best Wishes,

Photo courtesy of George Hall. Added handwriting courtesy of Diane Hall. George W. Bush courtesy of Supreme Court and Karl Rove. Karl Rove courtesy of Satan.